Building Cisco Multilayer Switched Networks

Karen Webb, CCIE

Cisco Press
201 West 103rd Street
Indianapolis, IN 46290 USA

Building Cisco Multilayer Switched Networks

Karen Webb

Copyright© 2000 Cisco Systems, Inc.

Cisco Press logo is a trademark of Cisco Systems, Inc.

Published by:

Cisco Press
201 West 103rd Street
Indianapolis, IN 46290 USA

Printed in the United States of America 4 5 6 7 8 9 0

4th Printing January 2001

Library of Congress Cataloging-in-Publication Number: 99-67900

ISBN: 1-57870-093-0

Warning and Disclaimer

This book is designed to provide information about Cisco multilayer switched networks. Every effort has been made to make this book as complete and as accurate as possible, but no warranty or fitness is implied.

The information is provided on an "as is" basis. The author, Cisco Press, and Cisco Systems, Inc., shall have neither liability nor responsibility to any person or entity with respect to any loss or damages arising from the information contained in this book or from the use of the discs or programs that may accompany it.

The opinions expressed in this book belong to the author and are not necessarily those of Cisco Systems, Inc.

Trademark Acknowledgments

All terms mentioned in this book that are known to be trademarks or service marks have been appropriately capitalized. Cisco Press or Cisco Systems, Inc., cannot attest to the accuracy of this information. Use of a term in this book should not be regarded as affecting the validity of any trademark or service mark.

Feedback Information

At Cisco Press, our goal is to create in-depth technical books of the highest quality and value. Each book is crafted with care and precision, undergoing rigorous development that involves the unique expertise of members from the professional technical community.

Reader feedback is a natural continuation of this process. If you have any comments regarding how we could improve the quality of this book, or otherwise alter it to better suit your needs, you can contact us through e-mail at ciscopress@mcp.com. Please make sure to include the book title and ISBN in your message.

We greatly appreciate your assistance.

through e-mail at ciscopress@mcp.com. Please make sure to include the book title and ISBN in your message.

We greatly appreciate your assistance.

Publisher	John Wait
Executive Editor	John Kane
Cisco Systems Program Manager	Jim LeValley
Managing Editor	Patrick Kanouse
Senior Acquisitions Editor	Brett Bartow
Development Editor	Andrew Cupp
Project Editor	Sheri Replin
Copy Editor	Gayle Johnson
Technical Editors	Hassan Jabi
	Paul Levasseur
	Kevin Schemery
Course Developers	Libby Goga
	Charles Newby
	Karen Webb
Team Coordinator	Amy Lewis
Book Designer	Gina Rexrode
Cover Designer	Louisa Klucznik
Compositor	Gina Rexrode
Indexer	Larry Sweazy

CISCO SYSTEMS

CISCO PRESS

Corporate Headquarters
Cisco Systems, Inc.
170 West Tasman Drive
San Jose, CA 95134-1706
USA
http://www.cisco.com
Tel: 408 526-4000
      800 553-NETS (6387)
Fax: 408 526-4100

European Headquarters
Cisco Systems Europe s.a.r.l.
Parc Evolic, Batiment L1/L2
16 Avenue du Quebec
Villebon, BP 706
91961 Courtaboeuf Cedex
France
http://www-europe.cisco.com
Tel: 33 1 69 18 61 00
Fax: 33 1 69 28 83 26

American Headquarters
Cisco Systems, Inc.
170 West Tasman Drive
San Jose, CA 95134-1706
USA
http://www.cisco.com
Tel: 408 526-7660
Fax: 408 527-0883

Asia Headquarters
Nihon Cisco Systems K.K.
Fuji Building, 9th Floor
3-2-3 Marunouchi
Chiyoda-ku, Tokyo 100
Japan
http://www.cisco.com
Tel: 81 3 5219 6250
Fax: 81 3 5219 6001

Cisco Systems has more than 200 offices in the following countries. Addresses, phone numbers, and fax numbers are listed on the Cisco Connection Online Web site at http://www.cisco.com/offices.

Argentina • Australia • Austria • Belgium • Brazil • Canada • Chile • China • Colombia • Costa Rica • Croatia • Czech Republic • Denmark • Dubai, UAE Finland • France • Germany • Greece • Hong Kong • Hungary • India • Indonesia • Ireland • Israel • Italy • Japan • Korea • Luxembourg • Malaysia • Mexico • The Netherlands • New Zealand • Norway • Peru • Philippines • Poland • Portugal • Puerto Rico • Romania • Russia • Saudi Arabia • Singapore • Slovakia • Slovenia • South Africa • Spain • Sweden • Switzerland • Taiwan • Thailand • Turkey • Ukraine • United Kingdom • United States • Venezuela

About the Author

Karen Webb, CCIE #3662, develops and delivers training solutions for Cisco products and technologies through The Meadow Network Training Corporation. She is also a Cisco Certified Systems Instructor and has taught many of the Cisco authorized courses. She is known for her dynamic classroom teaching style, her dedication to adult learning, and her in-depth knowledge of routing and switching protocols and concepts. Karen has been in the networking industry for over 13 years and has extensive network design and implementation experience in a wide variety of network technologies and protocols.

About the Technical Reviewers

Hassan Jabi is a Cisco Certified Systems Instructor and holds an electrical engineering bachelor degree. He has been working in the data communications field for 12 years providing training and consulting services throughout North America and Europe. Hassan can be reached at hjabi@geotrain.com.

Paul Levasseur was a Cisco Certified Systems Instructor teaching for Protocol Interface, GeoTrain, and Global Knowledge and is now a Course Developer/Project Manager for Netscreen Technologies.

Kevin Schemery has held various technical training and technical support positions in the internetworking industry for six years. His extensive experience includes LAN and WAN design, analysis, and project management. He has worked at the educational, district, regional, and national levels. He has been involved with several large switched Ethernet implementations in the insurance, government, educational, and private industries. In addition, Kevin teaches customized classes on switched Ethernet design and implementation. Currently, he works for AE Business Solutions, a Cisco Gold Partner in Middleton, Wisc.

Acknowledgments

I would like to acknowledge the following people who helped me put the book together:

The Cisco Press team. Many thanks to the Cisco Press team for all of their assistance and patience during the creation of this book. Drew Cupp, development editor, provided invaluable assistance with the editing of the material and always amazed me with his ability to improve the language and presentation as well as technical corrections. Many thanks as well to Paul Lavasseur, Kevin Schemery, and Hassan Jabi for their technical review and comments on every chapter.

The Cisco Systems team. I would like to thank the original developers of the BCMSN course, Libby Goga and Charles Newby for their truly wonderful course. Their work made the creation of this book so much easier.

My family and friends. To my children, my rays of sunshine, Alexandria and Samantha. You shine so brightly. Your curiosity, your beauty and laughter fill my heart with joy. To my father for his gentle words of wisdom, and to my mother for all she gave to her daughters. To Timothy Quinn for inspiring me to dream and for teaching me that who you are is more important than what you do.

"We find greatest joy, not in getting, but in expressing what we are. Men do not really live for honors or for pay; their gladness is not the taking and holding, but in doing, the striving, the building, the living. It is a higher joy to teach than to be taught. It is good to get justice, but better to do it; fun to have things but more to make them. The happy man is he who lives the life of love, not for the honors it may bring, but for the life itself."

—R.J. Baughan

In addition to the course developers (Libby Goga, Charles Newby, and Karen Webb), Cisco Press would like to acknowledge the following technical contributors whose input and assistance made the Cisco Systems BCMSN course a reality: Andre Wetsteyn, Stefan Sidl, Gilles Larivee, Peter Welcher, Ilona Serrao, Ken Crozier, Phillip Harris, and Faraz Aladin.

Contents at a Glance

Table of Contents

Foreword

In April 1998, Cisco Systems, Inc. announced a new professional development initiative called the Cisco Career Certifications. These certifications address the growing worldwide demand for more and better-trained computer networking experts. Building upon our highly successful Cisco Certified Inter-network Expert (CCIE) program—the industry's most respected networking certification vehicle—Cisco Career Certifications enable you to be certified at various technical proficiency levels.

Building Cisco Multilayer Switched Networks presents in book form all the topics covered in the challenging instructor-led and e-learning certification preparation courses of the same name. The BCMSN courses are designed to teach network professionals how to build campus networks using multilayer switching technologies over high-speed Ethernet. It is one of four recommended training courses for CCNP and CCDP certification. Whether you are studying to become CCNP- or CCDP-certified, or you are seeking to gain a better understanding of the products, services, and policies that enable you to build and manage effective multilayer switched networks, you will benefit from the information presented in this book.

Cisco and Cisco Press present this material in a text-based format to provide another learning vehicle for our customers and the broader user community in general. Although a publication does not duplicate the instructor-led or e-learning environments, we acknowledge that not everyone responds in the same way to the same delivery mechanism. It is our intent that presenting this material via a Cisco Press publication will enhance the transfer of knowledge to a broad audience of networking professionals.

This is the eighth in a series of course supplements planned for Cisco Press, following *Introduction to Cisco Router Configuration, Advanced Cisco Router Configuration, Building Cisco Remote Access Networks, Cisco Internetwork Troubleshooting, Designing Cisco Networks, Cisco Internetwork Design,* and *Interconnecting Cisco Network Devices.* Cisco will present existing and future courses through these coursebooks to help achieve Cisco Worldwide Training's principal objectives: to educate the Cisco community of networking professionals and to enable that community to build and maintain reliable, scalable networks. The Cisco Career Certifications and classes that support these certifications are directed toward meeting these objectives through a disciplined approach to progressive learning. The books Cisco creates in partnership with Cisco Press meet the same standards for content quality demanded of our courses and certifications. It is our intent that you will find this and subsequent Cisco Press certification and training publications of value as you build your networking knowledge base.

Thomas M. Kelly
Director, Worldwide Training
Cisco Systems, Inc.
February 2000

Introduction

Building Cisco Multilayer Switched Networks teaches you how to build an enterprise campus network utilizing Layer 2 devices such as switches and Layer 3 devices such as routers. As soon as your campus network is built, this coursebook further teaches you how to optimize routing, ensure network availability, and provide for multicast applications. From this book's extensive text, configuration examples, and in-depth case studies, you will learn to do the following:

- Select and cable the Cisco products that enable connectivity within the campus network
- Ensure network availability through redundant links and virtual default routers
- Enable multilayer switching to facilitate wire-speed data transmission
- Ensure routing reliability through the implementation of the Cisco Hot Standby Router Protocol
- Implement network services to obtain membership in multicast groups
- Control network traffic by implementing a network admission policy

Who Should Read This Book

This book is intended for network administrators who will be implementing a multilayer switched network in an enterprise. It is recommended for anyone who is interested in learning switching concepts at both Layer 2 and Layer 3. Of course, it is also intended to supplement the Building Cisco Multilayer Switched Networks (BCMSN) course and to prepare you for the corresponding certification exam on the Cisco Certified Network Professional (CCNP) or Cisco Certified Design Professional (CCDP) certification track.

The technologies taught in this book and the network diagrams used in the case studies are taken from Cisco recommended designs and from typical customer implementations. The majority of current customer implementations use Ethernet in the campus network and TCP/IP as the Layer 3 protocol. For this reason, the transmission media that are covered in this course are Ethernet, Fast Ethernet, and Gigabit Ethernet. The Layer 3 protocol discussed is TCP/IP.

The book first discusses design criteria for multilayer switched networks, including the current Cisco recommendation for designing a campus network. The network is built in the subsequent chapters, from cabling connections to implementing VLANs, Spanning Tree, and routing. After the network has been built, this book examines ways to optimize the network and to ensure its availability.

This book follows the typical progression of a new campus network installation, making it a useful tool for network administrators who are installing a campus network for the first time.

Prerequisites

This book is one in a series of books designed to prepare you for CCNP and CCDP certification. In order to be properly prepared for the material in this book, you should have a CCNA-level understanding of the following:

- Internetworking fundamentals
- Basic router configuration

- Basic switch configuration
- Basic VLAN configuration
- Spanning Tree protocol
- Inter-Switch Link configuration
- Standard access list configuration
- Routing protocol concepts

At the end of each chapter, you have a chance to review the concepts you learned by answering review questions and examining a case study. Each case study shows you how to implement a new portion of the network shown in Figure I-1.

Figure I-1   *Case Study Network*

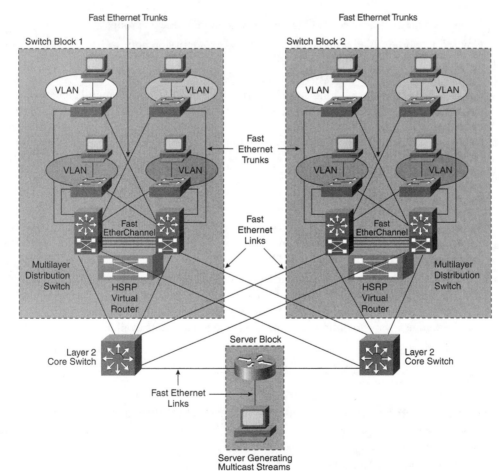

Figure I-1 represents the current most commonly recommended Cisco design for the enterprise campus network. Each chapter and its corresponding case study address building, optimizing, and securing a portion of this network.

Conventions Used in This Book

This book contains illustrations and configuration examples to aid in your understanding of multilayer switched networks. This section covers the conventions of the images and syntax found in this book.

Illustration Iconography

The icons displayed in Figure I-2 are used in the figures presented throughout this book.

Figure I-2   *Network Icons Used in This Book*

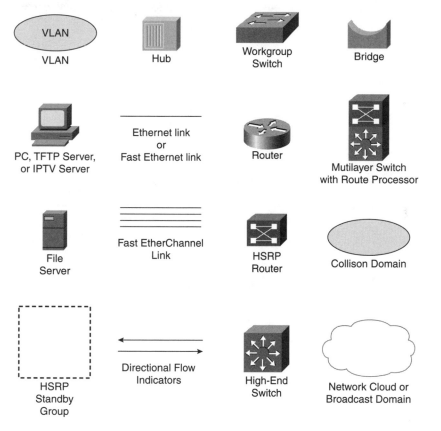

Command Syntax Conventions

The conventions used in the command syntax in this book are the same as those used in the IOS Command Reference. The Command Reference describes these conventions as follows:

- **Boldface** indicates commands or keywords that are typed in literally as shown. Note that in examples (not syntax), boldface indicates user input (such as a **show** command) or highlights portions of the example that pertain to the text.

- *Italics* indicates arguments for which you supply actual values.

- A vertical bar (|) separates alternative, mutually exclusive elements.

- Square brackets ([ ]) indicate an optional element.

- Braces ({ }) indicate a required choice.

- Braces within brackets ([{ }]) indicate a required choice with an optional element.

CHAPTER 1

Overview of a Campus Network

Today's campus networks are comprised of a combination of bridges and routers connected via either Ethernet or Token Ring. This chapter presents a new approach to campus networking called *multilayer switching*. Multilayer switching combines Layer 2 switching functions with Layer 3 routing. This chapter also includes a discussion of the correct placement of Layer 2, Layer 3, and multilayer devices in the campus network. Finally, this chapter shows how you can scale your campus network to meet the ever-increasing demands of your business.

This chapter describes a set of building blocks, which present a logical design for the network irrespective of any product that can be implemented. The success of any campus intranet is based on the placement of network services that, when applied correctly, will guarantee continued scalability.

This chapter covers the following topics:

- Campus network overview
- The emerging campus model
- Switching technologies
- The hierarchical model
- The building block approach
- Campus network availability example

Upon completion of this chapter, given a list of switching functions, you will be able to identify the correct Open System Interconnection (OSI) reference model layer associated with those functions. Given a list of characteristics, you will be able to identify the correct hierarchical model layer. And finally, given a set of user requirements, you will be able to identify the correct Cisco product solution.

Campus Network Overview

This section contains an overview of the traditional campus networks and describes some of the major issues and solutions that have changed the way networks operate. This section also discusses how network traffic patterns are changing. This section covers the following topics:

- The structure and characteristics of current campus networks
- Traditional network problems and the resulting solutions
- Existing and emerging traffic patterns

This section also deals with the demands on today's organizations that have brought about changes in the way campus networks are designed, as well as the components of a campus network and the technologies driving these changes.

Traditional Campus Networks

A *campus* is a building or group of buildings connected into one enterprise network that consists of many LANs. A campus is further defined as a company or a portion of a company contained in a fixed geographic area.

The distinct characteristic of a campus environment is that the company that owns the campus network usually owns the physical wires deployed in the campus. The campus network topology is primarily a LAN technology connecting all the end systems within the building or buildings. Campus networks generally use LAN technologies, such as Ethernet, Token Ring, and Fiber Distributed Data Interface (FDDI). Figure 1-1 shows a sample campus network.

Network designers generally deploy a campus design that is optimized for the fastest functional architecture that runs on the existing physical wire. This coursebook discusses the requirements of emerging applications and how higher-speed technologies, such as Fast Ethernet, Fast EtherChannel, and Gigabit Ethernet, along with multilayer switching (MLS), provide wire-speed data transfer to the desktop.

Regardless of the underlying technology, the main challenge facing network designers and administrators today is to have their campus LAN run effectively and efficiently. In order to achieve this goal, you must understand, implement, and manage the traffic flow throughout your network.

Originally, campus networks consisted of a single LAN to which new users were added. Because of distance limitations, campus networks usually were confined to a building or several buildings in close proximity to each other. The LAN was a physical network that connected the devices. In the case of Ethernet, all the devices shared the available half-duplex 10 Mbps. Because of the carrier sense multiple access collision detect (CSMA/CD) scheme used by the Ethernet, the whole LAN was considered a collision domain.

Figure 1-1 *A Traditional Campus Network*

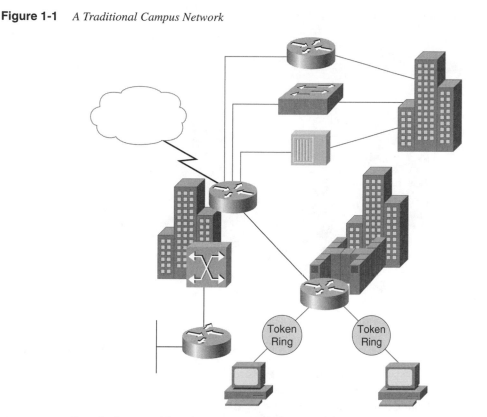

Few design considerations were needed to provide user access to the network backbone. Because of the limitations of Ethernet, physically adjacent users were connected to a single access device to minimize the number of taps into the backbone. Although hubs met this requirement and became standard devices for multiple network access, increased user demand quickly impacted the network's performance.

Traditional Campus Issues

The major problems with traditional networks are availability and performance. These two problems are impacted by the amount of bandwidth in the network.

In a single collision domain, frames are visible to all devices on the LAN and are free to collide. Multiport bridges segment the LAN into discrete collision domains. and forward Layer 2 data frames to only the segment that contains the destination address. Because bridge ports separate the LAN into distinct physical segments, bridges also help resolve Ethernet's distance limitations. Bridges must, however, forward broadcasts, multicasts, and unknown unicasts to all ports. Figure 1-2 shows that bridges terminate collision domains.

Figure 1-2   *A Bridge on a Traditional Campus Network*

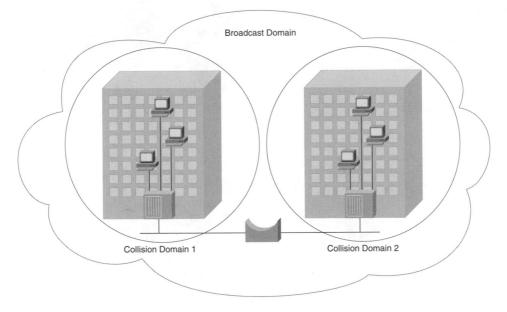

NOTE	A collision domain consists of all the devices that can see or be involved in a collision. A Layer 2 device such as a bridge or switch borders a collision domain. A collision domain is different from a broadcast domain. A broadcast domain consists of all the devices that can see the broadcast. A Layer 3 device such as a router borders a broadcast domain. By default, traditional bridge ports create separate collision domains but participate in the same broadcast domain.

Because bridges read only the Media Access Control (MAC) address in the frame, however, frames containing the broadcast MAC address still flood the entire network. Also, a single network device could malfunction and flood the network with indiscriminate jabber, virtually disabling the network. Because routers operate at the network layer, these devices can make intelligent decisions regarding the flow and type of information to and from a network subnet.

Examples of broadcasts that ask questions are IP Address Resolution Protocol (ARP) requests, NetBIOS name requests, and Internetwork Packet Exchange (IPX) Get Nearest Server requests. These types of broadcasts typically flood the entire subnet and have the target device respond directly to the broadcast. Figure 1-3 illustrates how multicasts, broadcasts, and even unknown unicasts become global events in the bridged network because each bridge processes the request for the MAC address for Server A.

Figure 1-3   *The Request for Server A's MAC Address Is Processed on Every Bridge in a Bridged Network*

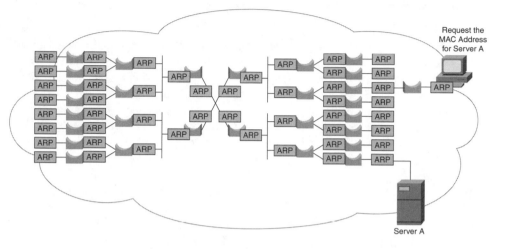

Examples of broadcasts that advertise are IPX Service Advertising Protocol (SAP) packets and routing protocols such as the Routing Information Protocol (RIP) and Interior Gateway Routing Protocol (IGRP).

Finally, multicast traffic can also consume bandwidth. Multicast traffic transmits to a specific group; however, depending on the number of users in a group or the type of application data contained in the multicast packet, this type of transmission can consume most, if not all, of the network resources. Examples of multicast implementations are the Cisco IPTV application using multicast packets to distribute multimedia data, and Novell 5 on IP using multicast packets to locate services.

As networks grow, so does broadcast traffic. Excessive broadcasts reduce the bandwidth available to the end users. In worst-case scenarios, broadcast storms can effectively shut down the network, because the broadcasts monopolize all the available bandwidth.

Also, in a bridge only network, all network-attached workstations and servers are forced to decode all broadcast frames. This action generates additional CPU interrupts and degrades application performance.

A Solution to Broadcast Domain Issues: Localize Traffic

There are two options for addressing the broadcast containment issue for large switched LAN sites.

The first option is to use routers to create many subnets, logically segmenting the traffic. LAN broadcasts do not pass through routers. Although this approach will filter broadcasts, traditional routers process each packet and can create a bottleneck in the network. For example, a Layer 2 bridge or switch can process millions of packets per second, while a traditional router will process in the hundreds of thousands of packets per second. This difference in packet processing speed can cause a bottleneck in the network if a large amount of traffic has to cross the Layer 3 device.

The second option is to implement virtual LANs (VLANs) within the switched network. For the purpose of this book, VLANs are defined as broadcast domains. A VLAN is a group of end devices, on multiple physical LAN segments or switches, that communicates as if these end devices were located on a single shared-media LAN segment. Devices on the same VLAN need not be physically colocated in the same part of the building or campus; however, Cisco recommends a one-to-one correspondence between VLANs and IP subnets. Figure 1-4 shows the usage of VLANs to separate the network into individual broadcast domains.

Figure 1-4 *VLANs*

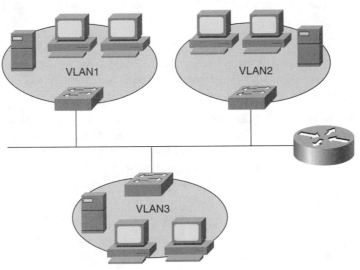

One of the primary benefits of VLANs is that LAN switches can be used to effectively contain broadcast traffic and separate traffic flows.

Because a VLAN is essentially a broadcast domain, the broadcast domain is now defined by a particular set of ports on switches. None of the switches in the set will bridge any frames between two VLANs. *It is important to note that routers are required to move traffic between broadcast domains.*

Current Campus Networks

Most campus networks now consist of two components: LAN switches and routers. By creating smaller Layer 2 broadcast domains and linking them using Layer 3 functionality, network administrators can filter broadcast traffic, interconnect multiprotocol workgroups, and offer a level of secure traffic.

Traffic in the Network

Devices and associated software applications running on the network all generate data traffic. Your network probably has at least the typical applications, such as word processing, file transfer, and electronic mail. These applications do not require much bandwidth, and their traffic patterns are intuitive.

However, emerging campus LANs have and need much more than these basic applications. Multifaceted applications, such as desktop publishing, videoconferencing, and WebTV multicast programs, are all gaining popularity. The characteristics of these applications are not always as easy to predict.

NOTE   It is recommended that you maintain a snapshot of the traffic on your network using a device such as a protocol analyzer or probe. Traffic patterns should be monitored on an ongoing basis, because they will change over time. A good understanding of your network's traffic patterns and applications is essential for planning and managing the network, as well as for future modifications such as quality of service (QoS).

The 80/20 Rule

Ideally, end users with common interests or work patterns are placed in the same logical network as the servers they access most often. With the definition of logical networks, most of the traffic within these workgroups is limited to the local segment. This simple task minimizes the load on the network backbone.

The 80/20 rule states that in a properly designed network environment, 80 percent of the traffic on a given network segment is local. Not more than 20 percent of the network traffic should move across a backbone. Backbone congestion indicates that traffic patterns are not meeting the 80/20 rule. In this case, rather than adding switches or upgrading hubs, network administrators can improve network performance by doing one of the following:

- Moving resources such as applications, software programs, and files from one server to another to contain traffic locally within a workgroup

- Moving users logically, if not physically, so that the workgroups more closely reflect the actual traffic patterns

- Adding servers so that users can access them locally without having to cross the backbone

The New 20/80 Rule

Traffic patterns are moving toward what is now referred to as the 20/80 model. In the 20/80 model, only 20 percent of traffic is local to the workgroup LAN, and 80 percent of the traffic is required to go off the local network.

Two factors contribute to these changing traffic patterns:

- With Web-based computing, such as Internet applications, a PC can be both a subscriber and a publisher of information. As a result, information can come from anywhere in the network, creating massive amounts of traffic that must travel across subnet boundaries. Users hop transparently between servers across the entire enterprise by using hyperlinks, without the need to know where the data is located.

- The second factor leading to the loss of locality is the move toward server consolidation. Enterprises are deploying centralized server farms because of the reduced cost of ownership, security, and ease of management. All traffic from the client subnets to these servers must travel across the campus backbone.

This change in traffic patterns means that 80 percent of the traffic now must cross a Layer 3 device. Because routing is a CPU-intensive process, the point where the Layer 3 processing takes place can lead to bottlenecks in the network. This change in traffic patterns requires the network Layer 3 performance to match the Layer 2 performance.

The new 20/80 rule makes it difficult for network administrators to manage VLANs. Network administrators do not want to spend their time tracking traffic patterns and redesigning the network. Because VLANs are created on the premise that most traffic is interworkgroup, end stations need to be in the same broadcast domain to take advantage of the switched infrastructure.

With the new 20/80 rule, end devices need access to multiple VLANs. However, these end devices still need to operate within their current VLANs.

With current and future traffic patterns moving away from the traditional 80/20 rule, more traffic must flow between subnets (VLANs). Also, access to specific devices needs to be controlled. To perform these functions, routing technology is required within the network.

All these factors together are redesigning the traditional networks into a new campus model.

The Emerging Campus Network

Customer requirements for the campus network are evolving. This section presents the features and technologies that can be used to respond to these requirements.

The key requirements placing pressure on the emerging campus designs are as follows:

- **Fast convergence**—This requirement stipulates that the network must adapt quickly to network topology changes. This requirement becomes critical as the campus network grows in geographic scope.
- **Deterministic paths**—This requirement demands the desirability of a given path to a destination for certain applications or user groups.
- **Deterministic failover**—This requirement specifies that a mechanism be in place to ensure that the network is operational at all times.
- **Scalable size and throughput**—This requirement orders that as the network grows and new applications are added, the infrastructure must handle the increased traffic demands.
- **Centralized applications**—This requirement dictates that centralized applications be available to support most or all users on the network.
- **The new 20/80 rule**—This requirement focuses on the shift in traditional traffic patterns.
- **Multiprotocol support**—This requirement specifies that campus networks must now support multiprotocol environments.
- **Multicasting**—This requirement demands that campus networks support IP multicast traffic in addition to IP unicast traffic.

Emerging Campus Structure

User demands and complex applications force network designers to focus on the traffic patterns in the network. No longer can networks be divided into subnetworks based only on the number of users. The emergence of servers that run global applications also has a direct effect on the load across the network. A higher traffic load across the entire network results in the need for more efficient routing and switching techniques.

In the new campus model, traffic patterns dictate the placement of the services required by the end user. Services can be separated into three separate categories:

- Local services
- Remote services
- Enterprise services

Local Services

A local service is when the entities that provide services reside on the same subnet, and therefore, the same virtual network as the user. Local services remain in specific areas of the network. Traffic to and from local services is confined between the server, switches, and end users. Local traffic does not enter the network backbone or move through a router.

To service the localized traffic, Layer 2 switches are moving to the edge of the network and into the wiring closets. These switches connect end-user devices and servers into common workgroups.

Remote Services

A remote service is an entity that might be geographically close to the end user but is not on the same subnet or VLAN as that user. Traffic to and from remote services might or might not cross the backbone. Because these services are remote to the requesting end user, however, requests for remote services will cross broadcast domain boundaries. Therefore, switches connect to Layer 3 devices to allow for cross-broadcast domain boundary traffic. The router also controls the type of traffic that crosses the network backbone.

Enterprise Services

Enterprise services are services common to all users. Examples of enterprise services are e-mail, Internet access, and videoconferencing. Because all users need to access enterprise services, these servers and services exist within a separate subnet placed close to the network's backbone. Because enterprise services exist outside the end user's broadcast domain, Layer 3 devices are required for access to these services. Enterprise services might or might not be grouped by Layer 2 switches.

Placing the enterprise servers close to the backbone ensures the same distance from each user; however, this also means that all traffic going to an enterprise server crosses the backbone.

Figure 1-5 shows the three services and how traffic patterns dictate the placement of these services.

Figure 1-5   *Sample Emerging Campus Network Structure*

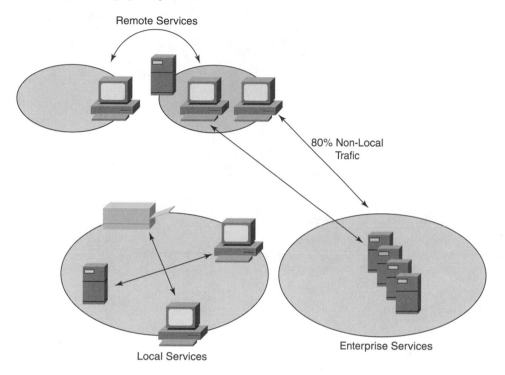

Switching Technologies

Due to the emerging 20/80 rule, network managers want to take advantage of the high throughput benefits of switching technology while still retaining Layer 3 functionality in the network. Therefore, a new model is required to support these requirements. This model employs a concept of providing switching techniques for Layer 2, 3, and 4 functions.

Basic Layer Terminology

Most communication environments use a model that separates the communications functions and applications processing into layers. Each layer serves a specific function. This coursebook focuses on Layers 2, 3, and 4 of this model. Figure 1-6 shows the basic layer terminology.

Figure 1-6   *Basic Layer Terminology*

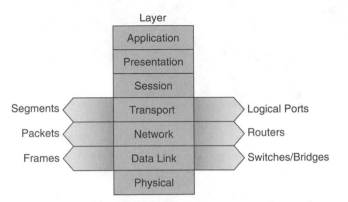

Each layer uses its own layer protocol to communicate with peer layers in another system. Each layer protocol exchanges information, called protocol data units (PDUs), between peer layers. A given layer can use a more specific name for its PDU. Table 1-1 gives examples of specific PDUs for Layers 2, 3, and 4 and the device types that process those PDUs.

Table 1-1   *PDU and Device Types Relating to the OSI Layers*

Model Layer	PDU Type	Device Type
Data Link (Layer 2)	Frames	Switches/bridges
Network (Layer 3)	Packets	Routers
Transport (Layer 4)	TCP segments	TCP ports

Each peer-layer protocol uses the services of the underlying layers. Thus, Transmission Control Protocol (TCP) segments are encapsulated in Layer 3 packets, and Layer 3 packets are encapsulated in Layer 2 frames. The layer-specific device processes only those PDU headers for which the device is responsible.

Layer 2 Switching

Layer 2 switching is hardware-based bridging. In a switch, frame forwarding is handled by specialized hardware called Application-Specific Integrated Circuits (ASICs). Because of ASIC technology, switches also provide scalability to gigabit speeds and low latency at costs significantly lower than Ethernet bridges.

NOTE   An ASIC is an Application-Specific Integrated Circuit. This means that an application or process has been implemented in hardware or an integrated circuit chip. ASICs are used in everything from switches to wireless phones. For more information on specific ASICs in Cisco switches, refer to Appendix B, "Switching Architectures and Functional Descriptions."

Layer 2 switches give network managers the ability to increase bandwidth without adding unnecessary complexity to the network. Layer 2 data frames consist of both infrastructure content, such as MAC addresses, and end-user content. At Layer 2, no modification is required to the packet infrastructure content when going between like Layer 1 interfaces, such as from Ethernet to Fast Ethernet. However, changes to infrastructure content might occur when bridging between unlike media types such as FDDI and Ethernet or Token Ring and Ethernet.

Workgroup connectivity and network segmentation are the two primary uses for Layer 2 switches. The high performance of a Layer 2 switch can produce network designs that decrease the number of hosts per physical segment. Decreasing the hosts per segment leads to a flatter network design with more segments in the campus.

However, for all its advantages, Layer 2 switching has all the same characteristics and limitations as bridging, as shown in Figure 1-7. Broadcast domains built with Layer 2 switches still experience the same scaling and performance issues as the large bridged networks of the past. The broadcast and multicast radius increases with the number of hosts, and broadcasts still interrupt all the end stations. The Spanning-Tree Protocol limitations of slow convergence and blocked links still apply.

Given the limitations of Layer 2 switching, there is still a need for Layer 3 functionality within the network.

NOTE   Although switches are much faster than the traditional bridge, Layer 2 switching and bridging are logically equivalent and are used synonymously in this book.

Figure 1-7 *Sample Network with Layer 2 Switching*

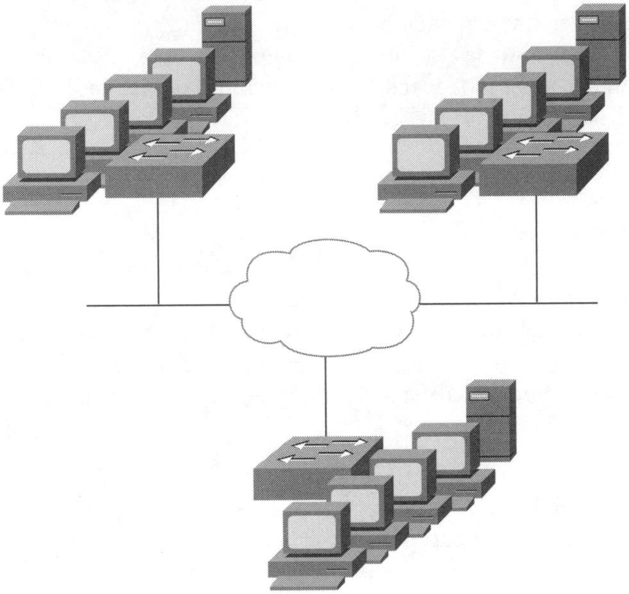

Benefits of Routing

Routers make optimal path decisions based on Layer 3 addressing. Routers improve network segmentation by determining the next network point to which a packet should be forwarded based on an optimal path decision. Routers do not forward Layer 2 broadcast frames, nor do routers forward multicast packets on a network that does not have any multicast clients.

Routing decisions must be performed for every packet received by the routing process. Incoming packets include a destination address (DA) field identifying a unique destination within the network. Routers use the DA to look up the next-hop router address and physical point in their routing tables.

After path determination is complete, packet forwarding is a well-defined set of packet manipulations. Figure 1-8 shows how routers make optimal path decisions based on Layer 3 protocols.

Figure 1-8   *An Example of a Optimized Routed Path*

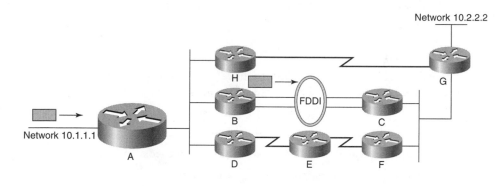

NOTE	Each routed packet undergoes a very similar process. This process includes determining the Layer 3 destination by looking at the DA in the Layer 3 packet. The router then looks up the destination in the routing table in order to find the next-hop Layer 3 address. After the next-hop Layer 3 address has been determined, the router looks up the Layer 2 address of the next hop in a table that maps Layer 3 addresses to Layer 2 addresses. This would be, for example, an ARP table for IP. After both of these lookups have occurred, the frame undergoes a process sometimes called an *inline rewrite*. This process overwrites the old Layer 2 information with the new information, including the new source and destination MAC addresses, and it decrements or increments the Time To Live in the Layer 3 packet. After all this is complete, the packet is forwarded out the egress interface.

A network layer address identifies an entity at the network layer of the OSI reference model and is called a *virtual address* or *logical address*. Routers and other internetworking devices require one network-layer address per physical network connection for each network-layer protocol supported.

Because routers map a single Layer 3 logical address to a single network device, routers limit or secure network traffic based on identifiable attributes within each packet. These options can be applied to inbound or outbound packets on any router interface.

Concurrent with the increasing acceptance of Layer 2 switching as an essential component of network infrastructure are two other developments:

- Migration of servers to server farms for increased security and management of data resources

- Deployment of intranets, with organization-wide client/server communications based on Web technology

These factors are moving data flows off local subnets and onto the routed network, where the limitations of router performance can increasingly lead to bottlenecks.

Layer 3 Switching

Layer 3 switching is hardware-based routing. In particular, packet forwarding is handled by specialized hardware ASICs. A Layer 3 switch does everything to a packet that a traditional router does, such as the following:

- Determines the forwarding path based on Layer 3 information
- Validates the integrity of the Layer 3 header via checksum
- Verifies packet expiration and updates accordingly
- Processes and responds to any option information
- Updates forwarding statistics in the Management Information Base (MIB)
- Applies security controls if required

The primary difference between the packet-switching operation of a router and a Layer 3 switch is the physical implementation. In general-purpose routers, microprocessor-based engines typically perform packet switching. A Layer 3 switch performs packet switching with hardware.

NOTE   A Layer 3 device, such as a router or switch, performs two basic functions. The first function is to make a path determination based on the information found in the Layer 3 address. This is done through the use of routing protocols to build routing tables. The routing tables are used to determine how a packet should move through the network. The second function that a router must perform is called *packet switching*. Packet switching is the process of rewriting the Layer 2 information, decrementing the Time To Live (TTL) field, and moving the frame from one interface to the next. This process of packet switching should not be confused with basic Layer 2 switching.

Cisco currently has two major implementations of Layer 3 switching for the Catalyst switch product: multilayer switching and Cisco Express Forwarding. Multilayer switching is covered in-depth in this book. Cisco Express Forwarding is covered in Appendix B.

High-performance packet-by-packet Layer 3 switching is achieved in different ways. For example, the Cisco 12000 Gigabit Switch Router (GSR) achieves wire-speed Layer 3 switching with a crossbar switch matrix. The Catalyst family of multilayer switches performs Layer 3 switching with special ASICs.

Because it is designed to handle high-performance LAN traffic, a Layer 3 switch can be placed anywhere within the network, cost-effectively replacing the traditional router.

NOTE	Layer 3 switching and routing are logically equivalent and are used synonymously in this book.

Layer 4 Switching

Layer 4 switching refers to Layer 3 hardware-based routing that considers the application. Information in packet headers typically includes Layer 2 and Layer 3 addressing and the Layer 3 protocol type, plus more fields relevant to Layer 3 devices, such as TTL and checksum. The packet also contains information relevant to the higher layers within the communicating hosts, such as the protocol type and port number.

A simple definition of Layer 4 switching is the ability to make forwarding decisions based on not just the MAC address or source/destination IP addresses but on these Layer 4 parameters. In TCP or User Datagram Protocol (UDP) flows, the application is encoded as a port number in the segment header. Layer 4 switching is vendor-neutral and is beneficial even when added to preexisting network environments.

Cisco routers can control traffic based on Layer 4 information. One method of controlling Layer 4 traffic is by using standard or extended access lists. Another method is to provide Layer 4 accounting of flows using NetFlow switching.

Finally, when performing Layer 4 functions, a switch reads the TCP and UDP fields to determine what type of information the packet is carrying. The network manager can program the switch to prioritize traffic by application. This function allows network managers to define a quality of service (QoS) for end users. When being used for QoS purposes, Layer 4 switching means that a videoconferencing application might be granted more bandwidth than an e-mail message.

Layer 4 switching is necessary if your policy dictates granular control of traffic by application, or if you require accounting of traffic by application.

However, it should be noted that switches performing Layer 4 switching need the ability to identify and store large numbers of forwarding table entries. This is especially true if the switch is within the core of an enterprise network. Many Layer 2 and Layer 3 switches have forwarding tables that are sized in proportion to the number of network devices.

With Layer 4 switches, the number of network devices must be multiplied by the number of different application protocols and conversations in use in the network. Thus, the size of the forwarding table can quickly grow as the numbers of end devices and types of applications increase. This large table capacity is essential to creating a high-performance switch that supports wire-speed forwarding of traffic at Layer 4.

Multilayer Switching

Multilayer switching combines Layer 2 switching and Layer 3 routing functionality. Multilayer switching moves campus traffic at wire speed while at the same time satisfying Layer 3 routing requirements. This combination not only solves throughput problems but also removes the conditions under which Layer 3 bottlenecks form. Multilayer switching is based on the "route once, switch many" model.

Multilayer switching in the Catalyst family of switches can operate as a Layer 3 switch or a Layer 4 switch. When operating as a Layer 3 switch, the Catalyst family of switches caches flows based on IP addresses. When operating as a Layer 4 switch, the Catalyst family of switches caches conversations based on source address, destination address, source port, and destination port.

Because Layer 3 or Layer 4 switching is performed in hardware, there is no performance difference between the two modes of operation.

Multilayer switching is discussed in more detail in Chapter 6, "Improving IP Routing Performance with Multilayer Switching."

The Hierarchical Model

Campus network designs have traditionally placed basic network-level intelligence and services at the center of the network and shared bandwidth at the user level. Over the past few years, distributed network services and switching have migrated to the user level, and a distinct model has taken shape.

Figure 1-9 illustrates the hierarchical model and the devices within that model. The layers are defined as follows:

- Access layer
- Distribution layer
- Core layer

This approach allows designers to define building blocks that interconnect users and services. The building block encompasses both distributed network services and network intelligence.

The best-managed campus networks are typically designed following the hierarchical model. This model simplifies the management of the network and allows for controlled growth. The following sections describe the components of the hierarchical model.

Figure 1-9   *The Hierarchical Model*

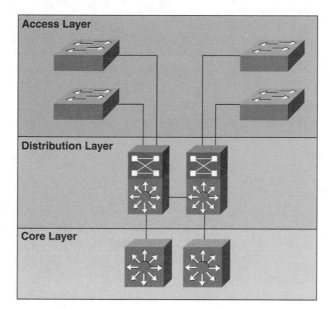

The Access Layer

The access layer of the network is the point at which end users are allowed into the network. This layer can provide further tuning in terms of filtering or access lists; however, the key function of this layer is to provide access for end users into the network. In the campus environment, some of the functions represented by the access layer are as follows:

- Shared bandwidth
- Switched bandwidth
- Layer 2 services, such as VLAN membership and traffic filtering based on broadcast or MAC addresses

The main criterion for access devices is to provide this functionality with low-cost, high-port density devices.

The Distribution Layer

The distribution layer of the network marks the point between the access and core layers of the network. The distribution layer also helps define and differentiate the core. This layer provides a boundary definition and designates where potentially expensive packet manipulations are handled. In the campus environment, the distribution layer can represent a multitude of functions, some of which are as follows:

- VLAN aggregation
- Departmental or workgroup access
- Broadcast or multicast domain definition
- Inter-VLAN routing
- Media translations
- Security

The distribution layer can be summarized as the layer that provides policy-based connectivity.

The Core Layer

The core layer is sometimes referred to as the backbone of a campus network. The primary purpose of the core layer is to switch traffic as fast as possible. This layer of the network should not be involved in expensive packet manipulation or any processing that slows down traffic switching. Functions such as access lists and packet filtering should be avoided in the core. The core layer is responsible for the following functions:

- Providing connectivity between switch blocks
- Providing access to other blocks, such as the WAN block
- Switching frames or packets as quickly as possible

Choosing a Cisco Product

Campus size is an important factor in network design. A large campus has several or many colocated buildings. A medium campus has one or several colocated buildings, and a small campus might have only one building.

The selection of Cisco products at a specific layer depends on the required functionality of each device. The following sections discuss each layer and the appropriate devices. For pictures and further explanation of the products explained in this section, see the Cisco Connection Online (CCO) Web site's product listings at http://www.cisco.com/public/products_prod.shtml.

Access Layer Switches

The Catalyst 1900 or 2820 series switch is an effective access device in a small or medium campus network, connecting individual desktops and 10BaseT hubs to distribution switches with high-speed connections.

The Catalyst 2900 series switch is also effective in providing network access to server clusters or end-user populations of less than 50 users that have high bandwidth requirements. In these types of applications, such as in CAD/CAM and IC design environments, the 2900 series switch provides up to 1000 Mbps throughput for client/server applications and enterprise servers.

The Catalyst 4000 series provides an advanced high-performance enterprise switching solution optimized for connecting up to 96 users and data center server environments that require up to 36 Gigabit Ethernet ports. The Catalyst 4000 series leverages a multigigabit architecture for 10/100/1000 Mbps Ethernet switching.

The Catalyst 5000 series is an effective access device in large campus networks that need to provide network access for more than 100 end users. This switch supports 10/100/1000 Mbps Ethernet switching.

Distribution Layer Switches

Because the distribution layer switch is the aggregation point for multiple access switches, it must be able to handle the total amount of traffic from these devices. The distribution layer switch also must be able to participate in multilayer switching with a route processor. Therefore, the most effective distribution switch devices are the Catalyst 5000 series and 2926G switches. For Layer 3 switching, the Catalyst 5000 series switches support an internal route processor module, and the 2926G switch works with an external router, such as the 4x00 and 7x00 series routers.

The Catalyst 6000 switches are effective at the distribution level, where users require very high densities of Fast or Gigabit Ethernet—up to 384 10/100, 192 100FX, and 130 Gigabit Ethernet ports.

NOTE   When choosing a distribution layer switch, remember to consider the amount of aggregate bandwidth to support the access layer devices and connectivity to the core layer. The Catalyst 5000 is best used in small to medium networks where the primary connectivity is 10/100 Mb Ethernet. The Catalyst 5000 has a 3.6 Gbps switch fabric, which can be oversubscribed if it supports many Gigabit Ethernet ports. The Catalyst 6000 is recommended in medium to large network environments due to its ability to handle Gigabit Ethernet better than the Catalyst 5000. The Catalyst 6000 has a 32 Gbps switch fabric, which allows it to handle a larger number of Gigabit Ethernet connections. Refer to Appendix B for a more detailed discussion of switch fabrics and oversubscription.

Core Layer Switches

For core backbone implementations, the Catalyst 6500 and 8500 series provide wire-speed multicast forwarding and routing, as well as the Protocol-Independent Multicast (PIM) protocol for scalable multicast routing.

Both of these switches provide the high bandwidth and performance that is required for a campus backbone. They are ideal for aggregating multiprotocol traffic from multiple wiring closets or from workgroup switches, such as the Catalyst 5000/6000.

The Building Block Approach

In an attempt to ease the design process of small to large campus networks, Cisco has created a set of building blocks for the network. These building blocks allow a design to scale as small or as large as is necessary.

Network building blocks can be any one of the following fundamental campus elements or contributing variables.

Campus elements:

- Switch block
- Core block

Contributing variables:

- Server block
- WAN block
- Mainframe block

The fundamental campus elements are described in this section. Figure 1-10 shows the campus elements as well as the contributing blocks, or variables, connected by the core block.

NOTE   For more information on the various components of the building blocks, refer to the Campus Network Design Case Study white paper, located at the CCO Web site (http://www.cisco.com).

Figure 1-10   *Campus Network Building Blocks*

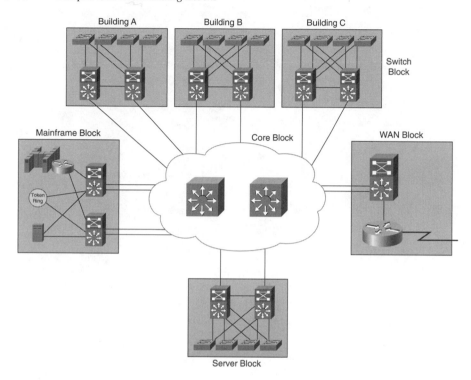

The Switch Block

The switch block contains a balanced implementation of scalable Layer 2 switching and Layer 3 services. Although the current generation of LAN switches is replacing shared media concentrators, LAN switches are not replacements for Layer 3 devices. Therefore, the switch block consists of both switch and router functionality. The switch block shown in Figure 1-11 prevents all broadcast traffic as well as network problems from traversing the core block and from reaching other switch blocks.

Figure 1-11   *The Switch Block*

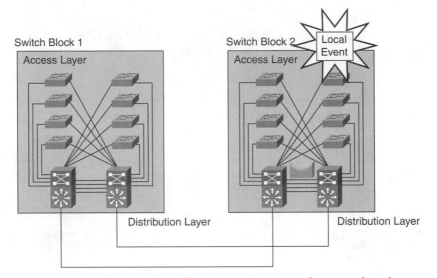

Layer 2 switches in the wiring closets connect users to the network at the access layer and provide dedicated bandwidth to each port. The Catalyst 2900 and 2820/1900 series switches provide cost-effective wiring closet connectivity.

The access devices merge into one or more distribution devices. The distribution device provides Layer 2 connectivity between access switches and acts as a central connection point for all of the switches in the wiring closets.

The distribution layer also provides Layer 3 functionality, which supports routing and networking services. The distribution layer shields the switch block against failures in other parts of the network.

The distribution device can be one of the following:

- A switch and external router combination
- A multilayer switch

These distribution layer devices are discussed in more detail in Chapter 5, "Inter-VLAN Routing."

If the switch block experiences a broadcast storm, the router prevents the storm from propagating into the core and into the rest of the network. Each block is protected from the other blocks when failures occur. However, the switch block, in which the broadcast storm occurs, still experiences network problems until the device generating the broadcasts is found and removed from the network.

NOTE   Cisco has attempted to address the problem of broadcast storms by adding broadcast thresholds to their switches. A broadcast threshold prevents the port from receiving broadcasts until the number of broadcasts drops below a specific number of broadcasts per second or a specific percentage of traffic. This prevents the broadcasts from overwhelming the device, such as a workstation, on the other end of the port.

Switch Block Characteristics

Access layer switches may support one or more subnets. A subnet must reside within one broadcast domain. This means that all stations residing in or ports configured on the same VLAN are assigned network addresses within the same subnet. However, a single VLAN can support multiple subnets.

The broadcast isolation feature of VLANs is the characteristic that allows VLANs to be identified with subnets. For example, the IP Address Resolution Protocol (ARP) propagates only within the VLAN of the originating request. All subnets terminate on Layer 3 devices, such as a router or a Route Switch Module (RSM). To connect to devices in other VLANs, the frame must traverse a router. In this model, VLANs should not extend beyond the distribution switch.

Access layer switches have redundant connections, or *uplinks,* to the distribution switch to maintain resiliency. The Spanning-Tree Protocol allows these redundant links to exist while preventing undesirable loops in the switch block. The Spanning-Tree Protocol terminates at the boundary of the switch block.

All switches in the network may be connected to a common management default subnet. VLAN management domains are discussed in greater detail in Chapter 3, "Defining Common Workgroups with VLANs."

NOTE   Cisco philosophy discourages trunking across the core unless discrete VLAN1 connections are made between the distribution and core switches.

Sizing the Switch Block

Although the size of a switch block is flexible, certain factors limit the size of this block. The number of switches that collapse into the distribution layer depends on several factors:

- Different types and patterns of traffic
- Amount of Layer 3 switching capacity at the distribution layer
- Number of users per access layer switch

- Extent to which subnets need to traverse geographical locations within the network
- Size to which the Spanning-Tree domains should be allowed to grow

There are two main factors in sizing the switch block:

- Traffic types and behavior
- Size and number of workgroups

NOTE   This model is based on no more than 2000 users per switch block.

A switch block is too large if

- A traffic bottleneck occurs in the routers at the distribution layer due to intensive CPU processing required by services such as access lists
- Broadcast or multicast traffic slows down the switches and routers

---

NOTE   The decision to break up the block should be based on the traffic going across the network, rather than the specific number of nodes in a building block. It is important to take periodic snapshots of traffic flows in order to be able to determine when to break up the switch block.

The Core Block

A core is required when there are two or more switch blocks. The core block is responsible for transferring cross-campus traffic without any processor-intensive operations, such as routing. All the traffic going to and from the switch blocks, the server blocks, the Internet, and the wide-area network passes through the core.

Traffic going from one switch block to another also must travel through the core. Because of these traffic patterns, the core handles much more traffic than any other block. Therefore, the core must be able to pass the traffic to and from the blocks as quickly as when there are two or more switch blocks.

In Figure 1-12, the core block supports frame, packet, or cell-based technologies, depending on your specific needs. This coursebook discusses and demonstrates an Ethernet core. Because the distribution switch provides Layer 3 functionality, individual subnets will connect all distribution and core devices.

Figure 1-12   *The Core Layer*

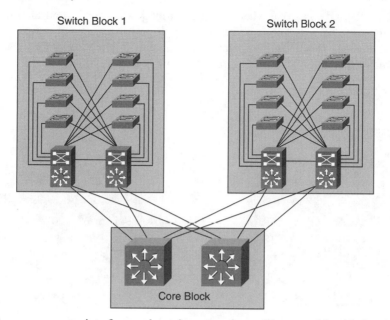

The core can consist of one subnet; however, for resiliency and load balancing, at least two subnets are configured. Because VLANs terminate at the distribution device, core links are not trunk links, and traffic is routed across the core. Therefore, core links do not carry multiple subnets per link.

One or more switches make up the core subnet; however, Cisco recommends that a minimum of two devices be present in the core to provide redundancy. The core block can consist of high-speed Layer 2 devices such as Catalyst 5500 or 6500 series switches or Layer 3 devices such as the 8500 series routers.

At a minimum, the media between the distribution switches and the core layer switches should be capable of supporting the amount of load handled by the distribution switch.

At a minimum, the links between core switches in the same core subnet should be sufficient to switch the aggregate amount of traffic with respect to the input aggregation switch traffic. The design of the core should consider average link utilization while still allowing for future traffic growth.

There are two basic core designs:

- Collapsed core
- Dual core

Collapsed Core

The collapsed core exists when both the distribution and core layer functions are performed in the same device. A collapsed core design is prevalent in small campus networks. Although the functions of each layer are contained in the same device, the functionality remains distinctly separate. Figure 1-13 shows a sample collapsed core.

Figure 1-13   *A Collapsed Core*

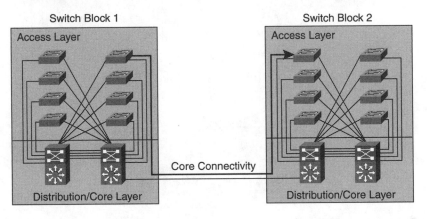

In a collapsed core design, each access layer switch has a redundant link to the distribution layer switch. Each access layer switch may support more than one subnet; however, all subnets terminate on Layer 3 ports on the distribution switch.

Redundant uplinks provide Layer 2 resiliency between the access and distribution switches. Spanning Tree blocks the redundant links to prevent loops.

Redundancy is provided at Layer 3 by the dual distribution switches with the Hot Standby Router Protocol (HSRP), providing transparent default gateway operations for IP. In the event that the primary routing process fails, connectivity to the core is maintained. HSRP is discussed in more detail in Chapter 7, "Configuring HSRP for Fault-Tolerant Routing."

Dual Core

A dual-core configuration is necessary when two or more switch blocks exist and redundant connections are required. Figure 1-14 shows a dual-core configuration in which the core contains only Layer 2 switches for the backbone. The core devices are not linked to avoid any bridging loops.

Figure 1-14   *A Dual Core*

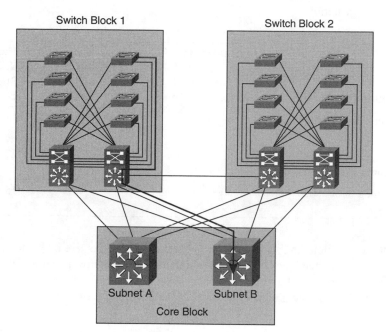

A dual-core topology provides two equal-cost paths and twice the bandwidth. Each core switch carries a symmetrical number of subnets to the Layer 3 function of the distribution device. Each switch block is redundantly linked to both core switches, allowing for two distinct and equal path links. If one core device fails, convergence is not an issue, because the routing tables in the distribution devices already have an established route to the remaining core device. The Layer 3 routing protocol provides the link determination across the core, and HSRP provides quick failover determination. Spanning Tree is not needed in the core, because there are no redundant links between the core switches.

Sizing the Core

Because Layer 3 devices isolate the core, routing protocols are used to maintain the current state of the network. As the routing protocol sends these updates and changes to the routers throughout the network, the network topology might also change. The more routers connected to the network, the longer it takes these updates and changes to propagate throughout the network and change the topology. Also, one or more of the routers might connect to a WAN or the Internet, which adds more sources of routing updates and topology changes.

The routing protocol used on the Layer 3 devices determines the number of distribution devices that can be attached to the core. Table 1-2 gives examples of some widely used protocols and the maximum number of peer routers for which these protocols can maintain state information.

Table 1-2   *Maximum Number of Supported Blocks by Routing Protocol*

Routing Protocol	Maximum Number of Supported Routing Peers	Number of Subnet Links to the Core	Maximum Number of Supported Blocks
Open Shortest Path First (OSPF)	50	2	25
Enhanced Interior Gateway Routing Protocol (EIGRP)	50	2	25
Routing Information Protocol (RIP)	30	2	15

All blocks, including server, WAN, and mainframe blocks, are included in the maximum number of switch blocks supported in Table 1-2. The figures given in Table 1-2 are very optimistic for the total number of peers supported by each of the routing protocols. In reality, the maximum number of peers for each of the routing protocols should be closer to 15.

Layer 2 Backbone Scaling

Switched Layer 2 Ethernet cores are very cost-effective and provide high-performance connectivity between switch blocks. The classic design model has several switch blocks, each supporting Layer 2 devices in a wiring closet terminating into a Layer 3 device. The Layer 3 devices are connected by a core composed of Layer 2 devices.

The Spanning-Tree Protocol represents a practical limit to the scale of a Layer 2 switched backbone. As you increase the number of core devices, you need to increase the number of links from the distribution switches to maintain redundancy. Because routing protocols dictate the number of equal-cost paths, the number of independent core switches is limited. Interconnecting the core switches creates bridging loops. Introducing the Spanning-Tree Protocol into the core compromises the high-performance connectivity between switch blocks. Ideally, Layer 2 switched backbones consist of two switches with no Spanning-Tree loops in the topology.

Figure 1-15 has eight distribution layer switches that connect to the core. The distribution layer switches have connections to each of the core layer switches. Note that the core layer switches are not connected to each other in order to prevent a loop. With the two core layer switches there are now two equal-cost paths to all VLAN destinations.

Figure 1-15   *Scaling the Core Block with Layer 2*

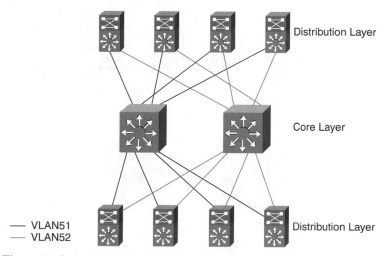

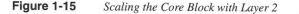

In Figure 1-15, the Layer 2 switched backbone provides redundancy without any Spanning-Tree loops. Because the two core switches are not linked, loops do not occur. Each distribution switch in every switch block has a separate path to each core switch. The dual connection between each core and distribution device provides each Layer 3 device with two equal-cost paths to every other router in the campus.

Layer 3 Backbone Scaling

Most of the designs successfully follow the model that has been presented so far, with Layer 2 at the access layer, Layer 3 at the distribution layer, and Layer 2 at the core layer. This is sometimes referred to as the Layer 2-Layer 3-Layer 2 model. However, there are designs in which having a Layer 3 core layer is advantageous.

You would implement a Layer 3 core for the following reasons:

- Fast convergence
- Automatic load balancing
- Eliminate peering problems

Figure 1-16 shows a Layer 3 core. Each connection from the distribution layer devices is a separate subnet, and the core layer devices are responsible for routing between each of these subnets.

Figure 1-16 *Layer 3 Backbone Scaling*

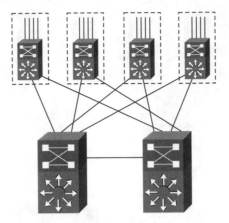

Fast Convergence

As you increase the number of switch blocks and servers, each distribution layer device must be connected to the core. Because there is a limit to the number of switch blocks to a dual Layer 2 core, increasing the number of connections means increasing the number of core devices. To maintain redundancy, the core devices must be connected. After you interconnect Layer 2 devices, bridging loops appear. To eliminate bridging loops in the core, you must enable the Spanning-Tree Protocol. The Spanning-Tree Protocol might have a convergence time of over 50 seconds. If there is a fault in the network's core, Spanning-Tree Protocol convergence can disable a network core for more than one minute.

With the implementation of Layer 3 devices in the core, the Spanning-Tree Protocol becomes unnecessary. In this design, routing protocols are used to maintain the network topology. Convergence for routing protocols takes anywhere from 5 to 10 seconds, depending on the routing protocol.

Automatic Load Balancing

Load balancing tries to achieve a traffic distribution pattern that will best utilize the multiple links that provide redundancy. With multiple, interconnected Layer 2 devices in the core, you must selectively choose the root for utilizing more than one path. You then manually configure the links to support specific VLAN traffic.

With Layer 3 devices in the core, the routing protocols can load balance over multiple equal-cost paths.

Eliminate Peering Problems

Another issue with the Layer 2 core in a very large network involves router peering. Router peering ensures that the routing protocol running within a router maintains state and reachability information about other neighboring routers. In this scenario, each distribution device becomes a peer with every other distribution device in the network. Scalability becomes an issue in the configuration, because each distribution device must maintain state for all other distribution devices.

With the implementation of Layer 3 devices in the core, a hierarchy is created, and the distribution device is not considered a peer with all other distribution devices. This type of core might appear in very large campus networks in which the network supports more than 100 switch blocks.

Implementing Layer 3 devices in the core is expensive. As stated earlier, the main purpose of the core is to move packets as quickly and efficiently as possible. Although Layer 3 devices can support the switching of some protocols, both performance and equipment cost become an issue.

Campus Network Availability Example

The design shown in Figure 1-17 consists of two buildings: North and South. Each building has 10 floors and 1000 users. Each floor is connected to an access switch in the wiring closet. Each access switch is linked to a distribution layer switch.

If a link from a wiring closet switch to the distribution-layer switch is disconnected, 100 users on a floor could lose their connections to the backbone. To prevent this, each access switch has a link to each distribution switch in the building. The Spanning-Tree Protocol blocks the redundant link to prevent loops.

Load balancing across the core is achieved by intelligent Layer 3 routing protocols implemented in the Cisco IOS software. In Figure 1-17, there are four equal-cost paths between the two buildings. The four paths from the North building to the South building are AXC, AYD, BXC, and BYD. These four Layer 2 paths are considered equal by Layer 3 routing protocols. Note that all paths from both buildings to the backbone are single, logical hops.

Figure 1-17 *A Campus Network Availability Example*

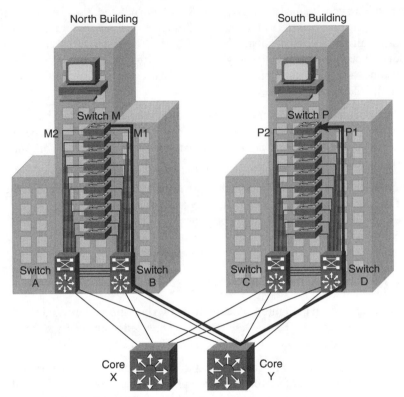

In this scenario, a user attached to access switch M wants to transfer data to a user attached to switch P. The active router is multilayer switch B, and HSRP is enabled. As shown in Figure 1-17, the logical path for the data from M to P is as follows:

* Access switch M switches the data over link M1 to multilayer switch B.

* Multilayer switch B routes the data out subnet BY to core Y.

* Core Y switches the information out link YD to multilayer switch D.

* Multilayer switch D switches the data over link P1 to access switch P.

If the M1 link fails, however, as shown in Figure 1-18, the redundant M2 link becomes the primary link, and the data path from M to P is as follows:

* Access switch M switches the data over link M2 to multilayer switch A.

* Multilayer switch A switches the data to the active HSRP router, multilayer switch B.

* Multilayer switch B routes the data out subnet BY to core Y.

* Core Y switches the information out link YD to multilayer switch D.

* Multilayer Switch D switches the data over link P1 to access switch P.

Figure 1-18   *Access Layer Switch Failure Causes Data to Fail Over to the Redundant Link*

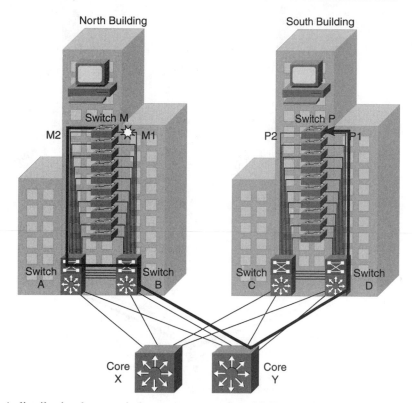

A distribution layer switch represents a point of failure at the building level. One thousand users in the North building could lose their connections to the backbone in the event of a disabled route processor. To provide fault-tolerant access to each user, redundant links connect access layer switches to a pair of Catalyst multilayer switches in the distribution layer, as shown in Figure 1-19.

In Figure 1-19, the route processors in both distribution devices are connected, and HSRP is configured. This configuration allows for fast failover at Layer 3 if one of the distribution switches fails. In this scenario, the data path from M to P is as follows:

- Access switch M switches the data over link M2 to multilayer switch A.

- Because multilayer switch B is disabled, multilayer switch A becomes the active HSRP router and routes the data out subnet AY to core Y.

- Core Y switches the information out link YD to multilayer switch D.

- Multilayer switch D switches the data over link P1 to access switch P.

Figure 1-19 *Redundancy in the Distribution Layer*

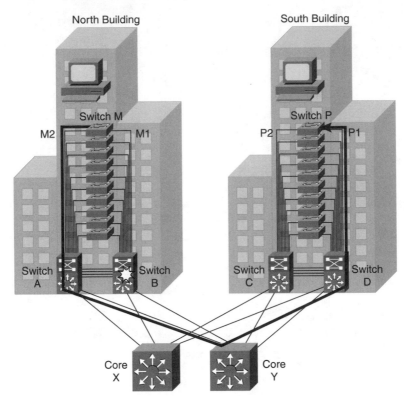

Redundancy in the backbone is achieved by installing two or more Catalyst switches in the core. Each link from the distribution switch to the core is an equal-cost path. This topology provides failover as well as load balancing from each distribution switch across the backbone.

Load balancing across the core is achieved by intelligent Layer 3 routing protocols implemented in the Cisco IOS software. Figure 1-20 shows an example.

If one switch in the core fails, the data path from M to P is as follows:

- Access switch M switches the data over link M2 to multilayer switch A. Link M1 is still disabled.

- Because multilayer switch B is disabled, multilayer switch A becomes the active HSRP router.

- Because core Y is disabled, the data is routed out subnet AX to core X.

- The path at the distribution layer depends on how the ports and VLANs on those devices are configured. In this scenario, the data core X switches the information out link XC to multilayer switch C.

- Multilayer switch C has the MAC address of workstation P in the CAM table, and it switches the data over link P2 to access switch P.

Figure 1-20   *Example of a Core Layer Failure*

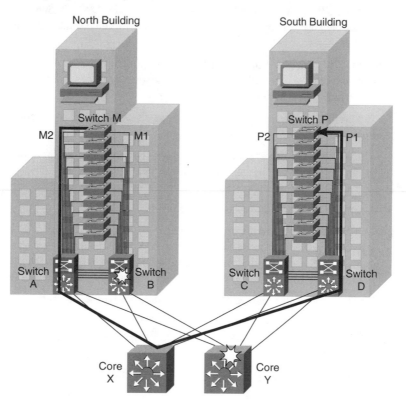

Summary

Many problems in the current campus networks can be solved with proper design and an understanding of the ever-changing traffic patterns. A redundant, well-planned design will provide users of the campus network with availability and fault tolerance and will provide the network administrator with a deterministic flow of traffic.

Here are some of the issues and solutions discussed in this chapter:

- Broadcasts are useful and necessary traffic; however, too much broadcast traffic can cause network performance problems. Managing broadcast traffic is a critical aspect of campus LAN design.

- The location of common workgroups and servers can have a significant impact on traffic patterns.

- Adding more bandwidth is not the long-term solution to meeting the needs of high-priority traffic.

- Multilayer switching combines Layer 2 switching and Layer 3 routing functionality.

- The multilayer design model is inherently scalable. Layer 3 switching performance scales because it is distributed. Backbone performance scales as you add more links or switches.

- A switch block is the unit that contains distributed network services and network intelligence. A switch block consists of Layer 2 switches, Layer 3 routers, and, sometimes, distributed servers.

- A core block is the unit that transfers cross-campus traffic. It can consist of Layer 2 or Layer 3 devices.

- The purpose of network link redundancy is to provide alternative physical pathways through the network in case one pathway fails.

- Routing updates and route changes might propagate to all of the routers on the campus, depending on which routing protocol is in use.

- The number of equal-cost paths supported by the routing protocol also determines the size of the core. For instance, if the routing protocol supports up to six equal-cost paths, these paths should be distributed over a different physical Layer 2 device to maintain a 1:1 redundancy. Hence, six equal-cost paths require six Layer 2 devices.

- Finally, at a minimum, the core layer switches must be capable of scaling to the following:

  $n \times$ amount of load per link at 100 percent capacity = total core switch capacity

  where n is equal to the number of distribution links.

Review Questions

The following questions test your retention of the material presented in this chapter. The answers to the Review Questions can be found in Appendix A, "Answers to Review Questions."

1 Discuss the various trends that have forced the redesign of campus networks.

2 Describe the different switching technologies and how they enable multilayer switching.

3 Explain the multilayer model and how it affects traffic flows in the network.

Written Exercises: Overview of a Campus Network

These exercises help you identify the different switching technologies implemented at OSI Layers 2, 3, and 4. The answers to each task can be found at the end of this chapter.

Task 1: Describing Layer 2, 3, and 4 and Multilayer Switching Functions

For each network function listed in the following table, choose the switching technology that most accurately supports each function, and place the letter of that switching technology next to the function. Each function can have more than one correct answer, so list all possible answers. The first answer is given as an example.

A. Layer 2 switching

B. Layer 3 switching

C. Layer 4 switching

D. Multilayer switching

B	Hardware-based routing
	Hardware-based bridging
	Forwards packets based on application port numbers
	Based on the principle of "route once, switch many"
	Promotes flatter network designs with fewer subnets
	Controls traffic using access lists based on port identifiers
	Provides traffic flow accounting through NetFlow switching
	Combines Layer 2 switching and Layer 3 routing functionality
	Uses frames to communicate with peer layers in another system
	Handles frame forwarding using specialized hardware called ASICs
	Uses packets to communicate with peer layers in another system
	Allows the switch to be programmed to prioritize traffic by application
	Interrogates the initial packet in a flow, which is then forwarded to a cache
	Allows the prioritization of traffic based on specific applications
	Does not modify frame infrastructure when moving frames between like media

	Reads the TCP or UDP field to determine what type of information the packet is carrying
	Repackages multiport bridging technology with significant performance improvements and increased scalability
	Implements a level of security, interrogating traffic based on the source address, destination addresses, and port number

Task 2: Identifying the Switch Layer Solution for a Given Network Requirement

Read each statement carefully. From the following list, choose the corresponding letter of the layer that best fits the description given in each statement. There is only one possible answer for each description:

A.   Access layer

B.   Distribution layer

C.   Core layer

1 This layer is responsible for routing traffic between VLANs.

2 The primary objective of this layer is to switch traffic as fast as possible.

3 This layer provides communication between switch blocks and to the enterprise servers.

4 The key function of this layer is to provide access for end users into the network.

5 This layer provides segmentation and terminates collision and broadcast domains.

6 This layer blocks or forwards traffic into or out of the switch block, based on Layer 3 parameters.

7 Some of the functions represented by this layer are shared bandwidth, VLAN membership, and traffic filtering based on broadcast addresses.

8 The main criterion for devices at this layer is to provide LAN segmentation with low-cost, high-port density devices.

Task 3: Given a Set of User Requirements, Identify the Correct Cisco Product Solution

Read the following scenarios and choose the most appropriate Cisco solution from the list following each scenario.

1 The ABC Company is a small widget-distributing company that wants to interconnect users on multiple floors in the same building. To date, the company has only 15 employees, but it plans to triple that number in the next two years. Because of the nature of the business, users need to access large files on the workgroup servers. What is the most appropriate device for the access layer?

A. Catalyst 8500 series switch

B Catalyst 5500 series switch with an internal RSM

C. Catalyst 1900 series switch with 10BaseT ports

D. Catalyst 2900 series switch with 100BaseTX ports

2 The Acme Engineering Company has redesigned its campus network to support three switch blocks containing 2000 end users in each block. The network administrator wants to control broadcast domains to each individual switch block while still allowing inter-VLAN routing within and between switch blocks. What is the most appropriate device for the distribution layer?

A Catalyst 8500 series switch

B. Catalyst 4000 series switch

C. Catalyst 5500 series switch with an internal RSM

D. Catalyst 1900 series switch with a two-port 100Base uplink module

3 The Tool & Die Manufacturing Company has experienced 300 percent growth over the last year and has recently installed a new multimedia center for distributing company information throughout the campus. The company has requirements for gigabit-speed data transfer, high availability, and inter-VLAN routing between the end users and the enterprise server farms. What is the most appropriate device for the distribution layer?

A Catalyst 8500 series switch

B. Catalyst 1900 series switch with 12 10BaseT ports

C Catalyst 4000 series switch with a six-port Gigabit Ethernet module

D. Catalyst 6000 series switch with a 16-port Gigabit Ethernet module

4 The Rataxes Toy Company needs to interconnect its four separate campus buildings with a high-speed, high-bandwidth backbone. Each building supports a separate department, and each department supports a different network protocol. The network designer has already recommended a Catalyst 6000 series switch at the distribution layer. What is the most appropriate device for the core layer?

A. Catalyst 8500 series switch

B. Catalyst 1900 series switch with 12 10BaseT ports

C. Catalyst 4000 series switch with a six-port Gigabit Ethernet module

D. Catalyst 5500 series switch with a 24-port group switched 100BaseT Ethernet module

Task 1 Answers: Describing Layer 2, 3, and 4 and Multilayer Switching Functions

The following table contains the correct answers for Task 1.

B	Hardware-based routing
A	Hardware-based bridging
B & C	Forwards packets based on application port numbers
D	Based on the principle of "route once, switch many"
A	Promotes flatter network designs with fewer subnets
B & C	Controls traffic using access lists based on port identifiers
B & C	Provides traffic flow accounting through NetFlow switching
D	Combines Layer 2 switching and Layer 3 routing functionality
A	Uses frames to communicate with peer layers in another system
A	Handles frame forwarding using specialized hardware called ASICs
B	Uses packets to communicate with peer layers in another system
C	Allows the switch to be programmed to prioritize traffic by application
D	Interrogates the initial packet in a flow, which is then forwarded to a cache
C	Allows the prioritization of traffic based on specific applications
A	Does not modify frame infrastructure when moving frames between like media
C	Reads the TCP or UDP field to determine what type of information the packet is carrying

A	Repackages multiport bridging technology with significant performance improvements and increased scalability
C	Implements a level of security, interrogating traffic based on the source address, destination addresses, and port number

Task 2 Answers: Identifying the Switch Layer Solution for a Given Network Requirement

The following are the correct answers for Task 2.

1 This layer is responsible for routing traffic between VLANs.

   B. Distribution layer

2 The primary objective of this layer is to switch traffic as fast as possible.

   C. Core layer

3 This layer provides communication between switch blocks and to the enterprise servers.

   C. Core layer

4 The key function of this layer is to provide access for end users into the network.

   A. Access layer

5 This layer provides segmentation and terminates collision and broadcast domains.

   B. Distribution layer

6 This layer blocks or forwards traffic into or out of the switch block, based on Layer 3 parameters.

   B. Distribution layer

7 Some of the functions represented by this layer are shared bandwidth, VLAN membership, and traffic filtering, based on broadcast addresses.

   A. Access layer

8 The main criterion for devices at this layer is to provide LAN segmentation with low-cost, high-port density devices.

   A. Access layer

Task 3 Answers: Given a Set of User Requirements, Identify the Correct Cisco Product Solution

The following are the correct answers for Task 3.

1   The ABC Company is a small widget-distributing company that wants to interconnect users on multiple floors in the same building. To date, the company has only 15 employees, but it plans to triple that number in the next two years. Because of the nature of the business, users need to access large files on the workgroup servers. What is the most appropriate device for the access layer?

   C.   **Catalyst 1900 series switch with 10BaseT ports**

2   The Acme Engineering Company has redesigned its campus network to support three switch blocks containing 2000 end users in each block. The network administrator wants to control broadcast domains to each individual switch block while still allowing inter-VLAN routing within and between switch blocks. What is the most appropriate device for the distribution layer?

   C.   **Catalyst 5500 series switch with an internal RSM**

3   The Tool & Die Manufacturing Company has experienced 300 percent growth over the last year and has recently installed a new multimedia center for distributing company information throughout the campus. The company has requirements for gigabit-speed data transfer, high availability, and inter-VLAN routing between the end users and the enterprise server farms. What is the most appropriate device for the distribution layer?

   D.   **Catalyst 6000 series switch with a 16-port Gigabit Ethernet module**

4   The Rataxes Toy Company needs to interconnect its four separate campus buildings with a high-speed, high-bandwidth backbone. Each building supports a separate department, and each department supports a different network protocol. The network designer has already recommended a Catalyst 6000 series switch at the distribution layer. What is the most appropriate device for the core layer?

   A.   **Catalyst 8500 series switch**

CHAPTER 2

Connecting the Switch Block

Campus networks carry a variety of traffic types. The growing numbers of users and the increasing size of graphical, collaborative, and multimedia applications now prevalent in campus networks are impacting performance on the traditional 10 Mbps Ethernet LANs.

This chapter discusses the various Ethernet technologies that can be used in the campus network and shows you how to establish connections within the switch block at the access layer.

This chapter covers the following topics:

- Cable media types
- Cabling switch block devices
- Configuring connectivity within the switch block

Upon completion of this chapter, you will be able to cable the physical links between devices within the switch block, configure connectivity from the end-user station to the access layer using Ethernet, provide connectivity from the access layer to the distribution layer using Fast Ethernet, ensure network availability by cabling and configuring backup links between the access layer and the distribution layer, and enable interblock communications by configuring high-speed links between the distribution and core switches.

Introduction to Connecting the Switch Block

As more applications and users are configured into the campus network, the need for available bandwidth increases. Choosing a media type involves more than just finding the highest possible bandwidth. Careful consideration should be given to matching the media type to the applications on the network, as well as matching the media type to the aggregate number of nodes that will be using a single server or host. Workstations serving a single user should not be given the same bandwidth as servers that service hundreds of users. To do so would allow a single workstation to monopolize the available bandwidth to the server. In addition, the latency tolerance of an application should be evaluated. Applications, such as file transfers, are very latency-tolerant, whereas other applications such as real-time video are latency-sensitive. Bandwidth requirements and latency tolerance should be carefully analyzed before an application is deployed.

Applications such as multimedia and real-time video are particularly demanding, as are applications such as Web browsing. Future e-commerce transmissions require dedicated connections to accommodate the high density of traffic they frequently generate. With more and more users requiring faster access to large database systems, tolerance for sluggish performance is waning.

The module design of the campus network topology allows for scaling bandwidth appropriately at every level. This approach provides advantages in configuring and managing any size of network.

Every network site is unique, and the performance of the network is a result of a number of different factors. One of those factors is the type and layout of the underlying cables that are used to interconnect the devices, and how the devices in the switch block are configured for basic operations. This chapter covers cable media types, focusing specifically on Ethernet, Fast Ethernet, and Gigabit Ethernet. Additionally, this chapter discusses cabling devices in the switch block.

Cable Media Types

A variety of cable media types have been deployed for local-area networks (LANs), including Ethernet, Token Ring, Arcnet, and FDDI, just to name a few. Most of these cable media types deploy a shared media architecture, meaning that only one device can use the cable segment at a time. As larger applications are added to the network, much work must be put into increasing the bandwidth available to the user. There are two predominant methods to increase the bandwidth to the user:

- Increase the overall bandwidth of the network.
- Decrease the number of devices on the same shared media cable segment.

In the past couple of years, Ethernet has become the most commonly implemented LAN standard. This book focuses only on variations of Ethernet for that reason.

Ethernet

One solution to the bandwidth crunch is Ethernet switching, which dynamically allocates dedicated 10 Mbps connections to each user on the network. Another option is full-duplex switched Ethernet.

Finally, increasing the speed of the link also increases network performance. Whereas Ethernet supports 10 megabits of data per second, Fast Ethernet supports 100 megabits of data per second, and Gigabit supports up to 1000 megabits of data per second.

Within the switch block, network performance is enhanced at the access layer by reducing the number of users per Ethernet segment. Segmentation provides each user, or a group of users connected by a hub, with a dedicated, collision-free 10 Mbps connection to any other node or LAN segment.

NOTE   Ethernet is a LAN technology that offers increased bandwidth to desktop users at the access layer. Ethernet transmits information between end-user devices at speeds of 10 million bits per second.

The availability of powerful, affordable personal computers and workstations has driven the requirement for speed and availability in the campus network. However, existing applications and a new generation of multimedia, imaging, and database products can easily overwhelm a network running at a traditional Ethernet speed of 10 Mbps. Table 2-1 describes the typical layers that utilize 10 Mbps Ethernet.

Table 2-1   *Ethernet 10BaseT Media Deployment Strategy*

Model Layer	Positioning
Access layer	Provides connectivity between the end-user device and the access switch.
Distribution layer	Not typically used at this layer.
Core layer	Not typically used at this layer.

Most cable installers recommend that the 100-meter rule be followed when installing unshielded twisted-pair (UTP) cable connections. The 100-meter rule is broken down into the following distances:

- Five meters from the switch to the patch panel
- Ninety meters from the patch panel to the office punch-down block
- Five meters from the punch-down block to the desktop connection

Short cables in a noisy wiring closet translate to less induced noise on the wire and less crosstalk in large multiple-cable bundles. However, short cables might restrict switch location in large wiring closets, so the 100-meter rule is often overlooked.

Fast Ethernet

For campuses with existing Ethernet installations, increasing the network speed from 10 Mbps to 100 Mbps is preferable to investing in a completely new LAN technology. This requirement forced the networking industry to specify a higher-speed Ethernet that operates at 100 Mbps and is known as Fast Ethernet.

Fast Ethernet technology can be used in a campus network in several different ways. Fast Ethernet is used as the link between the access and distribution-layer devices, supporting the aggregate traffic from each Ethernet segment on the access link.

Fast Ethernet links can also be used to provide the connection between the distribution layer and the core. Because the campus network model supports dual links between each distribution-layer router and core switch, the aggregated traffic from multiple access switches can be load-balanced across the links.

Many client/server networks suffer from too many clients trying to access the same server, creating a bottleneck where the server attaches to the LAN. To enhance client/server performance across the campus network, enterprise servers are connected by Fast Ethernet links to ensure the avoidance of bottlenecks at the server. Fast Ethernet, in combination with switched Ethernet, creates an effective solution for avoiding slow networks. Table 2-2 describes the layers that typically deploy Fast Ethernet.

Table 2-2   *Fast Ethernet Deployment Strategy*

Model Layer	Positioning
Access layer	Gives high-performance PC and workstations 100 Mbps access to the server.
Distribution layer	Provides connectivity between access and distribution layers. Provides connectivity from the distribution layer to the core layer. Provides connectivity from the server block to the core layer.
Core layer	Provides interswitch connectivity.

Fast Ethernet is based on carrier sense multiple access collision detect (CSMA/CD), the Ethernet transmission protocol, and it can use existing UTP or fiber cabling. However, Fast Ethernet reduces the duration of time each bit is transmitted by a factor of 10, allowing packet speed to increase tenfold from 10 Mbps to 100 Mbps. Data can move from 10 Mbps to 100 Mbps without protocol translation or changes to application and networking software. Fast Ethernet also maintains the 10BaseT error control functions, as well as the frame format and length.

Fast Ethernet can run over UTP and fiber. Table 2-3 shows the distance for each media type defined by the Fast Ethernet specification.

Table 2-3   *Distance Limitations for Fast Ethernet*

Technology	Wiring Category	Cable Length Switched Media
100BaseTX	EIA/TIA Category 5 (UTP) Unshielded twisted pair 2 pair	100 meters

Table 2-3   *Distance Limitations for Fast Ethernet (Continued)*

Technology	Wiring Category	Cable Length Switched Media
100BaseT4	EIA/TIA Category 3, 4, 5 (UTP) Unshielded twisted pair 4 pair	100 meters
100BaseFX	MMF cable, with a 62.5-micron fiber-optic core and 125-micron outer cladding (62.5/125)	400 meters

Fast Ethernet can deliver up to 100 Mbps throughput in each direction using full-duplex technology. Full duplex provides bidirectional communication, meaning that 100 Mbps is available for transmission in each direction.

Full-duplex communication is implemented by providing separate transmission paths for transmit and receive data. This implementation disables the collision detection and loopback functions, which are necessary to ensure communication in a shared medium. Switches offer full duplex to directly attached workstations or servers.

Users see greater performance improvements when full-duplex Fast Ethernet is implemented on a distribution-layer connection rather than on a client connection, because client/server applications primarily transmit read/write asymmetrical traffic. Many applications and operating systems have half-duplex conversations. This limits the amount of gain that a client/server station can achieve with the implementation of full duplex.

The Fast Ethernet specification describes a negotiation process that allows devices at each end of a network link to automatically exchange information about the link's capabilities. This negotiation process also affects the configuration necessary to operate together at a maximum common level. For example, autonegotiation can determine whether a 100 Mbps hub is connected to a 10 Mbps or 100 Mbps adapter and then adjust the mode of operation accordingly.

This autonegotiation activity identifies the highest physical-layer technology that can be used by both devices, such as 10BaseT, 100BaseT, 100BaseTX, or 100BaseT4. Table 2-4 lists the priorities from highest to lowest.

Table 2-4   *Autonegotiation Priority Resolution*

Priority Ranking	Physical-Layer Technology
A	100BaseTX full duplex
B	100BaseT4
C	100BaseTX
D	10BaseT full duplex
E	10BaseT

Table 2-4 indicates, for example, that if both devices on the link can support both 10BaseT and 100BaseTX, the autonegotiation process at both ends of the link will connect using 100BaseTX mode.

The autonegotiation definition also provides a parallel detection function that allows half- and full-duplex 10BaseT, half- and full-duplex 100BaseTX, and 100BaseT4 physical layers to be recognized, even if one of the connected devices does not offer autonegotiation capabilities. The full-duplex mode of operation is given priority over half duplex, because the full-duplex system can send more data than a half-duplex link operating at the same speed.

NOTE   Although the autonegotiation protocol allows devices to automatically exchange information about the link, the protocol is not well standardized. Autonegotiation can lead to connectivity problems, so Cisco recommends that the appropriate values of speed and duplex be configured in the switches.

Gigabit Ethernet

Gigabit Ethernet is effective in the switch block, the core block, and the server block.

In the switch block, Gigabit Ethernet is deployed for links that connect centrally located aggregation switches with each access switch. Each access switch has a Gigabit Ethernet uplink that connects to the distribution switch.

In the core block, Gigabit Ethernet links are used to connect distribution-layer switches in each building with a central campus core. Table 2-5 describes the most common deployment strategy of Gigabit Ethernet in the switch block.

Table 2-5   *Gigabit Deployment Strategy*

Model Layer	Positioning
Access layer	Not commonly used between the end-user device and the access switch, although more end stations or nodes are beginning to support Gigabit Ethernet uplinks.
Distribution layer	Provides high-speed connections between the access and distribution-layer devices.
Core layer	Provides high-speed connectivity to the distribution layer and the server block. Provides high-speed interconnectivity between core devices.

Gigabit Ethernet is also well-suited for connecting high-performance servers to the network. A high-performance UNIX or video server can easily flood three to four Fast Ethernet connections simultaneously. As servers are growing in power and throughput, and with the trend for centralizing servers within the campus network, Gigabit Ethernet can provide the required high-speed network connection. To achieve this connection, a Gigabit Ethernet switch is centrally located in the server block.

Gigabit Ethernet builds on top of the Ethernet protocol; however, data transfer speeds are increased tenfold over Fast Ethernet to 1000 Mbps, or 1 Gbps. This protocol is crucial to high-speed LAN backbones and server connectivity. Ethernet uses many of the original Ethernet specifications, so customers can leverage existing knowledge and technology to install, manage, and maintain gigabit networks.

In order to increase speeds from 100 Mbps Fast Ethernet to 1 Gbps, several changes were made to the physical interface. Gigabit Ethernet looks identical to Ethernet from the data link layer upward. As shown in Figure 2-1, the challenges involved in increasing to 1 Gbps have been resolved by merging two technologies: IEEE 802.3 Ethernet and American National Standards Institute (ANSI) X3T11 FiberChannel.

Figure 2-1   *Gigabit Ethernet Combines Standard Ethernet Technology with ANSI X3T11 FiberChannel*

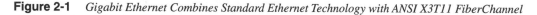

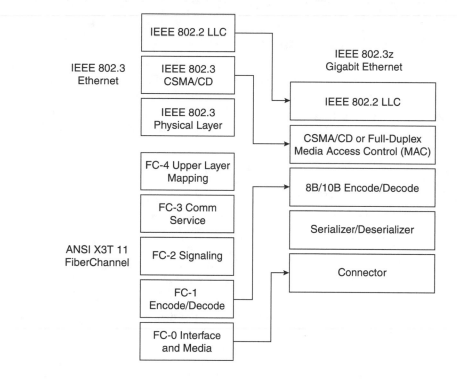

The Gigabit specification defines the distance for each media type listed in Table 2-6.

Table 2-6   *Distance Limitations for Gigabit Ethernet*

Technology	Wiring Category	Cable Length Switched Media
1000BaseCX	Copper shielded twisted pair	25 meters
1000BaseT	Copper EIA/TIA Category 5 (UTP) Unshielded twisted pair 4 pair	100 meters
1000BaseSX	Multimode fiber cable, with a 62.5-micron fiber-optic core and 50-micron fiber-optic core; 780 nanometer laser	260 meters
1000BaseLX	Single-mode fiber cable, 9-micron core, 1300-nanometer laser	3 km (Cisco supports up to 10 km)

Example of Subscribing Links

Determining the bandwidth needed for each link is done by determining the aggregate average bandwidth of all devices that will use that link. Figure 2-2 shows an example of a network topology using both Ethernet and Fast Ethernet links. Based on this network topology and information about the user's traffic patterns and network connections in the following sections, complete this section so that you can decide whether the 100 Mbps link is sufficient.

Subscribing Links Example User Statistics

The following are the user statistics for this example:

- There are 1000 users in a single building.

- Each floor houses 100 users.

- Each floor has one 24-port 10 Mbps switch, allowing four users per port. The users are attached to each port via a hub.

- Shared-media Ethernet can support 4 Mbps of data under load; therefore, each user has 1 Mbps of bandwidth.

Note   Shared Ethernet is traditionally rated at approximately 3.3 Mbps to 4 Mbps. This is a generalization used for this example only. Ethernet behaves differently under different load conditions and with a different number of stations.

- Applications are e-mail and word processing.
- Each floor is an IP subnet.

Figure 2-2   *Example of a Network Topology Using Ethernet and Fast Ethernet Links*

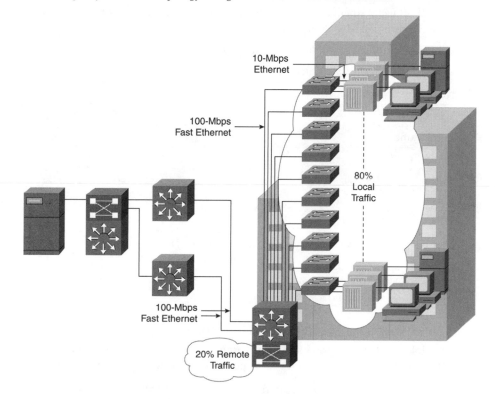

Subscribing Links Example Traffic Statistics

This section discusses the methodology of determining the amount of bandwidth that is needed at each link. The numbers used in the example are very generalized in order to make it easier to understand and calculate. These numbers do not necessarily reflect any real-life scenario.

Due to the ever-decreasing cost of bandwidth in campus networks, many corporations simply put as much bandwidth as possible in the uplinks from the access layer to the distribution layer and from the distribution layer to the core layer. In general terms, the aggregate bandwidth of the access layer devices should not exceed the bandwidth of the link that they use to get to their distribution switch. Furthermore, the aggregate of all the uplinks to the distribution switches should not exceed the bandwidth of the links to the core layer.

The traffic statistics for this example are as follows:

- Eighty percent of the traffic is local to the floor.

- Twenty percent of the traffic crosses the core to the e-mail server.

- If all users simultaneously accessed the network, the switch would receive 24 ports × 4 Mbps = 96 Mbps.

Table 2-7 graphically displays these statistics.

Table 2-7   *Subscribing Links Example Statistics*

Number of floors	10
Users per floor	100
Local traffic	80 percent
Remote traffic	20 percent
10BaseT ports per floor	24
Users per port	4
Usable bandwidth per port	4 Mbps
Maximum used bandwidth on trunks if traffic is 100 percent remote	96 Mbps
Used bandwidth on trunks	192 Mbps

Subscribing Links Example Access-Layer Requirements

The link between the access and distribution layer switches must be capable of carrying 96 Mbps of traffic. The decision for the type of link depends on the following factors:

- If the link is Fast Ethernet in full-duplex mode, it can carry 100 Mbps of traffic. This type of link would support a 96,182 Mbps load.

Note   You will frequently see full-duplex rated at twice the port's bandwidth capacity. This is not an entirely accurate representation of the link's capacity. For the purposes of this exercise, all links are rated at their true capacity even if they are in full-duplex mode.

- If the link is Ethernet in full-duplex mode, it can carry 10 Mbps of traffic. This capacity is one-tenth the offered load, and packets would be dropped after switch and port buffers were consumed. If this situation is unacceptable, Fast Ethernet must be chosen.

- If the link must operate in access or trunk mode, Fast Ethernet must be chosen. Trunk links are discussed in more detail in Chapter 3, "Defining Common Workgroups with VLANs."

Subscribing Links Example Distribution-Layer Requirements

In this scenario, the distribution layer must be capable of providing the following capacity:

- Total load at the distribution-layer switch is the number of access switches × 96 Mbps. In this scenario, there are 10 access switches or a 10 × 96 Mbps = 960 Mbps total bandwidth requirement at the distribution layer.

- Eighty percent of the traffic is local to the switch block and is not routed across the core.

- Twenty percent of the traffic is remote and is routed toward the core.

- Therefore, 20 percent × 960 Mbps = 192 Mbps of traffic to cross the core.

This sample topology supports a redundant core; therefore, each core subnet carries 50 percent of the traffic load or 96 Mbps of traffic (192 Mbps × 50 percent).

Given this amount of traffic, the distribution switch must be capable of switching the following number of packets per second:

96 Mbps at 64-byte packets = 187,000 packets per second

The Layer 3 component of the Distribution Layer is responsible for routing 20 percent of the traffic to the core. It must be capable of supporting the amount of traffic that has to be passed to the core.

The Route Switch Module in the Catalyst 5000 series switch is capable of handling 175,000 64-byte packets per second. The Catalyst 6000 series switches can switch up to 150 million 64-byte packets per second. In this example, a single Route Switch Module might not have the capacity to handle the number of packets it needs to route.

When designing a link strategy, you should consider the needs of a fault-tolerant network as well as the bandwidth requirements of each link and the capacity of the switch itself. The problem with this topology is that there is no redundancy between the end user and the core. As shown in Figure 2-3, if the link between an access switch and distribution device fails, 100 users have lost connectivity. If the distribution device fails, the entire building is disconnected from the network.

Figure 2-3 *The Lack of Redundancy Between the User and the Core*

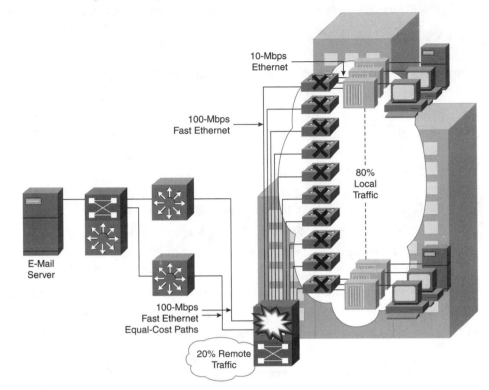

One way of resolving this dilemma is to add a second distribution switch with backup links to each access switch. This topology and how to manage it is covered in greater detail in the Chapter 4, "Managing Redundant Links."

Cabling Switch Block Devices

Before you can begin configuring your switch, you must first establish physical connectivity.

There are two types of cable connections: through the console port and through the Ethernet port. The console port is preconfigured and is used to configure the switch initially.

When connecting the switch's 10BaseT Ethernet ports to 10BaseT-compatible servers, routers, or workstations, use a straight-through Category 5 cable wired for 10BaseT. When connecting the 100BaseTX Ethernet ports to 100BaseT-compatible servers, routers, or workstations, use a straight-through Category 5 cable.

Connecting to the Console Port on an IOS Command-Based Switch

To connect a management terminal to the 1900/2800 or 2900 XL switch through the serial console, use the RJ-45-to-RJ-45 rollover cable supplied with the switch. Follow these steps to cable the two devices:

Step 1   Connect one end of the supplied rollover cable to the console port. As you can see in Figure 2-4, the 1900 and some 5000 series switches use an RJ-45 console connection. Older 5000 series switches use a DB-25 connection.

Figure 2-4   *Console Port Connection*

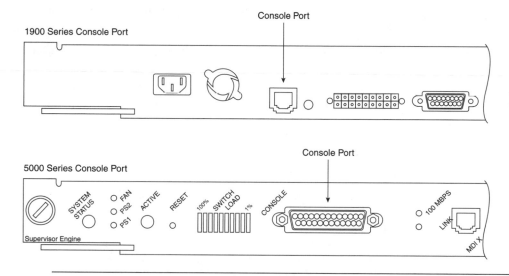

CAUTION   Do not connect an actual telephone line, a live Integrated Services Digital Network (ISDN) line, or an Ethernet cable to this console port. Damage to the switch can result. Make sure you use the supplied RJ-45-to-RJ-45 rollover cable and adapters to connect the console port to the management station or modem.

Step 2   Attach one of the following supplied adapters to a management station or modem:

— RJ-45-to-DB-9 female data terminal equipment (DTE) adapter (labeled Terminal) to connect a PC

— RJ-45-to-DB-25 female DTE adapter (labeled Terminal) to connect a UNIX workstation

— RJ-45-to-DB-25 male data communications equipment (DCE) adapter (labeled Modem) to connect a modem

Step 3   Connect the other end of the supplied rollover cable to the adapter.

Step 4   From your management station, start the terminal emulation program.

Connecting to the Console Port on a Catalyst 5000 Series Switch

To connect a management terminal to the Supervisor Engine III console port switch through the console, use the RJ-45-to-RJ-45 rollover cable and the appropriate adapter, both supplied with the switch. Follow these steps to cable the two devices:

Step 1   Connect one end of the supplied rollover cable to the console port.

Step 2   Attach one of the following supplied adapters to a management station or modem:

— RJ-45-to-DB-9 female DTE adapter (labeled Terminal) to connect a PC

— RJ-45-to-D-subminiature female adapter (labeled Terminal) to connect a UNIX workstation

— RJ-45-to-D-subminiature male adapter (labeled Modem) to connect a modem

Step 3   Connect the other end of the supplied rollover cable to the RJ-45 port.

Step 4   From your management station, start the terminal emulation program. Neither this book nor the BCMSN course covers cabling to a Gigabit Ethernet port.

Connecting to an Ethernet Port

On the Catalyst 1900 and 2800 series switches, the port types are fixed. All 10BaseT ports (ports 1x through 12x or ports 1x through 24x) can be connected to any 10BaseT-compatible device. The 100BaseTX ports (ports Ax and Bx) can be connected to any 100BaseTX-compatible device.

The Catalyst 5000 series switches have ports that can be configured for either 10BaseT or 100BaseT.

All UTP connections between the switch and the attached device(s) must be within 100 meters.

When connecting the switch to servers, workstations, and routers, ensure that you use a straight-through cable. When connecting to other switches or repeaters, ensure that you use a crossover cable. Figure 2-5 shows the RJ-45 ports on an Ethernet line module for a Catalyst 5000 series switch.

Figure 2-5   *Ethernet Line Module on a Catalyst 5000 Series Switch*

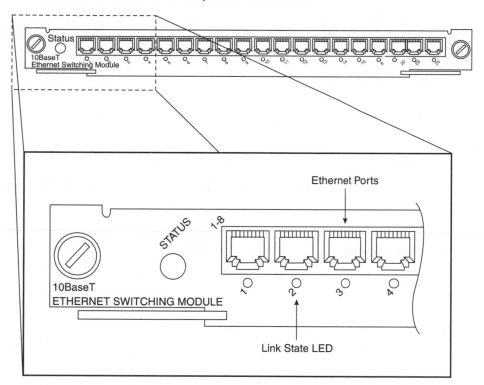

To connect a UTP cable on the switch to another device, follow these steps:

Step 1   Connect one end of the UTP cable to the port on the switch.

Step 2   Connect the other end of the UTP cable to the port of the target device.

The port status LED comes on when both the switch and the connected device are powered up. If the LED is not on, the device at the other end might not be turned on, there might be a problem with the adapter in the attached device or with the cable, or you might need to change the type of cable.

Configuring Connectivity within the Switch Block

After the switches have been physically cabled, some basic system settings should be assigned. These system settings include the following:

- Limiting access to the switch
- Setting the host or prompt name to the switch
- Defining the switch's IP address and subnet mask

- Identifying a port or an interface with a unique description
- Setting the port speed
- Defining the port duplex mode
- Verifying connectivity

Catalyst switches support one of two types of operating systems: Cisco IOS-based and set-based. The command-line interface (CLI) commands on some Cisco switches, such as the Catalyst 1900/2800 and 2900 XL series switches, are similar to the Cisco IOS command set used on Cisco routers. The CLI commands on some Cisco switches, such as the Catalyst 2926, 2926G, 1948G, 4000, 5000, and 6000 series switches, use a command set in which the commands **set** and **clear** are used to configure the switch.

This section discusses both command sets, where appropriate, when configuring the Catalyst switches.

Limiting Switch Access Using Passwords

By default, all ports on a switch are in the same broadcast domain. In order to manage the switch, you must first perform some basic configuration tasks on each device.

The first task you should perform when configuring a device is to secure it against unauthorized use. The simplest form of security in a campus network is to limit access to the switches in the switch block. By setting passwords, you can limit the level of access or completely exclude a user from logging on to an access or distribution switch. Cisco provides various methods for protecting devices and data within the campus network. Chapter 10, "Controlling Access to the Campus Network," discusses these topics in greater detail. This section deals with how to set a user- and privilege-level password on the switches in your network.

You can apply two types of login passwords to your devices. The login password requires users to verify authorization before accessing any line, including the console. The enable password requires authentication before you can set or change system operating parameters.

Cisco also provides levels of authority. A privilege level of 1 gives the user normal EXEC-mode user privileges. A privilege level of 15 is the level of access permitted by the enable password.

Limiting Access on a Cisco IOS Command-Based Switch

To set passwords on a Cisco IOS-based switch, enter the following commands in global configuration mode:

```
Switch(config)#enable password level 1 password
Switch(config)#enable password level 15 password
```

password is any set of alphanumeric characters. The password must be from four to eight (inclusive) characters long.

Example 2-1 shows a Catalyst 1912 series switch that requires the word **cisco** as a login to user EXEC level and the password **san-fran** as the privileged mode password.

Example 2-1   *Catalyst 1912 Series Switch*

```
Switch#show running-configuration
Building configuration...
Current configuration:
(text deleted)
!
enable password level 1 "CISCO"
enable password level 15 "SAN-FRAN"
```

To remove a password, enter the **no enable password** *level number* command.

Limiting Access on a Set Command-Based Switch

To set passwords on a set-based switch, enter the following commands in privileged mode:

```
Switch (enable) set password
Enter old password: old password
Enter new password: new password
Retype new password: new password
Password changed.
Switch (enable) set enablepass
Enter old password: old password
Enter new password: new password
Retype new password: new password
Password changed.
```

password is any set of alphanumeric characters.

NOTE   Passwords on these switches are case-sensitive.

Example 2-2 shows the configuration of a Catalyst 5000 series switch that has both a console login and enabled password set.

Example 2-2 *Catalyst 5000 that Has a Console Login and Enabled Password Set*

```
DSW111 (enable) show config
.....
..........
..........
.........
(text deleted)
begin
set password $1$9qGT$XSM6Mh//ygeee/g3t8NRV/
set enablepass $1$oI7d$01ZtlKtavKuXHycQ2wKsw/
```

Uniquely Defining the Switch

Every switch arrives from the factory with the same default prompt designation. In a large campus network, it is crucial to distinguish one switch from another, especially because most network administrators use Telnet to connect to many switches across the campus.

Setting a Host Name on a Cisco IOS Command-Based Switch

To set the host or system name on a 1900/2800 or 2900 XL series switch, enter the following command in global configuration mode:

```
Switch(config)#hostname name
```

name can be from 1 to 255 alphanumeric characters.

As soon as you execute the **hostname** command, the system prompt assumes the host name. To remove the system name, enter the **no hostname** command in global configuration mode.

Setting a System Prompt on a Set Command-Based Switch

If your switch is set-based, the name you assign for the system name is used to define the system prompt. However, you can assign a name to the CLI prompt that differs from the system name. To assign a unique name to the CLI prompt, enter the following command in privileged mode:

```
System(enable) set prompt name
```

name sets the CLI prompt.

Configuring Switch Remote Accessibility

Before you can Telnet to, ping, or globally manage the switch, you need to associate that switch with the management virtual LAN (VLAN). Although LAN switches are essentially Layer 2 devices, they do maintain an IP stack for administrative purposes. Assigning an IP address to the switch associates that switch with the management VLAN, providing that the subnet portion of the switch IP address matches the subnet number of the management VLAN.

Configuring Remote Accessibility on a Cisco IOS Command-Based Switch

To assign an IP address on a 1900/2800 or 2900 XL series switch, enter the following command in global configuration mode:

```
Switch(config)ip address ip address netmask
```

The **show ip** command displays the IP address and the subnet mask for the device. Example 2-3 shows that the management interface resides in VLAN1 and has a subnet mask of 255.255.0.0.

Example 2-3 *Management Interface Resides in VLAN1 and Has a Subnet Mask of 255.255.0.0*

```
Switch#show ip
IP Address: 172.16.1.87
Subnet Mask: 255.255.0.0
Default Gateway: 0.0.0.0
Management VLAN:  1
Domain name:
Name server 1: 0.0.0.0
Name server 2: 0.0.0.0
HTTP server : Enabled
HTTP port :  80
RIP : Enabled
```

To remove the IP address and subnet mask, enter the **no ip address** command in global configuration mode.

Configuring Remote Accessibility on a Set Command-Based Switch

If your switch is set-based, you assign the IP address to the in-band logical interface. To assign an IP address to this interface, enter the following command in privileged mode:

```
Switch(enable)set interface sc0 ip address netmask broadcast address
```

After you define the in-band management IP address, you assign the IP address to its associated management VLAN. The number of the VLAN must match the subnet number of the IP address. To associate the in-band logical interface to a specific VLAN, enter the following command in privileged mode:

```
Switch(enable)set interface sc0 vlan
```

If you do not specify a VLAN, the system automatically defaults to VLAN1.

The **show interface** command displays the IP address and the subnet mask for the device. Example 2-4 shows that the management interface resides in VLAN1 and has a subnet mask of 255.255.0.0.

Example 2-4   *The Management Interface Resides in VLAN1 and Has a Subnet Mask of 255.255.0.0*

```
Switch(enable)show interface
sl0:flags=51<UP,POINTOPOINT,RUNNING>
     slip 0.0.0.0 dest 0.0.0.0
sc0:flags=63<UP,BROADCAST,RUNNING>
     vlan 1 inet 172.16.1.144 netmask 255.255.0.0 broadcast 172.16.255.255
```

Uniquely Identifying Ports

You can add a description to an interface or port to help you remember specific information about that interface, such as what access- or distribution-layer device the interface services. This description is meant solely as a comment to help identify how the interface is being used. The description will appear in the output when you display the configuration information.

Uniquely Identifying an Interface on a Cisco IOS Command-Based Switch

To add a unique comment to an interface on a 1900/2800 or 2900 XL series switch, enter the following command in interface configuration mode:

```
Switch(config-if)#description description string
```

If you need to enter a description with spaces between characters, you must enclose the string in quotation marks:

```
Switch(config-if)#description "PC TO ASW44 PORT"
```

To clear a description, enter the **no description** command in interface configuration mode.

Uniquely Identifying a Port on a Set Command-Based Switch

If your access switch is set-based, you assign a description to a port by entering the following command in privileged mode:

```
Switch(enable) set port name module/number description
```

module specifies the target module on which the port resides.

number identifies the specific port.

description describes the specific text string.

The description must be less than 21 alphanumeric characters. Spaces can be entered in the description without special consideration.

To clear a port name, enter the **set port name** *module/number* command, followed by a carriage return in privileged mode. Because you don't define a port name, the value for this parameter is cleared.

Defining Link Speed

The speed of the ports is 10/100 Mbps on a Cisco IOS-based switch, and it cannot be altered. The Catalyst 1900 series switch has a fixed configuration of 12 or 24 10BaseT and one or two Fast Ethernet 100BaseTX ports. The Catalyst 2820 series switch has a fixed configuration of 24 10BaseT ports and two module slots for Fast Ethernet.

Configuring the Port Speed on a Set Command-Based Switch

If your access switch is set-based, enter the following command in privileged mode to configure the port speed on 10/100 Mbps Fast Ethernet modules:

```
Switch(enable) set port speed mod-num/port-num [10 |  100 | auto]
```

mod-num indicates the port's module number.

port-num indicates the port number.

10, **100**, and **auto** indicate the port's speed. **auto** places the port in autonegotiate speed mode.

NOTE   If the port speed is set to **auto** on a 10/100 Mbps Fast Ethernet port, both speed and duplex are autonegotiated.

Use the **show port** command to verify your configuration. Example 2-5 shows that the 10/100 Ethernet module 2 port 4 is connected and is operating at 100 Mbps.

Example 2-5   *The 10/100 Ethernet Module 2 Port 4 Is Connected and Is Operating at 100 Mbps*

```
Switch (enable)show port 2/4
Port  Name              Status     Vlan       Level  Duplex Speed Type
----- ----------------- ---------- ---------- ------ ------ ----- ------------
 2/4                    connected  1          normal full   100   10/100BaseTX
```

Maximizing Data Transmission

Full duplex is the simultaneous action of transmitting and receiving data by two devices. This operation can be achieved only if both connected devices support full-duplex mode.

Not only do full-duplex links double potential throughput, but they also eliminate collisions and the need for each station to wait until the other station finishes transmitting. If reads and writes on a full-duplex link are symmetric, data throughput can be doubled. In actual usage, however, bandwidth improvements are more modest. Full-duplex Ethernet and Fast Ethernet links are particularly useful for server-to-server, server-to-switch, and switch-to-switch connections.

Configuring the Line Mode on a Cisco IOS Command-Based Switch

To set the line mode on an interface on a 1900/2800 or 2900 XL series switch, enter the following command in interface configuration mode:

```
Switch(config-if)#duplex {auto | full | full-flow-control | half}
```

auto puts the 100BaseTX port into autonegotiation mode. This is the default for the 100BaseTX port. This argument is valid on 100BaseT ports only.

full forces the 10BaseT or 100BaseTX port into full-duplex mode.

full-flow-control forces the 100BaseTX port into full-duplex mode with flow control. This argument is valid on the 100BaseTX ports only.

half forces the 10BaseT or 100BaseTX port into half-duplex mode. This is the default for the 10BaseT port.

NOTE   Use the **auto** parameter only for fixed Fast Ethernet TX ports. In autonegotiation mode, the switch attempts to negotiate full-duplex connectivity with the connecting device. If negotiation is successful, the port operates in full-duplex mode. If the connecting device is unable to operate in full duplex, the port operates in half duplex. This process is repeated whenever there is a change in link status.

Example 2-6 shows that the fixed-port Ethernet 0/4 is configured for full-duplex mode.

Example 2-6   *The Fixed-Port Ethernet 0/4 Is Configured for Full-Duplex Mode*

```
Switch(config-if)#show interface ethernet 0/4
Ethernet 0/4 is Enabled
Hardware is Built-in 10Base-T
Address is 0090.8678.9743
MTU 1500 bytes, BW 10000 Kbits
802.1d STP State: Forwarding        Forward Transitions:  2
Port monitoring: Disabled
Unknown unicast flooding: Enabled
Unregistered multicast flooding: Enabled
```

Example 2-6 *The Fixed-Port Ethernet 0/4 Is Configured for Full-Duplex Mode (Continued)*

```
Description: PC_To_ACCESS_SWITCH
Duplex setting: Full duplex
Back pressure: Disabled
```

To return the **duplex** parameter to the default setting, enter the **no duplex** command in interface configuration mode.

Configuring the Line Mode on a Set Command-Based Switch

To set the port duplex mode on a set-based switch, enter the following command in privileged mode:

```
Switch(enable)set port duplex mod-num/port-num {full | half}
```

The following are the default duplex settings for Ethernet:

- Half-duplex mode is the default for 10 Mbps ports
- Full-duplex mode is the default for 100 Mbps ports

NOTE Set the speed first, and then set the ports' duplex mode.

Use the **show port** command to verify your configuration. Example 2-7 shows that the 10/100 Ethernet module 2 port 4 is connected and is operating in full-duplex mode.

Example 2-7 *The 10/100 Ethernet Module 2 Port 4 Is Connected and Is Operating in Full-Duplex Mode*

```
Switch (enable)show port 2/4
Port  Name              Status     Vlan       Level  Duplex Speed Type
----- ----------------- ---------- ---------- ------ ------ ----- -----------
 2/4                    connected  1          normal full   100   10/100BaseTX
```

NOTE The ports on a Catalyst 29xx, 4000, 5000, or 6000 series switch might or might not be automatically enabled. To activate a port, enter the **set port enable** command in privileged mode.

Verifying Connectivity

After the switch is assigned an IP address and at least one switch port is connected to the network and is properly configured, you can communicate with the switch from other nodes on the network. The switch needs an IP address in order to be managed from other nodes on the network, but it does not need an IP address in order to switch traffic.

To test connectivity to remote hosts, enter the following command in privileged mode:

```
Switch (enable)ping destination ip address
```

The **ping** command will return one of the following responses:

- **Success rate is 100 percent or *ip address* is alive**—This response occurs in 1 to 10 seconds, depending on network traffic and the number of Internet Control Message Protocol (ICMP) packets sent.

- **Destination does not respond**—No answer message is returned if the host does not respond.

- **Unknown host**—This response occurs if the targeted host does not exist.

- **Destination unreachable**—This response occurs if the default gateway cannot reach the specified network.

- **Network or host unreachable**—This response occurs if there is no entry in the route table for the host or network.

Example 2-8 states that the destination IP address 172.16.1.47 can be reached by the device generating the ping.

Example 2-8   *The Destination IP Address 172.16.1.47 Can Be Reached*

```
Switch#ping 172.16.1.47
Sending 5, 100-byte ICMP Echos to 172.16.1.47, time out is 2 seconds:
!!!!!
Success rate is 100 percent (5/5), round-trip min/avg/max 0/2/10/ ms
```

NOTE   If the access or distribution switch is a Catalyst 5000, 4000, 2948G, 2926G, or 2926 series switch, you can display a hop-by-hop path through an IP network from the source switch to a specific destination host. To enable this feature, enter the **traceroute** *destination ip address* command in privileged mode. For more information on the **traceroute** command, refer to the *Software Configuration Guide (4.4)*.

Note that the **traceroute** command shows only Layer 3 hops, not Layer 2 switch hops. **traceroute** relies on the decrementing of the TTL in the IP header in order to relay information about that hop. The switch does not decrement the TTL header, so it would never be seen with the **traceroute** command.

Summary

This chapter discussed the media types typically used in campus network connections, including Ethernet, Fast Ethernet, and Gigabit Ethernet, as well as where they are typically deployed. This chapter also covered how to configure each of these different connection types, as well as the basic configuration of the switch, including passwords and IP addresses.

Review Questions

The following questions test your retention of the material presented in this chapter. The answers to the Review Questions can be found in Appendix A, "Answers to Review Questions."

1 Describe the three major link technologies and where they are used in the campus network.

2 List the steps necessary to configure an Ethernet connection on an access-layer switch.

Case Study: Connecting the Switch Block

This case study shows the initial configuration of the switch block. This configuration will include configuring the Ethernet connections in the access layer and the fast Ethernet connections in both the distribution layer and the core layer.

NOTE   The switch block being used in this and all following case studies uses two different operating systems as specified in the chapter. The 1900 Series Switch commands will always be given in IOS and the 5000/6000 Series Switch commands will always be given in the set Command Line Interface.

Scenario

This case study shows you how to configure the connectivity for the entire switch block, including the access layer, the distribution layer, and the core layer. You will see how to ensure that the network ports are functioning correctly and that operating parameters, such as host name and passwords, have been set on each of the switches. Figure 2-6 shows the physical connections that will be configured.

Figure 2-6   *Switch Block Connections*

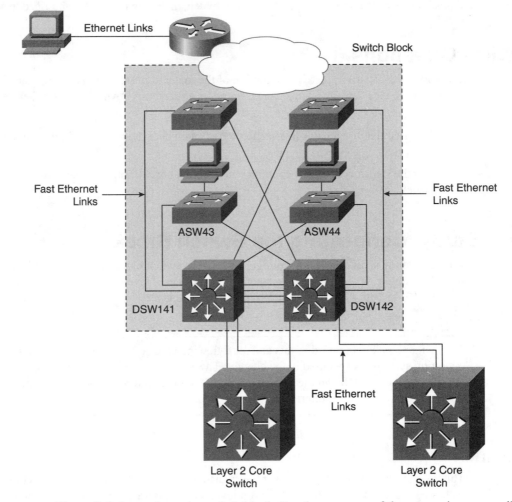

Figure 2-6 shows the entire switch block. For the purposes of these exercises, you will configure only a portion of the switch block. This portion will include a single PC, an access layer switch, and the two distribution layer switches. Figure 2-7 shows these four devices and their corresponding addresses and names.

Figure 2-7   *Host Names and IP Addresses*

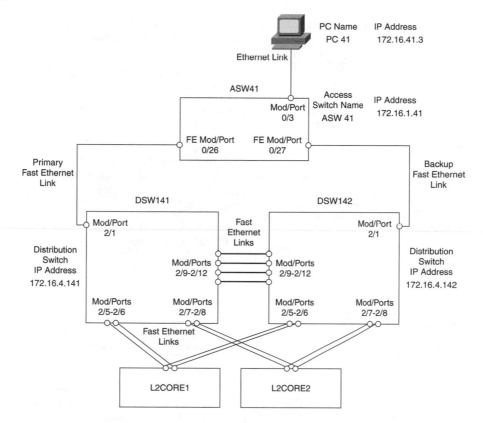

Command List

In this case study, you will see the following commands. Refer to Table 2-8 and Table 2-9 if you need an explanation of the commands during the case study.

Table 2-8   *Access Switch Commands*

Command	Description
hostname	Assigns a unique name to the Catalyst 1900/2800 series switch.
ip address *ip address*	Assigns a unique IP address to the Catalyst 1900/2800 series switch.
interface ethernet *mod/port*	Identifies a specific interface on the Catalyst 1900/2800 series switch.

continues

Table 2-8   *Access Switch Commands (Continued)*

Command	Description
duplex	Sets the duplex mode of the link. Options are half or full.
show run	Displays the running configuration of a Catalyst 1900/2800 series switch.
interface fastethernet *mod/port*	Identifies a specific Fast Ethernet port on a Catalyst 1900/2800 series switch.
enable password level *number*	Assigns a password to the system. The privilege level number indicates the types of commands you can access. Level 1 allows you user EXEC mode access. Level 15 allows you privileged EXEC mode status.
shutdown	Administratively disables an interface on a Catalyst 1900/2800 series switch.
Ctrl-Shift-6-x	Escape Sequence.

Table 2-9   *Distribution Switch Commands*

Command	Description
Ctrl-c	Stops a command during execution.
set prompt *name*	Assigns a unique name to the prompt for the set-based switch.
set interface sc0 *ip address subnet mask*	Assigns a unique IP address to the management interface for the set-based switch.
set password *password*	Sets the console login password.
set enablepass *password*	Sets the privileged mode password.
set port speed *speed*	Sets the media speed for a specific mod/port on a Set-based switch. Options are 10 or 100 Mbps.
set port duplex [**half** | **full**]	Sets the duplex mode of the link. Options are half or full.
show config	Displays the current configuration on the Set-based switch.
Ctrl-Shift-6-x	Escape Sequence.

Task 1: Configure the Access Layer Connection to the PC

In this task, you will configure two types of devices—the PC and the access layer switch. The access layer switches are 1900 Series switch with Enterprise software. They will be configured using IOS commands. Provide the PC with an IP address and subnet. Provide the access layer switches with a hostname, passwords, and port configurations to the PCs. You should be able to successfully ping the access layer switch from the PC when you are done with this task.

Step 1 From your Windows desktop, go to Start, Settings, Control Panel, Network.

Step 2 Double-click the TCP/IP Interface Adapter symbol. Perform the following substeps:

— You should see TCP/IP Properties.

— Click the IP Address tab.

— Click Specify IP Address.

— Enter your PC's assigned IP address and subnet mask.

— Click WINS Config Tab.

— Click Enable WINS.

— Enter both primary and secondary WINS addresses (identical).

— No entry in scope field.

— Click the DNS Configuration tab.

— Click Disable DNS.

— Click OK.

— Click OK.

— You will be prompted to restart your PC, click YES.

— Click YES to any prompts that might appear during windows closedown.

Note   The 1900 series switch supports both a menu-driven and command line interface. In this example, you will use the command line interface.

Step 3   Open a hyperterm session with the access layer switch.

Step 4   From the access switch menu, enter option **K** to enter CLI mode.

Step 5   In global configuration mode, enter the **enable password level 1**
password command to assign the password for user EXEC mode.

Step 6   In global configuration mode, enter the **enable password level 15**
password command to assign the password for privileged EXEC mode.

Step 7   In global configuration mode, enter the **hostname** *switch_name*
command to assign a unique name for your switch prompt.

Step 8   In global configuration mode, enter the **ip address** *ip address* command
to assign an IP address to your access switch.

Step 9   In global configuration mode, enter the **interface ethernet** *mod/port*
command to configure your Ethernet link to your PC.

Step 10 In interface configuration mode, enter the **description** command to
assign a unique description to this mod/port, for example, TO PC41.

Step 11 In interface configuration mode, enter the **duplex** command. Configure
the mod/port for full duplex.

Step 12 In privileged mode, enter the **show run** command to verify the
configuration.

Your configuration should resemble the output in Example 2-9.

Example 2-9   *Task 1 Running Configuration*

```
Switch#show run
Building configuration...
Current configuration:
!
hostname "ASW42"
!
ip address 172.16.1.42 255.255.0.0
enable password level 1 "CISCO"
enable password level 15 "SAN-FRAN"


 Text deleted

interface Ethernet 0/3
  duplex full
  description "TO PC42"
 !
```

Step 13 To verify the port configuration, enter the **show interface ethernet 0/3** command. Your configuration should resemble the output in Example 2-10.

Example 2-10   *Task 1 show interface Command Output*

```
Ethernet 0/3 is Enabled
Hardware is Built-in 10Base-T
Address is 0090.8678.9743
MTU 1500 bytes, BW 10000 Kbits
802.1d STP State:  Forwarding     Forward Transitions:  1
Port monitoring: Disabled
Unknown unicast flooding: Enabled
Unregistered multicast flooding: Enabled
Description: PC TO ASW11
Duplex setting: Full duplex
Back pressure: Disabled
```

Step 14 To verify connectivity, enter the **ping** *ip address* command, where *ip address* is the IP address of your PC.

You have successfully completed this task if you can ping your PC from your access switch.

Task 2: Configure the Connections Between the Access Layer Switches and the Distribution Layer Switches

In this task, you will provide for the initial configuration of the distribution layer switches including hostname, passwords, and IP addresses. In addition, you will configure the connection from the access layer switch to the distribution layer switch. You will have successfully completed this task when you can ping from the PCs and the access layer switches to the distribution layer switches and all appropriate parameters have been configured on the distribution switches.

In this task, you configure a Fast Ethernet mod/port on both your access and distribution switches. At the end of this task, you will verify your configurations. Execute the following steps to complete this task.

On the Access Layer Switch

Complete the following steps:

Step 1 In global configuration mode, enter the **interface fastethernet** *mod/port* command to configure your Fast Ethernet link.

Step 2 In interface configuration mode, enter the **description** command to assign a unique description to this port, for example, Trunk Link to DSW141.

Step 3   In interface configuration mode, enter the **duplex** command. Configure the mod/port for **full duplex**.

Step 4   In privileged mode, enter the **show run** command to verify the configuration. Your configuration should resemble the output in Example 2-11.

Example 2-11   *Task 2 Running Configuration—Access Layer Switch*

```
Switch#show run
Building configuration...
Current configuration:
!
(text deleted)
interface FastEthernet 0/26

  duplex full
  description "Trunk Link to DSW141"
!
interface FastEthernet 0/27

  duplex full
  description "Trunk Link to DSW142"
```

On the Distribution Layer Switch

Complete the following steps:

Step 1   Open a hyperterm session with the distribution layer switches.

Step 2   In privileged mode, enter the **set password** command to assign the login password to the distribution switch.

Step 3   In privileged mode, enter the **set enablepass** command to assign the enable password to the distribution switch.

Step 4   In privileged mode, enter the **set prompt** command to assign the unique name to the distribution switch prompt.

Step 5   In privileged mode, enter the **set interface sc0** command to assign the provided IP address to the distribution switch.

Step 6   In privileged mode, enter the **set port speed** command to configure your the distribution switch mod/ports. Set the speed to 100.

Step 7   In privileged mode, enter the **set port duplex** command to configure your distribution switch mod/port. Set the duplex to full.

Step 8   In privileged mode, enter the **set port name** *mod/num port name* to define a description for your distribution links, for example, FE TO ACCESS SWITCH.

Step 9 Repeat the above command for all access switch port connections on your distribution switch.

Step 10 In privileged mode, enter the **set port disable 2/5-8** to disable the ports to the core switches.

Step 11 In privilege mode, enter the **show port** command. The output from the command in Example 2-12 should display ports 2/5-8 as disabled.

Example 2-12   *Task 2 **show port** Command Output*

```
DSW141> (enable) show port 2
Port  Name                Status      Vlan    Level  Duplex Speed Type
----- ------------------- ----------- ------- ------ ------ ----- ------------
 2/1  "To ASW41"          connected   1       normal  full    100 10/100BaseTX
 2/2  "To ASW42"          connected   1       normal  full    100 10/100BaseTX
 2/3  "To ASW43"          connected   1       normal  full    100 10/100BaseTX
 2/4  "To ASW44"          connected   1       normal  full    100 10/100BaseTX
 2/5                      disabled    1       normal  auto   auto 10/100BaseTX
 2/6                      disabled    1       normal  auto   auto 10/100BaseTX
 2/7                      disabled    1       normal  auto   auto 10/100BaseTX
 2/8                      disabled    1       normal  auto   auto 10/100BaseTX
 2/9                      connected   1       normal a-full a-100 10/100BaseTX
```

Step 12 In privileged mode, enter the **show config** command to verify the configuration. Your configuration should resemble the output in Example 2-13.

Example 2-13   *Task 2 **show config** Command—Distribution Layer Switch*

```
begin
set password $1$FMFQ$HfZR5DUszVHIRhrz4h6V70
set enablepass $1$FMFQ$HfZR5DUszVHIRhrz4h6V70
set prompt DSW141
set length 24 default
set logout 20
set banner motd ^C^C
!
#system
set system baud  9600
set system modem disable
set system name
set system location
set system contact
(text deleted)
#ip
set interface sc0 1 172.16.1.141 255.255.0.0 172.16.1.255

set interface sc0 up
set interface sl0 0.0.0.0 0.0.0.0
set interface sl0 up
set arp agingtime 1200
set ip redirect    enable
```

continues

Example 2-13   *Task 2 **show config** Command—Distribution Layer Switch (Continued)*

```
set ip unreachable   enable
set ip fragmentation enable
set ip alias default      0.0.0.0
!
```

Step 13 In privileged mode, enter the **ping** *ip address* command, where *ip address* is the address of your access switches.

You have successfully completed this task if you can **ping** your access switches from your distribution switches.

Step 14 In privileged mode, enter the **show run** command to verify the configuration. Your con-figuration of each switch should resemble the output in Example 2-14 and Example 2-15.

Example 2-14   *Task 2 Running Configurations—Distribution Layer Switch*

```
Switch#show run
Building configuration...
Current configuration:
!
(text deleted)
interface FastEthernet 0/26

  duplex full
description "Trunk Link to DSW141"
  shutdown
!
interface FastEthernet 0/27

  duplex full
  description "Backup Trunk Link to DSW142"
```

Example 2-15   *Task 2 Running Configuration for ASW42—Distribution Layer Switch*

```
Switch#show run
Building configuration...
Current configuration:
!
(text deleted)
interface FastEthernet 0/27

  duplex full
description "Backup Trunk Link to DSW142"
```

Task 3: Configure the Connections from the Distribution Layer Switches to the Core Layer Switches

Configure the connections from the distribution layer switches to the core layer switches. In addition configure the core layer switches for hostname, IP addresses, and passwords. You have successfully completed this task when all connections between the distribution layer and the core layer are up and functional and you can ping from your PC to every switch inside of the switch block and the core layer.

Distribution to Core Connections

Complete the following steps:

Step 1 Connect to the distribution switches with a terminal emulation program.

Step 2 In privileged mode, enter the **set port speed** command to configure the distribution switch mod/ports that connect to the CORE switch. Set the speed to 100.

Step 3 In privileged mode, enter the **set port duplex** command to configure your distribution switch mod/ports that connect to your assigned CORE switch. Set the duplex to full.

Step 4 In privileged mode, enter the **set port name** *mod/num port-name* to define a description for the distribution links, for example, FE TO L2CORE1 or FE TO L2CORE2.

Distribution to Distribution Connections

Complete the following steps:

Step 1 Open a terminal session with the distribution switch that you are configuring.

Step 2 In privileged mode, enter the **set port speed** command to configure your distribution switch mod/ports that connect to the other distribution switch. Set the speed to 100.

Step 3 In privileged mode, enter the **set port duplex** command to configure the distribution switch mod/ports that connect to the other distribution switch. Set the duplex to full.

Step 4 In privileged mode, enter the **set port name** *mod num/port-name* to define a description for the distribution links, for example, FE TO DSW142 or FE TO DSW141.

Step 5 In privileged mode, enter the **ping** *address* command to test the connectivity between distribution switches in your block.

You have successfully completed Task 3 if the ports associated with the core links show connected when you use the **show port 2** command. Your configuration should resemble the output in Example 2-16.

Example 2-16   *Task 3 **show port 2** Command*

```
DSW141 (enable)show port 2
Port  Name                 Status     Vlan      Level  Duplex Speed Type
----- -------------------- ---------- --------- ------ ------ ----- -----------
 2/1  To ASW41             connected  1         normal full    100 10/100BaseTX
 2/2  To ASW42             connected  1         normal full    100 10/100BaseTX
```

continues

Example 2-16   *Task 3 **show port 2** Command (Continued)*

```
2/3   To ASW43          connected  1       normal   full   100 10/100BaseTX
2/4   To ASW44          connected  1       normal   full   100 10/100BaseTX
2/5   FE TO CORE1       connected  1       normal   full   100 10/100BaseTX
2/6   FE TO CORE1       connected  1       normal   full   100 10/100BaseTX
2/7   FE TO CORE2       connected  1       normal   full   100 10/100BaseTX
2/8   FE TO CORE2       connected  1       normal   full   100 10/100BaseTX
2/9   FE TO DSW142      connected  1       normal   full   100 10/100BaseTX
2/10  FE TO DSW142      connected  1       normal   full   100 10/100BaseTX
```

In addition, you should be able to ping all devices in the switch block and the core.

CHAPTER 3

Defining Common Workgroups with VLANs

In the preceding chapters, you learned about the campus model and made the connections in the switch block. In this chapter, you will learn how to break the Layer 2 switch block into separate broadcast domains called virtual LANs (VLANs). This chapter also defines different types of links in the campus network and the method of identifying VLANs on those links. Finally, this chapter introduces and shows you how to configure VLAN management tools, such as the VLAN Trunking Protocol (VTP).

This chapter covers the following topics:

- VLAN overview
- VLAN identification
- VLAN Trunking Protocol

VLANs have been designed to address two problems: the scalability issues of a flat network topology and the addition of network management through Layer 3 routing protocols. This chapter covers the process of defining campus network workgroups within a switch block. This chapter also presents an overview of the technologies associated with designing and configuring workgroups in VLANs, configuring VTP, and employing other techniques to ease the task of VLAN administration.

Upon completion of this chapter, you will be able to correctly associate VLANs and port numbers given a network diagram of your switch block, enable a single physical connection to carry multiple VLANs, ensure broadcast domain integrity by establishing VLANs in the switch block, and maintain VLAN configuration consistency using VTP domains.

VLANs

In order to understand the necessity of VLANs, it is important to understand the issues found in Layer 2 campus networks. The Layer 2 campus network presents the following challenges:

- **Flat network structure**—In a flat switched network, every device sees every packet that is transmitted. Because each port is in its own collision domain, the normal distance limitation rules of Ethernet no longer apply. This leads to Layer 2 switched networks that are considerably larger than traditional Ethernet networks. A Layer 2 switched network can even span several buildings. As the size of the Layer 2 switched network increases, so does the number of packets that each station must process. This becomes especially difficult if applications are sending large numbers of broadcasts. Every station must process every broadcast as if it were intended for that station.

- **Security**—In a Layer 2 environment, there is no easy way to provide security. Users have the ability to access all devices.

- **Managing multiple paths to a destination**—Layer 2 switches do not allow for redundant paths to a destination and are not capable of intelligently load-balancing traffic.

Switches use VLANs to solve many of the issues of a large Layer 2 environment. VLANs connected by routers limit the broadcast to the domain of origin, as shown in Figure 3-1.

Figure 3-1   *VLANs Establish Broadcast Domains*

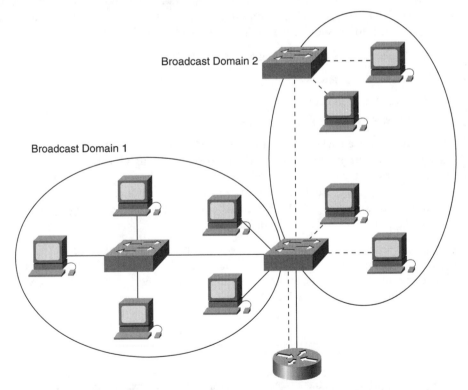

A VLAN has the following characteristics:

- All devices in a VLAN are members of the same broadcast domain. If a station transmits a broadcast, all other members of the VLAN will receive the broadcast. The broadcast is filtered from all ports or devices that are not members of the same VLAN.

- A VLAN is a logical subnet or segment made up of defined members. A VLAN is slightly different from a physical subnet. A physical subnet consists of the devices on a physical cable segment. A logical subnet, or VLAN, consists of devices that have been configured as members of that VLAN. These devices can exist anywhere in the switch block. Just as you must have a router to communicate between physical subnets, you must also have a router to communicate between logical subnets, or VLANs.

- VLAN membership is most commonly based on a switch port number, but VLANs can also be dynamically assigned based on the device's Media Access Control (MAC) address.

- The most common type of VLAN is a geographic VLAN. Geographic VLANs are defined in a specific geographic area. This area is usually a wiring closet.

- End-to-end VLANs are defined throughout the entire switch fabric. An end-to-end VLAN can span several wiring closets or even several buildings. End-to-end VLANs are usually associated with a workgroup such as a department or project team.

VLANs solve many of the Layer 2 issues that arise from a switched campus network, such as the following:

- **Efficient bandwidth utilization**—A VLAN solves the scalability problems found in large flat networks by dividing the network into smaller broadcast domains or subnets. All traffic, including broadcasts and multicasts, is contained within the subnet. In order for information to get to a different VLAN, it must be routed through a Layer 3 process.

- **Security**—VLANs provide for security by forcing the Layer 3 routing process to occur between VLANs. If inter-VLAN communication is configured, the router's traditional security and filtering functions can be used.

- **Load-balancing multiple paths**—VLANs allow a Layer 3 routing protocol to intelligently determine the best path to a destination, including the ability to load-balance when there are multiple paths to a destination.

- **Isolation of problem components**—One of the most important reasons to implement VLANs is to reduce the impact of network problems. In a flat network, a faulty device, internetworking loop, or broadcast-intensive application could potentially impact the entire network to the point of total failure. One of the most effective measures against such network failures is to properly segment the network with a router between segments. The router can effectively prevent problems from being propagated to other segments or VLANs. This isolates the problem to a limited number of devices on a single VLAN.

Defining VLAN Boundaries

The number of VLANs in the switch block will vary widely, depending on several factors, including traffic patterns, types of applications, network management needs, and group commonality.

Another factor to consider in defining the size of the switch block and the number of VLANs is the IP addressing scheme used.

For example, suppose your network uses a 24-bit mask to define a subnet. Given this criterion, a total of 254 host addresses are allowed in one subnet. Because Cisco Systems recommends a one-to-one correspondence between VLANs and IP subnets, there can be no more than 254 devices in one VLAN. It is further recommended that VLANs should not extend outside the Layer 2 domain of the distribution switch. With 1000 users in the building, and the recommended constraints, there will be a minimum of four VLANs in the switch block.

NOTE	Cisco Systems recommends that there be a one-to-one correspondence between IP subnets for ease of administration. There are instances, however, where you might need to have multiple IP subnets on one VLAN. For example, if you are migrating from one IP addressing scheme to another, you might have multiple subnets on one VLAN. Another example is when the number of devices on a VLAN exceeds the number of host addresses available in the configured IP subnet. In this case, a second IP subnet can be applied to the VLAN in order to increase the maximum number of host devices.

When scaling VLANs in the switch block, there are two basic methods of defining the VLAN boundaries:

- End-to-end VLANs
- Local VLANs

End-to-End VLANs

End-to-end VLANs allow the network to group devices based on a commonality, such as server usage, project team, or operational department. The goal of end-to-end VLANs is to maintain 80 percent of the traffic on the local VLAN. In Figure 3-2, the VLAN extends through the entire network in order to connect the server and the workstation on the same VLAN.

Figure 3-2   *End-to-End VLANs*

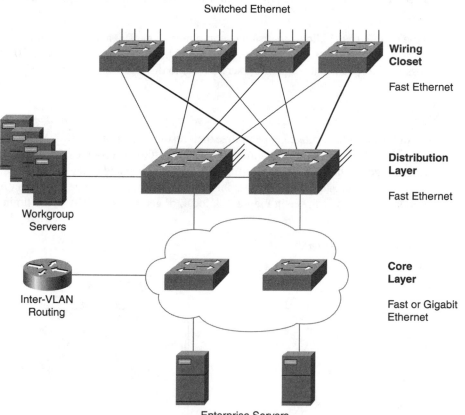

Switched Ethernet

Wiring
Closet

Fast Ethernet

Distribution
Layer

Fast Ethernet

Workgroup
Servers

Core
Layer

Fast or Gigabit
Ethernet

Inter-VLAN
Routing

Enterprise Servers

End-to-end VLANs span the entire switch fabric and are used to place users in the same subnet with the services they need. These services can now be physically placed anywhere inside a corporation, and their users will still appear to be on the same local subnet. An end-to-end VLAN network has the following characteristics:

- Users are grouped into VLANs independent of physical location.
- All users in a VLAN should have the same 80/20 traffic flow patterns.
- As a user moves around the campus, his or her VLAN membership remains the same.
- Each VLAN has a common set of security requirements for all members.

Starting in the wiring closet, 10 Mbps dedicated Ethernet ports are provisioned for each user. Each shade or style of line in Figure 3-2 represents a subnet, and, because people have moved around over time, each switch eventually becomes a member of all VLANs. Fast Ethernet Inter-Switch Link (ISL) is used to carry multiple VLAN information between the wiring closet and the distribution layer switches.

Workgroup servers serve users who operate in a client/server model, and attempts are made to keep users in the same VLAN as their server to maximize the performance of Layer 2 switching.

In the core, a router allows intersubnet communication. The network is engineered, based on traffic flow patterns, to have 80 percent of the traffic within a VLAN and 20 percent crossing the router to the enterprise servers and to the Internet and the WAN.

Local VLANs

As corporations have moved to centralize their resources, end-to-end VLANs have become more difficult to maintain. Users might use many different resources, including many that are no longer in their VLAN. Due to this shift in placement and usage of resources, VLANs are more often created around geographic or local boundaries rather than commonality boundaries. As you can see in Figure 3-3, local, or geographic, VLANs are limited to a physical location.

Figure 3-3   *Local or Geographic VLANs*

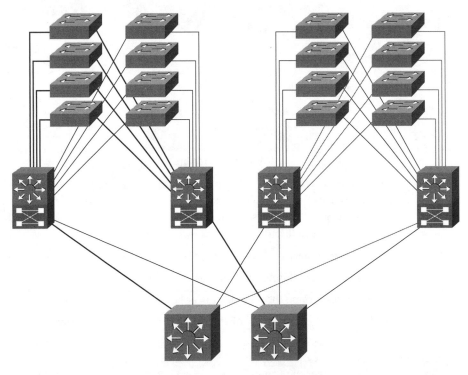

This geographic location can be as large as an entire building or as small as a single switch inside a wiring closet. In a geographic VLAN structure, it is typical to find 80 percent of the traffic remote to the user (server farms and so on) and 20 percent of the traffic local to the user (local server, printers, and so on). Although this topology means that the user must cross a Layer 3 device in order to reach 80 percent of the resources, this design allows the network to provide for a deterministic, consistent method of getting to resources.

Geographic VLANs are also easier to manage and conceptualize than VLANs that span different geographic areas.

Establishing VLAN Memberships

This section describes VLAN membership characteristics and shows you how to establish VLAN membership. The two common approaches to assigning VLAN membership are as follows:

- **Static VLANs**—This method is also called *port-based membership*. Static VLAN assignments are created by assigning a port to a VLAN. As a device enters the network, it automatically assumes the port's VLAN. If the user changes ports and needs access to the same VLAN, the network administrator must manually make a port-to-VLAN assignment for the new connection.

- **Dynamic VLANs**—Dynamic VLANs are created through the use of CiscoWorks 2000 or CiscoWorks for Switched Internetworks (CWSI). Dynamic VLANs currently allow for membership based on the device's MAC address. As a device enters the network, it queries a database for VLAN membership.

NOTE   Dynamic VLANs are not covered as part of this course and book. Dynamic VLANs are covered in the Managing Cisco Switched Internetworks (MCSI) course.

Membership by Ports

In port-based VLAN membership, the port is assigned to a specific VLAN independent of the user or system attached to the port. The network administrator typically performs the VLAN assignment. The port cannot be automatically changed to another VLAN without manual intervention. As you can see in Figure 3-4, all users of the same port must be in the same VLAN.

Figure 3-4 *Port-Based VLANs*

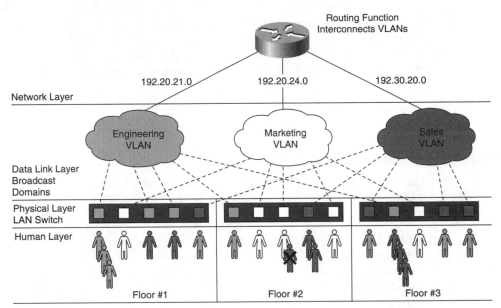

As in other VLAN approaches, the packets forwarded in this method do not leak into other VLAN domains on the network. After a port has been assigned to a VLAN, it cannot send to or receive from devices in another VLAN without the intervention of a Layer 3 device, such as a router.

The device that is attached to the port might not know that a VLAN exists. The device simply knows that it is a member of a subnet and that it should be able to talk to all other members of the subnet by simply sending information to the cable segment. The switch is responsible for specifying that the information came from a certain VLAN and for ensuring that the information gets to all other members of the VLAN. The switch is also responsible for ensuring that ports in a different VLAN do not receive the information.

This approach is quite simple, fast, and easy to manage because no complex lookup tables are required for VLAN segmentation. If port-to-VLAN association is done with an Application-Specific Integrated Circuit (ASIC), performance is very good. An ASIC allows the port-to-VLAN mapping to be done at the hardware level.

Configuring VLANs

Static VLANs are ports on a switch that you manually assign to a VLAN using a VLAN management application or by working directly within the switch. These ports maintain their assigned VLAN configuration until you change them. Although static VLANs require manual entry changes, they are secure, easy to configure, and straightforward to monitor.

This type of VLAN works well in networks where moves are controlled and manage where there is robust VLAN management software to configure the ports, and where it is not desirable to assume the additional overhead required to maintain end-station MAC addresses and custom filtering tables.

Enter the **set vlan** command to create a VLAN and the **clear vlan** command to delete a VLAN on a Catalyst 5*xxx* switch.

NOTE   VLANs support a number of parameters. This section covers only a few of these. For complete information on the **set vlan** command and its parameters, refer to the *Catalyst 5000 Series Command Reference*.

To create a VLAN on a set-based switch, enter the following command:

```
switch (enable) set vlan vlan_num mod_num/port_list
```

The following is an example of entering the **set vlan** command:

```
switch (enable) set vlan 41 2/1-10
```

Verifying VLAN Configuration

It is a good practice to verify your VLAN configuration by entering the **show vlan** command in privileged mode and observing the resultant display.

Example 3-1 shows sample output from using the **show vlan** command.

Example 3-1   *show vlan Command Output*

```
Switch (enable) show vlan
VLAN Name                          Status    IfIndex Mod/Ports, Vlans
---- -------------------------------- --------- --------- ------- --------
1    default                        active    104      2/1-24
41   Usergroup41                    active    117
42   Usergroup42                    active    118
(text deleted)
```

It helps to remember the following guidelines when creating VLANs:

- A created VLAN remains unused until it is mapped to switch ports. Use the **set vlan** command to map VLANs to ports.

- The default configuration has all Ethernet ports on VLAN 1. However, you can enter groups of ports as individual entries, such as 2/1, 3/3, 3/4, 3/5. You can also use a hyphenated format, such as 2/1, 3/3-5.

- Do not enter spaces between the port numbers. Doing so would generate an error message from the system, because it interprets spaces as separators for arguments.

VLAN Identification

In a traditional Ethernet environment, an interface or cable segment could be a member of only one subnet. Switches change this paradigm by allowing multiple VLANs to exist on the same switch and by allowing those VLANs to span to other switches. Each connection from switch to switch or switch to router must be able to carry traffic from different VLANs. The traditional Ethernet frame did not allow for an identification of the VLAN or subnet because it was assumed that this information would be carried in the Layer 3 portion of the packet.

In a campus network, users can be assigned to VLAN groups that span multiple connected switches. In this environment, a method by which switches identify frames belonging to a specific VLAN can direct those frames to the appropriate port.

Frame identification (frame tagging) uniquely assigns a user-defined ID, sometimes referred to as a VLAN ID or color, to each frame.

VLAN frame identification has been specifically developed for switched communications. VLAN frame identification places a unique identifier in the header of each frame as it is forwarded through the switch fabric on trunk links. Each switch examines this frame identifier to determine the frame's VLAN. Based on the VLAN identifier, the switch can make the appropriate decision to broadcast or transmit to other ports in this VLAN.

This section covers the different link types available on a switch, as well as the methods of identifying VLANs on physical links.

Link Types

There are two types of links in a switch environment: access and trunk. This section examines the differences between the two link types and also discusses a special link state called a hybrid link.

Access Links

An access link is a member of only one VLAN. This VLAN is called the port's native VLAN. The device that is attached to the port is completely unaware that a VLAN exists. The device simply assumes that it is part of a network or subnet based on the Layer 3 information that is configured on the device. In order to ensure that it does not have to understand that a VLAN exists, the switch is responsible for removing any VLAN information from the frame before it is sent to the end device.

An access link is a port that belongs to one, and only one, VLAN. The port can't receive information from another VLAN unless the information has been routed. The port can't send information to another VLAN unless the port has access to a router.

Trunk Links

A trunk link can carry multiple VLANs. A trunk link gets its name from the trunks of the telephone system, which can carry multiple telephone conversations. Trunk links are typically used to connect switches to other switches, or switches to routers. Cisco supports trunk lists on Fast Ethernet and Gigabit Ethernet ports.

The switch must have some way to identify which VLAN a frame belongs to when the VLAN receives the frame on a trunk link. The identification techniques currently used are as follows:

- Cisco Inter-Switch Link (ISL)
- IEEE 802.1Q standard

Both of these identification methods are covered later in this section.

A trunk link does not belong to a specific VLAN; rather, a trunk link transports VLANs between devices. The trunk link can be configured to transport all VLANs, or it can be limited to transporting a limited number of VLANs.

A trunk link can, however, have a native VLAN. The trunk's native VLAN is the VLAN that the trunk uses if the trunk link fails for any reason.

NOTE   Trunking capabilities are hardware-dependent. For example, the Catalyst 4000 series switch modules support only 802.1Q encapsulation. To determine whether your hardware supports trunking, and to determine which trunking encapsulations are supported, see your hardware documentation, or use the **show port capabilities** command.

Figure 3-5 shows that VLAN identification adds VLAN information to trunk links and removes VLAN information from access links. In Figure 3-5, Port A and Port B have been defined as access links on the same VLAN. By definition, they can belong to only this one VLAN and cannot receive frames with a VLAN identifier. As Switch Y receives traffic from Port A destined for Port B, Switch Y will not add an ISL encapsulation to the frame.

Figure 3-5   *VLAN Identification Using ISL*

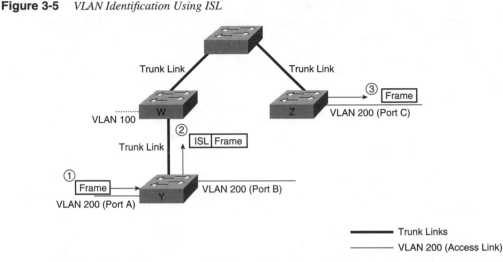

Port C is also an access link. Port C has been defined as a member of VLAN 200 as well. If Port A sends a frame destined for Port C, the switch does the following (the numbers in the following list correspond to the numbers in Figure 3-5):

1 Switch Y receives the frame and identifies it as traffic destined for VLAN 200 by the VLAN and port number association.

2 Switch Y encapsulates the frame with an ISL header identifying VLAN 200 and sends the frame through the intermediate switch on a trunk link. This process is repeated for every switch that the frame must transit as it moves to its final destination of Port C.

3 Switch Z receives the frame, removes the ISL header, and forwards the frame to Port C.

Hybrid Links

Some links are considered to be *hybrid* links—the link is both a trunk and an access link. Hybrid links carry both kinds of frames: frames with VLAN information (tagged frames) and frames without VLAN information (untagged frames).

A hybrid link can receive both tagged and untagged frames. If the received frame is tagged, it will be associated with the VLAN equal to VLAN_ID, which is in the VLAD_ID field of the tag in the frame itself. If the received frame is untagged or tagged but with a NULL VLAN_ID, it will be associated with the VLAN equal to PVID (Port VLAN). At frame transmission, all frames that are sent to the hybrid link should be tagged, except for those that have a VLAN equal to the port's PVID.

VLAN Frame Identification Methods

VLAN identification logically identifies which packets belong to which VLAN group. Cisco supports multiple trunking methodologies:

- **Inter-Switch Link (ISL)**—A Cisco proprietary encapsulation protocol for interconnecting multiple switches. This protocol is supported in Catalyst switches and routers.
- **IEEE 802.1Q**—An IEEE standard method for identifying VLANs by inserting a VLAN identifier into the frame header. This process is called *frame tagging*.
- **LAN Emulation (LANE)**—An IEEE standard method for transporting VLANs over Asynchronous Transfer Mode (ATM) networks.
- **802.10**—A Cisco proprietary method of transporting VLAN information inside the standard 802.10 frame (Fiber Distributed Data Interface [FDDI]). The VLAN information is written to the Security Association Identifier (SAID) portion of the 802.10 frame. This method is typically used to transport VLANs across FDDI backbones.

NOTE   This chapter discusses ISL and 802.1Q methods of VLAN identification only.

Table 3-1 summarizes frame tagging methods and encapsulation. The VLAN identification options of ISL and 802.1Q are discussed in more detail in the following sections.

Table 3-1   *Frame Tagging and Encapsulation Methods*

Identification Method	Encapsulation	Tagging (Insertion into Frame)	Media
802.1Q	No	Yes	Ethernet
ISL	Yes	No	Ethernet
802.10	No	No	FDDI
LANE	No	No	ATM

ISL

The ISL protocol is a way to multiplex VLANs over a trunk link through the use of an encapsulation around the frame.

ISL is a Cisco proprietary protocol for interconnecting multiple switches and maintaining VLAN information as traffic travels between switches on trunk links.

ISL is made up of three major components: a header, the original Ethernet frame, and a frame check sequence (FCS) at the end. With ISL, an Ethernet frame is encapsulated with a header that transports VLAN IDs between switches and routers. The 26-byte header containing a 10-bit VLAN ID is added to each frame. In addition, a 4-byte tail is added to the frame to perform a cyclic redundancy check (CRC). This CRC is in addition to any frame checking that the Ethernet frame performs. Figure 3-6 shows the ISL frame.

Figure 3-6 *The ISL Frame Identification Technique Adds 30 Bytes to the Standard Ethernet Frame*

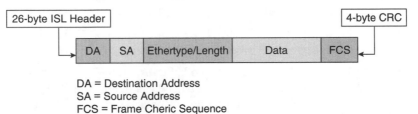

DA = Destination Address
SA = Source Address
FCS = Frame Cheric Sequence

A VLAN ID is added only if the frame is forwarded out a port configured as a trunk link. If the frame is to be forwarded out a port configured as an access link, the ISL encapsulation is removed.

Figure 3-6 shows the 30 additional bytes added to the Ethernet frame by the ISL encapsulation. It is important to note that the Ethernet frame is not modified in any way. The FCS at the end of the ISL encapsulation in Figure 3-7 is in addition to the original FCS of the Ethernet frame.

Figure 3-7 *ISL Frame Format—Shaded Areas Indicate ISL Tag Fields*

40 bits	4 bits	4 bits	48 bits	16 bits	24 bits	24 bits	15 bits	1 bit	16 bits	16 bits	Variable length	32 bits
DA	TYPE	USER	SA	LEN	SNAP/ LLC	HSA	VLAN ID	BPDU/ CDP	INDX	Reserved	Encapsulated Frame	FCS (CRC)

The fields of ISL encapsulation in Figure 3-7 are explained as follows:

- **Destination address (DA)**—The address is a multicast address and is currently set for 01.00.0c.00.00. The first 40 bits of the destination address signal the receiver that this is an ISL frame.

- **Frame type (TYPE)**—The TYPE field indicates the type of frame that is encapsulated and can be used in the future to indicate different encapsulation types. The following type codes have been defined:

  — 0000—Ethernet

  — 0001—Token Ring

  — 0010—FDDI

  — 0011—ATM

- **User-defined bits (USER)**—The user-defined bits are an extension of the TYPE field. The USER bits are used to extend the meaning of the TYPE field. For example, Token Ring frames can have more than one type. The default USER field value is 0000. For Ethernet frames, two USER field values have been defined. The USER field will be passed unchanged from the ISL packet to the internal packet headers in the switch.

  For Ethernet frames, the user field bits 0 and 1 indicate the packet's priority as it passes through the switch. Whenever traffic can be handled in a manner that allows it to be forwarded more quickly, packets that have this bit set should take advantage of this quick path. It is not required that such paths be provided.

Code	Meaning
XX00	Normal priority
XX01	Priority 1
XX10	Priority 2
XX11	Highest priority

- **Source address (SA)**—The SA field is the source address field of the ISL packet. It should be set to the 802.3 MAC address of the switch port transmitting the frame. It is a 48-bit value. The receiving device may ignore the frame's SA field if it has no reason to use the information.

- **Length (LEN)**—The LEN field is a 16-bit value of the length of the packet in bytes excluding the DA, TYPE, USER, SA, LEN, and CRC fields. The total length of the excluded fields is 18 bytes, so the LEN field is the total length minus 18 bytes. It is stored as a 16-bit value.

- **SNAP/LLC**—The SNAP field is an 24-bit constant value of 0xAAAA03.

- **High bits of the Source Address (HSA)**—The HSA field is the upper 3 bytes, the manufacturer's ID portion, of the SA field. It must contain the value 0x00.00.0C.

- **VLAN ID**—The VLAN field is the packet's virtual LAN ID. It is a 15-bit value that is used to distinguish frames on different VLANs. This field is often referred to as the color of the packet.

- **BPDU/CDP Indicator**—The BPDU (Bridge Protocol Data Unit) bit is set for all bridge protocol data units that are encapsulated by the ISL packet. The BPDUs are used by the Spanning Tree algorithm to determine information about the network's topology.

Note	The Bridge Protocol Data Unit is discussed in more detail in Chapter 4, "Managing Redundant Links."

- **Index (INDX)**—The INDX field indicates the port index of the source of the packet as it exits the switch. It is used for diagnostic purposes only and may be set to any value by other devices. It is a 16-bit value and is ignored in received packets.

- **Reserved for FDDI and Token Ring**—The RES field is used when Token Ring or FDDI packets are encapsulated with an ISL packet. In the case of Token Ring frames, the address copied (AC) and frame copied (FC) fields are placed here. In the case of FDDI, the FC field is placed in the least-significant byte of this field (for example, an FC of 0x12 would have a RES field of 0x0012). For Ethernet packets, the RES field should be set to all 0s.

- **Encapsulated Frame**—The ENCAP FRAME is the encapsulated frame, including its own CRC value, completely unmodified. The internal frame must have a CRC value that is valid after the ISL encapsulation fields are removed. The length of this field can be from 1 to 24,575 bytes to accommodate Ethernet, Token Ring, and FDDI frames. A receiving switch can strip off the ISL encapsulation fields and use this ENCAP FRAME as the frame is received, associating the appropriate VLAN and other values with the received frame for switching purposes.

- **Frame Check Sequence (FCS)**—The CRC is a standard 32-bit CRC value calculated on the entire encapsulated frame from the DA field to the ENCAP FRAME field. The receiving MAC checks this CRC and can discard packets that do not have a valid CRC. Note that this CRC is in addition to the one at the end of the ENCAP FRAME field.

NOTE

The ISL frame encapsulation is 30 bytes, and the minimum FDDI packet is 17 bytes, so the minimum ISL encapsulated packet is 47 bytes. The maximum Token Ring packet is 18,000 bytes, so the maximum ISL packet is 18,030 bytes.

If only Ethernet packets are encapsulated, the range of ISL frame sizes is from 94 to 1548 bytes.

IEEE 802.1Q

The official name of the IEEE 802.1Q protocol is Standard for Virtual Bridged Local-Area Networks. This refers to the ability to carry the traffic of more than one subnet down a single cable.

The IEEE 802.1Q frame-tagging format provides a standard method for identifying frames that belong to particular VLANs. This format helps ensure interoperability of multiple vendor VLAN implementations. The IEEE 802.1Q standard defines the following:

- An architecture for VLANs
- Services provided in VLANs
- Protocols and algorithms involved in the provision of those services

As Figure 3-8 indicates, frame identification with 802.1Q involves the addition of 4 bytes to the standard Ethernet frame.

Figure 3-8 *Frame Identification with 802.1Q*

Initial MAC Address	2-Byte TPID 2-Byte TCI	Initial Type/Data	New CRC

This 4-byte tag header contains the following:

- **2-byte Tag Protocol Identifier (TPID)**—Contains a fixed value of 0x8100. This particular TPID value indicates that the frame carries the 802.1Q/802.1p tag information.

- **2-byte Tag Control Information (TCI)**—Contains the following elements:

  — **3-bit user_priority**—This field allows the tagged frame to carry user_priority information across bridged LANs. The 3-bit value is interpreted as a binary number that can represent eight priority levels, 0 through 7. This field is used primarily by the 802.1p standard.

  — **1-bit Canonical Format Indicator (CFI)**—A CFI value of 0 indicates canonical format; a value of 1 indicates noncanonical format. It is used in Token Ring/Source-Routed FDDI media access methods to signal the bit order of address information carried in the encapsulated frame.

  — **12-bit VLAN Identifier (VID)**—This field uniquely identifies the VLAN to which the frame belongs. VID can uniquely define 4096 VLANs. However, VLANs 0 and 4095 are reserved. This field is used primarily by the 802.1Q standard. The current Cisco default for VLANs supports less than the maximum range of VLANs supported by 802.1Q.

Both ISL and IEEE 802.1Q tagging are explicit tagging, meaning that the frame is tagged with VLAN information explicitly.

The tagging mechanisms are quite different, however. IEEE 802.1Q uses an internal tagging process that modifies the existing Ethernet frame with the VLAN identification. This allows the 802.1Q frame identification process to work on both access links and trunk links as the frame appears to be a standard Ethernet frame.

ISL uses an external tagging process. With ISL external tagging, the original frame is not altered but is encapsulated with a new 26-byte ISL header (tag), and a new, extra 4-byte FCS is appended at the end of the frame. This means that only ISL-aware devices are capable of interpreting the frame. It also means that the frame can violate normal Ethernet conventions such as the maximum transmission unit size of 1518 bytes.

NOTE	Original Ethernet frames cannot exceed 1518 bytes. If a frame of the maximum size is tagged with 802.1Q, the resulting frame will be 1522 bytes. This frame is called a baby giant frame. The switch processes this frame successfully, although the switch might record it as an Ethernet error.

Trunk Negotiation

A trunk is a point-to-point link between two Catalyst switch ports, or between a Catalyst switch and a router. Trunks carry the traffic of multiple VLANs and allow you to extend VLANs from one Catalyst switch to another.

The Dynamic Trunking Protocol (DTP) manages trunk negotiation in Catalyst supervisor engine software release 4.2 and later. DTP supports autonegotiation of both ISL and IEEE 802.1Q trunks.

In prior releases, trunk negotiation was managed by the Dynamic Inter-Switch Link (DISL) protocol. DISL supports autonegotiation of ISL trunks only. In supervisor engine software release 4.1, you must manually configure IEEE 802.1Q trunks on both ends of the link. IEEE 802.1Q trunks were not supported prior to software release 4.1.

NOTE	For trunking to be autonegotiated on Fast Ethernet and Gigabit Ethernet ports, the ports must be in the same VTP domain. However, you can use on or nonegotiate mode to force a port to become a trunk, even if it is in a different domain.

During trunk negotiation, the port doesn't participate in Spanning-Tree Protocol.

NOTE	DTP is a point-to-point protocol. However, some internetworking devices might forward DTP frames improperly. To avoid this problem, ensure that trunking is turned off on ports connected to nonswitch devices if you do not intend to trunk across those links. When manually enabling a trunk on a link to a Cisco router, use the **nonegotiate** keyword of the **set trunk** command. This command allows the link to become a trunk, but it does not generate DTP frames. This keyword is discussed in the next section.

Configuring a Trunk Link

To create or configure a VLAN trunk, enter the **set trunk** command to configure the port on each end of the link as a trunk port and to identify the VLANs that will be transported on this trunk link. You can also enter the **set trunk** command to change a trunk's mode. The command syntax is as follows:

```
Switch (enable) set trunk mod_num/port_num [on | off | desirable | auto |
    nonegotiate] vlan_range [isl | dot1q | dot10 | lane | negotiate]
```

Fast Ethernet and Gigabit Ethernet trunking modes are as follows:

- **on**—Puts the port into permanent trunking. The port becomes a trunk port even if the neighboring port does not agree to the change. The on state does not allow for the negotiation of an encapsulation type. You must, therefore, specify the encapsulation in the configuration.

- **off**—Puts the port into permanent nontrunking mode and negotiates to convert the link into a nontrunk link. The port becomes a nontrunk port even if the neighboring port does not agree to the change.

- **desirable**—Makes the port actively attempt to convert the link to a trunk link. The port becomes a trunk port if the neighboring port is set to on, desirable, or auto mode.

- **auto**—Makes the port willing to convert the link to a trunk link. The port becomes a trunk port if the neighboring port is set to on or desirable mode. This is the default mode for Fast and Gigabit Ethernet ports. Notice that if the default setting is left on both sides of the trunk link, it will never become a trunk. Neither side will be the first to ask to convert to a trunk.

- **nonegotiate**—Puts the port into permanent trunking mode, but prevents the port from generating DTP frames. You must configure the neighboring port manually as a trunk port to establish a trunk link.

Clearing VLANs from a Trunk Link

By default, all VLANs are transported across a trunk link when you issue the **set trunk** command. However, there might be instances in which the trunk link should not carry all VLANs, such as the following:

- **Broadcast suppression**—All broadcasts must be sent to every port in a VLAN. A trunk link acts as a member port of the VLAN and, therefore, must pass all the broadcasts. Bandwidth and processing time are wasted if there is no port at the other end of the trunk link that is a member of that VLAN.

- **Topology change**—Changes that occur in the topology must also be propagated across the trunk link. If the VLAN is not used on the other end of the trunk link, there is no need for the overhead of a topology change.

NOTE   More information about topology change characteristics can be found in Chapter 4.

In order to remove a VLAN from a trunk link, use the following command:

```
Switch (enable) clear trunk mod_num/port_num vlan_range
```

If you want to remove many VLANs from the trunk link, it might be easier to clear all VLANs from the trunk link first, and then set just the VLANs that are supposed to be on the link.

NOTE   When you issue the **set trunk** command, VLANs 1 to 1000 are automatically transported, even if you specify a VLAN range. In order to limit VLANs on the trunk link, you must clear the VLANs from the link.

Verifying Trunk Link Configuration

Verify the trunking configuration by entering in privileged mode the **show trunk** [*mod_num/port_num*] command.

Example 3-2 shows how to verify the trunk configuration on a Catalyst 5*xxx* switch. This example assumes that the neighbor port is in auto mode.

Example 3-2   *The **show trunk** Command Verifies Trunk Configuration on Catalyst 5000 Series Switches*

```
switch (enable) show trunk 1/1
Port         Mode          Encapsulation  Status        Native vlan
--------     -----------   -------------  ------------  -----------
 1/1         desirable     isl            trunking      1
Port         Vlans allowed on trunk
--------     ----------------------------------------------------------------
 1/1         1-100,250,500-1005
Port         Vlans allowed and active in management domain
--------     ----------------------------------------------------------------
 1/1         1,521-524
Port         Vlans in spanning tree forwarding state and not pruned
--------     ----------------------------------------------------------------
 1/1         1,521-524
```

VLAN Trunking Protocol

In order to manage all the VLANs across the campus network, Cisco created the VLAN Trunking Protocol (VTP). VTP maintains VLAN configuration consistency throughout the network. VTP is a messaging protocol that uses Layer 2 trunk frames in order to manage the addition, deletion, and renaming of VLANs on a network-wide basis. VTP also allows you to make centralized changes that are communicated to all other switches in the network.

VTP minimizes the possible configuration inconsistencies that arise when changes are made. These inconsistencies result in security violations, because VLANs cross-connect when duplicate names are used and could become internally disconnected when VLANs are mapped from one LAN type to another (for example, Ethernet to ATM or FDDI).

VTP provides the following benefits:

- VLAN configuration consistency across the network
- Mapping scheme for going across mixed-media backbones to map Ethernet VLANs to a high-speed backbone VLAN such as ATM LANE or FDDI, allowing a VLAN to be trunked over mixed media
- Accurate tracking and monitoring of VLANs
- Dynamic reporting of added VLANs across the network
- "Plug-and-play" configuration when adding new VLANs

In order for VLANs to be created on a switch, you must first set up a VTP management domain so that it can verify the current VLANs on the network. All switches in the same management domain share their VLAN information, and a switch can participate in only one VTP management domain. Switches in different domains do not share VTP information.

Using VTP, each Catalyst family switch advertises the following on its trunk ports:

- Management domain
- Configuration revision number
- Known VLANs and their specific parameters

VTP Operation

A VTP domain is made up of one or more interconnected devices that share the same VTP domain name. A switch can be configured to be in one VTP domain only. Global VLAN information is propagated by way of connected switch trunk ports.

Switches can be configured not to accept VTP information. These switches will forward VTP information on trunk ports in order to ensure that other switches receive the update, but the switches will not modify their database, nor will they send out an update indicating a change in VLAN status. This is called transparent mode.

By default, management domains are set to a nonsecure mode without a password. Adding a password sets the management domain to secure mode. A password must be configured on every switch in the management domain before secure mode can be used.

Detecting the addition of VLANs within the advertisements acts as a notification to the switches (servers and clients) that they should be prepared to receive traffic on their trunk ports with the newly defined VLAN IDs, emulated LAN names, and 802.10 SAIDs.

In Figure 3-9, C5000-3 transmits a VTP database entry with additions or deletions to C5000-1 and C5000-2. The configuration database has a revision number that is notification+1 (N+1). A higher configuration revision number indicates that the VLAN information that is being sent is more current then the stored copy. Any time a switch receives an update that has a higher configuration revision number, the switch will overwrite the stored information with the new information being sent in the VTP update.

Figure 3-9   *VTP Database Entries Are Transmitted to Other Switches in the Same Domain*

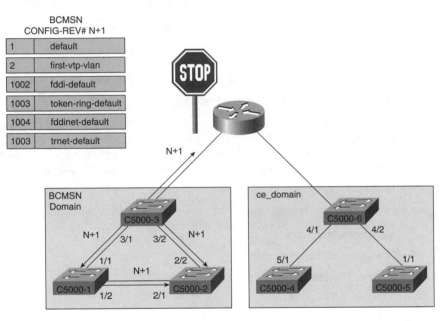

1	default
2	first-vtp-vlan
1002	fddi-default
1003	token-ring-default
1004	fddinet-default
1003	trnet-default

BCMSN
CONFIG-REV# N+1

NOTE	VTP has its own nonvolatile random-access memory (NVRAM). Therefore, the **clear config all** command does not really clear the entire configuration. In particular, the VTP information is still maintained, including the configuration revision number. The configuration revision number is cleared, or reset to 0, when the switch is power-cycled.

TIP   The behavior of the configuration revision number in VTP appears to vary from release to release of the **set** command-line interface. It is recommended that you test its behavior on your switches in order to ensure that VTP does not cause problems on your network. Some versions reset the configuration revision number on cold boot, but the latest versions appear not to. Earlier releases did not reset the configuration revision number with the issuance of a **clear config all** command, but the newest releases appear to do so. It appears that Cisco is modifying the behavior of the configuration revision number in order to address issues with its behavior.

VTP Modes of Operation

You can configure a Catalyst family switch to operate in any of the following VTP modes:

- **Server**—In VTP server mode, you can create, modify, and delete VLANs, as well as specify other configuration parameters (such as VTP version and VTP pruning) for the entire VTP domain. VTP servers advertise their VLAN configuration to other switches in the same VTP domain and synchronize the VLAN configuration with other switches based on advertisements received over trunk links. VTP server is the default mode.

- **Client**—VTP clients behave the same way as VTP servers, but you cannot create, change, or delete VLANs on a VTP client.

- **Transparent**—VTP transparent switches do not participate in VTP. A VTP transparent switch does not advertise its VLAN configuration and does not synchronize its VLAN configuration based on received advertisements. However, in VTP version 2, transparent switches do forward received VTP advertisements out their trunk ports.

Adding a Switch to an Existing Domain

Use caution when inserting a new switch into an existing domain. In order to prepare a switch to enter an existing VTP domain, follow these steps:

Step 1   Issue a **clear config all** command to remove the existing configuration. This will not clear the VTP configuration revision number.

Step 2   Power-cycle the switch to clear the VTP NVRAM. This will reset the configuration revision number to 0, ensuring that the new switch will not propagate the incorrect information.

Step 3   Determine the switch's VTP mode of operation and include the mode when setting the VTP domain information on the switch. The most common default for switches is server mode. If you leave the switch in server mode, verify that the configuration revision number is set to 0 before adding the switch to the VTP domain. Cisco Systems recommends that there be several servers with all other switches set to client mode for purposes of controlling VTP information.

Note	Cisco highly recommends that you assign a password to your VTP domain. This prevents unauthorized switches from adding themselves to your domain and passing incorrect VLAN information. After a password has been configured, all switches in the management domain must be assigned the same password. The management domain password must be assigned to allow VTP to pass VLAN information.

VTP Advertisements

With VTP, each switch advertises on its trunk ports its management domain, configuration revision number, the VLANs that it knows about, and certain parameters for each known VLAN. These advertisement frames are sent to a multicast address so that all neighboring devices can receive the frames; however, the frames are not forwarded by normal bridging procedures. All devices in the same management domain learn about any new VLANs now configured in the transmitting device. A new VLAN must be created and configured on one device only in the management domain. The information is automatically learned by all the other devices in the same management domain.

Advertisements on factory-default VLANs are based on media types. User ports should not be configured as VTP trunks.

Each advertisement starts as configuration revision number 0. When changes are made, the configuration revision number increments ($n + 1$).

There are two types of advertisements:

- Requests from clients that want information at bootup
- Responses from servers

There are three types of messages:

- **Advertisement requests from clients**—Clients request VLAN information; the server responds with summary and subset advertisements.
- **Summary advertisements**—Occur every 300 seconds on VLAN 1 and every time a topology change occurs.
- **Subset advertisements**—Contains detailed information about VLANs.

Figure 3-10 summarizes these three types of VTP advertisement content.

Figure 3-10   *The Three Types of VTP Advertisements—Requests, Summaries, and Subsets*

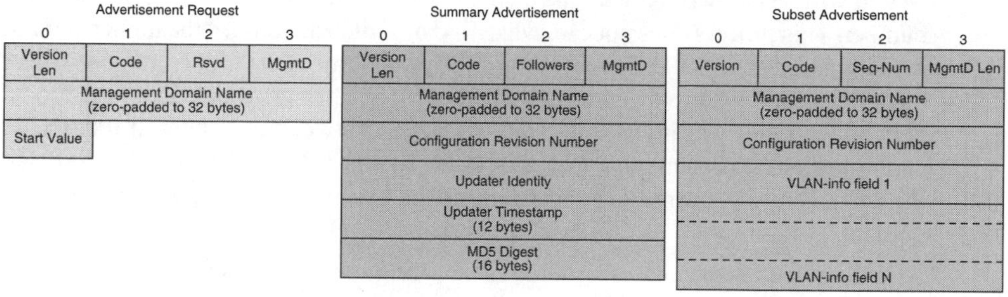

Advertisements can contain the following information:

- **Management domain name**—Advertisements with different names are ignored.

- **Configuration revision number**—The higher number indicates a more recent configuration.

- **MD5 Digest**—The MD5 Digest is the key that is sent with the VTP when a password has been assigned. If the key does not match, the update is ignored.

- **Updater identity**—The identity of the switch that is sending the VTP summary advertisement.

VTP Configuration Revision Number

One of the most critical components contained in the VTP advertisements is the configuration revision number.

Each time a VTP server modifies its VTP database, the server increments the configuration revision number by 1. The server then advertises its database with the new configuration revision number.

If the configuration revision number being advertised is higher than the number stored on the other devices in the VTP domain, the switch will make a request of the updater for a subset advertisement. The subset advertisement contains details of the VLANs that the updater has stored in its NVRAM. The switches will then overwrite their databases with the new information that is being advertised.

This overwrite process means that if the VTP server deleted all VLANs and had the higher configuration revision number, the other devices in the VTP domain would also delete their VLANs.

NOTE   Understanding the configuration revision number is critical to maintaining VTP. The configuration revision number determines which VLAN database the VTP domain decides to use. A higher configuration revision number means that the current database on the switch will be overwritten with the database that has the highest configuration revision number. This process does not care what kind of switch advertised the higher configuration revision number. It could be a client device that advertises the higher number. This occurs most frequently when a switch has been configured as a server outside of the production network and then was inserted into the production network as a client. If it has a higher configuration revision number than the current number of the VTP domain, the database of the new client will overwrite the database of the existing servers and clients in the VTP domain.

Also note that two databases with the same configuration number will not update each other, because they assume that they both contain the same information.

VTP Configuration Tasks and Guidelines

Before you configure VTP and VLANs on your network, you must make several decisions. This section discusses the guidelines for making those decisions and covers the configuration commands to implement VTP.

The following list outlines the basic tasks that you must consider before you configure VTP and VLANs on your network:

1 Determine the version number of VTP that will be running in your environment.

2 Decide if this switch is to be a member of an existing management domain or if a new domain should be created. If a management domain does exist, determine its name and password.

3 Choose a VTP mode for the switch.

Choosing a VTP Version

Two different versions of VTP can run in your management domain: VTP version 1 and VTP version 2. These two versions are not interoperable. If you choose to configure a switch in a domain for VTP version 2, you must configure all switches in the management domain to be in VTP version 2. VTP version 1 is the default. You might need to implement VTP version 2 if you need some of the specific features that VTP version 2 offers that are not offered in VTP version 1. The most common feature that is needed is Token Ring VLAN support.

Use the **set vtp v2 enable** command to change the VTP version number.

VTP version 2 supports the following features that are not supported in version 1:

• **Token Ring support**—VTP version 2 supports Token Ring LAN switching and VLANs.

- **Unrecognized Type-Length-Value (TLV) support**—A VTP server or client propagates configuration changes to its other trunks, even for TLVs that it can't parse. The unrecognized TLV is saved in NVRAM.

- **Version-dependent transparent mode**—In VTP version 1, a VTP transparent switch inspects VTP messages for the domain name and version and forwards a message only if the version and domain name match. Because only one domain is supported in the supervisor engine software, VTP version 2 forwards VTP messages in transparent mode without checking the version.

- **Consistency checks**—In VTP version 2, VLAN consistency checks (such as VLAN names and values) are performed only when you enter new information through the command-line interface (CLI) or Simple Network Management Protocol (SNMP). Consistency checks are not performed when new information is obtained from a VTP message or when information is read from NVRAM. If the digest on a received VTP message is correct, its information is accepted without consistency checks. A switch that can run VTP version 2 can operate in the same domain as a switch running VTP version 1 if VTP version 2 remains disabled on the VTP version 2-capable switch.

- **Token Ring environment**—You must use VTP version 2 if you are running VTP in a Token Ring environment.

- **Version number propagation**—If all switches in a domain can run VTP version 2, you need to enable VTP version 2 on only one switch (using the **set vtp v2 enable** command). The version number is propagated to the other VTP version 2-capable switches in the VTP domain.

Determining VTP Management Domain and Mode

If this is the first switch in the network, you will have to create the management domain. If other Catalyst switches exist, you will probably join an existing management domain. Verify the name of the management domain that you want to join. If the management domain has been secured, you will also need to get the password for the domain.

To create a management domain or to add yourself to a management domain, use the following command:

```
Switch (enable) set vtp domain domain_name password password
```

The domain name can be up to 32 characters. The password must be 8 to 64 characters long.

Configuring VTP and Choosing a VTP Mode for the Switch

You will need to choose one of the three available VTP modes for the switch. This section covers general guidelines for choosing the mode of your Catalyst switch.

If this is the first Catalyst switch in your management domain, and you intend to add more switches, set the mode to server. The additional switches will be able to learn VLAN information from this switch. You should have at least one server.

If there are any other Catalyst switches in the management domain, set your switch mode to client and power off the switch. This will prevent the new switch from accidentally propagating the incorrect information to your existing network. If you would like this switch to end up as a VTP server, change the switch's mode to server after it has learned the correct VLAN information from the network.

If the switch won't share VLAN information with any other switch on the network, set the switch to transparent mode. This will allow you to create, delete, and rename VLANs, but the switch will not propagate changes to other switches. If many people are configuring your environment, you run the risk of creating overlapping VLANs that have two different meanings in the network but the same VLAN identification.

To set the correct mode of your switch, use the following command:

```
Switch (enable) set vtp domain domain-name mode [server | client | transparent]
```

NOTE   The domain name used in this command is the same as the domain name and password that you configured before. You can issue all the options in one command, such as **set vtp domain** *domain-name* **password** *password* **mode** *mode* **v2 enable**.

It is generally recommended that there be at least two VTP servers and that the rest of the switches be VTP clients. Be aware that if the client loses power, it must contact the server to get VLAN information. If the server is not available due to power outages or a slow boot process, the client might not receive VLAN information. This means that the client switch will only know about VLAN 1, and all ports in VLANs other than VLAN 1 will be placed in an inactive state.

Verifying VTP Configuration

The following is an example of the **set vtp domain** command to change the local VTP mode to server:

```
switch (enable) set vtp domain bcmsn_block2 mode server
VTP domain bcmsn_block2 has been modified.
```

Example 3-3 shows a **show vtp domain** command example for the previous configuration.

Example 3-3   *show vtp domain Command Example*

```
switch (enable) show vtp domain
Domain Name      Domain Index  VTP Version       Local Mode  Password
-------------    ------------  ----------------  ----------  --------
bcmsn_block2     1             2                 server      -
Vlan-count Max-vlan-storage Config Revision Notifications
```

Example 3-3 *show vtp domain Command Example (Continued)*

```
---------- ---------------- ---------------- ------------
33          1023              0                disabled
Last Updater   V2 Mode  Pruning  PruneEligible on Vlans
--------------- -------- -------- ------------------------
172.20.52.124   disabled disabled 2-1000
```

NOTE   The **show vtp domain** command is very useful for verifying the current configuration
                revision number.

Another useful command for troubleshooting VTP is the **show vtp statistics** command.
This command shows a summary of VTP advertisement messages sent and received, as
well as configuration errors detected. Example 3-4 displays sample output from the **show
vtp statistics** command.

Example 3-4 *The **show vtp statistics** Command Displays a Summary of VTP Advertisement Traffic and Detects
Configuration Errors*

```
switch (enable) show vtp statistics
VTP statistics:
summary advts received      0
subset  advts received         0
request advts received         0
summary advts transmitted      0
subset  advts transmitted      0
request advts transmitted      10
No of config revision errors   0
No of config digest errors     0
```

To reset the values displayed with the **show vtp statistics** command, use the **clear vtp
statistics** command:

```
switch (enable) clear vtp statistics
vtp statistics cleared
```

VTP Pruning

By default, broadcasts for a VLAN are sent to every switch that has a trunk link that carries
that VLAN. This happens even if the switch has no ports in that VLAN. This process means
that trunk links will carry broadcast traffic that will ultimately be discarded by the switch.

VTP pruning enhances network bandwidth use by reducing unnecessary flooded traffic,
such as broadcast, multicast, unknown, and flooded unicast packets. VTP pruning increases
available bandwidth by restricting flooded traffic to those trunk links that the traffic must
use to access the appropriate network devices. This means that it restricts broadcasts,

multicasts, and flooded unicast traffic from switches that do not have ports assigned to that VLAN. By default, VTP pruning is disabled.

NOTE VTP pruning does not change a link's Spanning-Tree Protocol characteristics. Bridge Protocol Data Units will still be broadcast on the link in order to build a Spanning Tree for that VLAN, and the trunk link will still participate in Spanning Tree convergence. For that reason, it might be preferable to clear the VLAN from the trunk link. This will accomplish the same thing as VTP pruning, with the added benefit that the trunk link no longer has to participate in the Spanning-Tree Protocol for that VLAN.

VTP Pruning Overview

Figure 3-11 shows a switched network without VTP pruning enabled. Port 1 on Switch 1 and Port 2 on Switch 4 are assigned to VLAN 10. A broadcast is sent from the host connected to Switch 1.

Figure 3-11   *A Switched Network Without VTP Pruning*

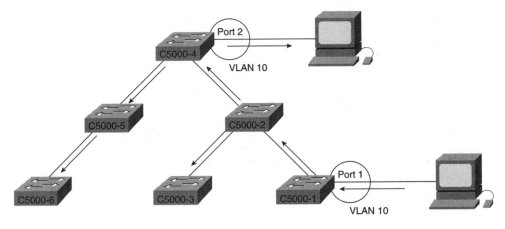

Switch 1 floods the broadcast, and every switch in the network receives this broadcast, even though Switches 3, 5, and 6 have no ports in VLAN 10.

Figure 3-12 shows the same switched network *with* VTP pruning enabled. The broadcast traffic from Switch 1 is not forwarded to Switches 3, 5, and 6 because traffic for VLAN 10 has been pruned on the links indicated (Port 5 on Switch 2 and Port 4 on Switch 4).

Figure 3-12   *A Switched Network with VTP Pruning*

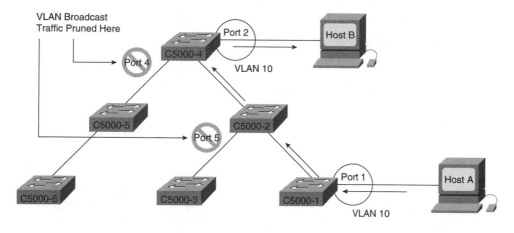

If you added a host to C5000-6 in the same VLAN as Host A and Host B from Figure 3-12, C5000-4, C5000-5, and C5000-6 would no longer be prune-eligible for that VLAN and would begin to receive all broadcast traffic for the VLAN.

Configuring VTP Pruning

Enabling VTP pruning on a VTP server allows pruning for the entire management domain. VTP pruning takes effect several seconds after you enable it. By default, VLANs 2 through 1000 are pruning-eligible. VTP pruning does not prune traffic from VLANs that are pruning-ineligible. VLAN 1 is always pruning-ineligible, so traffic from VLAN 1 cannot be pruned.

You have the option of making specific VLANs pruning-eligible or pruning-ineligible on the device. To make specific VLANs pruning-eligible, enter the following:

```
Switch (enable) set vtp pruneeligible vlan_range
```

To make specific VLANs pruning-ineligible, enter the following:

```
Switch (enable) clear vtp pruneeligible vlan_range
```

Verifying VTP Pruning Configuration

In order to verify the VLANs that are either pruned or not pruned, use the **show trunk** command. Example 3-5 shows sample output from this command.

Example 3-5   *The **show trunk** Command Verifies Whether VLANs Are Pruned*

```
switch (enable) show trunk 1/1
Port      Mode         Encapsulation  Status       Native vlan
--------  -----------  -------------  -----------  -----------
 1/1      desirable    isl            trunking     1
```

continues

Example 3-5   *The **show trunk** Command Verifies Whether VLANs Are Pruned (Continued)*

```
Port      Vlans allowed on trunk
-------   ----------------------------------------------------------------------
 1/1      1-100,250,500-1005
Port      Vlans allowed and active in management domain
-------   ----------------------------------------------------------------------
 1/1      1,521-524
Port      Vlans in spanning tree forwarding state and not pruned
-------   ----------------------------------------------------------------------
 1/1      1,521-524
```

Summary

VLANs solve many of the issues found in Layer 2 environments. These issues include broadcast control, isolation of problem components in the network, security, and load balancing through the use of a Layer 3 protocol between VLANs.

VLAN identification allows different VLANs to be carried on the same physical link, called a trunk link. There are two different types of frame identification methods: ISL and 802.1Q.

VLAN Trunking Protocol provides support for dynamic reporting of the addition, deletion, and renaming of VLANs across the switch fabric. This overwrite process would mean that if the server deleted all VLANs and had a higher configuration revision number, the other devices in the VTP domain would also delete their VLANs.

Review Questions

The following questions test your retention of the material presented in this chapter. The answers to the Review Questions can be found in Appendix A, "Answers to Review Questions."

1 Explain how VTP enables propagation of VLAN data across the network.

2 Discuss how frame identification enables VLAN membership association.

3 Define the three VTP modes of operation and describe how they work.

4 Describe the use of VTP pruning. Explore the same solution without VTP pruning.

Case Study: Defining Common Workgroups

Follow this case study as a review of information discussed in this chapter.

Scenario

This case study shows you how to configure VLANs on each of the access layer switches. VLANs must also be created for the segments that attach the distribution layer switches to the core layer. In addition to creating VLANs, you will see how to configure trunking on all the uplinks from the distribution layer switches to the access layer switches.

When the configuration is complete, each access switch should have ports that reside in one of two VLANs assigned to that access switch. Each distribution switch in the switch block should be configured to support all VLANs.

This case study assumes that the core layer devices have already been configured with the appropriate VTP and VLAN information and that only the access layer switches and the distribution layer switches have to be configured.

Figure 3-13 provides the visual objective for the case study and also gives values for VLANs and the VTP domain name that will be used in this case study.

Figure 3-13   *Visual Objective for the Case Study*

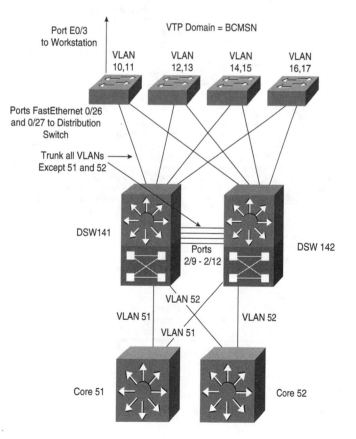

Command List

In this case study, you will see the following commands. Refer to Table 3-2 and Table 3-3 if you need an explanation of the commands used during the case study.

Table 3-2   *Access Switch Commands*

Command	Description
interface	Selects an interface to configure.
trunk	Enables trunking on a Fast Ethernet interface.
no trunk-vlan	Denies VLAN traffic from being carried on trunk.
vlan	Sets VLAN configuration.
vlan-membership	Sets VLAN membership configuration.
vtp *name*	Defines the VTP domain name.
vtp *mode*	Places the switch in chosen VTP mode (server, client, or transparent).
vtp password *password*	Sets a password for the VTP domain (optional).
show vtp	Displays the VTP configuration information.
show run	Displays configuration information.
Ctrl-Shift-6-x	Escapes sequence.

Table 3-3   *Distribution Switch Commands*

Command	Description
enable	Enters privileged mode.
set *port mod/ports*	Sets port parameters.
set vlan *vlan-num* [*name*]	Creates an Ethernet VLAN (if you do not specify a type, the default type is Ethernet).
set vlan *vlan-num mod/ports*	Assigns port(s) to a VLAN.
set trunk *mod/ports* [**on|off|desirable|auto|nonegotiate**] [*vlans*] [*trunk_type*]	Configures the trunk ports.
clear trunk *mod/ports vlans*	Clears trunk.
set vtp domain *name*	Defines the VTP domain name.
set vtp mode *mode*	Places the switch in chosen VTP mode (server, client, or transparent).
set vtp password *password*	Sets a password for the VTP domain (optional).
show vlan	Shows the VLANs configured on this switch.

Table 3-3   *Distribution Switch Commands (Continued)*

Command	Description
show vtp domain	Displays the VTP configuration information.
Ctrl-Shift-6-x	Escapes sequence.

Task 1: Configure the Access Layer Devices with VTP Domain, VLANs, and Trunks

In this task, you must configure two VLANs on each of the access layer switches. The VLANs should be unique for each switch and each switch should contain an odd and an even VLAN. You must further assign these VLANs to ports on the switch and configure trunking on the uplink ports that connect the access layer switch to the distribution layer.

Execute the following steps to complete this task.

Placing the Access Switch in a Management Domain

Complete the following steps:

Step 1 From your PC desktop, Telnet to your access switch.

Step 2 In global configuration mode, enter the **vtp** *mode* command to alter the VTP mode. Change the mode to server.

Step 3 In global configuration mode, enter the **vtp domain** *name* command to assign a VTP domain name to your access switch.

Step 4 In privileged mode, enter the **show vtp** command to verify the VTP domain name and mode. Your configuration should resemble the output in Example 3-6.

Example 3-6 *show vtp Command Output*

```
VTP version: 1
Configuration revision: 0
Maximum VLANs supported locally: 1005
Number of existing VLANs: 0
VTP domain name       : BCMSN
VTP password          :
VTP operating mode    : Server
VTP pruning mode      : Disabled
VTP traps generation  : Enabled
Configuration last modified by: 172.16.4.41 at 00-00-0000 00:00:00
```

Activating Trunking on the Access Switch

Complete the following steps:

Step 1 From your PC desktop, Telnet to your assigned access switch.

Step 2 In global configuration mode, enter the **interface fast 0/26** command to enter interface configuration mode.

Step 3 In interface configuration mode, enter the **trunk on** command to activate trunking.

Step 4 In interface configuration mode, enter the **no trunk-vlan 51 52** command to restrict vlans 51 and 52 from the trunk.

This prevents the core VLANs from being carried on this trunk link. The VLAN number that you specify will depend on the VLANs configured for the Core Layer connections.

Step 5 In global configuration mode, enter the **interface fast 0/27** command to enter interface configuration mode.

Step 6 In interface configuration mode, enter the **trunk on** command to activate trunking.

Step 7 In interface configuration mode, enter the **no trunk-vlan 51 52** command to restrict VLANs 51 and 52 from the trunk.

Step 8 In privileged mode, verify that trunking is active by entering the **show trunk** *trunk* command. Enter value **A** for trunk port 0/26, enter value **B** for trunk port 0/27. Your display should resemble the output in Example 3-7.

Example 3-7 *show **trunk** Command Output*

```
ASW21#show trunk A
DISL state: On, Trunking: On, Encapsulation type: ISL
ASW21#show trunk B
DISL state: On, Trunking: On, Encapsulation type: ISL
```

Step 9 In privileged mode, verify that trunking is configured for FastEthernet 0/26 and 0/27 by entering the **show run** command. The output is displayed in Example 3-8.

Example 3-8 *Task 1 **show run** Command Output*

```
interface FastEthernet 0/26

  duplex full
!
  trunk On
no trunk-vlan 51 52
!
  description "Trunk link to primary DSW121"
```

Example 3-8 *Task 1 **show run** Command Output (Continued)*

```
!
interface FastEthernet 0/27

  duplex full
!
  trunk On
no trunk-vlan 51 52
!
  description "trunk link secondary to DSW122"
```

You completed this part of the task if

- The **show run** command indicates both Fast Ethernet interfaces on your access switch have trunking configured.

- The **show trunk** command displays that Trunk A and Trunk B is trunking.

Creating and Naming VLANs on the Access Layer Switches

Complete the following steps:

Step 1 From your PC desktop, Telnet to your assigned access switch.

Step 2 In global configuration mode, enter **vlan** *vlan* **name** *vlan-name* command to create a VLAN. Create both VLANs using this command.

Step 3 In privilege mode, enter the **show vlan** command to display the parameters of the VLANs currently configured on the switch.

Step 4 Using the value of your VLAN enter the **show vlan** *vlan-number* command to display detail parameters of the VLAN you just configured on the switch. Enter the **show vlan** command to see all VLANs that currently exist on the switch. The output is displayed in Example 3-9.

Example 3-9 *show vlan Command Output*

```
ASW41#show vlan 10

VLAN Name              Status      Ports
----------------------------------------
10   Usergroup10       Enabled
----------------------------------------


VLAN Type    SAID    MTU    Parent RingNo BridgeNo Stp  Trans1 Trans2
---------------------------------------------------------------------
10   Ethernet 100010 1500    0      0      0        Unkn 0      0
---------------------------------------------------------------------
ASW41#
```

Assign VLANs to Ports on Access Layer Switch

Complete the following steps:

Step 1 In global configuration mode, enter **interface e 0/1** command to enter interface configuration mode.

Step 2 In interface configuration mode, enter the **vlan-membership static** *vlan-number* command to assign the interface to the appropriate native VLAN. Refer to Figure 3-13 for the VLAN number.

Step 3 Repeat Steps 1 and 2 to assign your Ethernet interfaces to all specified VLANs.

Step 4 In privilege mode, enter the **show run** command. Your configuration should resemble the following output. The output is displayed in Example 3-10.

Example 3-10 *show run Command Output*

```
text deleted

interface Ethernet 0/2

  vlan-membership static 10
!
interface Ethernet 0/3
interface Ethernet 0/3

  duplex full
  vlan-membership static 42
  description "To PC42"
!
interface Ethernet 0/4

  vlan-membership static 10
!
```

Step 5 In privileged mode, enter the **show vlan** command. Your display should resemble the output in Example 3-11.

Example 3-11 *show vlan Command Output*

```
ASW21#show vlan

VLAN Name          Status    Ports
-------------------------------------
1    default       Enabled   AUI, A, B
10   Usergroup41   Enabled   1-6
11   Usergroup45   Enabled   7-12
```

Task 2: Configuring the Distribution Layer Switches with VTP Domain and Trunks

In this task, you will configure the distribution layer switches to participate in the same VTP domain as the access layer switches. In addition, you will configure the trunks on the ports that connect the distribution layer switches to the access layer switches. Finally, you will create two VLANs for the core layer switch connections and will assign these VLANs statically to the ports that connect the distribution layer switches to the core layer switches.

Placing the Distribution Switch in a VTP Management Domain

Complete the following steps:

Step 1 In privileged mode, enter the **set vtp domain** *name* **mode** *mode* command to assign the VTP domain name and mode. Specify **server** for the VTP mode type.

Step 2 In privileged mode, enter the **show vtp domain** command to verify your configuration. Your configuration should resemble the output in Example 3-12. Output can vary depending on the name of your VTP domain.

Example 3-12   *show vtp domain Command Output*

```
Domain Name               Domain Index VTP Version Local Mode  Password
------------------------- ------------ ----------- ----------  ----------
BCMSN                          1            2          Server -

Vlan-count Max-vlan-storage Config Revision Notifications
---------- ---------------- --------------- -------------
5          1023                  0              disabled

Last Updater    V2 Mode  Pruning  PruneEligible on Vlans
--------------- -------- -------- ------------------------
disabled disabled 2-1000
```

Activating Trunking and Limiting VLAN Ranges on the Distribution Switches

Complete the following steps:

Step 1 In privileged mode, enter the **set trunk** *mod/port* **on isl** command to activate trunking on the distribution port supporting your access switch.

Step 2 In privileged mode, enter the **clear trunk** *mod/port vlan-range* command to limit the VLAN traffic permitted over this trunk. The range of permitted VLANs is 1-50,53-1005, or we would clear 51 to 52.

Step 3   In privileged mode, enter the **show trunk** command to verify your
configuration. Your configuration should resemble the output in Example
3-13. Output can vary depending on the VLANs configured.

Example 3-13   *show trunk Command Output*

```
DSW121 (enable) show trunk
Port      Mode          Encapsulation Status        Native vlan
--------  -----------   ------------- -----------   -----------
 2/1      on            isl           trunking      1
 2/2 on isl trunking 1
 2/3      on            isl           trunking      1
 2/4 on isl trunking 1

text deleted

Port      Vlans allowed on trunk
--------  -----------------------------------------------------
 2/1      1-50,53-1005
 2/3      1-50,53-1005

text deleted
Port      Vlans allowed on trunk
--------  -----------------------------------------------------
 2/1      1-50,53-1005
 2/2      1-50,53-1005
 2/3      1-50,53-1005
 2/4      1-50,53-1005
text deleted
```

You completed this part of the task if the **show trunk** command indicates the following:

- Each port supporting the link between the distribution switch and your access switch
  has trunking enabled.

- Each trunk between the distribution switch and your access switch permits traffic for
  the assigned VLANs.

Activating Trunking Between the Distribution Switches

Complete the following steps:

Step 1   In privileged mode, enter the **set trunk** *mod/port* **on isl** command to
activate trunking between the two distribution switches. You will need to
repeat this command for all four trunk connections.

Step 2   In privileged mode, enter the **clear trunk 2/9-12** *vlan-range* command to
limit VLAN traffic permitted over these trunks. The range of permitted
VLANs is 1-50,53-1005, or we would clear 51 to 52.

Step 3   In privileged mode, enter the **show trunk** command to verify your
configuration. Your configuration should resemble the output in Example
3-14.

Example 3-14   *show trunk Command Output*

```
DSW141> (enable) show trunk
Port      Mode          Encapsulation  Status        Native vlan
--------  -----------   -------------  ------------  -----------
  text deleted
 2/9      on            isl            trunking      1
 2/10     on            isl            trunking      1
 2/11     on            isl            trunking      1
 2/12     on            isl            trunking      1


Port      Vlans allowed on trunk
--------  -----------------------------------
  text deleted
 2/9      1-50,53-1005
 2/10     1-50,53-1005
 2/11     1-50,53-1005
 2/12     1-50,53-1005
```

You completed this portion of the task if the **show trunk** command indicates the following:

- Each port supporting the links between the two distribution switches has trunking
enabled.

- Each trunk between the distribution switches permits traffic for the assigned VLANs.

Creating and Configuring Global Parameters of the Core VLANs on the Distribution Layer Switch

Complete the following steps:

Step 1   In privileged mode, enter the **set vlan** *vlan number* **name** *vlan name*
command to create the core VLAN.

Step 2   In privileged mode, enter the **set vlan** *vlan number mod/ports* command
to assign the core ports to their native VLAN.

Step 3   In privileged mode, enter the **set port name** *mod/port* **"To Core** *xx***"**
command to assign the core ports a name, where *xx* is **51** or **52**.

Step 4   In privileged mode, enter the **show port** command to verify your configuration. Your configuration should resemble the output in Example 3-15. Output can vary depending on the number of VLANs configured.

Example 3-15   *show port Command Output*

```
DSW141> (enable) show port
Port  Name               Status      Vlan       Level  Duplex Speed Type
----- ------------------ ----------  ---------- ------ ------ ----- ------------
text deleted
 2/9  "To core51"        disabled    51         normal auto   auto  10/100BaseTX
 2/10 "To core51"        disabled    51         normal auto   auto  10/100BaseTX
 2/11 "To core52"        disabled    52         normal auto   auto  10/100BaseTX
 2/12 "To core52"        disabled    52         normal auto   auto  10/100BaseTX
text deleted
```

CHAPTER 4

Managing Redundant Links

Businesses today increasingly rely on data networks to deliver services required for their operations. Services such as inventory control, accounts receivable and payable, order processing, and the many other aspects of running a business efficiently all rely on data networks. The need for timely and accurate data is driving the demand for high network availability and reliability.

This chapter discusses techniques and technologies within a campus network that are targeted at increased network reliability. This chapter covers the operation, configuration, and verification of the Spanning-Tree Protocol. In addition, this chapter presents technologies associated with scaling the Spanning-Tree Protocol and campus redundancy. This chapter covers the following:

- Overview of transparent bridging
- Introduction to the Spanning-Tree Protocol
- VLANs and Spanning Tree
- Scaling Spanning Tree in the campus network

Upon completion of this chapter, you will be able to perform the following tasks in a Layer 2 switch environment: Determine the default Spanning Tree in a network topology, improve Spanning Tree convergence using the UplinkFast protocol, ensure timely host access to the network in a Spanning Tree environment using the PortFast protocol, and distribute the traffic load on parallel links with Fast EtherChannel.

Overview of Transparent Bridging

The basic functionality of a switch is identical to that of a transparent bridge. A switch implements many of the same technologies as a transparent bridge, including the Spanning-Tree Protocol. In order to understand the Spanning-Tree Protocol in a switch, you must first look at the behavior of a transparent bridge without Spanning Tree.

By definition, a transparent bridge must do the following:

- The bridge must not modify frames that it forwards.
- The bridge learns addresses by listening on a port for a device's source MAC address. If a source address comes in a specific port, it is learned that the source address can be found at that port. The bridge then builds a table indicating that it can reach the source by sending out the port it just learned. A bridge is always listening and learning.
- A bridge must forward the broadcasts it receives out all ports except for the port that initially received the broadcast.
- If a destination MAC address is unknown, sometimes called an *unknown unicast*, the bridge forwards the frame out all ports except for the port that initially received the frame.
- When a bridge receives a frame, it either filters it if the frame's destination is out the receiving port or forwards the frame if the destination is on a different port.

In Figure 4-1, the bridge learns the location of Station A and Station B by listening to the source address of their respective frames. The bridge then builds a table with the source MAC address and the port it learned for that MAC address. This table is called a CAM (content-addressable memory) table in a Cisco switch. When Station A transmits to Station B, the switch looks up the destination MAC address in its CAM table. It then forwards the frame out the correct port.

Figure 4-1   *A Transparent Bridge*

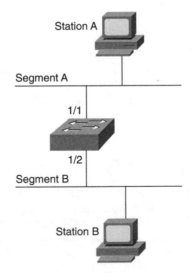

Transparent bridging by definition should be transparent to the devices on the network. It therefore should not make any modifications to the frame as it passes through the bridge.

The developers of transparent bridging wanted to make sure that end stations did not have to be modified to support the process of bridging.

In a simple bridge environment without any redundant links, transparent bridging works perfectly. Transparent bridging begins to have problems, however, as soon as a redundant path is added to the bridged network.

As you can see in Figure 4-2, Station A now has two potential paths to Station B by way of the switches.

Figure 4-2 *A Bridging Loop in a Network with a Redundant Path*

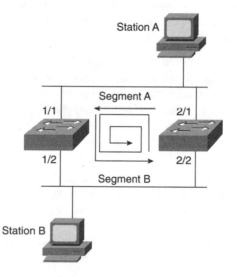

The following happens if Station A sends to Station B when neither of the switches has Station B in its address table:

Step 1 Station A transmits the frame to Segment A. Both bridges on Segment A pick up the frame on their ports—1/1 and 2/1, respectively. Both switches populate their respective address tables, indicating that Station A resides on Segment A out ports 1/1 and 2/1.

Step 2 The frame is forwarded by both switches to Segment B. Notice that not only will Station B receive the frame, but both switches will also see the frame coming from the other switch. Because one of the basic characteristics of transparent bridging is to listen to the source addresses in order to learn the correct port to use for that address, each switch relearns Station A as residing on ports 1/2 and 2/2. The switches now incorrectly assume that all frames for Station A should be sent to

Segment B. In addition, each switch sees another frame that needs to be forwarded without realizing that it is looking at the same frame it just transmitted.

Step 3   The packet is then forwarded again to Segment A, where the frame originated. The network now sees the beginning of a loop. Because neither switch is aware of the other, each switch continually forwards the frame on the other port. This loop goes on forever. The loop manifests itself as the ability to get to Station A and Station B some of the time. Some of the time, the information the switch has learned is correct, and the frame makes it to the destination. Other times, the switch is incorrect about its frame's destination, and it is sent in the completely wrong direction.

Notice that if Station A originally sent a broadcast, this problem would actually be much worse than just getting a bridging loop. The two behaviors of always retransmitting a broadcast and never marking the frame mean that the bridges actually create broadcasts in an exponential fashion when a bridge loop occurs. This process of creating new broadcasts does not stop until the loop is shut down. Eventually, in a broadcast-intensive network, the bridging loop effectively brings down the network through a broadcast storm.

NOTE   Switches typically hit a processor utilization of 80 to 100 percent during a bridge loop. Bridge loops also adversely affect routers, because these devices must also deal with the broadcasts created during a bridge loop.

Introduction to the Spanning-Tree Protocol

The Spanning-Tree Protocol (STP) was created to overcome the problems of transparent bridging in redundant networks. The purpose of STP is to avoid and eliminate loops in the network by negotiating a loop-free path through a root bridge, as shown in Figure 4-3. It does this by determining where there are loops in the network and blocking links that are redundant. In this way, it ensures that there will be only one path to every destination, so a bridging loop could never occur. In the case of a link failure, the root bridge would know that a redundant link existed and would bring up the link it previously shut down.

This means that some ports will need to be disabled or put into a nonforwarding mode. The ports remain aware of the network's topology and can be enabled if the link that is forwarding data ever fails.

Figure 4-3   *A Loop-Free Path Traced to the Root Bridge*

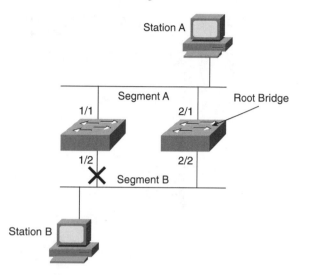

The Spanning-Tree Protocol executes an algorithm called the Spanning-Tree Algorithm (STA). In order to find the redundant links, the STA chooses a reference point, called a root bridge, in the network and then determines the available paths to that reference point. If it finds a redundant path, it chooses for the best path to forward and for all other redundant paths to block. This effectively severs the redundant links within the network.

To provide path redundancy, STP defines a tree that spans all switches in a subnet. STP forces certain redundant data paths into a standby (blocked) state (as indicated by the blocked paths in Figure 4-3). If one of the network segments in the Spanning Tree becomes unreachable, the Spanning-Tree Algorithm reconfigures the Spanning Tree topology and reestablishes the link by activating a standby path.

Bridge Protocol Data Units

All switches in an extended LAN participating in STP gather information on other switches in the network through an exchange of data messages. These messages are referred to as Bridge Protocol Data Units (BPDUs). A BPDU is shown in Figure 4-4. The left column indicates the number of bytes for each field, and the right column indicates the contents of the field.

Figure 4-4   *The BPDU Allows All Switches to Build the Spanning Tree*

Number of Bytes	Field Contents
2	Protocol ID
1	Version
1	Message Type
1	Flags (Including Topology Change)
2	Root Priority
6	Root ID
4	Path Cost
2	Bridge Priority
6	Bridge ID
1	Port Priority
1	Port ID
2	Message Age
2	Max Age
2	Hello Timer
2	Fwd Delay

BPDUs are sent out every two seconds on every port in order to ensure a stable, loop-free topology.

The Spanning-Tree Protocol uses each of the BPDU's fields. Each field will be discussed more in depth as we discuss the behavior of Spanning Tree. The following is an overview of the contents of the BPDU:

- **Root information**—The root information consists of a 2-byte root priority and a 6-byte root ID. The combination of this information indicates the device that has been elected to be the root bridge.

- **Path cost**—The path cost indicates how far from the root bridge this BPDU traveled. The path cost is used to determine which ports will forward and which ports will block.

- **Bridge information**—This is information on the bridge that sent the BPDU. It is used to indicate the neighbor bridge that sent the BPDU as well as the designated bridge that will be used to get to the root bridge. Bridge information consists of the bridge priority and bridge ID.

- **Port information**—The port information is comprised of a 1-byte port priority and a 1-byte port ID. The port information indicates information about the port that transmitted the BPDU. It is used to help determine which ports will forward and which will block.

- **Timers**—Timers are used to indicate how long Spanning Tree takes to perform each of its functions. These include message age, max age, hello, and fwd delay. Each of these timers is discussed in greater detail later in this chapter.

This exchange of BPDU messages results in the following:

- The election of a root switch for the stable Spanning-Tree network topology
- The election of a designated switch for every switched segment
- The removal of loops in the switched network by placing redundant switch ports in a backup state

Electing a Root Bridge

The first step in creating the loop-free Spanning Tree is to elect a root bridge. The root bridge is the reference point that all switches use to determine whether there are loops in the network.

At startup, the switch assumes that it is the root bridge and sets the bridge ID equal to the root ID. The bridge ID consists of two components:

- **A 2-byte priority**—The switch sets this number. By default, it is the same for all switches. The default priority on Cisco switches is 32,768 or 0x8000.
- **A 6-byte MAC address**—This is the MAC address of the switch or bridge.

The combination of these two numbers determines who will become the root bridge. The lower the number, the more likely it is that this switch will become the root. If a switch sees a root ID that is lower than its own, it begins to advertise that root ID in its BPDUs. By exchanging BPDUs, the switches determine which is the root bridge.

The combination of the priority and the bridge ID might look like this:

```
80.00.00.00.0c.12.34.56
```

The first two bytes are the priority. The last six bytes are the switch's MAC address.

Note that if all devices have the same priority, the bridge with the lowest MAC address becomes the root bridge. The lower the priority, the more likely it is that the bridge will become the root bridge.

Forming an Association with the Root Bridge

After the root bridge has been elected, each switch must form an association with the root bridge. It does this by listening to BPDUs as they come in on all ports. Receiving BPDUs on multiple ports indicates that it has a redundant path to the root bridge.

In order to choose which ports will forward data and which ports will block data, the switch looks at three components in the BPDU:

- Path cost
- Bridge information
- Port information

The switch looks at the path cost first to determine which port is receiving the lowest-cost path. The path cost is calculated based on link speed and the number of links that the BPDU crossed downstream from the root bridge. The cost is added in the outbound direction from the switch toward the root bridge. It can be changed by a switch port cost parameter. As shown in Figure 4-5, path cost is determined by the sum of path costs between source and destination.

Figure 4-5   *Path Cost Is the Sum of All Port Costs from the Root Bridge*

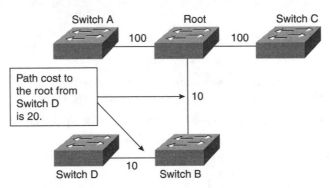

If one port has the lowest cost, it is placed in forwarding mode. All other ports that are receiving BPDUs are placed in blocking mode.

If the path costs of the received BPDUs are equal, the switch looks at the bridge ID to determine which port should forward. The port with the lowest bridge ID is chosen to forward, and all other ports block.

If the path cost and bridge IDs are equal, as in the case of parallel links, the bridge goes to the port ID as a tiebreaker. The lowest port ID forwards, and all other ports block.

NOTE   The cost associated with different bandwidths varies, depending on the device and the software release. In general, the higher a link's bandwidth, the lower the cost.

The result of the BPDU exchange is as follows:

- One switch is elected to be the root switch.

- The shortest distance to the root switch is calculated for each switch.

- A designated switch is selected. This is the switch closest to the root switch through which frames will be forwarded to the root. A designated switch is sometimes called a *parent switch*.

- A root port for each switch is selected. This is the port that provides the best path from the switch to the root switch (usually the lowest-cost path).

- Ports that will not be forwarding are placed in a blocked state. These ports will continue to send and receive BPDU information but will not be allowed to send or receive data.

Now that the basic process of the Spanning-Tree Protocol has been explained, the next section examines the various states through which the switch transitions as it builds a stable, loop-free network.

Spanning-Tree Port States

In order to build a loop-free network, Spanning Tree forces each port to transition through several different states:

- **Blocked**—All ports start in blocked mode in order to prevent the bridge from creating a bridging loop. The port stays in a blocked state if Spanning Tree determines that there is a better path to the root bridge.

- **Listen**—The port transitions from the blocked state to the listen state. It uses this time to attempt to learn whether there are any other paths to the root bridge. During the listen state, the port can listen to frames but cannot send or receive data. The port is also not allowed to put any of the information it hears into its address table. The listen state is really used to indicate that the port is getting ready to transmit but that it would like to listen for just a little longer to make sure it does not create a loop. The switch listens for a period of time called the fwd delay (forward delay).

- **Learn**—The learn state is very similar to the listen state, except that the port can add information it has learned to its address table. It is still not allowed to send or receive data. The switch learns for a period of time called the fwd delay.

- **Forward**—This state means that the port can send and receive data. A port is not placed in a forwarding state unless there are no redundant links or it is determined that it has the best path to the root.

- **Disabled**—The switch can disable a port for a variety of reasons. These include problems such as hardware failure, the deletion of the port's native VLAN, and being administratively disabled.

NOTE	In later versions of the Catalyst 5000 set command-line interface, there is a distinction between "disable" and "disabled." "Disable" means that the switch has disabled the port. "Disabled" means that the port is administratively disabled.

If the VLAN that is assigned to a port is deleted, the port is disabled. The port is enabled if it is assigned to a valid VLAN or if the VLAN that was deleted is recreated.

Spanning-Tree Timers

As BPDUs travel throughout the switched network, they might face propagation delays. These delays occur for a variety of reasons. They happen due to packet length, switch processing, bandwidth utilization, and other port-to-port delays encountered as a packet traverses the network. As a result of propagation delays, topology changes can take place at different times and at different places in a switched network. When a switch port transitions directly from nonparticipation in the stable topology to the forwarding state, the port can create temporary data loops if it doesn't know all the information about the network.

The Spanning-Tree Protocol implements timers to force the ports to wait for the correct topology information. The timers are set by default on the switch. The default timers have been calculated based on the assumption that the switch diameter is 7 and the hello timer is 2 seconds. Based on these assumptions, the network should always form a stable topology.

Defaults timer values are as follows:

- **Hello time**—2 seconds
- **Maximum time (max age)**—20 seconds
- **Forward delay (fwd delay)**—15 seconds

NOTE	The diameter is measured from the root bridge, with the root bridge counting as the first switch. Each switch out from the root bridge is added to come up with the diameter number. The root bridge can be configured with a diameter from 2 switches to 7 switches. Modifying the diameter changes the timer values that are advertised by the root to more accurately reflect the true network diameter. For example, a diameter of 2 yields a max age of 10 seconds and a fwd delay of 7 seconds. It is recommended that you change the diameter to correctly reflect your network rather than manually changing the timers.

Listening and learning are transitional states implemented by Spanning Tree to force the port to wait in order to get all BPDUs from other switches. Typical port transitions are as follows:

- From blocking to listening (20 seconds)
- From listening to learning (15 seconds)
- From learning to forwarding (15 seconds)
- From forwarding to disabled in the event of a failure

Figure 4-6 shows how Spanning Tree timers determine how long a port stays in each state. Spanning Tree uses the timers as it passes through the STP states.

Figure 4-6   *VLAN STP Timer Operation Using Default Values*

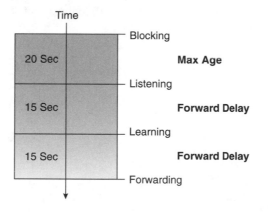

Each of these states can be modified by management software. When STP is enabled, every switch in the VLAN goes through the blocking state and the transitory states of listening and learning at power up.

The performance and operation of STP can be modified to affect its convergence time. Default timing is indicated in Figure 4-6.

The forward delay parameter can be set to a minimum value of 4 seconds. The default value is 15 seconds. If a switch can detect a fault at the physical level (direct fault), it might move a blocked port into the forwarding state in 8 seconds.

NOTE   It is recommended that you modify Spanning Tree timers only during periods of instability in Spanning Tree. During these times, the timers should be increased, not decreased, to give the network a chance to stabilize. The section "Scaling Spanning Tree in the Campus Network" later in this chapter covers other ways to handle Spanning Tree's convergence issues.

Handling Topology Changes in Spanning Tree

As discussed earlier, the Spanning-Tree Protocol implements a series of timers to prevent bridging loops from occurring in the network. It could be many seconds before the network converges to a new topology. During the time that the network is converging, MAC addresses that can no longer be reached still exist inside the CAM table. This means that each switch is attempting to forward frames to devices it can no longer reach. The Spanning-Tree topology change process forces the switch to purge MAC addresses in the CAM table faster in order to get rid of the MAC addresses that the device can no longer reach.

Figure 4-7 shows a link-state change between Switches D and E, which triggers a topology change condition, which in turn triggers a topology change BPDU to be generated in the direction of the root bridge. In order to get to the root bridge, each switch forwards the topology change BPDU out the root port (RP) to the designated bridge.

Figure 4-7 *A Network Topology Change in Spanning Tree*

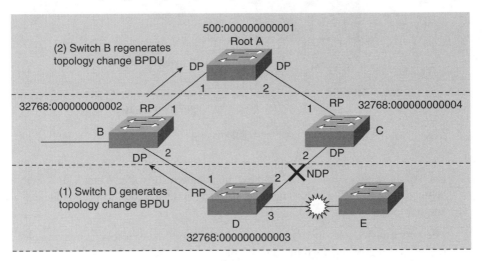

A topology change in the Spanning Tree network shown in Figure 4-7 occurs in this way:

Step 1 A bridge (Switch D) notices that a change has occurred to a link when the link between Switch D and Switch E fails.

Step 2 Switch D sends a topology change BPDU out its root port (RP), destined ultimately for the root bridge. The topology change BPDU is indicated by a change to the BPDU's 1-byte flag field. The bridge sends out the topology change BPDU until the designated bridge responds with a topology change acknowledgment (also in the 1-byte flag field).

Step 3   The designated bridge (Switch B) sends out a topology change acknowledgment to the originating bridge (Switch D). It also sends a topology change BPDU out its root port, destined for either its designated bridge or the root bridge.

Step 4   After the root bridge has received the topology change message, it changes its configuration message to indicate that a topology change is occurring. It sets the topology change in its configuration for a period of time equal to the sum of the fwd delay and max age parameters.

Step 5   A bridge receiving the topology change configuration message from the root bridge uses the fwd delay timer to age out entries in its address table. This allows it to age out entries faster than the normal five-minute default so that stations that are no longer available due to the topology change will be aged out faster. It does this until it no longer receives topology change configuration messages from the root bridge.

Spanning Tree Example

The Spanning-Tree Protocol is enabled by default on every switch. It first elects a root bridge or switch based on default settings. This means that the switch with the lowest MAC address becomes the root bridge. After the root bridge is elected, the shortest path to the root is calculated. This is also calculated based on default settings for path cost.

Figure 4-8 shows the switch block using default settings. Based on these settings, the access layer switch with a MAC address of **00-10-7b-00-08-00** becomes the root bridge. After the root bridge is elected, each switch uses the Spanning-Tree Protocol to determine the shortest path to the root bridge.

Based on the location of the root bridge, a port that is used to connect the distribution layer switches is placed in a blocked state. All other ports are in a forwarding state.

Figure 4-8 *Spanning Tree Sample Network*

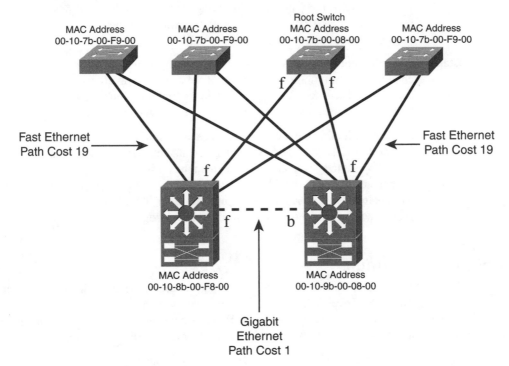

Enabling Spanning Tree

By default, the Spanning-Tree Protocol is enabled for every port on the switch. If for some reason it has been disabled, you can reenable it with the **set spantree enable** command.

You can also selectively enable or disable specific ports on the switch:

```
Switch (enable) set spantree enable mod_num/port_num
Switch (enable) set spantree disable mod_num/port_num
```

The following example shows how to enable STP and verify that it is enabled on a selected VLAN:

```
Switch> (enable) set spantree enable all
```

The console displays output similar to the following:

```
Spantree enabled.
```

NOTE   It is recommended that you leave Spanning-Tree Protocol enabled on the switch. It is particularly important that it be enabled on uplink ports where there is a chance that a bridging loop could be created.

You can verify the current Spanning Tree configuration with the following command:

```
Switch (enable) show spantree vlan
```

The **show spantree** command shows VLAN 1 by default. You can specify the VLAN number so that you can look at the Spanning Tree information for that VLAN. The ability to have different Spanning Trees for different VLANs is called Per-VLAN Spanning Tree (PVST) and is covered in the next section. Example 4-1 shows the output of the **show spantree** command. This output includes information on the elected root bridge, including its MAC address and priority. The final portion of the output gives information about this bridge. In addition, the output indicates the cost to get to the root bridge and which port it uses to get there. In this example, the cost to the root bridge is 0, indicating that this is in fact the root bridge. Another indicator that this is the root bridge is that the bridge's MAC address is the same as the root bridge's.

Example 4-1   *Verifying the Spanning Tree Configuration*

```
Switch> (enable) show spantree
VLAN 1
Spanning tree enabled
Spanning tree type          ieee
Designated Root             00-50-bd-18-a8-00
Designated Root Priority    8192
Designated Root Cost        0
Designated Root Port        1/0
Root Max Age    20 sec    Hello Time 2  sec    Forward Delay 15 sec
Bridge ID MAC ADDR          00-50-bd-18-a8-00
Bridge ID Priority          8192
Bridge Max Age 20 sec    Hello Time 2  sec    Forward Delay 15 sec

Port      Vlan  Port-State     Cost   Priority Fast-Start  Group-Method
--------- ----  -------------  -----  -------- ----------  ------------
  2/1        1  forwarding       19         32  disabled
  2/2        1  forwarding       19         32  disabled
```

The following is a description of each of the fields in Example 4-1:

- **Designated Root**—The 6-byte MAC address for the current designated root bridge.

- **Designated Root Priority**—The 2-byte priority setting for the root bridge. The priority in this example has been modified from the default of 32,768 to 8192.

- **Designated Root Cost**—This is the total cost to get to the root bridge through the shortest path. A root cost of 0 indicates that this bridge is the root bridge.

- **Designated Root Port**—The port that is used to get to the root bridge.

- **Root timers**—The timer values of the root bridge. The bridge always accepts the timers from the root bridge.

- **Bridge ID MAC ADDR**—The 6-byte address that this bridge is using for its bridge ID.

- **Bridge ID Priority**—The 2-byte priority of this bridge. Notice that the combination of the Bridge ID Priority and Bridge ID MAC Address are identical to the Designated Root. This is another indication that this is the root bridge.

- **Bridge timers**—The timer values for the bridge. These timers are not used in favor of the root bridge's timers.

- **Ports in the Spanning Tree**—Ports that are participating in this Spanning Tree are listed with their current state. Note that all ports on a root bridge will be forwarding.

The 1900/2800 series switches use the same command to view the Spanning Tree, but the output looks slightly different. Even though the output is different, the meaning of each of the major fields is the same. Example 4-2 shows the output of the **show spantree** command.

Example 4-2 *Verifying Spanning Tree on an IOS-Based Switch*

```
Switch#show spantree
VLAN1 is executing the IEEE compatible Spanning Tree Protocol
Bridge Identifier has priority 32768, address 0090.866F.D000
Configured hello time 2, max age 20, forward delay 15
Current root has priority 32768, address 0050.BD18.A800
Root port is FastEthernet 0/26, cost of root path is 10
Topology change flag not set, detected flag not set
Topology changes 60, last topology change occurred 0d14h15m09s ago
Times: hold 1, topology change 8960
      hello 2, max age 20, forward delay 15
    Timers: hello 2, topology change 35, notification 2
Port Ethernet 0/5 of VLAN1 is Forwarding
    Port path cost 100, Port priority 128
    Designated root has priority 32768, address 0050.BD18.A800
    Designated bridge has priority 32768, address 0090.866F.D000
    Designated port is Ethernet 0/5, path cost 10
    Timers: message age 20, forward delay 15, hold 1
Port Ethernet 0/25 of VLAN1 is Forwarding
    Port path cost 100, Port priority 128
    Designated root has priority 32768, address 0050.BD18.A800
    Designated bridge has priority 32768, address 0090.866F.D000
    Designated port is Ethernet 0/25, path cost 10
    Timers: message age 20, forward delay 15, hold 1
(text deleted)
```

Virtual LANs and Spanning Tree

One of the major differences between switches and transparent bridges is the implementation of VLANs on a switch. This section covers Spanning-Tree Protocol behavior as it relates to VLANs in the campus network.

This section discusses the following topics:

- Defining a separate STP for each VLAN
- Defining a common STP for all VLANs in a network
- Combining these two methods into one implementation

Cisco and the IEEE 802.1Q committee approach the Spanning Tree and VLAN issue in very different ways. Here are some of the major methods for reconciling STP and VLANs:

- **Per-VLAN Spanning Tree (PVST)**—PVST is a Cisco proprietary implementation. It requires Cisco ISL encapsulation in order to work. PVST runs a separate instance of the Spanning-Tree Protocol for every VLAN.

- **Common Spanning Tree (CST)**—CST is the IEEE 802.1Q solution to VLANs and Spanning Tree. CST defines a single instance of Spanning Tree for all VLANs. BPDU information runs on VLAN 1.

- **Per-VLAN Spanning Tree Plus (PVST+)**—PVST+ is a Cisco proprietary implementation that allows CST information to be passed correctly into PVST.

Per-VLAN Spanning Tree

A solution to the scaling and stability problems associated with large Spanning Tree networks is to create separate instances of Spanning Tree for each VLAN (referred to as Per-VLAN Spanning Tree [PVST]).

When creating fault-tolerant internetworks, a loop-free path must exist between all nodes in a network. The Spanning-Tree Algorithm calculates the best loop-free path throughout the switched network.

Because each VLAN is a logical LAN segment, one instance of STP maintains a loop-free topology in each VLAN. Although the Catalyst 2820 and Catalyst 1900 switches support a maximum of 1005 VLANs, you can enable STP on a maximum of only 64 VLANs at a time. If you configure more than 64 VLANs, you can still operate the other VLANs with STP disabled. By default, STP is enabled on VLANs 1 through 64.

Each VLAN has a unique STP topology (root, port cost, path cost, and priority). Figure 4-9 shows that PVST maintains a separate instance of Spanning Tree for every VLAN, allowing for optimization of all VLANs.

Figure 4-9 *Per-VLAN Spanning Tree*

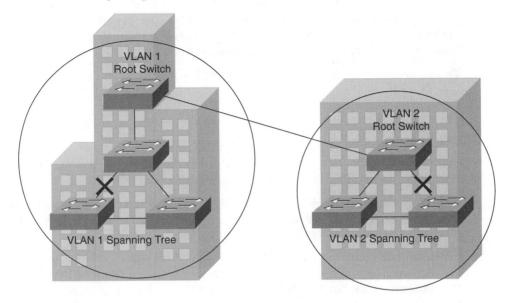

Having a separate instance of Spanning Tree for each VLAN reduces the recovery time for STP recalculation and thus increases the reliability of your network in the following ways:

- Overall size of Spanning-Tree topology is reduced

- Improves scalability and decreases convergence time

- Provides faster recovery and better reliability

Disadvantages of a PVST include the following:

- Utilization of a switch to support Spanning-Tree maintenance for VLAN

- Utilization of bandwidth on trunk links to support BPDUs for each VLAN

Common Spanning Tree

The IEEE 802.1Q standard uses an approach to VLANs referred to as Mono or Common Spanning Tree. The Spanning-Tree Protocol runs on VLAN 1, which is the default VLAN. All switches elect a single root bridge and form an association with that root bridge.

In Figure 4-10, a single root bridge has been elected for the Red and Green VLANs. Notice that the root bridge is optimized for the Red VLAN but some of the Green VLAN users must take a less-than-optimal path to get to their file servers. A Common Spanning Tree approach does not allow for optimization of the root bridge placement for each VLAN.

Figure 4-10   *Common or Mono Spanning Tree Can Result in Less-Than-Optimal Paths for Some Networks*

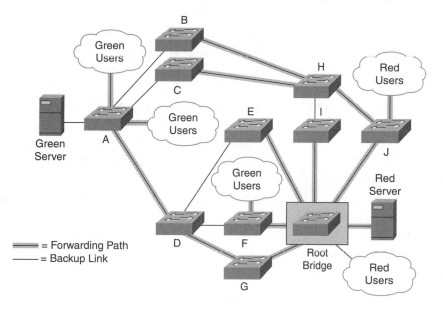

CST advantages include the following:

- Fewer BPDUs consuming bandwidth
- Less processing overhead on the switch

CST disadvantages are as follows:

- Single root bridge, which might mean less-than-optimal paths for some devices.
- Spanning-Tree topology grows to encompass all ports in the switch fabric. This can lead to longer convergence times and more frequent reconfiguration.

Per-VLAN Spanning Tree Plus

In order to support the IEEE 802.1Q standard, Cisco's existing PVST protocol has been extended to become the PVST+ protocol. PVST+ extends the PVST protocol by adding support for links across IEEE 802.1Q's Common Spanning Tree region. PVST+ is compatible with both IEEE 802.1Q's CST and the existing Cisco PVST protocols. In addition, PVST+ adds checking mechanisms to ensure that there is no configuration inconsistency with port trunking and VLAN_ID across switches. It is plug-and-play-compatible with PVST, with no requirement of new CLI commands or configuration.

PVST+ has the following characteristics:

- It interoperates with 802.1Q Common Spanning Tree (CST).

- It interoperates with 802.1Q-compliant switches on CST protocol through 802.1Q trunking. CST is on VLAN 1 by default. One CST's BPDU is transmitted or received with the IEEE Standard Bridge-Group MAC Address (01-80-c2-00-00-00) across an 802.1Q link.

- It tunnels PVST's BPDUs across the 802.1Q VLAN region as multicast data.

- For each VLAN on a trunk, a BPDU with Cisco's Shared Spanning-Tree Protocol (SSTP) MAC address (01-00-0c-cc-cd) is transmitted or received. For a VLAN equal to PVID (native port VLAN), BPDU is untagged; for all other VLANs, BPDUs are tagged.

- It is backward-compatible with the existing Cisco switch on PVST through ISL trunking.

- ISL-encapsulated BPDUs are transmitted or received through ISL trunking the same as the previous Cisco PVST.

- It checks port and VLAN inconsistencies.

- It blocks ports that receive inconsistent BPDUs in order to prevent forwarding loops from happening. It also notifies users via syslog messages about any inconsistency.

NOTE   PVST+ is available starting with the Catalyst 4.1 release. A Cisco Catalyst switch from release 4.1 or later is a Cisco PVST+ switch. A Cisco Catalyst switch from a pre-4.1 release is treated as a Cisco PVST switch. Cisco PVST+ switches are interoperable with both CST switches and Cisco PVST switches without user intervention.

Scaling Spanning Tree in the Campus Network

The previous sections covered why the Spanning-Tree Protocol is needed in your switch network. A Layer 2 bridged environment requires Spanning Tree to prevent loops in the network. Although Spanning Tree prevents bridge loop problems in a Layer 2 network, it can actually cause other problems.

This section looks at some of the ways to modify the behavior of Spanning Tree so that it can converge faster without running the risk of creating bridging loops.

This section discusses the following topics:

- How to select and maintain a root bridge

- How to determine the best loop-free path to the root

- Implementing Fast EtherChannel

Scaling the Spanning-Tree Protocol involves the following tasks:

- Providing for an optimal topology through the proper placement of the root bridge
- Providing for efficient workstation access through the use of the PortFast command
- Load-balance on redundant links through the use of technologies such as PortVlanPri and Fast EtherChannel
- Improve the convergence time of Spanning Tree during a network reconfiguration through the use of UplinkFast and BackboneFast

Establishing the Root Bridge

One of the most important decisions that must be made in the Spanning Tree network is the location(s) of the root bridge. Proper placement of the root bridge optimizes the path that is chosen by the Spanning-Tree Protocol. Proper placement also provides deterministic paths for data. Deterministic paths make troubleshooting and configuring the network easier.

You can manually configure the bridge that should be the root bridge, as well as the backup, or secondary, root bridge. The job of the secondary root bridge is to take over if the primary root bridge fails.

The Cisco switch software can be used to configure the STP operational parameters in a network. Use the **set spantree root** command to set the primary root for specific VLANs or for all the switch's VLANs. The **set spantree secondary** command allows you to configure a backup root bridge.

NOTE   Give careful consideration to switching paths before changing the root bridge. The root of your Spanning Tree should be close to the center of the network. For this reason, the root bridge is typically a distribution layer switch and not an access layer switch.

To configure the STP root switch on a Catalyst 5xxx switch, enter the following command in privileged mode:

```
Switch (enable) set spantree root vlan_list [dia network_diameter]
[hello hello_time]
```

Example 4-3 shows how to specify the primary root switch for VLANs 1 through 10.

Example 4-3   *Specifying the Primary Root Switch for a Range of VLANs*

```
Switch> (enable) set spantree root 1-10 dia 2
VLANs 1-10 bridge priority set to 8192
VLANs 1-10 bridge max aging time set to 10 seconds.
```

continues

Example 4-3   *Specifying the Primary Root Switch for a Range of VLANs (Continued)*

```
VLANs 1-10 bridge hello time set to 2 seconds.
VLANs 1-10 bridge forward delay set to 7 seconds.
Switch is now the root switch for active VLANs 1-10.
```

The **set spantree root** command reduces the bridge priority (the value associated with the switch) from the default (32,768 or 0x8000) to a significantly lower value of 8192 or 0x2000. This allows the switch to become the root bridge. Also notice that modifying the diameter changes the Spanning Tree timers that are advertised to the rest of the switches.

Table 4-1 lists the variables for the **set spantree root** and **set spantree secondary** commands.

Table 4-1   *set spantree root and set spantree secondary Command Variables*

Variable	Description
root	Keyword that designates this switch as the root switch.
secondary	(Optional) Keyword that designates this switch as a secondary root if the primary fails. This sets the priority of the bridge to 0x4000 or 16,384.
vlan_list	(Optional) Number of the VLAN. If you do not specify a VLAN number, VLAN 1 is used. Valid values are 1 to 1005.
dia *network_diameter*	(Optional) Keyword to specify the maximum number of bridges between any two points of attachment of end stations. Valid values of *network_diameter* are 2 to 7. The diameter should be measured from the root bridge, counting the root bridge as 1. The diameter will then correctly modify the timers to reflect the new diameter.
hello *hello_time*	(Optional) Keyword to specify in seconds the duration between the generation of configuration messages by the root switch. Valid values of *hello_time* are 1 to 10.

The switch software also provides commands that let you view the status of STP. Use the **show spantree** command in privileged mode to verify the operation and state of each port and VLAN:

```
Switch (enable) show spantree [vlan | mod_num/port_num] [active]
```

Example 4-4 displays sample show spantree output.

Example 4-4   *show spantree Command Verifies Port and VLAN Operation and State*

```
Switch> (enable) show spantree 10
VLAN 10
Spanning tree enabled
Spanning tree type        ieee
Designated Root           00-50-bd-18-a8-09
Designated Root Priority  8192
Designated Root Cost      0
```

Example 4-4 *show spantree Command Verifies Port and VLAN Operation and State (Continued)*

```
Designated Root Port       1/0
Root Max Age    10 sec   Hello Time 2  sec    Forward Delay 7 sec
Bridge ID MAC ADDR          00-50-bd-18-a8-09
Bridge ID Priority          8192
Bridge Max Age 10 sec    Hello Time 2  sec    Forward Delay 7 sec


Port      Vlan  Port-State     Cost   Priority  Fast-Start  Group-Method
--------- ----  -------------  -----  --------  ----------  ------------
 2/1      100   forwarding       19        32   disabled
 2/2      100   forwarding       19        32   disabled
```

Example 4-4 shows the Spanning Tree information for VLAN 10. Notice that the switch has been configured to be the root bridge of VLAN 10 and that its priority has been lowered to 8192. The timers also reflect the setting of a diameter of 2 for the Spanning Tree for VLAN 10.

Determining the Best Loop-Free Path to the Root

The switch examines all BPDUs that are being advertised into its ports. Ports connected to devices such as workstations and servers won't receive BPDUs because they have no path to the root bridge. Based on the information in the BPDU, Spanning Tree determines the best path to the root.

The Spanning-Tree Protocol uses these different fields, in order, in the BPDU to determine the best path to the root bridge:

- Path cost
- Bridge ID
- Port priority/port ID

The Spanning-Tree Protocol uses the information found in the BPDUs to determine which ports should be forwarding and which ports should be blocking. If costs are equal, the Spanning-Tree Protocol reads through the BPDU until it finds a parameter that is not equal. For example, in Figure 4-11, the BPDUs at Switch D are received with the same path cost of 38. Furthermore, they have the same bridge ID, because they are both being sent from Bridge B. The last field in the BPDU that is used to "break the tie" is the port ID field. The lower port ID becomes the forwarding port. The higher port ID is placed in a blocked state.

Figure 4-11   *Spanning-Tree Protocol Decision Process*

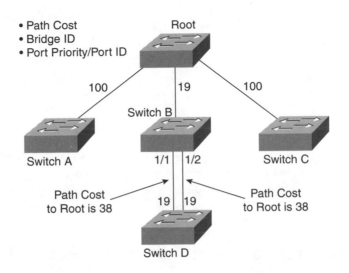

As the BPDU prepares to leave a port, it applies a *port cost*. The sum of all the port costs is the *path cost*. Spanning Tree looks first at the path cost to decide which ports should forward and which ports should block. The port that reports the lowest path cost is chosen to forward.

If the path cost is equal for multiple ports, Spanning Tree looks at the bridge ID. The port reporting the BPDU with the lowest bridge ID is allowed to forward, and all other ports block.

If the path cost and bridge ID are equal, as in the case of parallel links, Spanning Tree looks at the port ID to break the tie. The lower port ID has priority, making it the forwarding port. Cisco allows you to modify the first byte of the port ID through the change of a *port priority*.

Spanning Tree determines the best path to the root bridge by looking for the lowest value in each of the fields. As soon as it finds a lower value, it stops checking the BPDU and places the port with the lowest value in forwarding state. This means that a port with a lower path cost will be placed in forwarding state even if the bridge ID or port priority/port ID is lower.

Modifying the Port Cost

Path cost is the sum of costs between a switch and the root. STP calculates path cost based on the media speed of the links between switches and the port cost of each port forwarding frames.

If you want to change the path of frames between a particular switch and the root, carefully calculate the current path cost, and then change the port costs of the desired path. Make sure that you calculate the sum of potential alternate paths in addition to the desired path before making changes. This ensures a proper assessment of path costs before you make port cost changes and ensures that frames are forwarded over the chosen path.

You can change the port cost of switch ports. Ports with lower port costs are more likely to be chosen to forward frames.

Assign lower numbers to ports attached to faster media (such as full duplex) and higher numbers to ports attached to slower media. The possible range is 1 to 65,535. The default differs for different media. Path cost is typically 1000 divided by LAN speed in megabits per second, but it will vary with vendor and software release.

NOTE   Pay special attention to where you apply port cost. Path cost is advertised downstream from the root bridge and is calculated by taking the path cost of the root port and applying the port cost of the outgoing port. In order to influence the path cost, you must set the port cost on a switch higher in the Spanning Tree so that it advertises the port cost (via the path cost) to its downstream neighbor switch.

To change the port cost for a port on a Catalyst 5xxx switch, enter the **set spantree portcost** *mod_num/port_num cost* command in privileged mode. The following is an example of this command:

```
Console> set spantree portcost 2/1 10
Spantree port 2/1 path cost set to 10.
```

Verify the port cost setting by entering the **show spantree** [*mod_num/port_num*] command in privileged mode. The console returns a display similar to the preceding output for verifying port priority.

Example 4-5 shows how to change and verify port cost on a Catalyst 5xxx switch (**spantree enable** and **disable** are global commands).

Example 4-5   *Changing and Verifying Port Cost on a Catalyst 5xxx Switch*

```
switch> (enable) set spantree portcost 1/2 10
Spantree port 2/1 path cost set to 10.
switch> (enable) show spantree 1/2
Port      Vlan  Port-State     Cost    Priority  Fast-Start  Group-Method
--------- ----  ------------   -----   --------  ----------  ------------
  1/2      1    forwarding      10        32     disabled
  1/2      21   forwarding      10        32     disabled
  1/2      22   forwarding      10        32     disabled
  1/2      23   forwarding      10        32     disabled
  1/2      24   forwarding      10        32     disabled
  1/2      25   forwarding      10        32     disabled
```

continues

Example 4-5 *Changing and Verifying Port Cost on a Catalyst 5xxx Switch (Continued)*

```
  1/2     26     forwarding     10       32    disabled
  1/2     27     forwarding     10       32    disabled
  1/2     28     forwarding     10       32    disabled
  1/2     51     forwarding     10       32    disabled
  1/2     52     forwarding     10       32    disabled
  1/2    1003    not-connected  10       32    disabled
  1/2    1005    not-connected  10        4    disabled
switch> (enable)
```

NOTE   Port cost can also be changed on a per-VLAN basis using the command **set spantree portvlancost** *mod_num/port_num* **cost** *cost* [*vlans*]. This command allows you to influence the path of a specific VLAN rather than all VLANs.

Modifying Port Priority

You can change the port priority of switch ports. The port with the lowest-priority value forwards frames for all VLANs. The possible port priority range is 0 to 63. The default is 32. If all ports have the same priority value, the port with the lowest port number forwards frames.

To change the priority for a port, enter the command **set spantree portpri** *mod_num/port_num priority* [*vlans*] in privileged mode.

NOTE   The **set spantree portpri** command should be set on the upstream neighbor that is closest to the root bridge.

Verify the port priority setting by entering the **show spantree** [*mod_num/port_num*] command. Example 4-6 shows how to change the port priority for a port and verify the configuration.

Example 4-6 *Changing and Verifying Port Priority*

```
Console> (enable) set spantree portpri 1/2 20
Bridge port 1/2 port priority set to 20
Console> (enable) show spantree 1/2
Port      Vlan Port-State     Cost  Priority Fast-Start Group-method
--------- ---- -------------- ----- -------- ---------- ------------
  1/2     1    blocking        19      20    disabled
  1/2     100  forwarding      19      20    disabled
  1/2     521  blocking        19      20    disabled
  1/2     522  blocking        19      20    disabled
  1/2     523  blocking        19      20    disabled
```

Example 4-6 *Changing and Verifying Port Priority (Continued)*

```
1/2     524   blocking        19     20   disabled
1/2    1003   not-connected   19     20   disabled
Console> (enable)
```

Modifying Port Priority by VLAN

You can set the port priority for a port on a per-VLAN basis. The port with the lowest-priority value for a specific VLAN forwards frames for that VLAN. If all ports have the same priority value for a particular VLAN, the port with the lowest port number forwards frames for that VLAN. To modify the port priority on a per-VLAN basis, use the command **set spantree portvlanpri** *mod_num/port_num priority* [*vlans*].

This command can be very useful for load balancing across parallel paths. By default, if there is a parallel connection between two devices, Spanning Tree blocks one of the links. Traffic from all VLANs travels on one link, and the other link is used only as a backup. Figure 4-12 shows how port VLAN priority allows load sharing on links by allowing VLANs to individually determine which links forward and which block. The following commands were issued in order to get the VLANs to load balance in Figure 4-12:

```
set spantree portvlanpri 1/1 16 100-105
set spantree portvlanpri 1/2 16 106-110
```

Figure 4-12 *VLAN Port Priority*

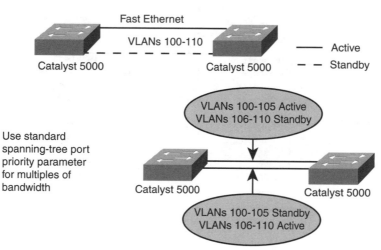

TIP   It is recommended that you set the priority for the VLANs on both switches. This will ensure that the switches will always load balance, even if something changes in the Spanning Tree network.

By changing the port priority for a specific group of VLANs, you can load balance the VLANs across the two links. In Figure 4-12, port 1/1 forwards for VLANs 100 to 105 and blocks for VLANs 106 to 110. The opposing port, 1/2, forwards for VLANs 106 to 110 and blocks for 100 to 105.

To change the port-VLAN priority for a port on a Catalyst 5*xxx* switch, enter the command **set spantree portvlanpri** *mod_num/port_num priority* [*vlans*] in privileged mode.

Verify the port-VLAN priority setting by entering the **show spantree** [*mod_num/port_num*] command in privileged mode.

Example 4-7 shows how to change the port-VLAN priority on a port and verify the configuration.

Example 4-7   *Changing and Verifying Port-VLAN Priority*

```
Console> (enable) set spantree portvlanpri 1/2 1 100
Port 1/2 vlans 1-99,101-1004 using portpri 32.
Port 1/2 vlans 100 using portpri 1.
Port 1/2 vlans 1005 using portpri 4.
Console> (enable) show spantree 1/2
Port      Vlan  Port-State      Cost    Priority  Fast-Start  Group-Method
--------- ----  -------------   -----   --------  ----------  ------------
  1/2     1     forwarding       19        32     disabled
  1/2     21    forwarding       19        32     disabled
  1/2     22    forwarding       19        32     disabled
  1/2     23    forwarding       19        32     disabled
  1/2     24    forwarding       19        32     disabled
  1/2     25    forwarding       19        32     disabled
  1/2     26    forwarding       19        32     disabled
  1/2     27    forwarding       19        32     disabled
  1/2     28    forwarding       19        32     disabled
  1/2     51    forwarding       19        32     disabled
  1/2     52    forwarding       19        32     disabled
  1/2     1003  not-connected    19        32     disabled
  1/2     1005  not-connected    19         4     disabled
Console> (enable)
```

Modifying Spanning-Tree Timers

The timers in Spanning Tree are necessary to prevent bridge loops from occurring in your network. They are put into place to give the network enough time to get all the correct information about the topology and to determine if there are redundant links.

The timers mean, however, that it could take up to 50 seconds after a link has failed for its redundant (or backup) link to take over. The length of time that it takes Spanning Tree to converge when a link has failed can be too much for some protocols and applications, resulting in lost connections, sessions, or data.

To set these timing parameters on a Catalyst 5xxx switch, enter the following commands in privileged mode (all times are in seconds):

- **Set the bridge forward delay for a VLAN**—Enter the command **set spantree fwddelay** *delay* [*vlan*]. This parameter indicates the interval during which a port moves from the listening to the learning state and then from the learning to the forwarding. The range is 4 to 30 seconds. The default is 15 seconds.

- **Set the bridge hello time for a VLAN**—Enter the command **set spantree hello** *interval*. The hello time parameter is the interval between the transmission of BPDUs from the root switch. It has a default value of 2 seconds and a minimum value of 1 second. Reducing the hello time from 2 seconds to 1 second doubles the number of BPDUs that must be lost before triggering an unwanted transition, but it also doubles the processing load on the switch CPUs.

- **Set the bridge maximum aging time for a VLAN**—Enter the command **set spantree maxage** *agingtime* [*vlan*]. The maximum age parameter expresses the lifetime of a BPDU. A BPDU is considered valid on a port for maxage seconds. If a new BPDU is not received in maxage seconds, the old BPDU is discarded. This parameter is important for a fault that cannot be detected at the physical level—for example, indirect faults. This parameter has a default value of 20 seconds and a minimum value of 6 seconds.

CAUTION   Use caution when modifying timers. The Spanning-Tree Protocol could place a port into a forwarding state before hearing all the BPDUs if the timers are too low. This would create a bridge loop in the switch network. It is recommended that you modify the diameter parameter when you define the root bridge. This will modify the timers to correctly reflect your network.

EtherChannel

Cisco provides another mechanism for redundant links in a Spanning Tree environment called Fast EtherChannel. Fast EtherChannel technology builds upon standards-based 802.3 full-duplex Fast Ethernet. Fast EtherChannel technology allows parallel links to be treated by Spanning Tree as one physical link. As Figure 4-13 shows, Fast EtherChannel and Gigabit EtherChannel allow for redundant links in a Spanning Tree environment by allowing the links to be treated as one link.

Figure 4-13 *Parallel Fast Ethernet Links*

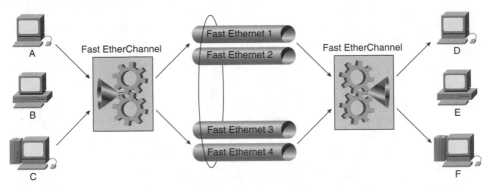

Fast EtherChannel offers bandwidth scalability within the campus by providing full-duplex bandwidth of 200 Mbps to 800 Mbps. The implementation of Fast EtherChannel technology, in addition to providing high bandwidth, provides load sharing and redundancy. This technology provides load balancing and management of each link by distributing traffic across the multiple links in the channel. Unicast, multicast, and broadcast traffic is distributed across the links in the channel. In addition, Fast EtherChannel technology provides redundancy in the event of link failure. If a link is lost in a Fast EtherChannel, traffic is rerouted on one of the other links in less than a few milliseconds, and the convergence is transparent to the user.

Fast EtherChannel and Gigabit EtherChannel use a load distribution algorithm based on the destination MAC address, as shown in Figure 4-14.

Figure 4-14 *Fast EtherChannel and Gigabit EtherChannel Use Load Distribution to Share Links*

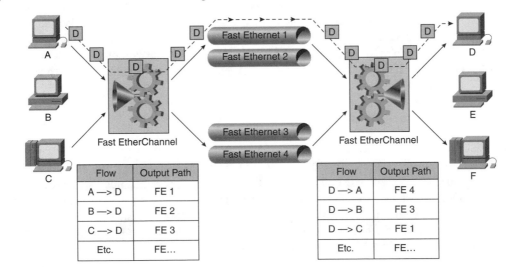

Flow	Output Path
A —> D	FE 1
B —> D	FE 2
C —> D	FE 3
Etc.	FE...

Flow	Output Path
D —> A	FE 4
D —> B	FE 3
D —> C	FE 1
Etc.	FE...

A *bundle* is a group of links managed by the Fast EtherChannel process. Fast EtherChannel technology provides statistical load distribution of connections over multiple links in a bundle. If one link in the bundle fails, the Ethernet Bundle Controller (EBC) informs the Enhanced Address Recognition Logic (EARL) entry of the failure, and the EARL ages out all addresses learned on that link. This condition allows the EBC and the EARL to recalculate in hardware the source-destination address pair on a different link. When a source address queries and the destination responds, the address is relearned on a different link in the bundle.

Failover time is the time it takes for the new address to be relearned. Assuming that one packet sent by the source results in an instant response, failover takes as little as 10 microseconds. It might take longer because of the windowing that the particular application uses to send packets before it expects an acknowledgment. Even then, relearning should not take more than a few milliseconds, and as a result, no application or session timeout will be seen that is caused by link failure.

Port Aggregation Protocol

The Port Aggregation Protocol (PAgP) adds additional features to Fast EtherChannel technology. PAgP aids in the automatic creation of Fast EtherChannel links. PAgP packets are sent between Fast EtherChannel-capable ports. The protocol learns the neighbors and their group capability dynamically and informs the neighbors of its group capability. After the protocol determines correctly paired, bidirectional, point-to-point links, it groups the ports that have the same neighbor device ID and neighbor group capability into a channel. Then the channel is added to Spanning Tree as a single bridge port.

Some restrictions have been deliberately introduced into PAgP. PAgP does not form a bundle on ports that are configured for dynamic VLANs. PAgP requires that all ports in the channel belong to the same VLAN or are configured as trunk ports.

Because dynamic VLANs can force the change of a port into a different VLAN, they are not included in EtherChannel participation. When a bundle already exists and a port's VLAN is modified, all ports in the bundle are modified to match that VLAN. PAgP does not group ports that operate at different speeds or port duplexes. If speed and duplex are changed when a bundle exists, PAgP changes the port speed and duplex for all ports in the bundle.

EtherChannel Guidelines

If improperly configured, some Fast EtherChannel ports are disabled automatically to avoid network loops and other problems. Use the following guidelines to avoid configuration problems:

- Assign all ports in a channel to the same VLAN, or configure them as trunk ports.

- If you configure the channel as a trunk, configure the same trunk mode on all the ports in the channel, on both ends of the link. Configuring ports in a channel in different trunk modes can have unexpected results.

- Configure all ports in a channel to operate at the same speed and duplex mode (full or half duplex).

- If you configure a broadcast limit on the ports, configure it as a percentage limit for the channeled ports. With a packets-per-second broadcast limit, unicast packets might get dropped for 1 second when the broadcast limit is exceeded.

- If the channel is composed of trunk ports, you must configure the same allowed VLAN range on all the ports. When the allowed VLAN range is not the same for all trunks in a channel, trunk ports on which a particular VLAN is not allowed drop the packets for that VLAN, and ports on which the VLAN is allowed transmit the traffic. If the allowed VLAN range is not the same on all ports in the channel, the ports do not form a channel when set to the auto or desirable mode with the **set port channel** command.

- Do not configure the ports in a channel as dynamic VLAN ports. Doing so can adversely affect switch performance.

- Make sure port security is disabled on channeled ports. If you enable port security on a channeled port, the port shuts down when it receives packets with source addresses that do not match the port's secure address.

- Enable all ports in a channel. If you disable a port in a channel, it is treated as a link failure, and its traffic is transferred to one or more of the remaining ports in the channel.

- Ensure that all ports in a channel have the same configuration on both ends of the channel.

- The hardware controlling channeling on the Catalyst 5xxx switches prevents certain ports or groups of ports from forming channels.

- Verify that a line card is capable of being channeled on a Catalyst 5xxx:

  ```
  Switch>(enable)show port capabilities [mod_num[/port_num]]
  ```

- Make sure that the ports you want to channel are configured correctly.

NOTE   Certain conditions must be met for the EtherChannel bundle to come up. Failure to meet these conditions might cause the ports to be automatically disabled.

Creating a Channel Group with Fast EtherChannel

Create a channel on the desired ports by entering the following command:

```
Switch> (enable)set port channel mod_num/ports [on | off | auto | desirable]
```

You should see the following output after issuing the set port channel command:

```
Port(s) 1/1-2 channel mode set to on.
04/05/1999,17:09:32:PAGP-5:Port 1/1 left bridge port 1/1.
04/05/1999,17:09:32:PAGP-5:Port 1/2 left bridge port 1/2.
04/05/1999,17:09:33:PAGP-5:Port 1/1 joined bridge port 1/1-2.
04/05/1999,17:09:33:PAGP-5:Port 1/2 joined bridge port 1/1-2.
Console> (enable)
```

To enable an EtherChannel bundle on an IOS-based switch, enter the following command:

```
Switch(config)#port-channel mode [on | off | auto | desirable]
```

This command creates a virtual port channel interface on the switch.

CAUTION   Before turning on port channeling for a group of ports, verify that all conditions for channeling have been met. If they have not, the ports will automatically disable, bringing the link down with them. If you are unsure whether all conditions have been met, remove the configuration from the links, channel the links, and then reapply the configuration.

Verify the EtherChannel configuration on a set-based switch, as shown in Example 4-8.

Example 4-8   *Verifying EtherChannel Configuration*

```
Switch> (enable) show port channel 1
Port    Status      Channel    Channel   Neighbor            Neighbor
                    mode       status    device              port
------  --------    --------   --------  ----------------    --------
1/1     connected   on         channel   WS-C5000 012345678    5/5
1/2     connected   on         channel   WS-C5000 012345678    5/6
------  --------    --------   --------  ------------------------------
Switch> (enable)
```

Verify the EtherChannel configuration on an IOS-based switch by entering the following:

```
Switch#show interface port-channel port-channel_group_number
```

Implementing PortFast

The Spanning-Tree Protocol runs on all ports of a switch. Many ports of a switch might connect to workstations or servers. These point-to-point connections are not part of the switch fabric, yet they must run Spanning Tree. The Spanning-Tree Algorithm makes each port wait up to 50 seconds before data is allowed to be sent on the port. This might cause problems with some protocols and applications.

PortFast should be implemented only for server or workstation connections, as shown in Figure 4-15.

Figure 4-15 *Implementing PortFast Decreases the Time a Port Is in the Listening and Learning States*

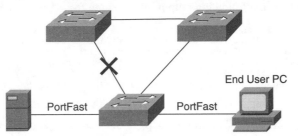

PortFast causes a port to enter the forwarding state almost immediately by dramatically decreasing the time of the listening and learning states. You can use PortFast on switch ports connected to a single workstation or server to allow those devices to connect to the network immediately, rather than waiting for Spanning Tree to converge. PortFast minimizes the time it takes for a server or workstation to come online. This prevents problems with applications such as DHCP, DNS, and Novell IPX server attachments.

NOTE   PortFast places the port into a forwarding state immediately. However, it still runs the Spanning-Tree Protocol. If a loop is detected, a port will be moved from a forwarding state into a blocked state in order to prevent the loop from occurring.

Enable PortFast using the set CLI to configure a switch port connected to a single workstation or server by entering the following command in privileged mode:

```
switch >(enable)set spantree portfast mod_num/port_num
```

Verify the PortFast setting by entering this command:

```
switch >(enable)show spantree mod_num/port_num
```

Enable PortFast on an IOS-based switch by entering this command:

```
switch(config-if)#spantree start-forwarding
```

PortFast should be used only when connecting a single end station to a switch port. Otherwise, you might create a network loop.

CAUTION   Some companies allow multiple workstations, through the use of a hub, at the user's desk. Use PortFast with caution on these connections, because the user might accidentally plug the hub into two different switch ports. If he does, he will create a loop between those two ports. PortFast is supposed to detect a bridge loop and block the port after the initial forwarding process. This would allow the loop to continue until Spanning Tree places it in a blocked state. There are instances, however, where ports configured for PortFast never go into a blocked state, even when a loop exists.

Configuring UplinkFast

STP ensures that a loop-free topology is maintained even in the face of topology changes. However, the convergence to a loop-free topology can be time-consuming. Implementing UplinkFast is one method to reduce this time by optimizing convergence times.

During the time it takes for STP to converge, some end stations might become inaccessible, depending on the STP state of the switch port to which the station is attached. This represents a major disruption in network connectivity. Thus, decreasing convergence time and reducing the length of the disruption is a major factor in deciding to deploy redundancy. UplinkFast was developed in response to the need for fast convergence.

UplinkFast allows a blocked port on a switch to almost immediately begin forwarding when it detects the failure of the forwarding link. UplinkFast must have direct knowledge of the link failure in order to move a blocked port into a forwarding state.

Specifically, an uplink group consists of the root port (which is forwarding) and a set of blocked ports, except for self-looping ports. The uplink group provides an alternate path in case the currently forwarding link fails.

The STP UplinkFast feature has been designed specifically for use with access layer switches. This feature is not designed for use within network cores.

The UplinkFast feature is not available in the 8500 series switch router. Figure 4-16 shows that UplinkFast allows a blocked port to almost immediately begin forwarding when it detects the failure of the forwarding link. UplinkFast should be configured only on the access layer switch in this figure. No other switches will participate in UplinkFast.

Figure 4-16   *UplinkFast Operation*

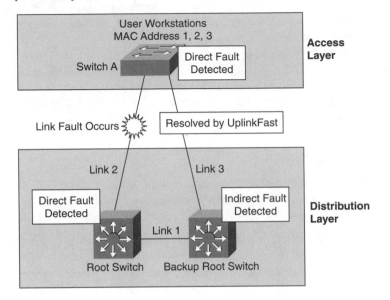

In Figure 4-16, the access switch has two uplinks to the distribution layer:

- One link connects the access switch to the distribution layer switch elected as the STP root bridge.

- The other link connects the switch to the distribution layer switch acting as the STP backup root bridge.

One of the uplinks is redundant and is blocked by STP. As soon as a switch detects a link down condition on the currently active link, UplinkFast moves the blocked port to the forwarding state. UplinkFast changes the port without passing through the listening and learning phases. Reconfiguration occurs within 3 to 4 seconds without going through the usual convergence time.

The conditions for UplinkFast to trigger a fast reconfiguration are as follows:

- UplinkFast must be enabled on the switch.

- The switch must have at least one blocked port.

- The failure must be on the root port.

UplinkFast initiates the reconfiguration as soon as the switch detects a link down on the root port. This process allows convergence to begin immediately without waiting for the max age timer to expire.

It is important to note that UplinkFast should be configured only on access layer switches, because quick transitions of the root port to its nondesignated backup(s) can be deterministically achieved only at the end leaf-node switches in a Spanning Tree topology.

If you are not using UplinkFast, it is strongly recommended that you use the Catalyst default settings. The UplinkFast feature checks to see if a switch is itself the root bridge.

Enable UplinkFast using the set command-line interface and by entering the **set spantree uplinkfast enable** command:

```
Switch>(enable)set spantree uplinkfast enable [rate station-update-rate]
    [all-protocols off | on]
```

Example 4-9 shows a demonstration.

Example 4-9 *UplinkFast*

```
VLANs 1-1005 bridge priority set to 49152.
The port cost and portvlancost of all ports set to above 3000.
Station update rate set to 15 packets/100ms.
uplinkfast all-protocols field set to off.
uplinkfast enabled for bridge.
```

To enable UplinkFast on IOS-based switches, in global configuration mode, enter the following command:

```
Switch(config)#uplink-fast
```

The **set spantree uplinkfast enable** command or the **uplink-fast** command increases the path cost of all ports on the switch, making it unlikely that the switch will become the root switch. The station-update-rate value represents the number of multicast packets transmitted per 100 milliseconds (the default is 15 packets per millisecond).

NOTE   When you use the **set spantree uplinkfast** command, it affects all VLANs on the switch. You cannot configure UplinkFast on an individual VLAN.

Example 4-10 shows how to verify UplinkFast using the set command-line interface. It also shows sample output.

Example 4-10   *Verifying UplinkFast Operation with the Set CLI*

```
Switch>(enable)show spantree uplinkfast
Station update rate set to 15 packets/100ms.
uplinkfast all-protocols field set to off.
VLAN          port list
---------------------------------------------
1             1/1(fwd),1/2
100           1/2(fwd)
521           1/1(fwd),1/2
522           1/1(fwd),1/2
523           1/1(fwd),1/2
524           1/1(fwd),1/2
```

Example 4-11 shows how to verify UplinkFast on IOS-based switches. It also shows sample output.

Example 4-11   *Verifying UplinkFast Operation with IOS*

```
Switch#show uplink-fast

Uplink fast Enabled
Uplink fast frame generation rate 15

Switch#show uplink-fast statistics

Uplink fast transitions 5
Uplink fast station learning frames 127
```

Configuring BackboneFast

BackboneFast is initiated when a root port or blocked port on a switch receives inferior BPDUs from its designated bridge. An inferior BPDU identifies one switch as both the root bridge and the designated bridge. Figure 4-17 shows that BackboneFast allows for faster failover when an indirect link fails.

Figure 4-17   *Example of an Indirect Link Failure*

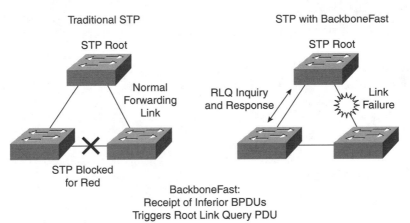

When a switch receives an inferior BPDU, it indicates that a link to which the switch is not directly connected (an indirect link) has failed (that is, the designated bridge has lost its connection to the root bridge). Under normal Spanning Tree rules, the switch ignores inferior BPDUs for the configured maximum aging time.

The switch tries to determine if it has an alternate path to the root bridge. If the inferior BPDU arrives on a blocked port, the root port and other blocked ports on the switch become alternate paths to the root bridge. If the inferior BPDU arrives on the root port, all blocked ports become alternate paths to the root bridge. If the inferior BPDU arrives on the root port and there are no blocked ports, the switch assumes that it has lost connectivity to the root bridge, causes the maximum aging time on the root to expire, and becomes the root switch according to normal Spanning Tree rules.

NOTE   BackboneFast is applicable in a limited number of environments. It must be deployed on all switches in the network, but not all switches support it. BackboneFast looks for an indirect link failure. If the network is configured in the traditional switch block with the root bridges at the distribution layer (such as in this book), an indirect link will never fail. The failure would be with a direct link. Finally, BackboneFast improves Spanning Tree performance by causing the max age timer to expire immediately. In a switch block with a diameter of 2, this saves 10 seconds in convergence time. The best use of BackboneFast is in environments that have a network diameter of 3 or greater and where all switches support the implementation of BackboneFast.

Root Link Query BPDU

If the switch has alternate paths to the root bridge, it uses these alternate paths to transmit a new kind of BPDU called the *root link query BPDU*. The switch sends the root link query BPDU out all alternate paths to the root bridge. If the switch determines that it still has an alternate path to the root, it causes the maximum aging time on the ports on which it received the inferior BPDU to expire. If all the alternate paths to the root bridge indicate that the switch has lost connectivity to the root bridge, the switch causes the maximum aging times on the ports on which it received an inferior BPDU to expire. If one or more alternate paths can still connect to the root bridge, the switch makes all ports on which it received an inferior BPDU its designated ports and moves them out of the blocking state (if they were in blocking state), through the listening and learning states, and finally into the forwarding state.

The following commands allow you to configure and verify BackboneFast in the switch block. The switch software also provides commands that allow you to configure the operation of BackboneFast. This feature enables faster convergence in the event of a backbone link failure.

Enable BackboneFast on the Catalyst 5xxx switch by entering the following command:

```
Switch>(enable)set spantree backbonefast
```

Verify that BackboneFast is enabled by entering the following command:

```
Switch>(enable)show spantree backbonefast
```

NOTE	For BackboneFast to work, you must enable it on all switches in the network. BackboneFast is not supported on Token Ring VLANs. This feature is also not supported for use with third-party switches.

Summary

The Spanning-Tree Protocol is one of the most important components of a bridged or switched network. The following summarizes the basic characteristics of the Spanning-Tree Protocol in the campus network:

- Spanning-Tree Protocol is a bridge-to-bridge link management protocol providing path redundancy while preventing loops in the network.

- The Spanning-Tree Algorithm feature of STP performs topology recalculations.

- STP communicates topology changes from switch to switch with BPDUs.

- BPDUs are not forwarded, but receipt of a topology change BPDU might cause a switch to generate and forward a topology change BPDU.

- When STP is enabled, a port is always in one of the following states: blocking, listening, learning, forwarding, or disabled.

- Spanning Tree PortFast causes a Spanning Tree port to enter the forwarding state immediately, bypassing the listen and learn states.

- EtherChannel allows parallel links to be bundled in order to achieve a higher aggregate throughput.

- You can use PortFast on switch ports connected to a single workstation or server to allow those devices to connect to the network immediately without waiting for Spanning Tree to converge.

- UplinkFast provides fast convergence after a Spanning Tree topology change and achieves load balancing between redundant links using uplink groups.

- BackboneFast is initiated when a root port or blocked port on a switch receives inferior BPDUs from its designated bridge.

Review Questions

The following questions test your retention of the material presented in this chapter. The answers to the Review Questions can be found in Appendix A, "Answers to Review Questions."

1 List the five Spanning Tree port states.

2 Identify at least one network problem caused by STP.

3 Explain the solutions developed to improve STP operation.

4 Discuss the purpose of an inferior BPDU.

5 Identify the purpose of PortFast, and describe its operation.

6 Explain the difference between BackboneFast and UplinkFast.

Case Study: Managing Redundant Links

Work through the following case study as a review of information discussed in this chapter.

Scenario

In this case study, you will see how to determine the default Spanning Tree that is created when no modifications are made to the switch. You will then see how to optimize the Spanning Tree by establishing the root switch and the secondary root switch for each of the VLANs. You will also see how to ensure a timely convergence by modifying the diameter of the switch network and implementing PortFast and UplinkFast. Finally, you will see how to configure the links between the distribution layer switches for EtherChannel.

NOTE   In the case study in Chapter 3, "Defining Common Workgroups with VLANs," you saw how to create two VLANs for each access layer switch. In this case study, you will define one distribution layer switch as the root bridge of the first VLAN and the other distribution layer switch as the root bridge of the second VLAN. This allows both of the links from the access layer devices to the distribution layer devices to be used. The first VLAN will forward on one link and block on the other. The second VLAN will forward on the link that is not being used by the first VLAN. This allows for load distribution of traffic from the access layer switch to the distribution layer. This case study will also determine the default Spanning Tree for VLAN1.

When the configuration is complete, each block will have (where possible) link redundancy with active multiline links, and enhancements to Spanning Tree operation to minimize the effects of link transitions. See Figure 4-18.

Figure 4-18 *Case Study Topology Information*

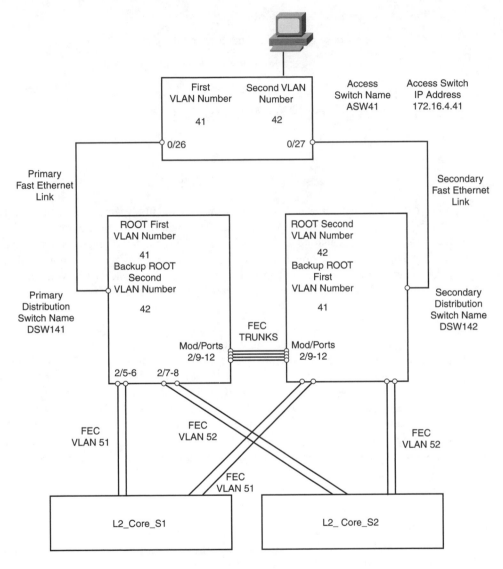

STP LAB Network Diagram

Command List

Tables 4-2 and 4-3 explain the important commands you will use in this case study.

Table 4-2   *Access Switch Commands*

Command	Description
interface	Selects an interface to configure.
vlan	VLAN configuration.
vlan-membership	VLAN membership configuration.
show spantree	Displays spantree information.
spantree start-forwarding	Enables PortFast on an interface.
uplink-fast	Enables UplinkFast on the switch.
shut	Administratively disables an interface.
show run	Displays configuration information.
Ctrl-Shift-6-x	Escape sequence.

Table 4-3   *Distribution Switch Commands*

Command	Description
enable	Enters privileged mode.
set port duplex *mod_num/port_num*	Sets port duplex parameters.
set port speed *mod_num/port_num*	Sets port speed parameters.
set port channel *port_list* **[on | off | desirable | auto]**	Sets a group of ports in channel mode.
set vlan *vlan_num mod_num/port_num*	Assigns port(s) to a VLAN.
set spantree root [secondary] *vlans*	Sets the root bridge priority for a primary or secondary value for a range of VLANs.
set trunk *mod_num/port_num*	Enables trunking on a link.
clear trunk *mod_num/port_num* [*vlans*]	Clears trunking.
show port *mod_num/port_num*	Displays current configuration information.
show spantree *vlan*	Displays current operational information.
show trunk	Displays information about trunk ports.
show vlan	Shows the VLANs configured on this switch.
Ctrl-Shift-6-x	Escape sequence.

Task 1: Verify Operation of the Spanning-Tree Protocol

In this task, you will verify STP operation so that it is enabled and determine the location of the root bridge when STP uses its default parameters.

NOTE   One of the easiest ways to perform this task is to re-create Figure 4-18 on a piece of paper. You should then check each switch for VLAN 1 to determine which switch has become the root bridge. After you have determined the root bridge, you should verify each of the ports to determine if they are forwarding or blocking. In the triangle created by the access layer switch and the two distribution switches, you should see only one port blocking. You will also see the four links between the distribution switches blocking in some way. The distribution switches will either block on three of the ports and forward on one, or they will block on all four ports. If the Spanning-Tree Protocol blocks on three ports and forwards on one, the block for the triangle occurs somewhere besides the link between the distribution layer switches. If the Spanning-Tree Protocol blocks on all four ports, the block for the triangle is the link between the switches.

Where the block occurs depends entirely on the location of the root bridge. In the default state, the location of the root bridge is determined entirely by the bridge's MAC address.

When you are determining the default Spanning Tree state, remember that only one side, or port, of a link will be blocked to stop the loop. For example, on the links that connect the distribution layer switches, you will see one side blocking the ports, and the other side will show as forwarding. In order to get a clear picture of the default Spanning Tree state, look at each port on each switch.

Follow these steps to complete this task:

Step 1   Open a console connection with your access switch.

Step 2   In global configuration mode, enter the **interface ethernet 0/3** command to enter interface configuration mode.

Step 3   Place the interface in VLAN 1 by using the **vlan-membership static 1** command. This will allow you to use the PC's Telnet application to access the switches via the management VLAN.

Step 4   In global configuration mode, enter the **interface fast 0/27** command to enter interface configuration mode. Repeat for interface 0/26.

Step 5   Place each interface in active mode by using the no **shutdown** command. You will now have two trunk links administratively up, but STP will have placed one in blocking mode.

Step 6 In privileged mode, enter the s**how spantree 1** command to verify that the STP is enabled for VLAN 1. Your configuration should resemble the output shown in Example 4-12.

Example 4-12   *show spantree 1 Command Output*

```
ASW41#show spantree 1
VLAN1 is executing the IEEE compatible Spanning Tree Protocol
   Bridge Identifier has priority 32768, address 0090.8678.3480
   Configured hello time 2, max age 20, forward delay 15
   Current root has priority 32768, address 0050.BD18.A800
   Root port is FastEthernet 0/27, cost of root path is 10
   Topology change flag not set, detected flag not set
   Topology changes 71, last topology change occured 0d01h30m20s ago
   Times:  hold 1, topology change 8960
           hello 2, max age 20, forward delay 15
   Timers: hello 2, topology change 35, notification 2
(text deleted)

Port FastEthernet 0/26 of VLAN1 is Forwarding
   Port path cost 10, Port priority 128
   Designated root has priority 32768, address 0050.BD18.A800
   Designated bridge has priority 32768, address 0090.8678.3480
   Designated port is FastEthernet 0/26, path cost 10
   Timers: message age 20, forward delay 15, hold 1
Port FastEthernet 0/27 of VLAN1 is Forwarding
   Port path cost 10, Port priority 128
   Designated root has priority 32768, address 0050.BD18.A800
   Designated bridge has priority 32768, address 0050.BD18.A800
   Designated port is , path cost 0
   Timers: message age 20, forward delay 15, hold 1
```

Step 7 Repeat Step 6 for your second assigned VLAN.

Step 8 Repeat the preceding steps for each of your switches, mapping out the Spanning Tree.

Task 2: Configure the Primary and Secondary Root Bridge for Your VLANs

In this task, you will configure a primary and secondary root bridge for each of the VLANs. The first VLAN should have a primary root bridge configured on DSW141, and DSW142 should be the secondary root bridge for that same VLAN. The second VLAN should have a primary root bridge configured on DSW142, and DSW141 should be the secondary root bridge. Additionally, each root bridge should be configured with the correct switch diameter.

Follow these steps:

Step 1   On your PC's desktop, form a connection with the distribution layer switch, DSW141.

Step 2   In privileged mode, enter the **set spantree root** *vlan* **dia 2** command, where *vlan* is the first VLAN number.

Step 3   In privileged mode, enter the **set spantree root secondary** *vlan* **dia 2** command, where *vlan* is the second VLAN number.

Step 4   Connect to your second distribution switch, DSW142.

Step 5   In privileged mode, enter the **set spantree root** *vlan* **dia 2** command, where *vlan* is the second VLAN number.

Step 6   In privileged mode, enter the **set spantree root secondary** *vlan* **dia 2** command, where *vlan* is the first VLAN number.

Step 7   In privileged mode, verify that the STP parameters have changed for both your VLANs and that the appropriate values of priority and root port are indicated. Your display should resemble the output shown in Example 4-13.

Example 4-13   *Verifying the STP Parameters*

```
DSW142> (enable) show spantree 41
VLAN 41
Spanning tree enabled
Spanning tree type           ieee

Designated Root              00-50-bd-18-a8-14
Designated Root Priority     8192
Designated Root Cost         19
Designated Root Port         2/9
Root Max Age   20 sec    Hello Time 2  sec   Forward Delay 15 sec

Bridge ID MAC ADDR           00-50-bd-18-ac-14
Bridge ID Priority           16384
Bridge Max Age 20 sec    Hello Time 2  sec   Forward Delay 15 sec

Port      Vlan  Port-State     Cost   Priority Fast-Start  Group-Method
--------- ----  -------------  -----  -------- ----------  -----------
  2/1      41   blocking          19        32  disabled
  2/2      41   blocking          19        32  disabled
  2/3      41   blocking          19        32  disabled
  2/4      41   blocking          19        32  disabled
  2/9      41   forwarding        19        32  disabled
  2/10     41   blocking          19        32  disabled
  2/11     41   blocking          19        32  disabled
  2/12     41   blocking          19        32  disabled
```

Step 8   Return to DSW141. Enter the **show spantree** command for your first VLAN. Your display should resemble the output shown in Example 4-14.

Example 4-14   *show spantree Command Output*

```
DSW141> (enable) show spantree 41
VLAN 41
Spanning tree enabled
Spanning tree type            ieee

Designated Root               00-50-bd-18-a8-14
Designated Root Priority      8192
Designated Root Cost          0
Designated Root Port          1/0
Root Max Age   20 sec    Hello Time 2  sec   Forward Delay 15 sec

Bridge ID MAC ADDR            00-50-bd-18-a8-14
Bridge ID Priority            8192
Bridge Max Age 20 sec    Hello Time 2  sec   Forward Delay 15 sec

Port      Vlan  Port-State      Cost    Priority  Fast-Start  Group Method
--------- ----  -------------   -----   --------  ----------  ------------
 2/1      41    forwarding       19        32      disabled
 2/2      41    forwarding       19        32      disabled
 2/3      41    forwarding       19        32      disabled
 2/4      41    forwarding       19        32      disabled
 2/9      41    forwarding       19        32      disabled
 2/10     41    forwarding       19        32      disabled
 2/11     41    forwarding       19        32      disabled
 2/12     41    forwarding       19        32      disabled
 3/1      41    not-connected     5        32      disabled
```

Step 9   Connect to your access layer switch.

Step 10   In privileged mode, enter the **show spantree** *vlan* command to display the forwarding status on the trunk links for your first VLAN. Your display should resemble the output shown in Example 4-15.

Example 4-15   *show spantree Command Output*

```
ASW41#show spantree 41
VLAN41 is executing the IEEE compatible Spanning Tree Protocol
   Bridge Identifier has priority 32768, address 0090.866F.D000
   Configured hello time 2, max age 20, forward delay 15
   Current root has priority 8192, address 0050.BD18.A814
   Root port is FastEthernet 0/26, cost of root path is 10
   Topology change flag not set, detected flag not set
   Topology changes 11, last topology change occured 0d00h20m47s ago
   Times:  hold 1, topology change 8960
           hello 2, max age 20, forward delay 15
   Timers: hello 2, topology change 35, notification 2

(text deleted)
```

Example 4-15 *show spantree Command Output (Continued)*

```
Port FastEthernet 0/26 of VLAN41 is Forwarding
    Port path cost 10, Port priority 128
    Designated root has priority 8192, address 0050.BD18.A814
    Designated bridge has priority 8192, address 0050.BD18.A814
    Designated port is , path cost 0
    Timers: message age 20, forward delay 15, hold 1
Port FastEthernet 0/27 of VLAN41 is Forwarding
    Port path cost 10, Port priority 128
    Designated root has priority 8192, address 0050.BD18.A814
    Designated bridge has priority 32768, address 0090.866F.D000
    Designated port is FastEthernet 0/27, path cost 10
    Timers: message age 20, forward delay 15, hold 1
```

Step 11 Repeat Step 10 for your second VLAN.

You have successfully completed this task if the **show spantree** output indicates that you have root port on Fa0/26 for your first VLAN and root port on Fa0/27 for your second VLAN.

Task 3: Configure Fast EtherChannel

In this task, you will configure a Fast EtherChannel trunk between the distribution switches and Fast EtherChannel to the core layer switches. To perform this task, complete the following steps.

Configure Fast EtherChannel Between Distribution Switches

These steps are the same for both distribution switches:

Step 1 On your PC's desktop, form a connection with your access layer switch.

Step 2 In privileged mode, enter the **show port** *line-module-number* command. In this example, the line module number is 2. This command will display the parameters of the ports on module 2. Your display should resemble the output shown in Example 4-16.

Example 4-16 *show port Command Output*

```
DSW141> (enable) show port 2
Port  Name     Status      Vlan     Level  Duplex Speed Type
----- -------- ----------  -------- ------ ------ ----- -----------
 2/1           connected   trunk    normal  full   100  10/100BaseTX
 2/2           connected   trunk    normal  full   100  10/100BaseTX
 2/3           connected   trunk    normal  full   100  10/100BaseTX
 2/4           connected   trunk    normal  full   100  10/100BaseTX
 2/5           connected   1        normal a-half a-100 10/100BaseTX
 2/6           connected   1        normal a-half a-100 10/100BaseTX
```

continues

Example 4-16   *show port Command Output (Continued)*

```
2/7           connected  1       normal a-half a-100 10/100BaseTX
2/8           connected  1       normal a-half a-100 10/100BaseTX
2/9           connected  trunk   normal a-full a-100 10/100BaseTX
2/10          connected  trunk   normal a-full a-100 10/100BaseTX
2/11          connected  trunk   normal a-full a-100 10/100BaseTX
2/12          connected  trunk   normal a-full a-100 10/100BaseTX

(text deleted)
```

Step 3   In privileged mode, enter the **show trunk** command. Your display should resemble the output shown in Example 4-17.

Example 4-17   *show trunk Command Output*

```
DSW141> (enable) show trunk
Port      Mode           Encapsulation  Status        Native vlan
--------  -------------  -------------  ------------  -----------
  2/1     on             isl            trunking      1
  2/2     on             isl            trunking      1
  2/3     on             isl            trunking      1
  2/4     on             isl            trunking      1
  2/9     on             isl            trunking      1
  2/10    on             isl            trunking      1
  2/11    on             isl            trunking      1
  2/12    on             isl            trunking      1
  3/1     on             isl            trunking      1


Port      Vlans allowed on trunk
--------  -------------------------------------------------------
  2/1     1-30,1001-1005
  2/2     1-30,1001-1005
  2/3     1-30,1001-1005
  2/4     1-30,1001-1005
  2/9     1-30,1001-1005
  2/10    1-30,1001-1005
  2/11    1-30,1001-1005
  2/12    1-30,1001-1005

(text deleted)
```

Step 4   Verify that the parameters of the ports are identical in all respects.

Step 5   In privileged mode, enter the **set port channel 2/9-12 on** command.

Step 6   In privileged mode, enter the **show port channel** command. Your display should resemble the output shown in Example 4-18.

Example 4-18   *show port channel Command Output*

```
DSW142> (enable) show port channel
Port   Status      Channel   Channel   Neighbor               Neighbor
                   mode      status    device                 port
-----  ----------  --------  --------- -------------------    ---------
2/9    connected   on        channel   WS-C5505   066523936   2/9
2/10   connected   on        channel   WS-C5505   066523936   2/10
2/11   connected   on        channel   WS-C5505   066523936   2/11
2/12   connected   on        channel   WS-C5505   066523936   2/12
-----  ----------  --------  --------- -------------------    ---------
```

Step 7   Repeat the preceding step after two minutes. You should get the same output.

Step 8   In privileged mode, enter the **show trunk** command. Your display should resemble the output shown in Example 4-19.

Example 4-19   *show trunk Command Output*

```
DSW142> (enable) show trunk
Port     Mode         Encapsulation  Status        Native vlan
-------- ------------ -------------- ------------- -----------
2/1      on           isl            trunking      1
2/2      on           isl            trunking      1
2/3      on           isl            trunking      1
2/4      on           isl            trunking      1
2/9      on           isl            trunking      1
2/10     on           isl            trunking      1
2/11     on           isl            trunking      1
2/12     on           isl            trunking      1
3/1      on           isl            trunking      1


Port     Vlans allowed on trunk
-------- -------------------------------------------------
2/1      1-30,1001-1005
2/2      1-30,1001-1005
2/3      1-30,1001-1005
2/4      1-30,1001-1005
2/9      1-30,1001-1005
2/10     1-30,1001-1005
2/11     1-30,1001-1005
2/12     1-30,1001-1005
```

You have successfully completed this task if the **show port channel** command indicates that you have created a four-port Fast EtherChannel that is channeling and that continues to do so without error messages. This Fast EtherChannel trunk should have the same limited VLAN range as the discrete links had before this task.

Configure Fast EtherChannel Links to the Core Switches

These steps are the same for all groups:

Step 1 Complete the same steps as in the preceding section for the connections to the core layer switches.

Step 2 Configure Fast EtherChannel links to have identical port parameters.

Step 3 The core switches have the ports configured as **fixed 100** and fixed **full duplex**. It is essential that the ports on the distribution switches match this.

Step 4 In privileged mode, enter the **show port channel** and **show port 2** commands. Your display should resemble the output shown in Example 4-20.

Example 4-20   *show port Command Output*

```
DSW142> (enable) show port channel
Port  Status     Channel   Channel     Neighbor                  Neighbor
                 mode      status      device                    port
----- ---------- --------- ----------- ------------------------- --
 2/5  connected  on        channel     WS-C5500   069051961      2/7
 2/6  connected  on        channel     WS-C5500   069051961      2/8
----- ---------- --------- ----------- ------------------------- ---
 2/9  connected  on        channel     WS-C5505   066523936      2/9
 2/10 connected  on        channel     WS-C5505   066523936      2/10
 2/11 connected  on        channel     WS-C5505   066523936      2/11
 2/12 connected  on        channel     WS-C5505   066523936      2/12
----- ---------- --------- ----------- ------------------------- --


DSW142> (enable) show port 2
Port  Name    Status     Vlan        Level  Duplex Speed Type
----- ------- ---------- ----------- ------ ------ ----- ------------
 2/1          connected  trunk       normal   full   100 10/100BaseTX
 2/2          connected  trunk       normal   full   100 10/100BaseTX
 2/3          connected  trunk       normal   full   100 10/100BaseTX
 2/4          connected  trunk       normal   full   100 10/100BaseTX
 2/5          connected  51          normal   full   100 10/100BaseTX
 2/6          connected  51          normal   full   100 10/100BaseTX
 2/7          connected  1           normal   full   100 10/100BaseTX
 2/8          connected  1           normal   full   100 10/100BaseTX
 2/9          connected  trunk       normal a-full a-100 10/100BaseTX
(text deleted)
```

You have successfully completed this task if the **show channel** command on your assigned distribution switch displays the ports in channel mode and in the appropriate native VLAN.

Task 4: Configure PortFast and UplinkFast

In this task, you will complete the Spanning Tree configuration by enabling UplinkFast on the access layer switch and PortFast on the access layer switch port that connects to the PC.

NOTE   You might want to test Spanning Tree's failover time before you implement both UplinkFast and PortFast. In order to do this, you should cut the active (or forwarding) connection from the access layer switch to the distribution layer switch. You should then note how long it takes for the backup link to move from a blocked state to a forwarding state. Watch carefully—this time should be approximately 40 to 50 seconds. You can also start a continuous ping that uses the active link (perhaps from the workstation to the distribution layer switch) and watch how long it takes for the ping to return after the link has failed. After you implement UplinkFast, perform the same test and record your results. You should notice a very different failover time. The delay in the failover is a delay that is imposed by the detection of the link failure. This should be no more than 3 seconds.

PortFast is enabled on the 1900/2800 switch by default. To verify that PortFast is enabled, perform the following steps.

Connect to Your Access Layer Switch

Step 1   In privileged mode, enter the **show run** command. Your display should resemble the output shown in Example 4-21. You will see that there is no indication of the **start-forwarding** command under the interface output.

Example 4-21   *show run Command Output*

```
ASW42#show run
Building configuration...
Current configuration:

(text deleted)
!
interface Ethernet 0/3

  duplex full
  description "To PC 42"
!
(text deleted)
Disable PortFast
```

Step 2   In global configuration mode, enter the **interface e 0/3** command.

Step 3   In interface configuration mode, enter the **no spantree start-forwarding** command to turn off the default configuration.

Step 4   In privileged mode, enter the **show run** command. Your display should resemble the output shown in Example 4-22. You will see that now the **no spantree start-forwarding** command appears under the interface output.

Example 4-22   *show run Command Output*

```
!
interface Ethernet 0/3

  duplex full
  no spantree start-forwarding
  description "To PC 42"
!
```

Test the Operation of PortFast

Step 1   Return to your PC. In Windows mode, go to Start, Run to bring up an MS-DOS window. Use the **ping** command with the address of your primary distribution switch and the **-t** option. This will send a continuous sequence of pings to the distribution switch, until interrupted by Ctrl-C.

```
C:\WINDOWS\Desktop>ping -t 172.16.4.141
```

Step 2   Leave the ping running, and use Hyperterm to view the console of your access layer switch. In interface configuration mode, use the **shut** and **no shut** commands on the e 0/3 interface. You should observe that the ping sequence on your PC window is timing out. Note how long it takes to resume.

Step 3   In global configuration mode, enter the **interface ethernet 0/3** command.

Step 4   In interface configuration mode, enter the **spantree start-forwarding** command to reestablish the default configuration.

Step 5   Connect to your access switch via the console port using Hyperterm. In interface configuration mode, use the **shut** and **no shut** commands on the e 0/3 interface. You should observe that the ping sequence on your PC command window is timing out. Note how long it takes to resume.

Step 6   You should observe that, with PortFast reenabled, the interruption to the ping sequence was very short (less than a second).

Test Uplink Disruption Prior to Configuring UplinkFast on Your Access Switch

Step 1   Return to your PC. Using the MS-DOS command window, reenter the **ping** command with the address of your primary distribution switch and the **-t** option. This will send a continuous sequence of pings to the distribution switch.

```
C:\WINDOWS\Desktop>ping -t 172.16.4.141
```

Step 2   On your access switch, enter the **show spantree 1** command, and observe which of your trunks is forwarding for VLAN 1. Use this interface in the following command.

Step 3   In interface configuration mode, use the **shut** command on your active trunk interface. You should observe that the ping sequence on your PC command window is timing out. Note how long it takes to resume.

Step 4   In interface configuration mode, use the **no shut** command on the interface you just shut. You should observe that the ping sequence on your PC command window is timing out. Note how long it takes to resume.

Configure UplinkFast on Your Access Switch

Step 1   In global configuration mode, enter the **uplink-fast** command.

Step 2   Test UplinkFast on your access switch.

Step 3   On your access switch, enter the **show spantree 1** command, and confirm which of the trunks is forwarding for VLAN 1. Use this interface in the following command.

Step 4   In interface configuration mode, use the **shut** command on the active trunk interface. You should observe that the ping sequence on your PC command window is unaffected.

Step 5   In interface configuration mode, use the **no shut** command on the trunk interface. You should observe that the ping sequence on your PC command window is still unaffected.

Step 6   Return to your PC, and close the MS-DOS window.

You have successfully completed this task if you have done the following:

- Demonstrated that PortFast's effect on the ping sequence was to make connectivity immediate after an access interface transition.
- Configured and tested UplinkFast, demonstrating the immediate transition to the other trunk in the event that the forwarding links fails.

CHAPTER 5

Inter-VLAN Routing

Configuring virtual LANs (VLANs) helps control the size of the broadcast domain and keeps local traffic from crossing into the core layer or into other switch blocks. VLANs are associated with individual networks or subnetworks; therefore, network devices in different VLANs cannot communicate with one another without the use of a Layer 3 device such as a router.

A router is required when an end station in one VLAN needs to communicate with an end station in another VLAN. This communication is referred to as *inter-VLAN routing*. You configure one or more routers to route traffic to the appropriate destination VLAN.

This chapter covers the following topics:

- Inter-VLAN routing issues and solutions
- Distribution layer topology
- Configuring inter-VLAN routing

Upon completion of this chapter, you will be able to identify the network devices required to effect inter-VLAN routing given a network diagram, configure a route processor to facilitate inter-VLAN routing, and configure a default gateway to ensure network reachability.

Inter-VLAN Routing Issues and Solutions

The following are a few of the most common issues and solutions that arise in routing between VLANs. These issues and solutions are not intended to be all-inclusive:

- Isolated broadcast domains and how route processors solve the problem
- Where end-user devices send nonlocal packets and how default routes solve the problem
- Supporting multiple VLAN traffic across VLAN boundaries and how Inter-Switch Link (ISL) solves the problem

Isolated Broadcast Domains

As discussed in Chapter 3, "Defining Common Workgroups with VLANs," VLANs are designed to control the size of the broadcast domain and keep local traffic local. Because VLANs isolate traffic to a defined broadcast domain or subnet, network devices in different VLANs cannot communicate with one another without some intervening device to forward packets between subnets. Figure 5-1 shows that a router is required to communicate between VLANs.

Figure 5-1 *Inter-VLAN Routing*

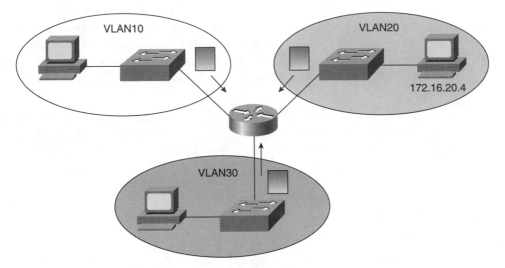

In switched networks, route processors are used to provide communications between VLANs. Route processors provide VLAN access to shared resources and connect to other parts of the network that are either logically segmented with the more traditional subnet approach or that require access to remote sites across wide-area links.

Before you can configure routing between VLANs, you must have defined the VLANs on the switches in your network. Issues related to network design and VLAN definition should be addressed during your network design. The issues that you need to consider are the following:

- Sharing resources between VLANs
- Load balancing
- Redundant links
- Addressing
- Segmenting networks with VLANs

NOTE   These topics are not covered in the BCMSN course or this book. For more in-depth coverage, refer to the *Cisco Internetworking Design* coursebook from Cisco Press.

Finding the Route

Connecting the separate subnets through a route processor introduces the issue of how end-user devices can communicate with other devices through multiple LAN segments. Some network devices use routing tables to identify where to deliver packets outside of the local network segment. Even though it is not the responsibility of end-user devices to route data, these devices still must be able to send data to addresses on subnets other than their own. Figure 5-2 shows that workstations send traffic that is not on their local subnet to a default gateway or router.

Figure 5-2   *Default Gateways*

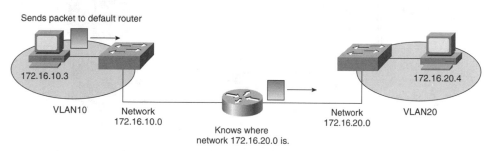

So that each end device does not have to manage its own routing tables, most devices are configured with the IP address of a designated route processor. This designated route processor is the default router to which all nonlocal network packets are sent. The route processor then forwards the packets toward the right destination. Each network device can have the same IP address for the default route processor. However, it is possible that there are multiple routers on a VLAN that are capable of acting as the default gateway or router.

If the route processor has no knowledge of that network segment, the route processor forwards the packet to the next-hop router.

Supporting Multiple VLAN Traffic

Another issue of routing between VLANs occurs when an external router is used. An external router traditionally supports one subnet or broadcast domain to a physical interface. Using traditional techniques, an external router would have to have a separate physical connection to a single switch for each VLAN that it was routing for that switch. This means that a switch with four VLANs would have to have four physical connections between the switch and the external router, as shown in Figure 5-3. In order to alleviate the issue of multiple physical connections, an external router must have a way to identify the different VLANs on one physical link.

Figure 5-3   *Supporting Multiple VLANs on Separate Physical Links*

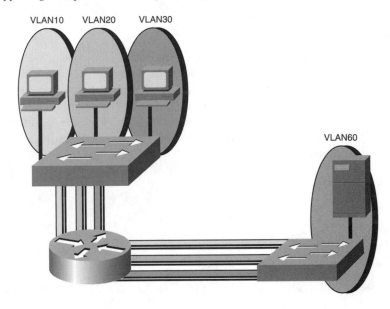

Another solution is to carry multiple VLAN traffic over a single link. In order to maintain integrity between VLAN traffic, a mechanism is required to identify each VLAN's packet. The Inter-Switch Link (ISL) protocol is used to interconnect two VLAN-capable Fast Ethernet devices, such as the Catalyst 5000 or Cisco 7500 routers. The ISL protocol is a frame-tagging protocol that contains a standard Ethernet frame and the VLAN information associated with that frame.

ISL is currently supported over Fast Ethernet links, but a single ISL link, or trunk, can carry traffic from multiple VLANs.

The concept of ISL is discussed in Chapter 3. Configuring ISL links is discussed later in this chapter. Figure 5-4 shows that the router can support an ISL or 802.1Q trunk connection for multiple VLANs.

Figure 5-4   *Supporting Multiple VLANs on a Single Physical Connection*

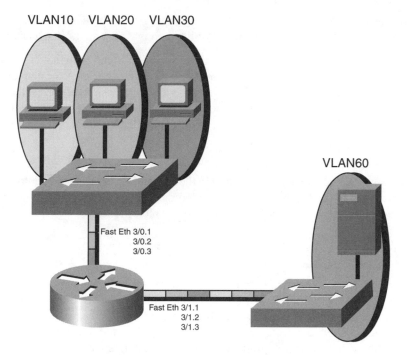

In Figure 5-4, the clients—on VLANs 10, 20, and 30—all need to establish sessions with a server that is attached to a port designated to be in VLAN 60. Because the file server resides in a different VLAN than any of the requestors, you need to configure inter-VLAN routing. The route processor would perform this function in the following way:

1 The route processor accepts the packets from each VLAN because the route processor is configured to route VLAN10, VLAN20, and VLAN30 traffic.

2 The route processor then classifies the packet based on the destination network address. The route processor encapsulates the packet with an ISL VLAN header appropriate to the destination subnet (in this case, ISL = 60). This encapsulation action is what differentiates this as a routing process rather than a switching process.

3 The router then routes the packets to the appropriate interface—in this case, to Fast Ethernet 3/1.

Distribution Layer Topology

As covered in Chapter 1, "Overview of a Campus Network," the distribution layer provides a broadcast or multicast boundary definition and is where inter-VLAN routing occurs.

The distribution layer consists of a combination of high-end switches and route processors. Because of its Layer 3 capabilities, the distribution layer becomes the demarcation between networks in the access layer and networks in the core. Each wiring closet hub corresponds to a logical network or subnet that homes to the route processor, allowing the route processors in the distribution layer to provide broadcast control and segmentation as well as terminating collision domains.

The switch/route processor model is straightforward to configure and maintain because of modularity. Each route processor within the distribution layer is programmed with the same features and functionality. Common configuration elements can be copied across the layer, allowing for predictable behavior and easier troubleshooting.

External Route Processors

You can use your existing Cisco high-end routers in conjunction with the Netflow Feature Card (NFFC) or NFFC II on a Catalyst 5000 family switch to implement multilayer switching. The router must be directly attached to the Catalyst switch either by multiple Ethernet connections (one per subnet) or by a Fast Ethernet connection using an ISL. Figure 5-5 shows that an external router can be used to communicate between VLAN 41 and VLAN 42.

Figure 5-5 illustrates the external router configuration. In Figure 5-5, all the traffic traverses the switches when traveling from clients on Switch A to clients on Switch B because the clients on both switches belong to network 172.16.41.0. The data goes through the router only when the traffic must cross over to another network. For example, if users on Switch A belong to Network 172.16.41.0, and users on Switch C belong to Network 172.16.42.0, communications between the end devices on Switch A and Switch C must go through the router.

The Cisco high-end routers supporting multilayer switching include the Cisco 7500, 7200, 4500, and 4700 series routers. These routers must have the Multilayer Switch Protocol (MLSP) software and Cisco IOS 11.3.4 or later software installed to provide the Layer 3 services to the switch.

Figure 5-5 *External Route Processor*

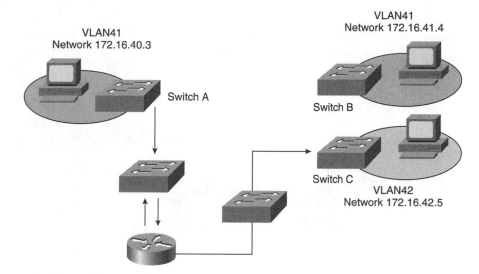

- An external Cisco high-end router and a Catalyst 5000 switch with an NFFC or NFFCII
- Connected by multiple ethernet connections or an ISL Link

Internal Route Processors

An alternative to using a Layer 2 switch and a Layer 3 router is to use the next generation of LAN switches, called Layer 3 switches. These new switches integrate Layer 2 and Layer 3 functionality in a single box. A multilayer switch can be a Catalyst 5000 series switch equipped with a Route Switch Module (RSM), a Catalyst 5000 series switch equipped with a Route Switch Feature Card (RSFC), or a Catalyst 6000/6500 series with a Multilayer Switch Module (MSM) or Multilayer Switch Feature Card (MSFC). Figure 5-6 shows how multilayer switches integrate Layer 2 and Layer 3 functionality in the same box.

Figure 5-6 *Internal Route Processors*

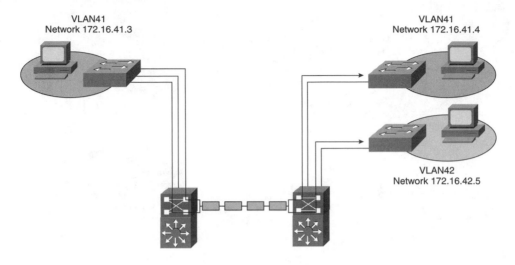

VLAN41
Network 172.16.41.3

VLAN41
Network 172.16.41.4

VLAN42
Network 172.16.42.5

NOTE	Chapter 1 discusses the differences between Layer 3 routers and Layer 3 switches. One of the largest differences is that Layer 3 routers perform routing in software, whereas Layer 3 switches perform routing in hardware. A Route Switch Module (RSM) in a Catalyst 5000 without a Netflow Feature Card (NFFC) is considered to be a Layer 3 router. That is, routing is performed in software by the RSM. The addition of an NFFC allows routing to be performed in hardware. This makes the Catalyst 5000 with RSM and NFFC a Layer 3 switch. The NFFC and the capabilities of routing in hardware are discussed in detail in Chapter 6, "Improving IP Routing Performance with Multilayer Switching."

The RSM is a router module running normal Cisco IOS router software. The router module plugs directly into the Catalyst 5000 series switch backplane, providing multiprotocol routing for the Catalyst 5000 series Ethernet interfaces. From the perspective of the Catalyst 5000 series switches, the RSM appears as a module with a single 800 Mb half-duplex trunk port and one Media Access Control (MAC) address. However, this port is unlike other Catalyst module ports in that it has no external attributes such as media type or speed.

The RSFC is a full-function Cisco IOS router installed as an integrated daughter card option for the Catalyst 5000 series Supervisor Engine II G and Supervisor Engine III G cards.

The MSM connects to the switching bus through four full-duplex Gigabit Ethernet interfaces. The Catalyst switch sees the MSM as an external router connected to the switch through the four interfaces. Four Gigabit interfaces can be grouped into a single Gigabit EtherChannel or configured as an independent interface. If channeled, the channel supports trunking through 802.1Q or ISL. After a channel is configured and the trunk type is specified, the port-channel interface on the MSM is configured with one subinterface for every VLAN on the switch, providing inter-VLAN routing. Alternatively, each gigabit interface can be configured independently as a separate VLAN trunk or nontrunked routed interface.

NOTE	The command set used for the RSM, RSFC, and MSM is identical. In this book, the RSM is used for demonstration purposes.

The RSM provides multilayer switching and inter-VLAN routing services between switched VLANs. Cisco has several different internal route processors, including the 5000's RSM, and the RSFC for the Catalyst 5000 and 6000 series switches.

The Catalyst 5500 switch has 13 slots. Slot 1 is reserved for the supervisor engine module. If a redundant supervisor engine module is used, it goes in slot 2; otherwise, slot 2 can be used for other modules. Slot 13 is a dedicated slot, reserved for the ATM Switch Processor (ASP) module. The RSM can be installed in any of the remaining slots. The Route Switch Module can be field-upgraded to support an optional Catalyst Versatile Interface Processor 2 (VIP2) module. Earlier versions of the RSM have a slot restriction that should be taken into consideration when installing the RSM in a Catalyst 5500. This slot restriction is *only* for RSMs that will be upgraded with the optional Catalyst VIP2.

If you plan on upgrading RSM hardware revision 2.0 (73-2119-05) or earlier with the Catalyst VIP2, you must install the RSM in slots 3 through 8 and leave the slot immediately above it empty. This prevents you from shuffling modules between slots when upgrading the RSM with the Catalyst VIP2.

If you are not upgrading with the Catalyst VIP2, there are no slot restrictions—you can install the RSM in slots 2 through 12.

NOTE	The maximum number of RSM modules for the Catalyst 5500 switch is seven. However, this number may be reduced, depending on the number of Asynchronous Transfer Mode (ATM) modules present. You can use any combination of ATM and RSM modules as long as the total does not exceed seven.

The RSM interface to the Catalyst 5000 series switch backplane is through VLAN 0 and VLAN 1. VLAN 0 is mapped to channel 0, and VLAN 1 is mapped to channel 1. VLAN 0 is used for communication between the RSM and the Catalyst 5000 series switch and is not accessible to the user. VLAN 1 is the default VLAN for the Catalyst 5000 series switch.

Additional VLANs are toggled between the two channels as they are created. A VLAN can be mapped to a specific channel to balance each channel's load.

The MAC addresses available to the RSM are assigned as follows:

- VLAN 0 (channel 0) is assigned the MAC address of a programmable ROM (PROM) on the RSM line communication processor (LCP). This MAC address is used for diagnostics and to identify the RSM physical slot. VLAN 0 is inaccessible to the user.

- VLAN 1 and additional VLANs are assigned the base MAC address from a MAC address PROM on the RSM that contains 512 MAC addresses. All routing interfaces except VLAN 0 use the base MAC address.

Configuring Inter-VLAN Routing

The Catalyst 5000, 4000, 2926G, and 2926 series switches are multimodule systems. You can see what modules are installed, as well as the MAC address ranges and version numbers for each module. To display information about the installed modules, enter the following command in privileged mode on the switch:

```
Switch(enable) show module mod_num
```

Entering the **show module** command without specifying a module number displays information on all modules installed in the system. Specifying a particular module number displays information on that module. Example 5-1 shows sample output from the **show module** command.

Example 5-1 *show module Sample Output*

```
DSW142 (enable) show module
Mod Module-Name         Ports Module-Type          Model     Serial-Num Status
--- ------------------- ----- -------------------- --------- ---------- -------
1                       0     Supervisor III       WS-X5530  010827944  ok
2                       24    10/100BaseTX Ethernet WS-X5225R 012152170  ok
3                       1     Route Switch         WS-X5302  007572460  ok


Mod MAC-Address(es)                         Hw     Fw         Sw
--- --------------------------------------- ------ ---------- ------------------
1   00-50-e2-80-54-00 to 00-50-e2-80-57-ff 2.0    3.1.2      4.3(1a)
2   00-10-7b-03-5d-58 to 00-10-7b-03-5d-6f 3.1    4.3(1)     4.3(1a)
3   00-e0-1e-91-dc-66 to 00-e0-1e-91-dc-67 5.0    20.14      11.3(6)WA4(9)


Mod Sub-Type Sub-Model Sub-Serial Sub-Hw
--- -------- --------- ---------- ------
1   NFFC     WS-F5521  0010839900 1.1
```

NOTE	The Catalyst 4912G, 2948G, 2926G, and 2926 series switches are fixed-configuration switches but are logically modular. You must apply configuration commands to the appropriate module. For example, on a Catalyst 2926G series switch, the 24 Fast Ethernet ports belong logically to module 2. Refer to the *Catalyst 2900 Series Configuration Guide and Command Reference* and *Switch Software Documentation, Release 5.1* publications for more information.

Loading and Accessing the Route Processor

You can eliminate the need to connect a terminal directly to the RSM console port by accessing the RSM from the switch. To access the RSM from the switch prompt, enter the following command:

```
Switch> session mod-num
```

mod-num is the module number of the RSM. The module number can be obtained by issuing the **show module** command on the switch.

After the **session** command executes, the switch responds with the Enter Password prompt for the RSM, if a password is configured. Once you enter the password for the RSM, you are logged in to the route processor. At this point, you are in user EXEC command mode on the route processor, and you have direct access only to the RSM with which you have established a session.

To exit from the router command-line interface and go back to the switch CLI, enter the **exit** command at the Router> prompt.

The following shows how to access the RSM from the switch CLI, and how to exit the router CLI and return to the switch CLI:

```
Switch> session 3
Switch> Enter Password: cisco
Router> exit
```

One of the first tasks in configuring your route processor is to name it. Naming your router helps you better manage your network by being able to uniquely identify each route processor within the network. The name of the route processor is considered to be the host name and is the name displayed at the system prompt. If no name is configured, the system default router name is Router followed by an angle bracket (>) for EXEC mode or a pound sign (#) for privileged EXEC mode.

To configure a host name, enter the following command in global configuration mode:

```
Router(config)#hostname name
```

name is the identifying system name between 1 and 255 in alphanumeric characters.

The output in Example 5-2 shows that the host name of the route processor is RSM143#.

Example 5-2 *Output Displaying the Host Name*

```
RSM143#show running-config
Building configuration...

Current configuration:
!
version 11.3
service timestamps debug uptime
service timestamps log uptime
no service password-encryption
!
hostname RSM143

-text deleted-
```

To clear the host name, enter the **no hostname** command in global configuration mode.

NOTE   Do not expect case to be preserved. Uppercase and lowercase characters look the same to many Internet software applications (often under the assumption that the application is doing you a favor). It might seem appropriate to capitalize a name the same way you would in English, but conventions dictate that computer names appear in all-lowercase. For more information, refer to RFC 1178, "Choosing a Name for Your Computer."

The name must also follow the rules for ARPANET host names. They must start with a letter, end with a letter or digit, and contain only letters, digits, and hyphens. Names must have 63 or fewer characters. For more information, refer to RFC 1035, "Domain Names—Implementation and Specification."

Enabling an IP Routing Protocol

All devices in a network communicate with each other over routes. A *route* is a path from the sending device to the receiving device. If the destination device is on the same network as the sending device, the sending device simply transmits the packet directly to the destination. When a destination is not on the local network, a sending device forwards the packet to a route processor.

Route processors can route in the following two basic ways:

- Use preprogrammed static routes
- Dynamically calculate routes using any one of a number of dynamic routing protocols

Routing protocols determine optimal paths through internetworks using routing algorithms, and they transport information across these paths.

NOTE	Discussion of IP routing protocols and their operations is beyond the scope of this book and the BCMSN course. The *Advanced Cisco Router Configuration* coursebook from Cisco Press discusses network routing and routing protocols in greater detail.

To assign a routing protocol to a route processor, enter the following commands in global configuration mode:

```
Router(config)#ip routing
Router(config)#router ip_routing_protocol
```

After the routing protocol has been specified, you must inform the routing protocol which interfaces will participate in the sending and receiving of routing updates. To initiate the routing protocol on the route processor interfaces, enter the following command in router configuration mode:

```
Router(config-router)#network network-number
```

network-number indicates the interfaces that will participate in this internal routing protocol. The network number must identify a network to which the router is physically connected. This command also allows the route processor to announce a route for that network to other route processors.

In the following example, RSM141 is configured with the Interior Gateway Routing Protocol (IGRP), in autonomous system number 1, and the RSM is routing for network 172.16.0.0:

```
RSM141#show running-config
Building configuration...

Current configuration:
!
(text deleted)
router igrp 1
 network 172.16.0.0
!
```

Configuring an Interface

The primary difference between traditional routing and VLAN routing configuration occurs at the interface. This is also true of the differences between internal and external route processors. This section examines how interfaces are configured on both types of route processors.

Configuring an Internal Route Processor

Configuring inter-VLAN routing on the RSM consists of two main procedures:

- Creating and configuring VLANs on the switch and assigning VLAN membership to switch ports.

- Creating and configuring VLAN interfaces for inter-VLAN routing on the RSM. A VLAN interface must be configured for each VLAN between which traffic is to be routed.

As discussed in Chapter 3, VLANs are *created* at the switch level to group ports into virtual LANs. However, VLANs are *controlled* at the route processor level. VLAN interfaces on the RSM are virtual interfaces, but you configure them much as you do a physical router interface. To specify a VLAN interface on the RSM, enter the following command in global configuration mode:

```
Router(config)#interface vlan-interface-number
```

To specify a VLAN interface other than 0 or 1, use the VLAN number as the *vlan-interface-number*. The interface number configured on the route processor corresponds to the VLAN number configured on the Catalyst 5000 series switch. For example, **interface VLAN 10** corresponds to VLAN 10 on the Catalyst 5000 series switch. The RSM can route up to 256 VLANs.

After you define the VLAN interface, you must assign a unique IP address to that interface. To assign a unique IP address and subnet mask to an interface, enter the following command in interface configuration mode:

```
Router(config-if)#ip address ip-address subnet-mask
```

NOTE   The VLAN interface will be administratively down until the **no shutdown** command is entered. Enter this command only if you are configuring the VLAN interface for the first time.

Each VLAN that the RSM is routing appears as a separate virtual interface. Therefore, the RSM's configuration file has an interface configuration for each VLAN, as shown in Example 5-3.

Example 5-3 *Internal Route Processor Interface Configuration*

```
RSM141#show running-config
Building configuration...

Current configuration:
!
version 11.3
(text deleted)
```

Example 5-3 *Internal Route Processor Interface Configuration (Continued)*

```
!
hostname RSM141
!
enable password san-fran
!
!
!
interface Vlan1
 ip address 172.16.1.141 255.255.255.0
!
interface Vlan11
 ip address 172.16.41.141 255.255.255.0
!
interface Vlan12
ip address 172.16.41.141 255.255.255.0
```

The RSM has one global MAC address that applies to all interfaces on that device. Specifying a unique MAC address for each interface enhances the operations of the RSM interface when working with some Catalyst switches. Assigning a unique MAC address for each interface has the following benefits:

- Makes best use of Fast EtherChannel and load distribution, because Fast EtherChannel uses a portion of the MAC address to determine which link the data uses.

- Enhances multilayer switching management by providing unique MAC addresses for each interface in the Multilayer Switching (MLS) cache.

- Avoids Catalyst 1900 switch operation problems by assigning unique MAC addresses in the 1900 switch content-addressable memory (CAM) table.

External Route Processor

On an external router, an interface can be logically divided into multiple virtual subinterfaces. Subinterfaces provide a flexible solution for routing multiple data streams through a single physical interface. To accomplish this goal, you need to customize the subinterface to create the environment in which the subinterface is used. To define subinterfaces on a physical interface, perform the following tasks:

- Identify the interface.
- Define the VLAN encapsulation.
- Assign an IP address to the interface.

To identify the interface, enter the following command in global configuration mode:

```
Router(config)#interface ethernet slot-number/port-number.subinterface-number
```

slot-number/port-number.subinterface-number identifies the physical and logical interfaces.

NOTE   The subinterface number that is used can be any number. It has no significance to the router. The router does not look at this number in order to determine the VLAN number. It is, however, standard practice to make the subinterface number the same as the VLAN in order to make it easier to manage the router.

To define the VLAN encapsulation, enter the following command in interface configuration mode:

```
Router(config-if)#encapsulation isl vlan-number
```

vlan-number identifies the VLAN for which the subinterface will carry traffic. A VLAN ID is added to the frame anytime the frame is sent out the interface. Each VLAN frame carries the VLAN ID within the packet header.

NOTE   Encapsulation type can be either ISL or dot1q, depending on the encapsulation technique used at the switch.

To assign the IP address to the interface, enter the following command in interface configuration mode:

```
Router(config-if)#ip address ip-address subnet-mask
```

ip-address and *subnet-mask* are the 32-bit network address and mask of the specific interface.

In Example 5-4, route processor Router144 has two subinterfaces configured on Fast Ethernet interface 0/1. These two interfaces are identified as 0/1.1 and 0/1.2. Both interfaces are encapsulated for ISL. Interface 0/1.1 is routing packets for VLAN 10, whereas interface 0/1.2 is routing packets for VLAN 20.

Example 5-4   *Interface Configuration on an External Route Processor*

```
RSM144#show running-config
Building configuration...
Current configuration:
!
!
hostname "Router144"
!
(text deleted)
```

Example 5-4   *Interface Configuration on an External Route Processor (Continued)*

```
interface fastethernet 0/1.1
encapsulation isl 10
ip address 172.16.10.3 255.255.255.0

interface fastethernet 0/1.2
encapsulation isl 20
ip address 172.16.20.3 255.255.255.0
```

Defining the Default Gateway

In order to forward a datagram, the sending device must first know which routers are connected to the local network and which route processor maintains the shortest path to the destination device. Because it is not the responsibility of the end-user device to create and maintain routing tables, a default gateway is used to forward all nonlocal packets.

Defining a Default Gateway on a Cisco IOS Command-Based Switch

To define a gateway on a Cisco IOS-based series switch, enter the following command in global configuration mode:

```
Switch (config) ip default-gateway ip-address
```

ip-address is the IP address of the default route processor.

Defining a Default Gateway on a Set Command-Based Switch

A switch acts like any other IP end station. It must have a default gateway configured so that the switch can communicate with devices in other IP subnets. To do this, a default route must be added that points to the gateway router in the same subnet/VLAN as the sc0 interface on the switch.

To configure a default route on a set command-based system, enter the following command in privileged mode:

```
Switch (enable) set ip route destination gateway metric
```

Table 5-1 describes the variables in this command.

Table 5-1   *set ip route Command Variables*

Variable	Description
destination	IP address or IP alias of the network or specific host to be added. Use **default** as the destination to set the new entry as the default route.
gateway	IP address or IP alias of the router.
metric	(Optional) Value used to indicate whether the destination network is local or remote. Use **0** for local and **1** for remote.

NOTE   You can add several routes to the switch, including the default route. The addition of routes to the switch with the **set ip route** command does not make the switch a router, nor does this command affect the switching of IP packets through the switch. This command is solely for IP communications to the switch, not for data through the switch.

This section contains two examples of verifying the default gateway. Example 5-5 shows the output from the **show ip** command on a Cisco IOS-based switch.

Example 5-5   *Verifying the Default Gateway with the **show ip** Command*

```
Access41#show ip
IP Address: 172.16.1.41
Subnet Mask: 255.255.0.0
Default Gateway: 172.16.1.143
Management VLAN:  1
Domain name:
Name server 1: 0.0.0.0
Name server 2: 0.0.0.0
HTTP server : Enabled
HTTP port :  80
RIP : Enabled
```

Example 5-6 shows the configuration output that results from the **show ip route** command on a set-based switch.

Example 5-6   *Verifying the Default Gateway with the **show ip route** Command*

```
DSW141 (enable) show ip route
Fragmentation    Redirect    Unreachable
-------------    --------    -----------
enabled          enabled     enabled

The primary gateway: 172.16.1.143
Destination      Gateway         Flags   Use          Interface
--------------   -------------   ------  ----------   ---------
default          172.16.1.143    UG      2004         sc0
172.16.1.0       172.16.1.141    U       11           sc0
default          default         UH      0            sl0
```

Testing the Link

After the route processor is properly configured and connected to the network, the route processor can communicate with other nodes on the network.

To test connectivity to remote hosts, enter the following command in privileged mode:

```
Switch (enable) ping destination-ip-address
```

The **ping** command will return one of the following responses:

- **Success rate is 100 percent, or *destination-ip-address* is alive**—This response occurs in 1 to 10 seconds, depending on network traffic and the number of Internet Control Message Protocol (ICMP) packets sent.

- **Destination does not respond**—No answer message is returned if the host does not exist.

- **Unknown host**—This response occurs if the targeted host does not exist.

- **Destination unreachable**—This response occurs if the default gateway cannot reach the specified network.

- **Network or host unreachable**—This response occurs if there is no entry in the route table for the host or network.

NOTE   You can also test the routes that packets will take from the route processor to a specific destination. To track a router, enter the **trace ip** *destination* command in privileged mode, where *destination* is the IP address of the target device. For more information on the **trace ip** command, refer to the *Cisco IOS Release 12.0 Command Summary* publication.

Summary

VLANs are an important component of the campus network. In order for VLANs to communicate with each other, inter-VLAN routing must be present. The following summarizes the major characteristics of routing between VLANs:

- Inter-VLAN routing is a requirement to enable communication between devices in separate VLANs.

- Most devices are configured with the IP address of a default router to which all nonlocal network packets are sent.

- The Inter-Switch Link (ISL) protocol is used to facilitate multiple VLAN traffic over a single link.

- The distribution layer routing processor can be an internal or external router/switch topology.

Review Questions

The following questions test your retention of the material presented in this chapter. The answers to the Review Questions can be found in Appendix A, "Answers to Review Questions."

1 List at least two problems that can impede communications between VLANs, and identify a solution for each problem.

2 Identify at least two Cisco platform solutions for an internal route processor topology at the distribution layer.

3 Compare and contrast the steps used to configure an interface on an RSM and an ISL link on an external router.

Case Study: Inter-VLAN Routing

Work though this case study to practice what you learned in this chapter.

Scenario

In this case study, you will see how to route between the VLANs created in Chapter 3. Routing will be configured on the RSMs on each of the distribution layer switches. In addition, you will configure a default gateway for the PC workstation.

When you have completed this case study, each VLAN should be capable of communicating with all other VLANs. Figure 5-7 shows the visual objective of the case study.

Figure 5-7   *Case Study Visual Objective*

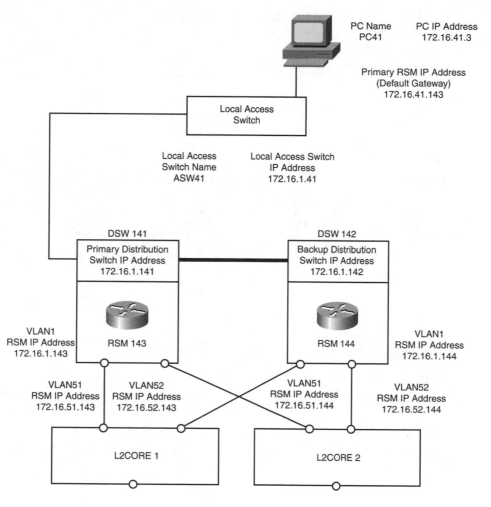

Command List

In this case study, you will use the commands listed in Tables 5-2 through 5-4. Refer to these tables for an explanation of the commands used in this case study.

Table 5-2 *Access Switch Commands*

Command	Description
interface	Selects an interface to configure.
ip address *ip-address subnet-mask*	Assigns an IP address and subnet mask to the access switch.
ip default-gateway *ip-address*	Assigns a router IP address as the default gateway.
ping *ip-address*	Sends an ICMP message to the designated IP address.
show ip	Displays the current IP settings.
show run	Displays the running configuration in memory.
vlan-membership	Specifies the VLAN membership configuration.
Ctrl-Shift-6-x	Escape sequence to return to the terminal server or switch block menu.

Table 5-3 *Distribution Switch Commands*

Command	Description
session *module-number*	Connects the CLI to a session on a module.
set interface sc0 *ip-address subnet-mask*	Assigns an IP address and subnet mask to the SC0 interface on the distribution switch.
set ip route default	Configures the default route.
show config	Displays the configuration of the switch.
show interface	Displays the current configuration of sc0 and sl0.
show module	Displays the module numbers of the cards in your distribution switch.
Ctrl-Shift-6-x	Escape sequence to return to the terminal server or switch block menu.

Table 5-4   *Distribution Route Switch Module Commands*

Command	Description
enable password	Assigns a password to privileged EXEC mode.
copy run start	Saves the running configuration in memory to NVRAM.
hostname	Assigns a unique name to the RSM.
interface vlan *number*	Enables interface configuration mode for the specified VLAN interface.
ip address *ip-address subnet-mask*	Assigns an IP address and subnet mask to an interface.
line console 0	Enters line console mode.
line vty 0 4	Enters vty line mode.
password *password*	Sets a password in line or vty mode.
login	Requires that a password be supplied when using a line.
mac-addresss	Set a specific MAC address on an interface.
network	Associates a network number with a routing protocol.
no ip classless	Restores the classful method of interpreting IP network addresses, masks, and behavior.
no shutdown	Administratively enables an interface.
ping *ip-address*	Sends an ICMP message to the designated IP address.
router igrp *autonomous-system*	Configures the IGRP routing process.
show ip route	Displays the IP route table entries.
show run	Displays the current system configuration in memory.
Ctrl-Shift-6-x	Escape sequence to return to the terminal server or switch block menu.

Task 1: Perform Basic Router Setup

In this task, you will perform basic router configuration on the RSM in each of the distribution layer switches, including hostname and login and enable passwords. Follow these steps:

Step 1   Open a console session with your distribution switch.

Step 2   In privileged mode on your distribution switch, enter the **show module** command to display the module number of your primary route processor. Your display should resemble the output shown in Example 5-7.

Example 5-7   *show module Command Output*

```
Mod Module-Name        Ports Module-Type         Model       Serial-Num Status
--- ------------------ ----- ------------------- ----------- ---------- -------
1                      0     Supervisor III      WS-X5530    010821493 ok
2                      24    10/100BaseTX Ethernet WS-X5225R 012145458 ok
3                      1     Route Switch         WS-X5302   006825295 ok

Mod MAC-Address(es)                         Hw     Fw         Sw
--- --------------------------------------- ------ ---------- ----------------
1   00-50-e2-80-a0-00 to 00-50-e2-80-a3-ff 2.0    3.1.2      4.3(1a)
2   00-50-a2-f1-42-c8 to 00-50-a2-f1-42-df 3.1    4.3(1)     4.3(1a)
3   00-e0-1e-91-ba-0a to 00-e0-1e-91-ba-0b 4.5    20.14      11.3(6)WA4(9)

Mod Sub-Type Sub-Model Sub-Serial Sub-Hw
--- -------- --------- ---------- ------
1   NFFC     WS-F5521  0010828703 1.1
```

Step 3   Locate the module number of your RSM.

Step 4   In privilege mode, enter the **session** *module-number* command, where *module-number* is equal to your RSM number.

Basic RSM Configuration

The following steps should be completed for each of your RSMs:

Step 1   In global configuration mode on your RSM, enter the **hostname** *hostname* command, where *hostname* is the name of your RSM.

Step 2   In global configuration mode, enter the **line console 0** command to assign a login password to your console port.

Step 3   In line configuration mode, enter the **login** command to require a login password to your console port.

Step 4   In global configuration mode, enter the **line vty 0 4** command to assign a login password to your Telnet ports 0 through 4.

Step 5   In global configuration mode, enter the **enable password** command to assign a password to privileged mode.

Task 2: Configure Routing on the Route Switch Module

In this task, you will enable routing on the RSM. These steps should be completed for each of the RSMs:

Step 1   In global configuration mode, enter the **router igrp 1** command to enable IP routing on the distribution router.

Step 2   In router configuration mode, enter the **network** *network-number* command to assign a network address to the router. Use IP network address 172.16.0.0.

Configure a VLAN Interface

Complete the following steps:

Step 1   In global configuration mode, enter the **interface vlan1** command to create and configure that interface.

Step 2   In interface configuration mode, enter the **ip address** *ip-address subnet-mask* command to assign an IP address to the VLAN1 interface. Use a subnet mask of 255.255.255.0.

Step 3   In interface configuration mode, enter the **no shutdown** command to administratively enable the interface.

Configure Core VLAN Interfaces

Repeat the steps listed in the "Configure a VLAN Interface" section for interfaces VLAN51 and VLAN52.

Check the Configuration

Follow these steps:

Step 1   In privileged mode, enter the **show run** command to display your configuration. Your configuration should resemble the output shown in Example 5-8.

Example 5-8   *show run Command Output*

```
Building configuration...

Current configuration:
!
version 11.3
service timestamps debug uptime
service timestamps log uptime
no service password-encryption
```

continues

Example 5-8 *show run Command Output (Continued)*

```
!
hostname RSM144
!
enable password san-fran
!
prompt RSM144
!
!
interface Vlan1
.mac-address 4004.0144.0001
 ip address 172.16.1.144 255.255.255.0

(text deleted)

interface Vlan51
.mac-address 4004.0144.0051
 ip address 172.16.51.144 255.255.255.0
!
interface Vlan52
mac-address 4004.0144.0052
 ip address 172.16.52.144 255.255.255.0
!
router igrp 1
 network 172.16.0.0
!
no ip classless

(text deleted)

line con 0
 password cisco
 login
line aux 0
line vty 0 4
 password cisco
 login
```

> **Step 2** In privileged mode, enter the **show ip route** command to display your
> route table. Your configuration should resemble the output shown in
> Example 5-9.

Example 5-9 *show ip route Command Output*

```
RSM143#show ip route
Codes: C - connected, S - static, I - IGRP, R - RIP, M - mobile, B - BGP
       D - EIGRP, EX - EIGRP external, O - OSPF, IA - OSPF inter area
       N1 - OSPF NSSA external type 1, N2 - OSPF NSSA external type 2
       E1 - OSPF external type 1, E2 - OSPF external type 2, E - EGP
       i - IS-IS, L1 - IS-IS level-1, L2 - IS-IS level-2, * - candidate default
       U - per-user static route, o - ODR
```

Example 5-9 *show ip route Command Output (Continued)*

```
Gateway of last resort is not set

     172.16.0.0/24 is subnetted, 4 subnets
C       172.16.52.0 is directly connected, Vlan52
I       172.16.53.0 [100/120] via 172.16.51.3, 00:00:08, Vlan51
                    [100/120] via 172.16.52.3, 00:00:08, Vlan52
C       172.16.51.0 is directly connected, Vlan51
C       172.16.2.0 is directly connected, Vlan1
C     127.0.0.0/8 is directly connected, Vlan0
RSM143#
```

Step 3   In privileged mode, enter the **copy run start** command to save your
configuration.

Task 3: Verify IP Addresses and Establish a Default Gateway for the Workstation

In this task, you will ensure that all devices have the correct IP address and gateway
information with a subnet mask of 255.255.255.0. Complete the following steps.

Modify Your PC IP Settings

Step 1   Close any open windows or applications.

Step 2   From your Windows desktop, select Start, Settings, Control Panel,
Network, and click the icon.

Step 3   Click the TCP/IP Interface Adapter symbol.

Step 4   Click the Properties button.

Step 5   From the TCP/IP Properties menu, select the IP Address tab and change
your subnet mask to 255.255.255.0.

Step 6   From the TCP/IP Properties menu, select the Gateway tab.

Step 7   In the New Gateway dialog box, enter your assigned default gateway IP
address.

Step 8   Click the Add button.

Step 9   Click the OK button (TCP/IP Properties).

Step 10 Click the OK button (Network).

Step 11 Enter **yes** to restart Windows, and answer **yes** to any and all prompts.

Step 12 Wait for Windows to restart.

Step 13 From your Windows desktop, select Start, Run.

Step 14 Enter **command** to open an MS-DOS window.

Step 15 At the DOS prompt, enter the **ping** *ip-address* command.

Step 16 From your PC desktop, open a hyperterm session to your assigned distribution switch.

Step 17 In privileged enable mode, use the **show interface** command to display the current values of the IP address and subnet mask.

Step 18 In privileged enable mode, use the **set interface sc0** *ip-address subnet-mask* command to use the current IP address, but change the mask to 255.255.255.0.

Step 19 In global configuration mode, enter the **set ip route default** *ip-address* command, where *ip-address* is the VLAN1 IP address of one of the RSMs.

Step 20 In privileged mode, enter the **show config** command to verify your configuration. Your configuration should resemble the output shown in Example 5-10.

Example 5-10   *show config Command Output*

```
begin
set password $1$9qGT$XSM6Mh//ygeee/g3t8NRV/
set enablepass $1$qmW5$yT2/Hz95oSCLFRd98Qznw0
set prompt DSW141

(text deleted)

!
#ip
set interface sc0 1 172.16.1.141 255.255.255.0 172.16.1.255

set interface sc0 up
set interface sl0 0.0.0.0 0.0.0.0
set interface sl0 up
set arp agingtime 1200
set ip redirect    enable
set ip unreachable    enable
set ip fragmentation enable
set ip route 0.0.0.0          172.16.1.143     1
set ip alias default        0.0.0.0
```

Step 21 Verify your configuration with a ping test to the following:

— The default gateway interface

— Your workstation

You completed the task if your output for **show interface** displays a subnet mask of 255.255.255.0 and you can successfully ping the assigned devices.

You have completed this case study when you can ping from your workstation to any of your switches.

CHAPTER 6

Improving IP Routing Performance with Multilayer Switching

Chapter 1 discussed the new 20/80 rule for designing campus networks. Based on this general rule, 80 percent of your users' traffic must cross a Layer 3 device. The speed at which this device can transmit data is extremely important. Cisco has developed several switching techniques in order to speed up the process of moving through a Layer 3 device. The primary method deployed inside the campus network is called *multilayer switching* (MLS). Multilayer switching is an important emerging technology that combines the best of switching and routing, bringing new levels of performance and scalability to campus networks. In light of changing traffic patterns and increasing loads being placed on the networks to access centralized resources and server farms, it becomes imperative for the platforms used in the campus design to provide appropriate Layer 3 performance.

This chapter discusses the following topics:

- Multilayer switching fundamentals
- Configuring the Multilayer Switching Route Processor
- Applying flow masks
- Configuring the multilayer switching switch engine
- MLS topology examples
- Other Layer 3 switching technologies

Upon completion of this chapter, you will be able to perform the following tasks: identify the network devices required to run multilayer switch IP traffic between two end-user devices, configure the distribution layer route processor to participate in multilayer switching, configure the distribution layer switching engine to participate in multilayer switching, verify existing flow entries in the MLS cache, and apply flow masks to determine how MLS entries are created in the MLS cache.

Multilayer Switching Fundamentals

Multilayer switching is one of the techniques used to increase IP routing performance by handling the Layer 3 packet switching and rewrite function in hardware. The Cisco Systems implementation of MLS supports all the traditional routing protocols; however, the frame forwarding and rewrite process functions previously handled by a router have been moved to switch hardware.

Before discussing how multilayer switching works, it is helpful to discuss what must happen during the routing of a packet.

The following must occur when a device sends data destined for another subnet:

- The packet is encapsulated at Layer 2 with a source MAC address of the sending station and a destination MAC address of the default gateway or router.

- The Layer 3 information contains the source IP address of the sending station and the IP address of the final destination.

- The router receives the frame based on the Layer 2 information. The interface is checked for an inbound access list. If there is an access list, it is checked for a match and is either permitted or denied based on the contents of the access list.

- The router then looks at the routing table to determine the next-hop address for the destination packet.

- After the router has determined the next-hop logical address (Layer 3 address), it consults the ARP cache table to find the Layer 2 address of the next hop.

- The frame is rewritten with the Layer 2 encapsulation information, and the TTL is decremented.

NOTE   This is a simplistic view of what happens inside the router. The intent of stepping through the basic mechanics of passing through a router is to explain how multilayer switching works.

In the multilayer switching process, a switch monitors a frame destined for the router's MAC address. It determines where the router sends the destination packet and then caches the packet information and the port it used to exit the switch. For this reason, multilayer switching is frequently referred to as a "route-once, switch-many" process.

Layer 3 protocols, such as IP, are connectionless, delivering each packet independently of the others. However, actual network traffic consists of many end-to-end conversations, or flows, between users or applications.

A flow is a specific conversation, consisting of many packets, between a network source and destination within a specific period of time. For example, Hypertext Transfer Protocol (HTTP) Web packets from a particular source to a particular destination are a flow separate from File Transfer Protocol (FTP) file transfer packets between the same pair of hosts. Flows may be unicast or multicast traffic. Multilayer switching identifies the information in the flow and caches it in the switch with the port assignment to the destination. As frames enter the switch, they are switched based on the information cached about the flow to the correct port. A Layer 2 device can now handle traffic that traditionally had to always pass to a Layer 3 device.

Hardware and Software Requirements

Multilayer switching can be implemented using a Layer 3 switch or an external router topology. MLS requires the following software and hardware:

- Catalyst 5000 or 6000 series switch with Supervisor Engine software release 4.1(1) or later
- Cisco IOS release 11.3(2)WA4(4) or later
- Supervisor Engine III or III F with the NFFC II, or Supervisor Engine II G or III G
- Route Switch Feature Card (RSFC)

You can also implement MLS with an external router/Catalyst switch combination. The following equipment is necessary when implementing MLS with an external router/ Catalyst switch combination:

- Catalyst 5000 or 6000 series switch with Supervisor Engine software release 4.1(1) or later
- Supervisor Engine III or III F with the NFFC II, or Supervisor Engine II G or III G
- Cisco high-end routers, such as Cisco 7500, 7200, 4500, 4700, or 8500 series
- Cisco IOS release 11.3(2)WA4(4) or later

NOTE   The Catalyst 8540 does not currently support multilayer switching. It utilizes a Layer 3 switching mechanism called Cisco Express Forwarding.

The connection between the external router and the switch can be multiple Ethernet links or Fast Ethernet with the Inter-Switch Link (ISL).

MLS Components

The Cisco multilayer switching implementation includes the following components:

- **Multilayer Switching Switch Engine (MLS-SE)**—The switching entity that handles the function of moving and rewriting packets. The MLS-SE is a NetFlow Feature Card residing on a Supervisor Engine III card in a Catalyst switch.

- **Multilayer Switching Route Processor (MLS-RP)**—A Route Switch Module or an externally connected Cisco 7500, 7200, 4500, 4700, or 8500 series router with software that supports multilayer switching. The MLS-RP sends MLS configuration information and updates, such as the router MAC address and virtual LAN (VLAN) number flow mask, and routing and access list changes.

- **Multilayer Switching Protocol (MLSP)**—This protocol operates between the MLS-SE and MLS-RP to enable multilayer switching. The MLSP is the method in which the RSM or router advertises routing changes and the VLANs or MAC addresses of the interfaces that are participating in MLS.

Figure 6-1 shows the icons used throughout this book for MLS-RP and MLS-SE.

Figure 6-1   *MLS Components—A Layer 3 Routing Component and a Layer 2 Switch Component*

MLS-RP—Multilayer
Switching Route Processor

MLS-SE—Multilayer
Switching Switch Engine

How MLS Works

The preceding section discussed the components of MLS. This section discusses the mechanics of MLS. This includes the communication between Layer 2 and Layer 3 devices, caching Layer 3 information in the Layer 2 switch, and switching packets through a switch. The following topics are discussed:

- MLS-RP advertisements
- MLSP hello messages
- Assigning XTAGs
- Establishing an MLS cache entry
- Switching frames in a flow

MLS-RP Advertisements

When an MLS-RP is activated in a campus network, the MLS-RP sends out a multicast hello message every 15 seconds. This message is sent to all switches in the network, and it contains the following:

- The MAC addresses used by the MLS-RP on its interfaces that are participating in MLS
- Access list information
- Additions and deletions of routes

MLSP uses the Cisco Group Management Protocol (CGMP) multicast address as the destination address of the hello message. This address ensures interoperability with the Cisco switches in the network. Although this address is the same as that used by CGMP, the message contains a different protocol type so that the switch can distinguish these messages from other multicast packets.

MLSP Hello Messages

Because all Cisco switches listen to the well-known multicast address, they all receive the hello message. However, only switches that have Layer 3 capabilities process the hello message. Switches without Layer 3 capabilities pass these frames to downstream switches.

When an MLS-SE receives the frame, the device extracts all the MAC addresses received in the frame, along with the associated interface or VLAN ID for that address. The MLS-SE records the addresses of the MLS-RPs in the MLS-SE content-addressable memory (CAM) table.

Assigning XTAGs

If there are multiple MLS-RPs attached to a switch, the MLS-SE distinguishes the MAC address entries of each MLS-RP by assigning an XTAG value to these addresses. The XTAG value is a locally generated one-byte value that the MLS-SE attaches to all the MAC addresses learned from the same MLS-RP via the MLSP frames.

The XTAG is also useful in deleting a specific set of Layer 3 entries from the Layer 3 table when an MLS-RP fails or exits the network.

Establishing an MLS Cache Entry

Multilayer switching is based on individual flows. The MLS-SE maintains a cache for MLS flows and stores statistics for each flow. All packets in a flow are compared to the cache.

NOTE   MLS cache entries support unidirectional flows. The unidirectional nature of a flow means that there is an MLS cache entry for the flow between Host A and Host B, and another MLS cache entry for the flow between Host B and Host A.

If the MLS cache contains an entry that matches the packet in the flow, the MLS-SE layer switches the packet, bypassing the router. If the MLS does not contain an entry that matches the packet, the following steps outline the process in establishing an MLS cache entry for a flow. Figures 6-2 though 6-4 include corresponding numbers that illustrate these steps.

Figure 6-2 *Establishing an MLS Cache Entry—Steps 1 Through 4*

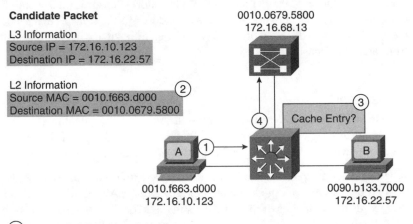

1. The MLS-SE receives initial frame.

2. The MLS-SE reads and recognizes the destination MAC address.

3. The MLS-SE checks the MLS cache for like entries.

4. The MLS-SE forwards the frame to the MLS–RP.

Step 1 A switch receives an incoming frame and looks at the frame's destination MAC address.

Step 2 The switch recognizes the frame's destination address as the address of the MLS-RP because the switch initially received this destination address in a Layer 3 hello message and programmed that MAC address in the CAM table.

Step 3 The MLS-SE checks the MLS cache to determine if an MLS flow is already established for this flow. If the frame is the first in a flow, there will not be an entry in the cache. Because the frame contained a route processor destination address, the switch recognizes the potential for Layer 3 switching for that frame.

Step 4 On the initial packet, the switch does not have all the information for a Layer 3 switch for the frame. Therefore, the switch forwards the frame to the addressed route processor.

This process of sending the frame to the addressed route processor creates a candidate entry in the MLS cache.

Figure 6-3   *Establishing an MLS Cache Entry—Steps 5 Through 8*

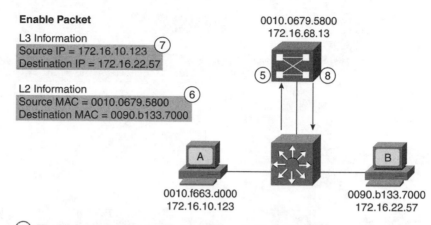

(5) The MLS-RP receives the frame and consults the routing table.

(6) The MLS-RP rewrites the header with the new destination MAC address.

(7) The MLS-RP enters its own MAC address for the source address.

(8) The MLS-RP forwards the frame to the MLS-SE.

Step 5   The route processor receives the frame and consults the routing table to determine if, in fact, the route processor has knowledge of a route for the destination address.

Step 6   If the route processor finds the destination address in the routing table, the route processor constructs a new Layer 2 header, which now contains the route processor's own MAC address as the source MAC address.

Step 7   The route processor also enters the MAC address of the destination host or next-hop route processor in the destination MAC address field of the Layer 2 frame.

Step 8   The route processor forwards the frame back to the MLS-SE.

Figure 6-4 *Establishing an MLS Cache Entry—Steps 9 Through 12*

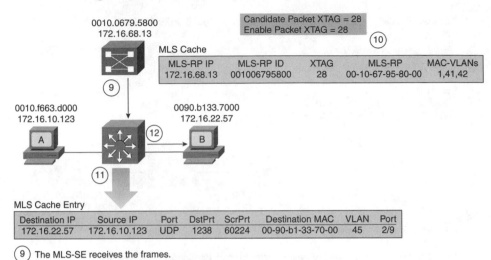

(9) The MLS-SE receives the frames.

(10) The MLS-SE compares the XTAG of the candidate and enable packets.

(11) The MLS-SE records the enable packet information in the MLS cache.

(12) The MLS-SE forwards the frame to the destination.

Step 9 When the switch receives the frame, the switch knows which port needs to forward the frame, based on the CAM table. Moreover, the switch also recognizes the MAC address in the source field and knows that this destination belongs to the route processor.

Step 10 This recognition triggers the process of checking the MLS cache to see if there is an entry for this route processor. The switch compares the XTAGs for both the candidate entry in the MLS cache and the returned frame. If the two XTAGs match, the frame came from the same route processor for the same flow.

Step 11 The switch records the information from the returned frame in the MLS cache.

Step 12 The switch forwards the frame out the appropriate port using the destination MAC address.

This second frame becomes the enable entry in the MLS cache, and the partial entry for that flow is completed.

NOTE   It is important to remember that the MLS-SE must see both sides of the flow going from the source to the destination in order to perform Layer 3 switching.

Switching Frames in a Flow

When the switch receives subsequent packets in the flow, it recognizes that the frames contain the MAC address of the route processor. Subsequent frames in a flow get switched at Layer 2 after checking the MLS cache. The following steps take place when switching subsequent frames in a flow. Figure 6-5 includes corresponding numbers that illustrate these steps.

Figure 6-5   *Switching Subsequent Frames in a Flow*

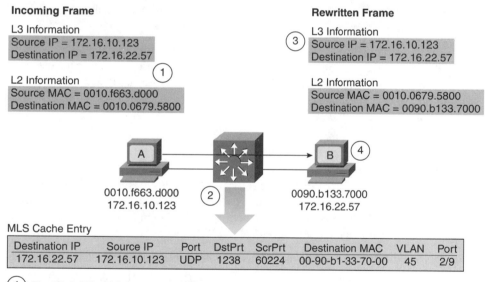

(1) The MLS-SE receives subsequent frames in the flow.

(2) The MLS-SE compares the incoming frame with the MLS cache entry.

(3) The MLS-SE rewrites the frame header.

(4) The MLS-SE forwards the frame to the destination.

Step 1   The switch receives subsequent frames in a flow.

Step 2   The switch checks the MLS cache and finds the entry matching the flow in question.

Step 3   The switch rewrites the Layer 2 frame header, changing the destination MAC address to the MAC address of Host B, and the source MAC address to the MAC address of the MLS-RP. The Layer 3 IP addresses remain the same, but the IP header Time To Live (TTL) is decremented and the checksum is recomputed. The MLS-SE rewrites the switched Layer 3 packets so that they appear to have been routed by a route processor.

NOTE   The switch rewrites the frame to look exactly as if the route processor processed the frame. The final destination sees the frame exactly as if the router processed the frame.

Step 4   After the MLS-SE performs the packet rewrite, the switch forwards the rewritten frame to the destination MAC address.

The state and identity of the flow are maintained while traffic is active; when traffic for a flow ceases, the entry ages out. Partial, or candidate, entries remain in the cache for 5 seconds with no enabled entry before timing out. Cache entries that are complete—those in which the switch captures both the candidate and the enabling packet—remain in the cache as long as packets in that flow are detected.

Commands That Disable MLS

Some IP commands require that the routing processor must manipulate every packet in the flow. Any command that requires each packet to be manipulated by the route processor precludes the multilayer switching function. The following are some IP commands that disable MLS on an interface:

- **no ip routing**—Purges all MLS cache entries and disables MLS on the MLS-RP.
- **ip security** (all forms of this command)—Disables MLS on the interface.
- **ip tcp compression-connections**—Disables MLS on the interface.
- **ip tcp header-compression**—Disables MLS on the interface.
- **clear ip-route**—Removes the MLS cache entries in all switches performing Layer 3 switching for this MLS-RP.

Configuring the Multilayer Switch Route Processor

You can complete the configuration of the MLS-RP in a few simple steps:

Step 1 Globally enable MLS on the route processor for a specific routing protocol.

Step 2 Assign an MLS VTP domain at the interface.

Step 3 Enable MLS on the route processor for a specific interface.

Step 4 Create a Null Domain.

Step 5 Specify an MLS management interface.

Step 6 (Optional) Assign a VLAN ID to an interface.

Globally Enabling MLS on the Route Processor

Before you can configure multilayer switching for a specific VLAN or interface, you must globally enable the MLSP that operates between the route processor and the switch.

To enable MLSP on the route processor, enter the following command in global configuration mode:

```
Router(config)#mls rp ip
```

The running configuration in Example 6-1 shows that the MLS-RP is configured to MLS routed IP packets.

NOTE   As of IOS release 12.0, MLS also routes Internetwork Packet Exchange (IPX) packets.

Example 6-1 *Example of IOS MLS-RP IP Configuration*

```
Router# show running-config
Building configuration...
Current configuration:
!
version 11.3
service timestamps debug uptime
service timestamps log uptime
no service password-encryption
!
hostname Router
!
!
mls rp ip
!
```

To disable multilayer switching on the route processor/RSM, enter the **no mls rp ip** command in global configuration mode.

NOTE	Cisco's implementation of MLS supports the Layer 3 switching of IP and IPX. All other routing protocols are routed at Layer 3 in software.

Assigning an MLS Interface to a VTP Domain

After you determine which route processor interfaces will be MLS interfaces, you must add them to the same VLAN Trunking Protocol (VTP) domain as the switch. Both the switch and the MLS interfaces must be in the same domain. If the switch is not assigned to the VTP domain, you do not need to perform this task.

To place an external route processor interface in the same VTP domain as the switch, enter the following commands in interface configuration mode:

```
Router(config) interface vlan vlan_number
Router(config-if)# mls rp vtp-domain domain-name
```

domain-name is the name of the VTP domain in which the switch resides.

NOTE	For an ISL interface, enter this command only on the primary interface. All subinterfaces that are part of the primary interface inherit the VTP domain of the primary interface.

The running configuration in Example 6-2 shows that the VLAN41 interface of the MLS-RP is configured to reside in the Rigel2 VTP domain.

Example 6-2 *Example of MLS-RP VTP Domain Configuration*

```
Router# show running-config
Building configuration...
(text deleted)
mls rp ip
!
!
interface Vlan1
 ip address 172.16.41.168 255.255.255.0
!
interface Vlan41
 ip address 172.16.41.168 255.255.255.0
 mls rp vtp-domain Rigel2
```

To remove the MLS interface from a VTP domain, enter the **no mls rp vtp-domain** *domain-name* command.

To view information about a specific VTP domain, enter the following command in privileged EXEC mode:

```
Router# show mls rp vtp-domain vtp-domain-name
```

The display resulting from this command shows a subset of the **show mls rp** command display. The following information is a result of issuing the **show mls rp vtp-domain** command:

- The name of the VTP domain(s) in which the MLS-RP interfaces reside
- Statistical information for each VTP domain
- The number of management interfaces defined for the MLS-RP
- The number of VLANs in this domain configured for MLS
- The ID of each VLAN configured for this domain MAC address
- The number of MLS-SEs that the router or RSM has knowledge of in this domain
- The MAC address of each switch in this domain

Enabling MLS on an Interface

Putting an MLS interface into a VTP domain does not activate MLS on the interface. MLS must be explicitly entered on the interface. Because of the one-to-one relationship between VLANs and subnets, each interface that is to participate in Layer 3 switching must be enabled for multilayer switching.

To enable an RSM interface for multilayer switching, enter the following command in interface configuration mode:

```
Router (config-if)#mls rp ip
```

The running configuration in Example 6-3 shows that the VLAN41 interface of the MLS-RP is enabled to participate in multilayer switching.

Example 6-3 *Enabling MLS at the Interface*

```
Router# show running-config
Building configuration...
(text deleted)
mls rp ip
!
!
interface Vlan1
 ip address 172.16.1.168 255.255.255.0
!
interface Vlan41
```

continues

Example 6-3 *Enabling MLS at the Interface (Continued)*

```
ip address 172.16.41.168 255.255.255.0
mls rp vtp-domain bcmsn
mls rp ip
```

To disable multilayer switching on an interface, enter the **no mls rp ip** command.

Creating a Null Domain

When a route processor resides in a VTP domain other than the domain in which the switch resides, the switch cannot multilayer switch frames for that router. There are several ways in which a route processor and switch can end up in different VTP domains:

- You can purposely place both devices in separate domains.

- You can misname or mistype the VTP domain when configuring either the switch or the route processor.

- You can enter the MLS interface command prior to putting the interface in a VTP domain.

Configuring an interface for multilayer switching by assigning an interface to a VTP domain prior to assigning the interface to a VTP domain places that interface in the null domain. When the interface resides in a null domain, it cannot participate in multilayer switching with the switch.

To remove the MLS interface from a null VTP domain, disable MLS on the interface.

Assigning an MLS Management Interface

When an RSM or router is configured to participate in multilayer switching, the device uses the MLSP to send hello messages, advertise routing changes, and announce the VLANs or MAC addresses of those interfaces on the devices that are participating in MLS. One interface on the MLS-RP must be identified as the management interface through which MLSP packets are sent and received. The MLSP management interface can be any MLS interface connected to the switch.

Only one management interface needs be specified; however, if no management interface is configured, MLSP messages will not be sent.

NOTE   Multiple interfaces on the same route processor can be configured as management interfaces; however, this action increases the management overhead per route processor. Cisco does not recommend this practice.

To identify a management interface on an RSM or router, enter the following command in interface configuration mode:

```
Router(config-if)#mls rp management-interface
```

To disable the management interface, enter the **no mls rp management-interface** command in interface configuration mode.

The running configuration in Example 6-4 shows that the VLAN41 interface on the MLS-RP is configured as the management interface.

Example 6-4 *Configuring the Management Interface*

```
Router# show running-config
Building configuration...

(text deleted)
mls rp ip
!
!
interface Vlan1
 ip address 172.16.1.168 255.255.255.0
!
interface Vlan41
 ip address 172.16.41.168 255.255.255.0
 mls rp vtp-domain bcmsn
 mls rp management-interface
 mls rp ip
```

Assigning a VLAN ID to an Interface on an External Router

Multilayer switching is inter-VLAN routing. Multilayer switches make forwarding decisions based on which ports are configured for which VLANs. Internal route processors and ISL-configured links inherently use VLAN IDs to identify interfaces. External route processor interfaces have knowledge regarding subnets but not VLANs. Therefore, MLS requires that each external route processor interface have a VLAN ID assigned to it.

To assign a VLAN ID to a route processor interface, enter the following commands in interface configuration mode:

```
Router (config)#interface interface number
Router (config-if)#mls rp vlan-id vlan-id-number
```

vlan-id-number represents the VLAN assigned to this interface.

To remove an interface from a VLAN, enter the **no mls rp vlan-id** *vlan-id-number* command.

Removing the VLAN ID from an interface disables MLS for that interface.

Verifying the Configuration

To verify the MLS configuration for an MLS-RP, enter the following command in privileged EXEC mode:

```
Router# show mls rp
```

Figure 6-6 shows an example of the **show mls rp** command output.

Figure 6-6   *Verifying the MLS-RP Configuration*

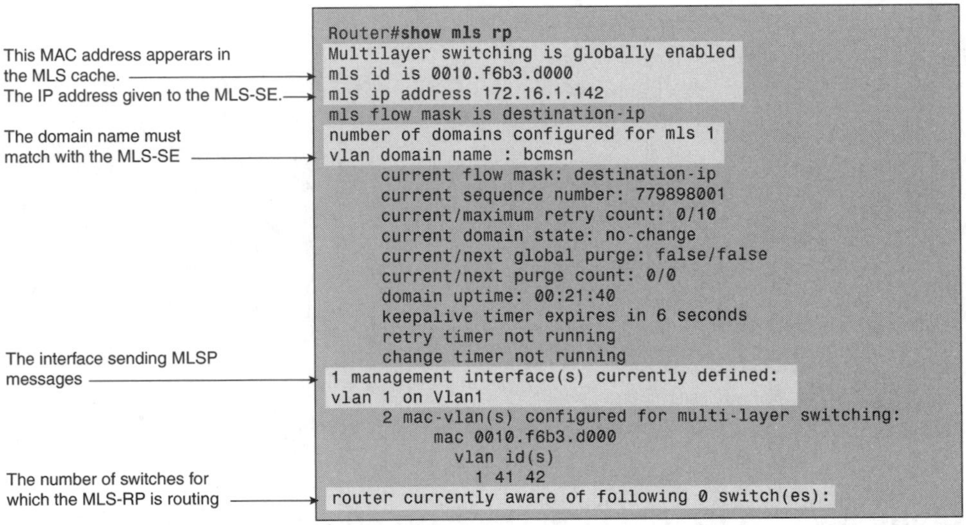

```
Router#show mls rp
Multilayer switching is globally enabled
mls id is 0010.f6b3.d000
mls ip address 172.16.1.142
mls flow mask is destination-ip
number of domains configured for mls 1
vlan domain name : bcmsn
        current flow mask: destination-ip
        current sequence number: 779898001
        current/maximum retry count: 0/10
        current domain state: no-change
        current/next global purge: false/false
        current/next purge count: 0/0
        domain uptime: 00:21:40
        keepalive timer expires in 6 seconds
        retry timer not running
        change timer not running
1 management interface(s) currently defined:
vlan 1 on Vlan1
        2 mac-vlan(s) configured for multi-layer switching:
              mac 0010.f6b3.d000
                  vlan id(s)
                  1 41 42
router currently aware of following 0 switch(es):
```

Annotations:
- This MAC address apperars in the MLS cache.
- The IP address given to the MLS-SE.
- The domain name must match with the MLS-SE
- The interface sending MLSP messages
- The number of switches for which the MLS-RP is routing

The display resulting from the **show mls rp** command shows the following information:

- Whether multilayer switching is globally enabled or disabled
- The MLS ID for this MLS-RP
- The MLS IP address for this MLS-RP
- The MLS flow mask
- The name of the VTP domain(s) where the MLS-RP interfaces reside
- Statistical information for each VTP domain
- The number of management interfaces defined for the MLS-RP
- The number of VLANs configured for MLS
- The ID of each VLAN configured for this MAC address
- The number of MLS-SEs to which the router or RSM is connected
- The MAC address of each switch

Each MLSP-RP is identified to the switch by both the MLS ID and the MLS IP address of the route processor. The MLS ID is the MAC address of the route processor. The MLS-RP automatically selects the IP address of one of its interfaces and uses that IP address as its MLS IP address.

The MLS-SE uses the MLS ID as a determining factor for establishing entries in the MLS cache.

This MLS IP address is used in the following situations:

- By the MLS-RP and the MLS-SE when sending MLS statistics to a data collection application
- In the included MLS route processor list on the switch

To verify the MLS configuration for a specific interface, enter the following command in privileged EXEC mode:

```
Router# show mls rp interface interface number
```

The display resulting from this command shows the following information:

- Whether multilayer switching is configured on the interface
- The VTP domain in which the VLAN ID resides
- Whether this interface is configured as the management interface for the MLS-RP

If the interface is not configured for multilayer switching, this **show** command displays a message such as the following:

```
Router# show mls rp ip interface Vlan41
mls not configured on Vlan41
```

Applying Flow Masks

The MLS-SE uses flow mask modes to determine how packets are compared to MLS entries in the MLS cache. The flow mask mode is based on the access lists configured on the MLS router interfaces. The MLS-SE learns of the flow mask through MLSP messages from each MLS-RP for which the MLS-SE is performing Layer 3 switching.

NOTE   Most Cisco documentation explains flow masks as a way to determine how packets are compared to entries in the MLS cache. This is inaccurate. Flow masks are actually used to determine how much information about the packet is placed in the MLS cache. The flow mask is not used to compare packets to existing entries in the MLS cache.

MLS-SE supports only one flow mask for all MLS-RPs that are serviced by the MLS-SE. If the MLS-SE detects different flow masks from different MLS-RPs for which the MLS-SE is performing Layer 3 switching, the MLS-SE changes its flow mask to the most specific flow mask detected. However, if a more-specific flow mask is in effect, a less-specific flow mask is applied.

The MLS-SE supports three flow mask modes:

- Destination-IP
- Source-Destination-IP
- IP-Flow

When the MLS-SE flow mask changes, the entire MLS cache is purged.

NOTE You can set a flow mask on the MLS-SE without applying an access list on the route processor. You do this when you want to cache entries on a specific set of criteria to export flow statistics but you don't want to set an access list on an interface. To set the flow mask on the MLS-SE without setting an access list on a route processor interface, enter the **set mls flow** [*destination* | *destination-source* | **full**] command in privileged mode.

Destination-IP Flow Mask

The default flow mask is the Destination-IP mode. This mode represents the least-specific flow mask. The MLS-SE maintains one MLS entry for each destination IP address. All flows to a given destination IP address use this MLS entry. This mode is used if no access lists are configured on any of the MLS router interfaces.

The following example shows an entry in the MLS cache for an IP flow. Notice that the example has fields for all the Layer 3 and Layer 4 information, as well as the source IP address. However, these fields are either blank or filled with zeros. The destination IP flow indicates that MLS should cache only the information about the destination IP address. When a packet enters the switch, it is compared to the destination IP address in the MLS cache.

```
Destination IP  Source IP  Port    DstPrt SrcPrt  Destination Mac    Vlan  Port
172.16.22.57    0.0.0.0    -       -              00-90-b1-33-70-00  45    2/9
```

Source-Destination-IP Flow Mask

The second type of flow mask is the Source-Destination-IP mode. The MLS-SE maintains one MLS entry for each source and destination IP address pair. All flows between a given source and destination use this MLS entry, regardless of the IP protocol ports. This mode is used if there is a standard access list on any of the MLS interfaces.

The following example shows an MLS cache entry for a source-destination IP flow. The only change is the addition of the source address in the MLS cache entry. When the switch checks the MLS cache to see if it has an entry that matches the packet, it looks only at the destination address for the match. The source address is not used in the comparison, even though it is listed in the MLS cache entry.

```
Destination IP  Source IP     Port  DstPrt  SrcPrt  Destination Mac     Vlan  Port
172.16.22.57    172.16.10.123 -     -       -       00-90-b1-33-70-00   45    2/9
```

IP-Flow Mask

The final flow mask is the IP-Flow mode. This mode represents the most specific flow mask. The MLS-SE creates and maintains a separate MLS cache entry for every IP flow. An IP-Flow entry includes the source IP address, destination IP address, protocol, and protocol ports. This mode is used if there is an extended access list on any MLS interface.

The following example shows an MLS cache entry when an IP flow mask has been applied. An IP flow mask indicates that the cache entry should contain all Layer 4 information, including protocol type as well as source and destination port number. This is in addition to the destination and source IP addresses. When the switch checks the MLS cache to see if it has an entry that matches the packet, it looks only at the destination address for the match. It does not compare the packet against the source IP address, the protocol type, or the source and destination ports.

```
Destination IP  Source IP     Port  DstPrt  SrcPrt  Destination Mac     Vlan  Port
172.16.22.57    172.16.10.123 UDP   1238    60224   00-90-b1-33-70-00   45    2/9
```

Output Access Lists and Flow Masks

In Figure 6-7, a flow is established between Hosts A and B, and packets in that flow are switched by the MLS-SE.

If an extended access list is applied to the router interface, the MLS-RP tells the MLS-SE to purge all cache entries in order to enforce the access list. Subsequent entries are relearned by being sent first to the route processor as candidate packets and then being cached in the MLS cache when they return from the route processor. If the packet is denied by the access list, it never makes it back to the switch as an enable packet and therefore is never cached. The extended access list indicates that the MLS cache should be maintained with an IP flow mask. This means that the cache should contain all of the Layer 3 and Layer 4 information.

Figure 6-7 *New Packets in the Flow Are Placed in the MLS Cache Only After They Pass the Access List*

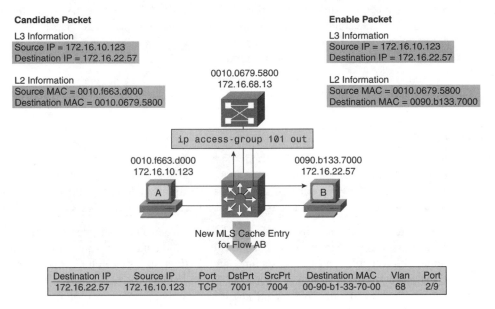

NOTE   The security implemented here works only for the first packet; it doesn't work for all subsequent packets. The following is an example of exactly how the flow cache works.

An extended IP access list is applied to the router interface. It allows ICMP from Workstation A to Workstation B but denies everything else:

```
Access-list 101 permit icmp host 172.16.10.123 host 172.16.22.57 eq echo
Access-list 101 permit icmp host 172.16.10.123 host 172.16.22.57 eq echo-reply
Access-list 101 deny any any
```

Workstation A talks to Workstation B for the first time by issuing the command **ping 172.16.22.57**. The MLS-SE sends the packet to the MLS-RP because there is currently no entry in the MLS cache for the destination address. The MLS-RP routes the packet to the correct subnet and checks it against access list 101. The packet is an ICMP echo, so it is permitted by the access list. The packet goes back to the MLS-SE, where the entry is completed inside the MLS cache:

```
Destination IP Source IP      Port DstPrt SrcPrt Destination Mac    Vlan Port
172.16.22.57   172.16.10.123 ICMP 7001    7004   00-90-b1-33-70-00 68   2/9
```

Now Workstation A attempts to open an FTP session with Workstation B. Workstation A sends the packet to the MLS-SE, which checks the MLS cache to see if there is a matching flow. The MLS-SE checks only the destination IP address. There is an entry in the cache for the destination IP address of 172.16.22.57. Based on this information, the MLS-SE immediately switches the packet to the destination port of 2/9. It also adds another entry to the MLS cache because the complete information of this packet is different than the information that was contained inside the cache. The MLS cache entry now looks like this:

```
Destination IP Source IP       Port DstPrt SrcPrt Destination Mac   Vlan Port
172.16.22.57   172.16.10.123   ICMP 7001    7004  00-90-b1-33-70-00  68  2/9
172.16.22.57   172.16.10.123   TCP  23       1180  00-90-b1-33-70-00  68  2/9
```

The MLS-SE switches a packet by comparing its destination address to what it has in cache. After it has determined that it knows the destination, it switches the packet without ever sending the packet to the MLS-RP.

This example shows that there could be a potential security hole with the use of access lists and MLS. The information that is cached for MLS is useful for determining traffic patterns and accounting. It is not, however, used to compare packets all the way through the Layer 4 information to ensure security. Cisco has solved this security problem in the Catalyst 6000/6500 Series switch with the creation of the Policy Feature Card (PFC). The PFC allows for the creation of the VLAN access control lists (VACLs) that determine if the switch should permit or deny a Layer 3 packet or a Layer 2 frame. You will find more information on access control ist usage on the Catalyst 6000 Series switch at the following URL: http://www.cisco.com/univercd/cc/td/doc/product/lan/cat6000/sw_5_3/msfc/acc_list.htm

New entries are placed in the MLS cache after the initial packet in the flow passes the test conditions in the output access control list (ACL).

NOTE   Using options such as **log**, **reflexive**, and **established** forces the router to examine every packet before routing. Under MLS, the router does not examine every packet; therefore, these options are not allowed.

Input Access Lists and Flow Masks

As with output access lists, placing an input access list on an MLS-enabled interface purges the MLS cache of all existing flows for that interface.

However, because the default behavior for the input access list is to examine and route all incoming packets, all subsequent packets in the flow between Hosts A and B are routed.

NOTE   Most input access lists can be implemented as output access lists to achieve the same effect.

Routers configured with Cisco IOS Release 11.3 or later do not automatically support input access lists on an interface configured for MLS. If an interface is configured with an input access list, all packets for a flow that are destined for that interface go through the router. Even if the router allows that flow, the flow is not Layer 3 switched.

To enable multilayer switching to cooperate with input access lists, enter the following command in global configuration mode:

```
Router(config)#mls rp ip input-acl
```

Example 6-5 shows that input ACLs on the MLS-RP are configured to work in a multilayer switching environment.

Example 6-5   *Input ACL MLS Configuration*

```
Router# show running-config
Building configuration...

Current configuration:
!
version 11.3
(text deleted)
mls rp ip input-acl
mls rp ip
```

To remove support for input access lists in a multilayer switching environment, enter the **no mls rp ip input-acl** command in global configuration mode.

Configuring the Multilayer Switch Switching Engine

MLS is enabled by default on Catalyst series switches that support Layer 3 switching. If the MLS-RP is the RSM, no configuration is needed for the switch. Configuring the switch is necessary when the following are true:

- The MLS-RP is an external router.
- The aging time for MLS cache entries is something other than the default.

Enabling MLS on the Switch

If a switch has been disabled for Layer 3 switching, enter the following command in privileged EXEC mode on the switch:

```
Switch(enable)#set mls enable
```

The following example shows that the MLS-SE is configured to support multilayer switching:

```
Switch(enable)#show config
(text deleted)
#mls
set mls enable
```

Enter the **set mls disable** command to disable MLS on the MLS-SE. This command stops the MLS-SE from processing the MLSP messages from the MLS-RP and purges all existing MLS cache entries in the switch.

Aging Out Cache Entries on the Switch

Because the MLS cache has a size limitation, MLS entries are deleted from the cache if certain conditions are met. This deletion (or aging) process happens for the following reasons:

- Candidate entries remain in the cache for 5 seconds with no enabled entry before timing out. A candidate entry with no corresponding enable entry means that the packet did not make it through the router. This could be because the destination was unknown or because an access list denying the packet was applied to the router.

- An MLS entry is deleted from the cache if a flow for that entry has not been detected for the specified aging time. The default aging time is 256 seconds.

Other events, such as applying access lists, routing changes, or disabling MLS on the switch, can cause MLS entries to be purged.

Managing Short-Lived Flows

The amount of time an MLS entry remains in the cache can be modified by the user. To alter the value of the aging time, enter the following command in privileged EXEC mode:

```
Switch(enable)#set mls agingtime agingtime
```

agingtime is the amount of time an entry remains in the cache before it is deleted. The range of the aging time value is from 8 to 2032 seconds. The default value is 256 seconds.

The following running configuration example shows that entries in which no packets have been detected for a period of 5 minutes will be deleted from the cache:

```
Switch(enable)show config
(text deleted)
#mls
set mls enable
set mls agingtime 304
```

NOTE   *agingtime* values are entered in 8-second increments. Any *agingtime* value that is not a multiple of 8 is adjusted to the closest multiple of 8. This means that a time interval of 300 seconds, or 5 minutes, would automatically be adjusted to 304.

Some MLS flows are sporadic or short-lived. An example of a sporadic or short-lived flow is packets that are sent to or received from a Domain Name System (DNS) or Trivial File Transfer Protocol (TFTP) server. Because the connection may be closed after one request and one reply cycle, that MLS entry in the cache is used only once. However, that MLS entry still consumes valuable cache space until the entry is aged out. Detecting and aging out these entries quickly can save MLS entry space for real data traffic.

To solve the problem of short-lived entries in the cache, a different type of aging mechanism, called fast aging, is available. This type of aging states that if the MLS-SE does not detect a specified number of packets in a certain time period, that entry is removed from the cache.

To configure the fast aging option, enter the following command in privileged EXEC mode:

```
Switch(enable)# set mls agingtime fast fastagingtime pkt_threshold
```

fastagingtime indicates the amount of time an entry remains in the cache before it is deleted. Allowable configuration values are 32, 64, 96, and 128 seconds. The default is 0 seconds.

pkt_threshold indicates the number of packets that must be detected within the specified amount of time. Allowable configuration values are 0, 1, 3, 7, 15, 31, and 63 packets. The default is 0 packets.

Example 6-6 shows that entries in which no more than seven packets have been detected for a period of 64 seconds will be deleted from the cache.

Example 6-6 *Example of Timer Configuration*

```
Switch (enable)show config
(text deleted)
#mls
set mls enable
set mls agingtime 304
set mls agingtime fast 64 7
```

Adding External Router MLS IDs

If the switch supports an externally attached MLS-RP, it must be manually configured to recognize that MLS-RP. To manually include an external MLS-RP, enter the following command in privileged EXEC mode on the switch:

```
Switch (enable) set mls include ip-addr
```

ip-addr is the MLS IP address of the external router. To determine the IP address of the MLS-RP, enter the **show mls rp** command on the MLS-RP.

NOTE Use this command *only* for external routers. The MLS-SE automatically includes the IP address of coresident RSMs in the switch inclusion list. When the RSM is physically removed from the switch chassis or MLS is disabled on an RSM, the RSM IP address is removed from the inclusion list. The auto-included RSM cannot be cleared using the **clear mls include** command.

Example 6-7 shows that an external MLS-RP with the IP address of 172.16.41.168 has been added to the MLS include list.

Example 6-7   *Including an External Router*

```
Switch (enable)show config
(text deleted)
#mls
set mls enable
set mls agingtime 256
set mls agingtime fast 0 0
set mls include 172.16.41.168
```

To remove the MLS-RP from the switch inclusion list, enter the **clear mls include** command. A single MLS-RP can be removed by entering the IP address of a specific MLS-RP. All externally connected MLS-RPs can be removed from the switch inclusion list by entering the **clear mls include all** command.

To display the contents of the switch inclusion list, enter the following command in privileged EXEC mode:

```
Switch (enable) show mls include
```

The resulting display returns the IP addresses of all MLS-RPs that are participating in multilayer switching with the MLS-SE.

If the IP address of an MLS-RP does not appear in the switch inclusion list, the MLS-SE will not Layer 3 switch for the MLS-RP. If the MLS-SE is supposed to be Layer 3 switching for a specific router and its IP address is not listed in the inclusion list, check the following:

- If the router for which you manually entered the MLS IP address is external.
- If the router is an RSM, an RSM must be resident and functional.
- Multilayer switching is globally enabled on the MLS-RP.

Verifying the Configuration

To display information about multilayer switching on an MLS-SE, enter the following command in privileged EXEC mode:

```
Switch (enable) show mls
```

The display resulting from this command returns the information shown in Example 6-8.

Example 6-8 *The Output of the **show mls** Command*

```
Switch (enable) show mls

Multilayer switching enabled
Multilayer switching aging time = 304 seconds
Multilayer switching fast aging time = 64 seconds, packet threshold = 7
Full flow
Total packets switched = 101892
Active shortcuts = 2138
Netflow Data Export disabled
Netflow Data Export port/host is not configured.
Total packets exported = 0

MLS-RP IP        MLS-RP ID     XTAG     MLS-RP MAC-Vlans
---------        ----------    ----     ------------------------
172.16.41.168    0010f6b3d000  28       00-10-f6-b3-d0-00  1,41-42
```

The **show mls** command gives you the following information:

- Whether multilayer switching is enabled on the switch.
- The aging time, in seconds, for an MLS cache entry.
- The fast aging time, in seconds, and the packet threshold for a flow.
- The flow mask.
- Total packets switched.
- The number of active MLS entries in the cache.
- Whether NetFlow data export is enabled and, if so, for which port and host.
- The MLS-RP IP address, MAC address, XTAG, and supported VLANs.
- To display information about a specific MLS-RP, enter the **show mls rp** command and designate the IP address of the target MLS-RP.

NOTE   Do not confuse the **show mls rp** command for the MLS-SE with the **show mls rp** command entered on the MLS-RP. The MLS-SE command requires a specific MLS-RP IP address and displays information used by the switch with regard to Layer 3 switching packets destined for this MLS-RP.

To display the MLS cache entries, enter the following command in privileged EXEC mode:

```
Switch (enable) show mls entry
```

In Example 6-9, the result of the command displays MLS cache entries using a full flow mask.

Example 6-9 *MLS Cache with IP Flow Mask*

```
Switch (enable) show mls entry

Destination IP  Source IP       Prot DstPrt SrcPrt Destination Mac    Vlan Port
--------------- --------------- ---- ------ ------ ----------------- ---- -----
MLS-RP 172.16.1.142:
172.16.53.1     172.16.87.3     UDP  1238   60224  00-10-7b-ee-94-70 1    2/9
172.16.53.1     172.16.87.3     UDP  69     60224  00-10-7b-ee-94-70 1    2/9
172.16.53.1     172.16.87.3     UDP  69     36776  00-10-7b-ee-94-70 1    2/9

MLS-RP 172.16.41.168:
172.16.41.17    172.16.53.1     UDP  60224  1238   00-00-0c-06-5b-1e 41   2/1
172.16.41.17    172.16.53.1     UDP  36776  69     00-00-0c-06-5b-1e 41   2/1
```

This command can be further defined to show MLS cache entries for the following parameters:

- **show mls entry destination** *ip-address*—For a specific destination IP address
- **show mls entry source** *ip-address*—For a specific source IP address
- **show mls entry rp** *ip-address*—For a specific MLS_RP ID
- **show mls entry flow** *protocol source-port destination-port*—For a specific IP flow

To remove entries from the MLS cache, enter the **clear mls entry** command in privileged EXEC mode. Example 6-10 shows that all entries to a destination of 172.16.1.142 begin cleared from the MLS cache.

Example 6-10 *Clear a Specific MLS Entry*

```
Switch (enable) clear mls entry destination 172.16.1.142

Switch (enable) show mls entry
Destination IP  Source IP       Prot DstPrt SrcPrt Destination Mac    Vlan Port
--------------- --------------- ---- ------ ------ ----------------- ---- -----
MLS-RP 172.16.41.168:
172.16.41.17    172.16.53.1     UDP  60224  1238   00-00-0c-06-5b-1e 41   2/1
172.16.41.17    172.16.53.1     UDP  36776  69     00-00-0c-06-5b-1e 41   2/1
```

MLS cache entries can be removed using the following commands:

- **clear mls entry source** *ip-address*—Removes all entries from a specific source IP address

- **clear mls entry destination** *ip-address*—Removes all entries to a specific destination IP address

- **clear mls entry flow** *protocol src-port dst-port*—Removes all entries in a specific flow

Refer to the "Configuring Multilayer Switching" section of the *Catalyst Series Switch Configuration Guide (4.3)* for details on how to format this command for each of these instances.

MLS Topology Examples

There is a dependency between the router and the switch at the distribution layer. How these devices are placed in relationship to each other is critical to multilayer switching. This section discusses the various configurations that participate in multilayer switching. This section also describes several configurations that don't allow MLS.

Topology Example

Figure 6-8 illustrates multilayer switching in a configuration that contains external routers and a hierarchy of MLS-SEs. Both Host A and Host B are connected through MLS-SE1.

Figure 6-8 *Multilayer Switching Can Be Configured Through a Hierarchy of Switches*

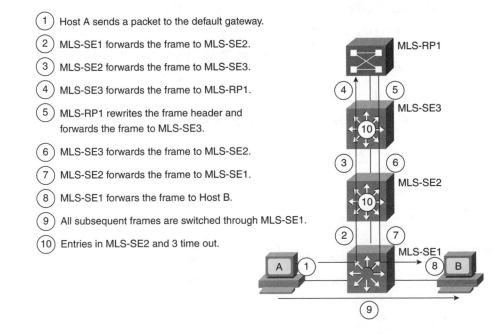

1. Host A sends a packet to the default gateway.
2. MLS-SE1 forwards the frame to MLS-SE2.
3. MLS-SE2 forwards the frame to MLS-SE3.
4. MLS-SE3 forwards the frame to MLS-RP1.
5. MLS-RP1 rewrites the frame header and forwards the frame to MLS-SE3.
6. MLS-SE3 forwards the frame to MLS-SE2.
7. MLS-SE2 forwards the frame to MLS-SE1.
8. MLS-SE1 forwars the frame to Host B.
9. All subsequent frames are switched through MLS-SE1.
10. Entries in MLS-SE2 and 3 time out.

Figure 6-8 summarizes the following sequence:

Step 1   To communicate with Host B, Host A addresses the frame to the default gateway MLS-RP.

Step 2   MLS-SE1 recognizes this frame as a candidate packet, and a partial entry is created in the MLS cache of MLS-SE1.

Step 3   The frame is then sent to MLS-SE2. MLS-SE2 recognizes this frame as a candidate packet, and a partial entry is created in the MLS cache of MLS-SE2.

Step 4   This process is repeated for MLS-SE3.

Step 5   MLS-SE3 sends the frame to the MLS-RP, which rewrites the destination and source MAC addresses in the frame and sends the frame back to MLS-SE3. The frame now meets the criteria of an enabling packet, and the MLS entry is completed in the cache.

Step 6   This process is repeated in MLS-SE2.

Step 7   This process is repeated in MLS-SE1.

Step 8   MLS-SE1 forwards the frame to Host B.

Step 9   A Layer 3 entry switch for the flow between Host A and Host B is established in all three switches. When subsequent packets in this flow come to MLS-SE1, a match is found in the MLS cache and forwarded to Host B.

Step 10 MLS-SE2 and MLS-SE3 never receive subsequent frames in this flow, and the entries in those MLS caches age out.

Topology Changes and Routing Impacts

Routing is an integral part of MLS; however, routing is still the responsibility of the MLS-RP. When Layer 3 switching is enabled, the MLS-RP still runs all the routing protocols and maintains a real-time routing table. Changes to the routing table might affect the behavior of MLS.

Changes that occur to the routing table, such as route modifications or the application of access lists, result in a notification from the router to the switch to purge the affected entries.

Modifications to the switch, such as moving a device from one port to another, result in the purge of entries destined for that port.

Topology Quiz

Figure 6-9 illustrates MLS in a configuration where multiple Layer 2 paths exist between the source and destination devices. It also shows how Spanning Tree operates with this configuration.

Figure 6-9   *Consider the Layer 2 Path That Will Be Taken in This Multilayer Switched Network*

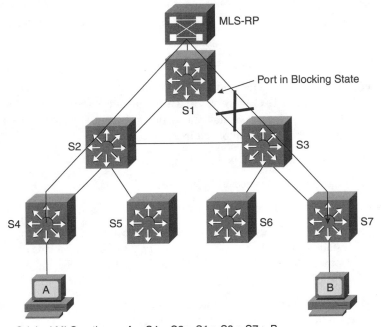

- Original MLS path was A→S4→S2→S1→S3→S7→ B.
- Spanning Tree blocked the link between S1 and S3.

As in the previous examples, communication is between Host A and Host B. From a Spanning-Tree perspective, the link between switches S2 and S3 is in blocking mode.

Study Figure 6-9 and answer the following questions:

1 What path will the flow between Host A and Host B now take?

2 Which switches will cache candidate packets?

3 Which switches will cache enable packets?

Figure 6-10 shows the path that traffic from Host A to Host B will have to take. A candidate packet will be sent from S4 to S2 to S1. Each switch moves the packet in the direction of the MLS-RP. The MLS-RP sends the packet back out to S1, which directs it to S2. S1 and S2 complete the MLS cache entry because they received the enable packet from the MLS-RP. S4 never receives the enable packet, so it drops the entry from cache in five seconds.

Figure 6-10 *Quiz Answer—Packets from A to B in This Multilayer Switched Network Take a Less-Than-Optimal Route*

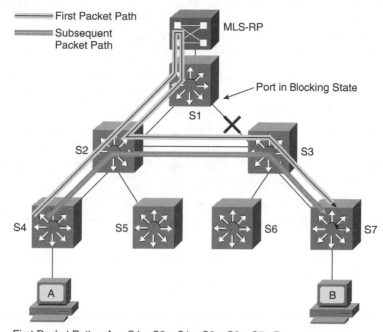

First Packet Path = A → S4 → S2 → S1 → S2 → S3 → S7 → B
Subsequent Packet Path = A → S4 → S2 → S3 → S7 → B

Other Layer 3 Switching Technologies

Multilayer switching is merely one of the new Layer 2/Layer 3 switching techniques being implemented by Cisco in order to make the Layer 3 routing process occur at close to wire speeds. At the time this book was published, these were the three most prevalent techniques for providing Layer 3 switching:

- Multilayer switching
- Cisco Express Forwarding
- Tag switching

Multilayer switching is covered in this book. Cisco Express Forwarding is covered in Appendix B, "Switching Architectures and Functional Descriptions." Tag switching is a predominantly ATM switching technique and therefore is not covered as part of this book or the BCMSN course. A search on CCO under "tag switching" will reveal a wealth of information on this switching technique.

Summary

Multilayer switching is a technique used to increase IP routing performance by handling the packet switching and rewrite function in ASICs. The Cisco multilayer switching implementation consists of a Multilayer Switching Switch Engine, a Multilayer Switching Route Processor, and a Multilayer Switching Protocol.

The MLS-RP uses multicast Layer 3 hello messages to inform the MLS-SE of the MAC addresses that are participating in MLS, access list information, and routing table updates and changes.

The MLS-SE maintains a cache for MLS flows and stores statistics for each flow. MLS-SE distinguishes the MAC address entries of each MLS-RP by assigning an XTAG value to these addresses. To create an MLS cache entry, the MLS-SE must detect both the candidate and enable packet for a specific flow.

The MLS-SE uses flow mask modes to determine how MLS entries are created in the MLS cache. MLS-SE supports only one flow mask for all MLS-RPs that are serviced by the MLS-SE.

Access lists affect how MLS cache entries are created and maintained.

MLS is enabled by default on the Catalyst series switches that support Layer 3 switching.

When Layer 3 switching is enabled, the MLS-RP still runs all the routing protocols and maintains a real-time routing table. Changes to the routing table might affect the behavior of MLS.

Review Questions

The following questions test your retention of the material presented in this chapter. The answers to the Review Questions can be found in Appendix A, "Answers to Review Questions."

1 Explain how the routing and switching functions of a Cisco MLS switch work together to enable multilayer switching.

2 Describe the three flow mask modes and the impact that ACLs have on those modes.

3 Discuss how various router/switch configurations can affect multilayer switching.

Case Study: Improving IP Routing Performance with Multilayer Switching

Work though the case study to practice what you learned in this chapter.

Scenario

In this case study, you will configure the MLS-RP and the MLS-SE for multilayer switching. You will also apply an access list in order to track data flow through the Catalyst switch.

When you have completed the job, routed IP data flow to or from an end user in the switch block must be Layer 3 switched. Evidence of the flows must be recorded in the MLS cache of the appropriate Catalyst 5505 switch.

Figure 6-11 represents the actions you will take in this case study.

Figure 6-11 *Case Study Visual Objective*

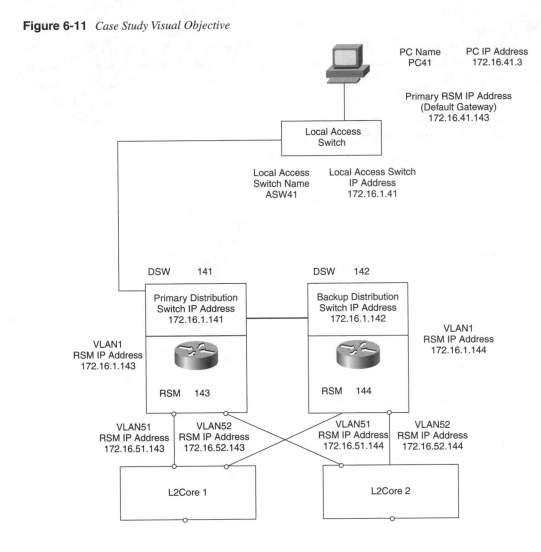

Command List

In this case study, you will use the commands listed in Tables 6-1 and 6-2. Refer to these tables if you need configuration command assistance during the case study.

Table 6-1   *Distribution Router Commands*

Command	Description
access-list *access-list-number*	Creates an access list.
ip access-group *access-list-number*	Assigns an access list to an interface.
mls rp input-acl	Supports the creation of MLS flow entries from interfaces with input ACLs.
mls rp ip	Enables multilayer switching on an MLS-RP and on a specific interface.
mls rp management-interface	Establishes a management interface through which MLSP messages are sent.
mls rp vtp-domain *vtp-domain-name*	Assigns an interface to a VTP domain.
show mls rp	Displays the MLS configuration on the MLS-RP.
show run	Displays the current configuration on the router.
Ctrl-Shift-6-x	Escape sequence.

Table 6-2   *Distribution Switch Commands*

Command	Description
access-list *access-list-number*	Creates an access list.
ip access-group *access-list-number*	Assigns an access list to an interface.
mls rp input-acl	Supports the creation of MLS flow entries from interfaces with input ACLs.
mls rp ip	Enables multilayer switching on an MLS-RP and on a specific interface.
mls rp management-interface	Establishes a management interface through which MLSP messages are sent.
mls rp vtp-domain *vtp-domain-name*	Assigns an interface to a VTP domain.
set mls agingtime *seconds*	Alters the time in which MLS entries are maintained in the MLS cache.
set mls enable	Enables multilayer switching on the MLS-SE.
show mls	Displays the MLS configuration on the MLS-SE.
show mls include	Displays the switch MLS-RP inclusion list.
show mls entry	Displays the MLS cache.

continues

Table 6-2   *Distribution Switch Commands (Continued)*

Command	Description
show mls rp	Displays the MLS configuration on the MLS-RP.
show run	Displays the current configuration on the router.

Task 1: Configure the Distribution Layer Route Processor to Participate in Multilayer Switching

In this task, you will configure the RSM residing in the distribution switch to participate as an MLS-RP in multilayer switching. At the end of this task, you will verify your configuration. In order to complete the configuration, follow these steps:

Step 1   In global configuration mode, enter the **mls rp ip** command to enable global multilayer switching on the MLS-RP.

Step 2   Enter the **interface vlan VLAN1** command to enter interface configuration mode.

NOTE   Make sure you configure your interface in a VTP domain before you enable MLS on the interface. If you do not, you will create a null domain.

Step 3   In interface configuration mode, enter the **mls rp** *vtp-domain vtp-domain-name* command to assign your interface to the VTP domain.

Step 4   In interface configuration mode, enter the **mls rp ip** command to enable multilayer switching on the VLAN1 interface.

Step 5   In interface configuration mode, enter the **mls rp management-interface** command to set the interface as a management interface.

Step 6   Repeat Steps 1 through 4 for all your VLANs. Do not enter the **mls rp management-interface** command on these interfaces.

Step 7   In privileged EXEC mode on the RSM, enter the **show mls rp** command to display the current MLS configuration for the route processor. Your configuration should resemble the output shown in Example 6-11.

Example 6-11   *show mls rp Command Output*

```
RSM143#show mls rp
multilayer switching is globally enabled
mls id is 0090.b133.7000
mls ip address 172.16.2.143
mls flow mask is destination-ip
```

Example 6-11   *show mls rp Command Output (Continued)*

```
number of domains configured for mls 1

vlan domain name: bcmsn
   current flow mask: destination-ip
   current sequence number: 1852101893
   current/maximum retry count: 0/10
   current domain state: no-change
   current/next global purge: false/false
   current/next purge count: 0/0
   domain uptime: 00:03:14
   keepalive timer expires in 2 seconds
   retry timer not running
   change timer not running

   1 management interface(s) currently defined:
      vlan 1 on Vlan1

   3 mac-vlan(s) configured for multi-layer switching:

      mac 4004.0123.0001
         vlan id(s)
         1

      mac 4004.0123.0051
         vlan id(s)
         51

      mac 4004.0123.0052
         vlan id(s)
         52

   router currently aware of following 1 switch(es):
      switch id 0050.bd18.abff
```

Step 8   Use the **copy run start** command to save your configuration.

You have completed this task if the results of the **show mls rp** command on both your distribution route processors displays the following information:

- You have one domain configured for MLS.

- The VLAN domain name is bcmsn (this name will depend on what you called your VTP domain).

- VLAN1 is configured as the management interface.

- The route processor has three MAC-VLANs configured for MLS.

- The route processor is aware of one switch.

Task 2: Configure the Distribution Layer Switching Engine to Participate in Multilayer Switching

In this task, you will configure the distribution layer switch to participate in MLS. The switch should recognize both of the Route Switch Modules as MLS-RPs that can perform the Layer 3 routing function. Follow these steps:

Step 1 In privileged mode, enter the **show mls** command to display the current multilayer switching configuration for the switching engine. Your configuration should resemble the output shown in Example 6-12.

Example 6-12 *show mls Command Output*

```
DSW141 (enable) show mls
Multilayer switching enabled
Multilayer switching aging time = 256 seconds
Multilayer switching fast aging time = 0 seconds, packet threshold = 0
Current flow mask is Destination flow
Configured flow mask is Destination flow
Total packets switched = 298
Active shortcuts = 2
Netflow Data Export disabled
Netflow Data Export port/host is not configured.
Total packets exported = 0

MLS-RP IP          MLS-RP ID      XTAG MLS-RP MAC-Vlans
----------------   ------------   ---- --------------------------------
172.16.4.143       0090b1337000      3 40-04-01-43-00-01  1
                                       40-04-01-43-00-21  41
                                       40-04-01-43-00-22  42
                                       40-04-01-43-00-23  43
                                       40-04-01-43-00-24  44
                                       40-04-01-43-00-51  51
                                       40-04-01-43-00-52  52

DSW141> (enable)
```

Step 2 In privileged mode, enter the **set mls include** *ip-address* command to add the IP address of the other MLS-RP to the MLS-RP IP list.

Step 3 Wait a few seconds until a console message says that the route processor has been added.

Step 4 In privileged mode, enter the **show mls** command to display the current multilayer switching configuration for the switching engine. Your configuration should now resemble the output shown in Example 6-13.

Example 6-13 *show mls Command Output*

```
DSW141> (enable) show mls
Multilayer switching enabled
Multilayer switching aging time = 256 seconds
Multilayer switching fast aging time = 0 seconds, packet threshold = 0
```

Example 6-13   *show mls Command Output (Continued)*

```
Current flow mask is Destination flow

(text deleted)

MLS-RP IP          MLS-RP ID      XTAG MLS-RP MAC-Vlans
----------------   ------------   ---- --------------------------------
172.16.4.144       0090b1314000     4 40-04-01-44-00-01  1
                                      40-04-01-44-00-21  41
                                      40-04-01-44-00-22  42
                                      40-04-01-44-00-23  43
                                      40-04-01-44-00-24  44
                                      40-04-01-44-00-51  51
                                      40-04-01-44-00-52  52
172.16.4.143       0090b1337000     3 40-04-01-43-00-01  1
                                      40-04-01-43-00-21  41
(text deleted)
```

Step 5   In privileged EXEC mode, enter the **show mls include** command to display the route processor for which your MLS-SE is switching packets. Your configuration should resemble the output shown in Example 6-14. Output can vary, depending on the number of resident RSMs configured for MLS.

Example 6-14   *show mls include and show mls rp Command Output*

```
Included MLS-RP
----------------------
172.16.4.143
172.16.4.144

RSM143#show mls rp
multilayer switching is globally enabled
mls id is 0090.b133.7000
mls ip address 172.16.4.143
mls flow mask is destination-ip
number of domains configured for mls 1

vlan domain name: bcmsn
    current flow mask: destination-ip

(text deleted)

    router currently aware of following 2 switch(es):
        switch id 0050.bd18.abff
        switch id 0050.bd18.afff
```

NOTE	If no switch ID appears in the output, check the VTP domain name for the switch. See if the VTP domain for the switch is the same VTP domain in which the route processor resides. See if MLS is enabled on the switch.

Task 3: Verify MLS Flow Cache

In this task, you will ping across the router in order to verify that MLS creates an entry in cache for this Layer 3 destination. Follow these steps:

Step 1   From your PC desktop, open an MS-DOS window.

Step 2   At the DOS prompt, enter the **ping** *ip address* **-n 100** command, where *ip address* is the IP address of a device on a different subnet.

Display an MLS Cache Entry for the Flow Just Created

Follow these steps:

Step 1   Connect to your primary distribution switch.

Step 2   In privileged EXEC mode, enter the **show mls entry** command to display the MLS cache. Your display should resemble the output shown in Example 6-15. Output can vary, depending on the number of flow entries in the cache.

Example 6-15   *show mls entry Command Output*

```
DSW141> (enable) show mls entry
                Last Used      Last    Used
Destination IP  Source IP      Prot DstPrt SrcPrt Destination Mac   Vlan Port
--------------- --------------- ---- ------ ------ ----------------- ---- -----
MLS-RP 172.16.4.143:

172.16.44.3     0.0.0.0        -      -      -     00-10-83-00-ed-45 24   2/9-12
172.16.41.3     0.0.0.0        -      -      -     00-10-7b-e1-2a-01 21   2/1
172.16.42.3     0.0.0.0        -      -      -     00-60-b0-fb-ed-02 22   2/9-12
172.16.4.121    0.0.0.0        -      -      -     00-50-bd-18-ab-ff 1    1/9
```

If no access list is applied, you should see only the source address cached in the flow. You might want to apply different access lists to your interfaces and watch the flow change. A standard access list adds the source IP address to the flow cache. An extended access list adds all the Layer 4 information.

You have completed this task if the MLS cache on your distribution switch displays an entry for the flow between your PC and your assigned target end-user device.

CHAPTER 7

Configuring HSRP for Fault-Tolerant Routing

As more and more organizations seek the economic benefits of campus networks for mission-critical communications, high reliability becomes increasingly crucial. Within the campus network, attention has been focused on providing a network infrastructure that is available 24 hours a day, seven days a week. However, one of the greatest challenges comes not from the network infrastructure, but from the workstations and network equipment at the user level.

This chapter focuses on a solution from Cisco called Hot Standby Routing Protocol (HSRP). It allows network administrators to create a virtual default gateway address and assign it to redundant routers on a LAN segment, ensuring fault-tolerant behavior for workstations and network equipment at the user level.

This chapter covers the following topics:

- HSRP overview
- HSRP operations
- Configuring HSRP

Upon completion of this chapter, you will be able to identify the virtual router for a given set of switch block devices, configure HSRP on the switch block devices to ensure continual inter-VLAN routing, maintain graceful packet forwarding by changing the active and standby HSRP router roles, and ensure the role of the active router by assigning a preempt status.

HSRP Overview

The Hot Standby Routing Protocol provides fault tolerance and enhanced routing performance for IP networks. HSRP allows Cisco IOS routers to monitor each other's operational status and very quickly assume packet forwarding responsibility in the event that the current forwarding device in the HSRP group fails or is taken down for maintenance. The standby mechanism remains transparent to the attached hosts and can be deployed on any LAN type. With multiple hot-standby groups, routers can simultaneously provide redundant backup and perform load sharing across different IP subnets.

| NOTE | Additional information on HSRP can be found in RFC 2281. |

The primary purpose of the campus network is to give end users access to their data and applications. End users perceive the campus network as a total system and typically do not care which routers and LAN switches are operational. By building various levels of redundancy into the network, the network designer permits the network, as a total system, to maintain connections and converge around failures.

Routing Issues in a Redundant Network

Workstations or host devices typically send information only to their own subnet or cable segment. They rely on a router to find the best path for their data whenever they need to send to a subnet other than their own. There are several different ways that hosts are told about the router they are supposed to use:

- Default gateways
- Proxy ARP
- Routing protocol

Default Gateways

One of the most common ways of allowing the host to find a subnet is setting a default gateway. The default gateway is used anytime the workstation attempts to send a packet that it determines is not in its own subnet. Most operating systems, such as Windows 95/98, allow only one default gateway to be used. The workstation sends an ARP request to find this router's MAC address, and that MAC address is used anytime the workstation sends data to another device on a different subnet. If the router that is being used as the default gateway fails, the workstation is unable to send packets anywhere else. This is true even if another router on the subnet could be used to make it to the final destination.

The hierarchical campus model builds in redundancy at the switch block level. Primary and secondary paths between the access layer and the distribution switch provide continual access despite a link failure at the access layer. Primary and secondary paths between the distribution router and the core provide continual operations should a link fail at the distribution layer. The network infrastructure might be able to converge quickly, but the host can't.

In Figure 7-1, Router A is responsible for routing packets for Subnet A, and Router B is responsible for handling packets on Subnet B. If Router A becomes unavailable to the PC, fast converging routing protocols can respond within seconds. After convergence, Router B is prepared to transfer packets that would otherwise have gone through Router A.

Figure 7-1   *Default Gateway Example*

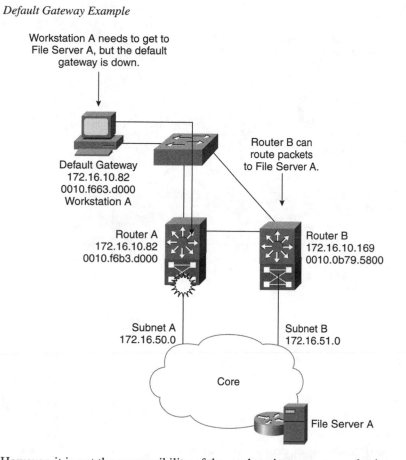

However, it is not the responsibility of the workstation, servers, and printers to exchange dynamic routing information, nor is routing by such devices a good design. These devices typically are configured with a single default gateway IP address. If the router that is the default gateway fails, the device is limited to communicating only on the local IP network segment and is effectively disconnected from the rest of the network. Even if a redundant router exists that could serve as a default gateway, there is no dynamic method that these devices can use to switch to a new default gateway IP address.

Proxy ARP

Figure 7-2 shows that a router can respond to ARP requests in proxy for the destination if its routing table indicates that the subnet is can be reached.

Figure 7-2 *Using Proxy ARP*

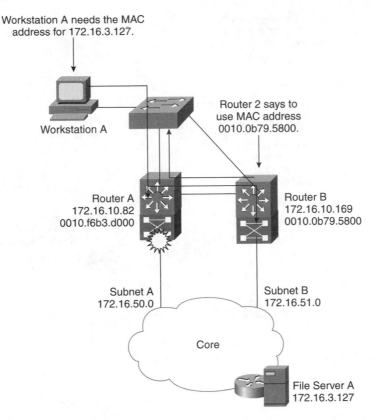

Some IP hosts rely on proxy Address Resolution Protocol (ARP) to select a router. The end-user station would send an ARP request for the IP address to the destination. The responsible router would respond with its own Media Access Control (MAC) address to the ARP request.

NOTE   In order to use proxy ARP in a Windows 95/98 environment, the default gateway must be set to the IP address of the host device.

With proxy ARP, the end-user station behaves as if the destination device were connected to the same segment of the network. The end-user station has an ARP cache showing every remote device with the router's MAC address. If the responsible router fails, the source end station continues to send packets for the destination to that router's MAC address. Those packets subsequently are dropped from the network.

To acquire the MAC address of the failover router, the source end station must either initiate another ARP request or be rebooted. In either case, the source end station cannot communicate with the destination for a significant period of time, even though the routing protocol has converged. The interval during which the source cannot communicate with the destination is calculated by the ARP protocol using the ARP update plus the ARP flush time entry. This means that the PC's ARP cache might not be timed out for hours.

Using RIP at the Host

Some IP hosts use the Routing Information Protocol (RIP) to discover routers. The end-user station maintains a table of which routers have a path to the destination. The end-user station uses the most expedient path.

The drawback of using RIP is that it is slow to adapt to changes in the topology. If the source end station is configured to use RIP, a period of three times the update interval might elapse before RIP makes another router available.

Solution to Routing Issues: Hot Standby Routing Protocol

Cisco routers can use HSRP, which allows end stations to continue communicating throughout the network even when the default gateway becomes unavailable.

With HSRP, a set of routers works together to represent a single virtual standby router. The standby group functions as a single router configured with a virtual IP and MAC address. From the viewpoint of the end system, the virtual router is a single target router with its own IP and MAC address, distinct from the physical routers in the network.

Because the routers in the standby group route packets sent to a virtual address, packets are still routed through the network even when the router originally forwarding the packets fails.

HSRP allows one router to automatically assume the function of another router if that router fails. HSRP is particularly useful when the users on one subnet require continuous access to resources in the network.

HSRP Group Members

The standby group is comprised of the following entities (see Figure 7-3):

- One active router
- One standby router
- One virtual router
- Other routers

Figure 7-3   *HSRP Group Members*

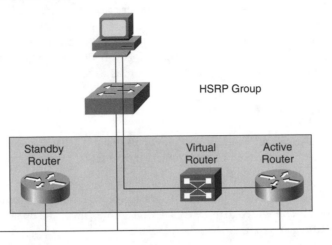

The function of the active router is to forward packets sent to the virtual router. Another router in the group is elected as the standby router. The active router assumes and maintains its active role through the transmission of hello messages.

The function of the standby router is to monitor the operational status of the HSRP group and quickly assume packet-forwarding responsibility if the active router becomes inoperable. The standby router also transmits hello messages to inform all other routers in the group of the standby router role and status.

The function of the virtual router is to present a consistently available router to the end user. The virtual router is assigned its own IP and MAC address, but it does not forward packets.

An HSRP standby group may contain other routers. These routers monitor the hello messages but do not respond. These routers forward any packets addressed to their IP addresses but do not forward packets that are addressed for the virtual router.

When the active router fails, the other HSRP routers stop receiving hello messages, and the standby router assumes the role of the active router.

Because the new active router assumes both the IP and MAC addresses of the virtual router, the end stations see little disruption in service. The end-user stations continue to send packets to the virtual router MAC address, and the new active router delivers the packets to the destination.

In the event that both the active and standby routers fail, all routers in the group contend for the active and standby router roles. By default, the lowest MAC address becomes the active router.

To facilitate load sharing, a single router can be a member of multiple HSRP standby groups on a single segment. Each standby group emulates a single virtual router.

NOTE	Increasing the number of groups in which a router participates increases the load on the router and can affect the router's performance. There can be up to 255 standby groups on any LAN.

In Figure 7-4, both Router A and Router B are members of Groups 1 and 2. However, Router A is the active forwarding router for Group 1 and the standby router for Group 2. Router B is the active forwarding router for Group 2 and the standby router for Group 1.

Figure 7-4 *Routers Can Be Members of Multiple HSRP Groups*

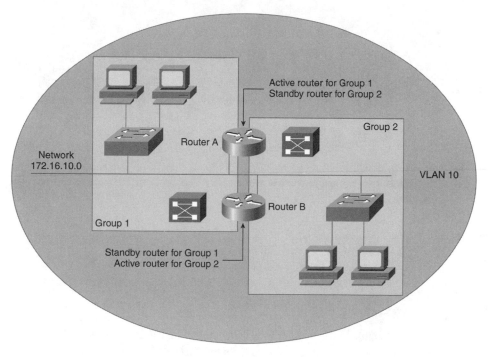

Routers can simultaneously provide redundant backup and perform load sharing across different IP subnets, as shown in Figure 7-5.

For each standby group, an IP address and a single well-known MAC address with a unique group identifier are allocated to the group.

The IP address of a group is in the range of addresses belonging to the subnet in use on the LAN. However, the IP address of the group must differ from the addresses allocated as interface addresses on all routers and hosts on the LAN, including virtual IP addresses assigned to other HSRP groups.

Figure 7-5 *Routers Can Perform Both Active and Standby Roles for Different Standby Groups*

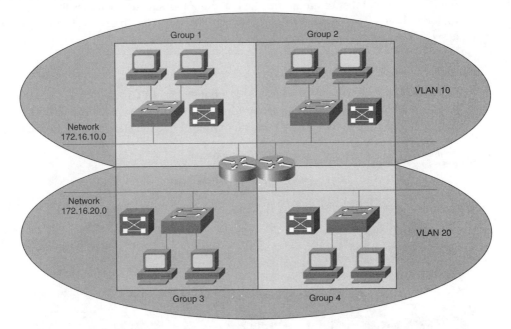

Although multiple routers can exist in an HSRP group, only the active router forwards the packets sent to the virtual router.

NOTE   A separate HSRP group is configured for each VLAN subnet.

HSRP Operations

Within the standby group, one router is elected to be the active router. The active router forwards the packets sent to the virtual router. The router with the highest standby priority in the group becomes the active router. The default priority for an HSRP router is 100. This is a user-configurable option.

The active router responds to traffic for the virtual router. If an end station sends a packet to the virtual router MAC address, the active router receives and processes that packet. If an end station sends an ARP request with the virtual router IP address, the active router replies with the virtual router MAC address.

In Figure 7-6, Router A has a priority of 200, and Router B has a default priority of 100. Router A assumes the active router role and forwards all frames addressed to the well-known HSRP MAC address.

Figure 7-6   *The Router with the Highest HSRP Priority Becomes the Active Router*

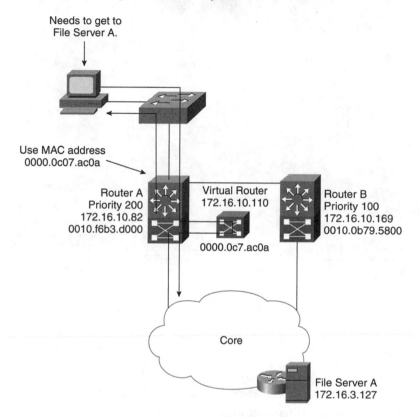

Locating the Virtual Router MAC Address

ARP establishes correspondences between network addresses, such as between an IP address and a hardware Ethernet address. Each router maintains a table of resolved addresses. The router checks this ARP cache before attempting to contact a device to determine if the address has already been resolved. The IP address and corresponding MAC address of the virtual router are maintained in the ARP table of each router in an HSRP standby group. Figure 7-7 shows the ARP cache and MAC address used by the virtual router.

Figure 7-7 *The MAC Address Is a Combination of Vendor Code, HSRP Code, and Group Number*

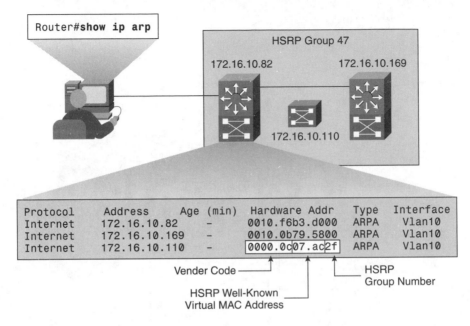

The MAC address used by the virtual router is made up of three components, as shown in Figure 7-7:

- **Vendor ID (Vendor code)**—The vendor ID is the first three bytes of the MAC address. In this case, the vendor ID of 0000.0c indicates that this is a Cisco device.

- **HSRP code (HSRP well-known virtual MAC address)**—The fact that the MAC address is for an HSRP virtual router is indicated in the next two bytes of the address. The HSRP code is always 07.ac.

- **Group ID (HSRP group number)**—The last byte of the MAC address is the group's identification number. For example, the group 47 would be translated to 2f in hexadecimal and would make up the last byte of the address.

The complete MAC address of the virtual router is therefore 00.00.0c.07.ac.2f.

To display the ARP cache on a router in order to view the MAC address being used, enter the following command in privileged EXEC mode:

```
Router# show ip arp
```

The resulting output from this command displays the information listed in Table 7-1.

Table 7-1   *Information Contained in the ARP Cache*

Field	Description
Protocol	Protocol for the network address in the Address field
Address	The network address that corresponds to Hardware Addr
Age (min)	Age, in minutes, of the cache entry
Hardware Addr	MAC address that corresponds to the network address
Type	Type of encapsulation: ARPA (Ethernet), SNAP (RFC 1042), or SAP (IEEE 802.3)
Interface	Interface to which this address mapping has been assigned

In Figure 7-7, the output displays an ARP cache for a Route Switch Module (RSM) that is a member of HSRP standby group 47 in VLAN10. The virtual router for VLAN10 is identified as 172.16.10.110. The well-known MAC address that corresponds to this IP address is 0000.0c07.ac2f, where 2f is the HSRP group identifier for standby group 47.

HSRP Messages

All routers in a standby group send and/or receive HSRP messages. These messages are used to determine and maintain the router roles within the group. HSRP messages are encapsulated in the data portion of User Datagram Protocol (UDP) packets, and they use port number 1985. These packets are addressed to an all-router multicast address of 224.0.0.2 with a Time-To-Live (TTL) of 1. Figure 7-8 shows the format of the HSRP message.

Figure 7-8   *HSRP Message Format*

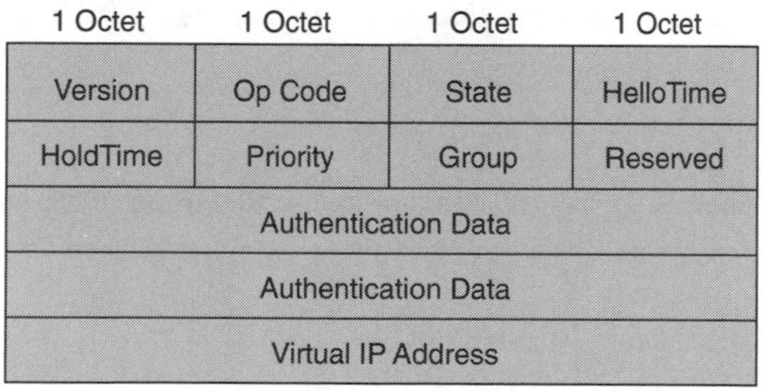

The HSRP message contains the following information (as shown in Figure 7-8):

- The Version field indicates the version of the HSRP.

- The Op Code describes the type of message contained in this packet. Possible values are as follows:

> — **Hello messages**—Sent to indicate that a router is running and is capable of becoming either the active or standby router.
>
> — **Coup messages**—Sent when a router wants to become the active router.
>
> — **Resign messages**—Sent when a router no longer wants to be the active router.

- Internally, each router in the standby group implements a state machine. The State field describes the current state of the router sending the message.

- The HelloTime field is meaningful only in hello messages. This field contains the approximate period between the hello messages that the router sends. The time is given in seconds.

- The HoldTime field is meaningful only in hello messages. This field contains the amount of time that the current hello message should be valid. The time is given in seconds.

- The Priority field is used to elect the active and standby routers. When the priorities of two different routers are compared, the router with the numerically higher priority wins. In the case of routers with equal priority, the router with the higher IP address wins.

- The Group field identifies the standby group. Values 0 through 255, inclusive, are valid.

- The Authentication Data field contains a cleartext eight-character reused password.

- The Virtual IP Address field contains the IP address of the virtual router used by this group.

To minimize traffic, only the active and standby routers send periodic HSRP messages as soon as the protocol has completed the election process. If the active router fails, the standby router takes over as the active router. If the standby router fails or becomes the active router, another router is elected as the standby router.

NOTE   A router uses its IP address as the source address in the periodic hello multicasts. This allows each of the routers to be uniquely identified in the standby group.

HSRP States

HSRP defines six states in which an HSRP configured router can exist. When a router exists in one of these states, it performs the necessary actions required in that state. The HSRP states are as follows:

- Initial state
- Learn state

- Listen state
- Speak state
- Standby state
- Active state

Not all HSRP routers transition through all states. For example, a router that is not the standby or active router does not enter the standby or active states.

Initial State

All routers begin in the initial state. This is the starting state, and it indicates that HSRP is not running. This state is entered via a configuration change or when an interface first comes up.

Learn State

In the learn state, the router is still waiting to hear from the active router. The router has not yet seen a hello message from the active router, nor has it learned the IP address of the virtual router.

Listen State

In the listen state, the router knows the virtual IP address but is neither the active router nor the standby router. The router listens for hello messages from those routers. Routers other than the active and standby router remain in listen state.

Speak State

In the speak state, the router sends periodic hello messages and actively participates in the election of the active and/or standby router. A router cannot enter the speak state unless it has the IP address of the virtual router.

Standby State

In the standby state, the router is a candidate to become the next active router, and it sends periodic hello messages. There must be one, and only one, standby router in the HSRP group.

Active State

In the active state, the router is currently forwarding packets that are sent to the group's virtual MAC address. The active router sends periodic hello messages. There must be one, and only one, active router in the HSRP group.

Configuring HSRP

This section covers the following topics:

- Configuring an interface to participate in an HSRP standby group
- Assigning HSRP standby priority
- Configuring HSRP standby preempt
- Configuring HSRP over trunk links
- Configuring hello message timers
- HSRP interface tracking
- Displaying the status of HSRP

To configure a router as a member of an HSRP standby group, enter the following command in interface configuration mode:

```
Router(config-if)# standby group-number ip virtual-ip-address
```

group-number (optional) indicates the HSRP group to which this interface belongs. Specifying a unique group number in the standby commands enables the creation of multiple HSRP groups. The default group is 0.

virtual-ip-address indicates the IP address of the virtual HSRP router.

NOTE   While running HSRP, it is important that the end-user stations do not discover the actual MAC addresses of the routers in the standby group. Any protocol that informs a host of the router's actual address must be disabled. To ensure that the actual addresses of the participating HSRP routers are not discovered, enabling HSRP on a Cisco router interface automatically disables ICMP redirects on that interface.

After the **standby ip** command is issued, the interface changes to the appropriate state. The following is an example of the state message that is generated. This message is automatically generated upon successful execution of the command:

```
3w1d    : %STANDBY-6-STATECHANGE: Standby: 47: Vlan10 state Speak      -> Standby
3w1d    : %STANDBY-6-STATECHANGE: Standby: 47: Vlan10 state Standby    -> Active
```

Example 7-1 shows that interface VLAN10 is a member of the HSRP standby group 47, the virtual router IP address for that group is 172.16.10.10, and ICMP redirects are disabled.

Example 7-1 *Setting the Virtual IP Address and Standby Group*

```
Router#show running-config
Building configuration...
Current configuration:
!
(text deleted)
interface Vlan10
ip address 172.16.10.82 255.255.255.0
no ip redirects
standby 47 ip 172.16.10.10
!
```

To remove an interface from an HSRP group, enter the **no standby** *group* **ip** command.

Assigning HSRP Standby Priority

Each standby group has its own active and standby routers. The network administrator can assign a priority value to each router in a standby group, allowing the administrator to control the order in which active routers for that group are selected.

To set a router's priority value, enter the following command in interface configuration mode:

```
Router#(config-if) standby group-number priority priority-value
```

group-number indicates the HSRP standby group. This number can be in the range of 0 to 255.

priority-value indicates the number that prioritizes a potential hot standby router. The range is 0 to 255; the default is 100.

The router in an HSRP group with the highest priority becomes the forwarding router.

Example 7-2 shows that interface VLAN10 has a priority value of 150 in HSRP standby group 47. If this priority value is the highest number in that HSRP standby group, the RSM on which this interface resides is the active router for that group.

Example 7-2 *Assigning the Standby Priority*

```
Router#show run
Building configuration...
Current configuration:
!
(text deleted)
interface Vlan10
ip address 172.16.10.10 255.255.255.0
```

continues

Example 7-2 *Assigning the Standby Priority (Continued)*

```
no ip redirects
standby 47 priority 150
standby 47 ip 172.16.10.1
```

To reinstate the default standby priority value, enter the **no standby priority** command.

NOTE   The default standby priority is 100. If the priorities are the same, the router with the highest IP address becomes the active router. IP addresses are learned during the exchange of hello packets as the router uses its interface's IP address as the source of the multicast.

Configuring HSRP Standby Preempt

The standby router automatically assumes the active router role when the active router fails or is removed from service. This new active router remains the forwarding router even when the former active router with the higher priority regains service in the network.

The former active router can be configured to resume the forwarding router role from a router with a lower priority. To make a router resume the forwarding router role, enter the following command in interface configuration mode:

```
Router(config-if)#standby group-number preempt
```

After the **standby preempt** command is issued, the interface changes to the appropriate state. The following is an example of the state message that is generated. This message is automatically generated as soon as the router becomes active in the network:

```
3w1d     : %STANDBY-6-STATECHANGE: Standby: 47: Vlan10 state Standby    -> Active
```

Example 7-3 shows that interface VLAN10 is configured to resume its role as the active router in HSRP group 47, assuming that interface VLAN10 on this router has the highest priority in that standby group.

Example 7-3 *Example of Preempt Configuration*

```
Router#show running-config
Building configuration...
Current configuration:
!
(text deleted)
interface Vlan10
ip address 172.16.10.82 255.255.255.0
no ip redirects
standby 47 priority 150
standby 47 preempt
standby 47 ip 172.16.10.1
```

To remove the interface from preempt status, enter the **no standby** *group* **preempt** command.

Configuring HSRP Over Trunk Links

Figure 7-9 shows the configuration for two HSRP-enabled routers participating in two separate virtual LANs using Inter-Switch Link. Running HSRP over ISL allows users to configure redundancy between multiple routers that are configured as front ends for VLAN IP subnets. By configuring HSRP over ISLs, users can eliminate situations in which a single point of failure causes traffic interruptions. This feature inherently provides some improvement in overall networking resilience by providing load balancing and redundancy capabilities between subnets and VLANs.

Figure 7-9   *HSRP Can Be Configured Between Two Routers Connected Via Trunk Links*

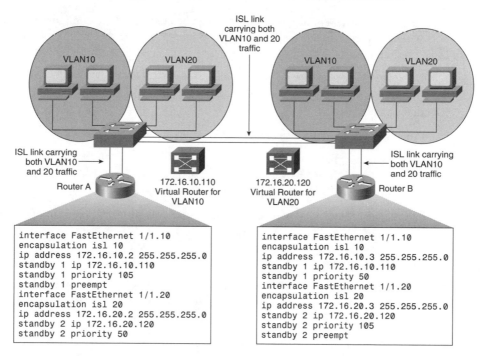

To configure HSRP over an ISL link between VLANs, perform the following tasks:

* Define the encapsulation format
* Define the IP address
* Enable HSRP

The first two steps are discussed in Chapter 5, "Inter-VLAN Routing." You enable HSRP using the exact same steps discussed earlier.

Configuring Hello Message Timers

An HSRP-enabled router sends hello messages to indicate that the router is running and is capable of becoming either the active or standby router. The hello message contains the router's priority, as well as a hellotime and holdtime value. The hellotime value indicates the interval between the hello messages that the router sends. The holdtime value contains the amount of time that the current hello message is considered valid.

If an active router sends a hello message, receiving routers consider that hello message to be valid for one holdtime.

NOTE   The holdtime should be at least three times the value of the hellotime.

Both the hellotime and holdtime parameters can be configured. To configure the time between hellos and the time before other group routers declare the active or standby router to be nonfunctioning, enter the following command in interface configuration mode:

```
Router(config-if)#standby group-number timers hellotime holdtime
```

group-number (optional) is the group number on the interface to which the timers apply. The default is 0.

hellotime is the hello interval in seconds. This is an integer from 1 to 255. The default is 3 seconds.

holdtime is the time, in seconds, before the active or standby router is declared to be down. This is an integer from 1 to 255. The default is 10 seconds.

To reinstate the default standby timer values, enter the **no standby** *group* **timers** command.

HSRP Interface Tracking

In some situations, the status of an interface directly affects which router needs to become the active router. This is particularly true when each of the routers in an HSRP group has a different path to resources within the campus network.

In Figure 7-10, Router A and Router B reside in a branch office. These two routers each support a T1 link to headquarters. Router A has the higher priority and is the active forwarding router for standby group 47. Router B is the standby router for that group. Router A and Router B exchange hello messages through their E0 interfaces.

Figure 7-10 *HSRP Interface Tracking*

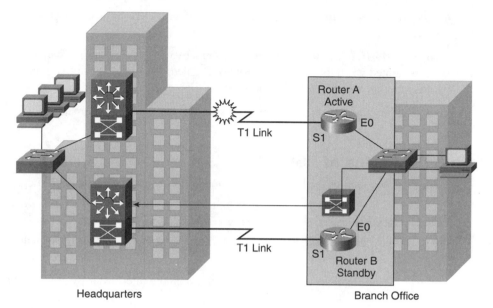

However, the T1 link between the active forwarding router for the standby group and headquarters experiences a failure. Without HSRP enabled, Router A would detect the failed link and send an ICMP redirect to Router B. However, when HSRP is enabled, ICMP redirects are disabled. Therefore, neither Router A nor the virtual router sends an ICMP redirect and, although the S1 interface on Router A is no longer functional, Router A still communicates hello messages out interface E0, indicating that Router A is still the active router. Packets sent to the virtual router for forwarding to headquarters cannot be routed.

Interface tracking lets the priority of a standby group router be automatically adjusted based on the availability of that router's interfaces. When a tracked interface becomes unavailable, the router's HSRP priority is decreased. The HSRP tracking feature reduces the likelihood that a router with an unavailable key interface will remain the active router.

In this campus LAN example, the E0 interface on Router A tracks the S1 interface. If the link between the S1 interface and headquarters fails, the router automatically decrements its priority on that interface and stops transmitting hello messages out interface E0. Router B assumes the active router role when no hello messages are detected for the specific holdtime period.

To configure HSRP tracking, enter the following command in interface configuration mode:

```
Router(config-if)#standby group-number track type number interface-priority
```

group-number (optional) indicates the group number on the interface to which the tracking applies. The default is 0.

type indicates the interface type (combined with the interface number) that will be tracked.

number indicates the interface number (combined with the interface type) that will be tracked.

interface-priority (optional) indicates the amount by which the router's hot standby priority is decremented when the interface becomes disabled. The router's priority is incremented by this amount when the interface becomes available. The default value is 10.

To disable interface tracking, enter the **no standby** *group* **track** command.

Displaying the Status of HSRP

To display the status of the HSRP router, enter the following command in privileged EXEC mode:

```
Router#show standby type-number group brief
```

type-number (optional) indicates the target interface type and number for which output is displayed.

group (optional) indicates a specific HSRP group on the interface for which output is displayed.

brief (optional) displays a single line of output summarizing each standby group.

If these optional interface parameters are not indicated, the **show standby** command displays HSRP information for all interfaces. Example 7-4 shows the sample output that results when the *type-number* and *group* parameters are specified.

Example 7-4 *Output of the show standby Command*

```
Router#show standby Vlan10 47
Vlan11 - Group 47
  Local state is Active, priority 150, may preempt
  Hellotime 3 holdtime 10
  Next hello sent in 00:00:02.944
  Hot standby IP address is 172.16.10.1 configured
  Active router is local
  Standby router is 172.16.10.82 expires in 00:00:08
  Standby virtual mac address is 0000.0c07.ac0b
  Tracking interface states for 1 interface, 1 up:
    Up  Vlan51 Priority decrement: 40
```

Example 7-5 shows the sample output that results when the **brief** parameter is specified.

Example 7-5 *Output of the show standby brief Command*

```
Router#show standby brief
Interface   Grp   Prio P State    Active addr     Standby addr    Group addr
Vl10        47    150  P Active   local           172.16.10.82    172.16.11.1
Vl12        12    100    Standby  172.16.12.82    local           172.16.12.1
```

| NOTE | When specifying a group, you must designate an interface. |

The Cisco IOS implementation of HSRP supports the **debug** command. Enabling the debug facility displays the HSRP state changes and debugging information regarding transmission and receipt of HSRP packets. To enable HSRP debugging, enter the following command in privileged EXEC mode:

```
Router#debug standby
```

| CAUTION | Because debugging output is assigned high priority in the CPU process, this command can render the system unusable. It should be used with extreme caution in a production network. |

Example 7-6 displays the **debug standby** command output as the router with IP address 172.16.10.82 initializes and negotiates for the role of the active router.

Example 7-6   *The debug standby Command*

```
Router#debug standby
3w1d : %STANDBY-6-STATECHANGE: Standby: 0: Vlan10 state Init     -> Listen
3w1d : %STANDBY-6-STATECHANGE: Standby: 0: Vlan10 state Listen   -> Speak
3w1d :SB0:Vlan10 Hello out 172.16.10.82 Speak pri 150 hel 3 hol 10 ip 172.16.10.1
3w1d :SB0:Vlan10 Hello out 172.16.10.82 Speak pri 150 hel 3 hol 10 ip 172.16.10.1
3w1d :SB0:Vlan10 Hello out 172.16.10.82 Speak pri 150 hel 3 hol 10 ip 172.16.10.1
3w1d :SB0:Vlan10 Hello out 172.16.10.82 Speak pri 150 hel 3 hol 10 ip 172.16.10.1
3w1d : %STANDBY-6-STATECHANGE: Standby: 0: Vlan10 state Speak    -> Standby
3w1d : %STANDBY-6-STATECHANGE: Standby: 0: Vlan10 state Standby    -> Active
3w1d : SB: Vlan10 Adding 0000.0c07.ac00 to address filter
```

To disable the debugging feature, enter either the **no debug standby** or **no debug all** command.

| NOTE | A shorthand version of the disable debug command is **u all**. |

Summary

Many end-user devices are configured statically with the address of a single router. These devices do not automatically assume a new default gateway when routing protocols converge after a router failure. HSRP provides an automatic router backup when configured for Cisco routers that run IP over Ethernet.

With HSRP, a set of routers works together to present the illusion of a single virtual router to the hosts on the LAN. HSRP has the following characteristics:

- Although multiple routers can exist in an HSRP group, only the active router forwards the packets sent to the virtual router.

- The router with the highest standby priority in the group becomes the active router.

- The standby router automatically assumes the function of the active router if the active router fails.

- Routers participating in an HSRP group communicate to each other via a multicast UDP-based hello packet.

- Routers receive hello messages from the active router and consider that hello message to be valid for one holdtime.

- HSRP defines six states in which a router can exist. When a router exists in one of these states, it performs the necessary actions required in that state.

- Multiple hot standby groups may coexist on a LAN segment. There can be up to 255 standby groups on any LAN.

- While running HSRP, the end-user station must not discover the primary MAC addresses of the routers in the standby group. Any protocol that informs a host of the router's primary address must be disabled.

Review Questions

The following questions test your retention of the material presented in this chapter. The answers to the Review Questions can be found in Appendix A, "Answers to Review Questions."

1   Discuss the basic tasks required to configure HSRP in the network.

2   Explain the purpose of active and standby routers and how these two entities interact.

3   Describe the six HSRP router states and the actions an HSRP router takes in each state.

Case Study

Work though the case study to practice what you learned in this chapter.

Scenario

This case study shows the configuration of HSRP between two distribution layer RSMs. This will ensure continual network access regardless of the availability status of the route processor. Figure 7-11 shows the visual objective for this case study. The virtual router will have an IP address of 172.16.41.145. The VLAN interface that will be configured on each RSM is VLAN 41. Each workstation will be configured for a default gateway of the virtual router.

Figure 7-11 *Case Study Visual Objective*

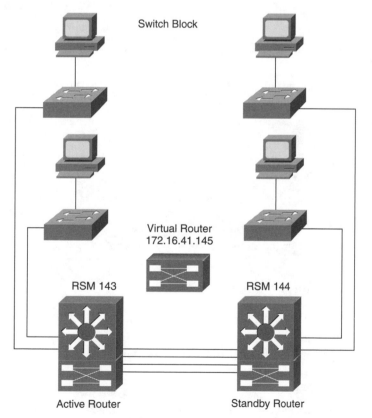

In order to complete this scenario, you must complete the following tasks:

- Configure HSRP on switch block devices to ensure continual inter-VLAN routing.
- Ensure the role of the active router by assigning a preempt status.

Command List

This case study uses the commands listed in Table 7-2.

Table 7-2   *Distribution Route Processor Commands*

Command	Description
interface vlan *number*	Enables interface configuration mode for the specified VLAN interface.
show arp	Displays the ARP table in the router.
shutdown	Disables the interface.
show standby vlan *vlan-number*	Displays HSRP information for the specified VLAN interface.
standby *group-number* **ip** *virtual-router-ip-address*	Assigns a standby group number and virtual router IP address to an interface.
standby *group-number* **preempt**	Gives the router the ability to take the active role from another router for this interface.
standby *group-number* **priority** *priority-number*	Manually assigns a standby priority to an interface.

Task 1: Configure HSRP

Complete the following steps to accomplish this task.

Configure HSRP on RSM143

Follow these steps to complete the configuration of HSRP on the first RSM:

Step 1   In global configuration mode, enter the **interface vlan** *vlan-number* command to enter interface configuration mode. The VLAN number used in this case study is 41.

Step 2   In interface configuration mode, enter the **standby** *group-number* **ip** *virtual-router-ip address* command. Use your VLAN number as the HSRP *group-number*. The virtual router's IP address is 172.16.41.145. Remember that this address must be the same for all routers in the same standby group, and it must be a valid IP address in the interface's subnet.

Step 3   Enter the **standby** *group-number* **priority** *priority-number* command to set the HSRP standby priority on your router. Use the HSRP priority of 150 for your first distribution router. The priority of 150 will be used to determine which router will become the active router. The default priority is 100. If all other routers are left at the default, this router becomes the active router.

Step 4   Exit all configuration modes. In privileged EXEC mode, enter the **show standby vlan** command to display the HSRP configuration on your primary router. Your configuration should resemble the output shown in Example 7-7.

Example 7-7   *show standby vlan Command Output*

```
Vlan41 - Group 41
  Local state is Active, priority 150
  Hellotime 3 holdtime 10
  Next hello sent in 00:00:02.396
  Hot standby IP address is 172.16.41.145 configured
  Active router is local
  Standby router is unknown expired
  Standby virtual mac address is 0000.0c07.ac29
```

Configure HSRP on RSM144

Follow these steps:

Step 1   Telnet to your secondary distribution router.

Step 2   In global configuration mode, enter the **interface vlan** *vlan-number* command to enter interface configuration mode. This case study uses VLAN41.

Step 3   In interface configuration mode, enter the **standby** *group-number* **ip** *virtual-router-ip-address* command. Use your VLAN number as the HSRP *group-number*. Remember that all routers in the standby group must agree on the same IP address for the virtual router. The IP address used in this example is 172.16.41.145.

Step 4   Enter the **standby** *group-number* **priority** *priority-number* command to set the HSRP standby priority on your secondary route processor. Use an HSRP priority of 50 for your secondary distribution router.

Step 5 In privileged EXEC mode, enter the **show standby vlan** command to display the HSRP configuration on your secondary route processor. Your configuration should resemble the output shown in Example 7-8. Note that the standby virtual MAC address is the same as the primary RSM.

Example 7-8 *show standby vlan Command Output*

```
Vlan41 - Group 41
  Local state is Standby, priority 50
  Hellotime 3 holdtime 10
  Next hello sent in 00:00:00.076
  Hot standby IP address is 172.16.41.145 configured
  Active router is 172.16.41.143 expires in 00:00:08
  Standby router is local
  Standby virtual mac address is 0000.0c07.ac29
```

Step 6 Save your configuration.

Step 7 Return to your primary distribution route processor.

Configure the Default Gateway on Your PC

Follow these steps:

Step 1 From your Windows desktop, select Start, Settings, Control Panel, and double-click the Network icon.

Step 2 Select the Configuration tab.

Step 3 Double-click the TCP/IP Interface Adapter symbol.

Step 4 From the TCP/IP Properties menu, do the following:

— Select the Gateway tab.

— In the Installed Gateways window, select the existing gateway IP address.

— Click the Remove button.

— In the New gateway box, enter the IP address of your HSRP virtual router. Use the address of 172.16.41.145.

— Click the Add button.

— Click the OK button twice.

Step 5 Click Yes to restart Windows, and answer Yes to any other prompts.

Step 6 Wait for Windows to restart.

Step 7 From your Windows desktop, select Start, Run.

Step 8   Enter **command** to open an MS-DOS window.

Step 9   From the DOS prompt, enter the **ping** *ip-address* command, where *ip-address* is equal to the IP address of an end user residing on a VLAN other than your own.

You have completed this task if you can ping an end user residing outside your native VLAN.

Task 2: Ensure the Role of the Active Router by Assigning a Preempt Status

In this task, you will configure your primary RSM VLAN interface to automatically reestablish itself as the active router by using the standby preempt feature. You verify the resumption of the active router role through the RSM **show standby** command.

Step 1   Enter the **standby** *group-number* **preempt** command to force this interface to resume active router status. Use your VLAN number as the HSRP *group-number*. Entering the **show standby** command results in the output shown in Example 7-9.

Example 7-9   *show standby Command Output*

```
Vlan41 - Group 41
  Local state is Active, priority 150, may preempt
  Hellotime 3 holdtime 10
  Next hello sent in 00:00:02.772
  Hot standby IP address is 172.16.41.145 configured
  Active router is local
  Standby router is 172.16.41.144 expires in 00:00:08
  Standby virtual mac address is 0000.0c07.ac29
```

Step 2   In interface configuration mode, enter the **standby** *group-number* **preempt** command to configure this interface to resume active router status should it be the highest priority. Use your VLAN number as the HSRP *group-number*.

You have successfully completed this task if the **show standby** *vlan* command shows that your primary VLAN interface has assumed the active router role.

CHAPTER 8

Multicast Overview

Most campus networks today support intranet applications that operate between one sender and one receiver. However, this paradigm is rapidly changing. In the emerging campus network, there is a demand for intranet and multimedia applications in which one sender transmits to a group of receivers simultaneously. These types of applications include transmitting a corporate message to employees, video and audio broadcasting, interactive video distance learning, transmitting data from a centralized data warehouse to multiple departments, communicating stock quotes to brokers, and collaborative computing. For example, an internal technical support facility might use multicast file transfer software to send software updates to multiple users in the campus simultaneously in one stream of data.

Sending from a single source to multiple destinations in one data stream is called *multicasting*. This chapter discusses multicasting and looks at its routing methods and some of its common protocols.

This chapter covers the following topics:

- Introduction to multicasting
- Addressing in an IP multicast environment
- Managing multicast traffic in a campus network
- Routing multicast traffic
- Multicast routing protocols

Upon completion of this chapter, you will be able to match the correct transmission method to the appropriate definition when given a list of transmission characteristics, correctly reconcile a list of multicast IP addresses to Ethernet addresses, compare and contrast the functional differences between IGMPv1 and IGMPv2, describe the setup procedure in which routers and switches facilitate multicast traffic, and select the appropriate multicast routing protocol for a given set of network requirements.

Introduction to Multicasting

Multimedia applications offer the integration of sound, graphics, animation, text, and video. These types of applications have become increasingly popular in the network as ways of conducting business become more complex. The bandwidth required to support an application increases as the application's sophistication increases. Some applications, such as stock market feeds, can produce up to 1000 packets per second. If not controlled, these applications can easily overwhelm a network.

Multimedia traffic can work its way through the network using one of several methods:

- Unicast
- Broadcast
- Multicast

Each one of these transmission methods has a different effect on network bandwidth.

Unicast Traffic

With a unicast design, an application sends one copy of each packet to every client unicast address. Unicast transmission has significant scaling restrictions. If the group is large, the same information must be carried multiple times, even on shared links. Figure 8-1 shows that unicast transmission requires that a separate transmission occur for every receiver.

Figure 8-1 *Unicast Traffic*

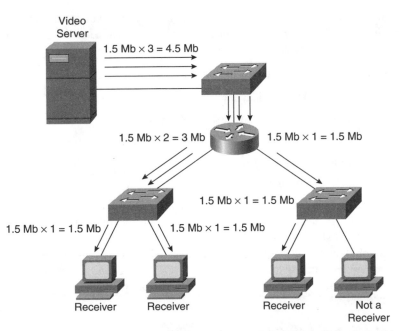

With technology, it is possible to afford the cost of making a unicast connection with every user who wants to see a specific Web page. However, a server sending audio and video requires a huge amount of bandwidth when compared with Web applications.

Two areas of unicast traffic are of concern to network managers:

- Number of user connections
- Amount of replicated unicast transmissions

A server in a unicast environment must send a separate video stream for each client requesting access to the application. For example, a video server sends a single channel of broadcast content to each client in the network. To support full-motion, full-screen viewing, the video stream requires approximately 1.5 Mbps of server-to-client bandwidth. The required bandwidth for this operation is as follows:

$1.5 \times n =$ Mbps of link bandwidth, where n is equal to the number of client viewers

With a 10 Mbps Ethernet interface on the server, six or seven server-to-client streams completely saturate the network interface. Even with a Gigabit Ethernet interface on a high-performance server, the practical limit is from 250 to 300 1.5 Mbps video streams.

Replicated unicast transmissions consume bandwidth within the network. The path between server and client must take into account the number of router and switch hops that occur between the two points. As routers are added to the path, the data is replicated across the link.

If 100 clients are separated from the server by two router hops and two switch hops, as in Figure 8-2, a single multiunicast channel consumes 300 Mbps of router bandwidth and 300 Mbps of switch bandwidth.

Figure 8-2   *A 10 Mbps Ethernet Network Is Quickly Saturated When the Application Is a Full-Motion, Full-Screen Video*

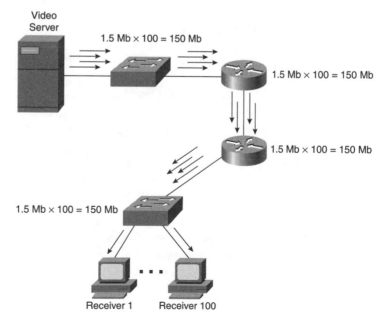

Even if the video stream bandwidth is scaled back to 100 Kbps, which provides acceptable quality in smaller windows on the end-station screen, the multiunicast consumes 20 Mbps of both router and switch bandwidth.

Because there are other choices for sending multimedia traffic, unicast multimedia is used on a limited basis. Replicated unicast cannot scale up to efficiently deliver traffic to large numbers of end stations, but it might be suitable for small numbers of destinations.

Broadcast Traffic

In a broadcast design, an application sends only one copy of each packet using a broadcast address. However, if this technique is used, broadcasts must be either stopped at the broadcast domain boundary with a Layer 3 device or transmitted to all devices in the campus network, as shown in Figure 8-3. Broadcasting a packet to all devices can be inefficient if only a small group in the network actually needs to see the packet.

Figure 8-3   *Broadcast Traffic*

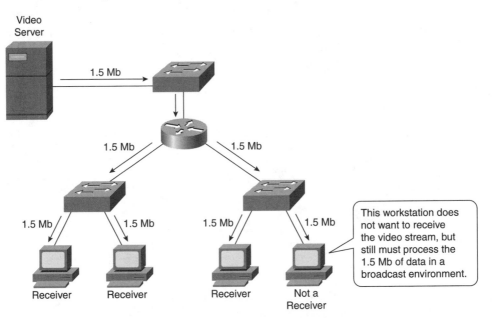

Broadcast multimedia is dispersed throughout the network just like normal broadcast traffic. As with normal broadcasts, every client has to process the broadcast multimedia data frame. However, unlike standard broadcast frames, which are generally small, multimedia broadcasts can reach as high as 7 Mbps or more of data. Even if an end station is not using a multimedia application, the device still processes the broadcast traffic. This requirement can use up most, if not all, of the allocated bandwidth for each device. For this reason, the broadcast multimedia method is rarely implemented.

Multicast Traffic

The most efficient solution is one in which a multimedia server sends one copy of each packet, addressing each packet to a special address. Unlike the unicast environment, a multicast server sends out a single data stream to multiple clients. Unlike the broadcast environment, the client device decides whether or not to listen to the multicast address. Multicasting saves bandwidth and controls network traffic by forcing the network to replicate packets only when necessary. By eliminating traffic redundancy, multicasting reduces network and host processing.

In Figure 8-4, the video server transmits a single video stream for each multicast group. A multicast (or host) group is defined as a set of host devices listening to a specific multicast address. The video stream is then replicated as required by the multicast routers and switches. This technique allows an arbitrary number of clients to subscribe to the multicast address and receive the broadcast.

Figure 8-4   *Multicast Traffic*

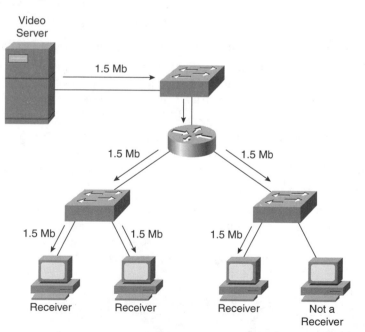

In the multicast scenario, only 1.5 Mbps of server-to-network bandwidth is utilized, leaving the remaining bandwidth free for other uses. Within the network, the multicast transmission offers similar efficiency, consuming only 1/*n*th of the bandwidth, where *n* equals the number of users receiving the video stream.

IP multicasting is the transmission of an IP data frame to a host group that is defined by a single IP address. IP reduces network traffic by simultaneously delivering a single stream of information to multiple recipients. This technology is an extension to the standard IP network-level protocol and is described in RFC 1112, "Host Extensions for IP Multicasting."

IP Multicast Characteristics

IP multicasting has the following characteristics:

- It facilitates transmission of an IP datagram to a host group comprised of zero or more hosts identified by a single IP destination address.
- It delivers a multicast datagram to all members of the destination host group with the same best-effort reliability as regular unicast IP datagrams.
- It supports dynamic membership of a host group.
- It supports all host groups regardless of the location or number of members.
- It supports the membership of a single host in one or more multicast groups.
- It upholds multiple data streams at the application level for a single group address.
- It supports a single group address for multiple applications on a host.
- In IP multicasting, the variability in delivery time is limited to the differences in end-to-end network delay along the complete server-to-client path. In a unicast scenario, the server sequences through transmission of multiple copies of the data, so variability in delivery time is large, especially for large transmissions or distribution lists.

Another unique feature of multicasting is that the server does not know the unicast network address of any particular recipient of the transmission. All recipients share the same multicast network address and therefore can join a multicast group while maintaining anonymity.

Multicast traffic is handled at the transport layer using the User Datagram Protocol (UDP). Unlike the Transmission Control Protocol (TCP), UDP adds no reliability, flow control, or error recovery functions to IP. Because of the simplicity of UDP, data packet headers contain fewer bytes and consume less network overhead than TCP.

Addressing in an IP Multicast Environment

IP multicasting is the transmission of an IP data frame to a host group, which is identified by a single IP address. Because the host group is identified by a single IP address rule, the IP multicast datagram contains a specific combination of the destination MAC address and a destination IP address.

IP Multicast Address Structure

The range of IP addresses is divided into classes based on the high-order bits of a 32-bit IP address. IP multicasting uses Class D addresses. A Class D address consists of 1110 as the higher-order bits in the first octet, followed by a 28-bit group address. Unlike Class A, B, and C IP addresses, the last 28 bits of a Class D address are unstructured.

These remaining 28 bits of the IP address identify the multicast group ID. This multicast group ID is a single address typically written as decimal numbers in the range 224.0.0.0 through 239.255.255.255. The high-order bits in the first octet identify this 224-base address.

Multicast addresses can be dynamically or statically allocated. Dynamic multicast addressing provides applications with a group address on demand. Because dynamic multicast addresses have a specific lifetime, applications must request this type of address only for as long as the address is needed.

Statically allocated addresses are reserved for specific protocols that require well-known addresses. The Internet Assigned Numbers Authority (IANA) assigns these well-known addresses. These addresses are called permanent host groups and are similar in concept to the well-known TCP and UDP port numbers. Table 8-1 lists some of the well-known Class D addresses.

Table 8-1   *Well-Known Class D Addresses*

Class D Address	Purpose
224.0.0.1	All hosts on a subnet
224.0.0.2	All routers on a subnet
224.0.0.4	All Distance Vector Multicast Routing Protocol (DVMRP) routers
224.0.0.5	All Open Shortest Path First (OSPF) routers
224.0.0.6	All OSPF designated routers
224.0.0.9	All Routing Information Protocol version 2 (RIPv2) routers
224.0.0.13	All Protocol-Independent Multicast (PIM) routers

Address 224.0.0.1 identifies the all-hosts group. Every multicast-capable host must join this group at the start. If a **ping** command is issued using this address, all multicast-capable hosts on the network must answer the ping request.

Address 224.0.0.2 identifies the all-routers group. Multicast routers must join that group on all multicast-capable interfaces.

Addresses ranging from 224.0.0.0 through 224.0.0.255 are reserved for local purposes, such as administrative and maintenance tasks. Multicast routers do not forward datagrams destined to this range of addresses.

Similarly, the address range 239.0.0.0 to 239.255.255.255 is reserved for administrative scoping. An administrative scope zone is defined by a set of routers surrounding a region within the network. These routers are configured to keep multicast traffic in a particular address range from entering or leaving the zone. This technique is useful in containing high-bandwidth traffic to a specific region in the campus network. Administrative scoping is outlined in RFC 2365, "Administratively Scoped IP Multicast."

A document containing the current list of multicast-assigned address can be retrieved from ftp://ftp.isi.edu/in-notes/iana/assignments/.

Mapping MAC Addresses to IP Multicast Addresses

Ethernet frames have a 48-bit destination address field. In order to avoid invoking the Address Resolution Protocol (ARP) to map multicast IP addresses to Ethernet addresses, the IANA designated a range of Ethernet addresses for multicasting. The lower 23 bits of the Class D address are mapped into a block of Ethernet addresses that have been reserved for multicasting. This block includes addresses in the range 01:00:5e:00:00:00 through 01:00:5e:ff:ff:ff. The IANA allocates half of this block for multicast addresses. Given that the first byte of any Ethernet address must be 01 to specify a multicast address, Ethernet addresses corresponding to IP multicasting are in the range 01:00:5e:00:00:00 through 01:00:5e:7f:ff:ff. Figure 8-5 shows how the IP multicast address is translated to an Ethernet MAC address.

Figure 8-5   *IP Addresses Map to Ethernet MAC Addresses Using the Last 23 Bits of the IP Address*

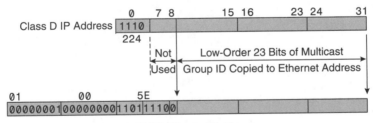

48-Bit Ethernet Address

The prefix 01-00-5e identifies the frame as multicast; the next bit is always 0, leaving only 23 bits for the multicast address. Because IP multicast groups are 28 bits long, the mapping cannot be one-to-one. Only the 23 least-significant bits of the IP multicast group are placed in the frame. The remaining five high-order bits are ignored, resulting in 32 different multicast groups being mapped to the same Ethernet address. For example, if the IP multicast group address is 224.10.8.5, the destination MAC address becomes 01-00-5E-0A-8-5.

Because 32 multicast addresses can be mapped to a single Ethernet address, the address is not unique. This correlation means that a host receiving multicasts needs to filter out multicast packets destined to multicast groups with the same MAC layer multicast address.

Figure 8-6 illustrates how the multicast group address 224.138.8.5, or EA-8A-08-05 expressed in hex, is mapped into an IEEE-802 multicast address. In multicast addressing, the high-order 9 bits of the IP address are not mapped into the MAC-layer multicast address. In this example, the mapping places the low-order 23 bits of the IP multicast group ID into the low-order 23 bits of the IEEE-802 multicast address.

Figure 8-6   *224.10.8.5 Translates to a MAC Address of 01.00.5e.0a.08.05*

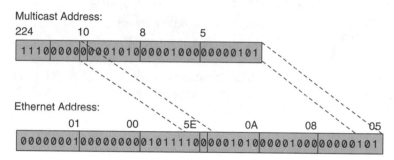

Because the upper 5 bits of the IP Class D address are not used, the mapping can correlate multiple IP groups into the same EEE-802 address. Therefore, there is a 32-to-1 ratio of IP Class D addresses to valid MAC-layer multicast addresses.

The Class D addresses 224.10.8.5 and 225.138.8.5 map to the same IEEE-802 MAC-layer multicast address (01-00-5E-0A-08-05).

The IP host group addresses 224.10.8.5 and 234.138.8.5 have the same MAC address of 01-00-5E-0A-8-5. However, the two groups remain separate because they have different IP host group addresses.

There is a small chance of collisions should multiple groups happen to have Class D addresses that map to the same MAC layer multicast address. Usually, higher-layer protocols let hosts interpret which packets are for the application. It's extremely unlikely that two different groups would pick the same Class D address and the same set of UDP ports.

Managing Multicast Traffic in a Campus Network

Multicasting on a single physical segment is simple. The sending process specifies a destination address that is defined as a multicast address. The device driver in the sending server converts this address to the corresponding Ethernet address and sends the package out on the network. The receiving devices, or clients, must indicate that they want to receive datagrams destined for a given multicast address.

Complications arise when multicasting is extended beyond a single physical network and multicast packets pass through routers.

Sending and receiving multimedia requires coordination from all devices participating in the multicast. These devices include the server, the host, the router, and the switch. Here are some of the issues in facilitating multimedia traffic in the campus network:

- Coordinating the multicast operations of the different devices in the network
- Establishing a path between source and destination devices
- Forwarding multicast traffic through the network

IP multicast traffic for a particular source/destination group pair is transmitted from the source to the host group via a distribution tree. This distribution tree connects all the hosts in the group. Different IP multicast routing protocols use different techniques to construct these multicast Spanning Trees; however, after the tree is constructed, all multicast traffic for a specific group is distributed over this tree.

Before multicast traffic can traverse the network, routers need to know which hosts (if any) on a specific physical network belong to a given multicast group.

Subscribing and Maintaining Groups

The first task in implementing multicasting in the campus network is to define who receives the multicast. As receivers or hosts request a specific multicast service, they must have the ability to let the network know that they are supposed to receive that multicast address.

The Internet Group Management Protocol (IGMP) provides a means to automatically control and limit the flow of multicast traffic through the network. IGMP version 1 is defined in RFC 1112, "Host Extensions for IP Multicasting." IGMP version 2 is documented in RFC 2236.

IGMP manages multicast traffic throughout networks with the use of special multicast queriers and hosts. A querier is a network device, such as a router, that sends queries. A set of queriers and hosts that receive multicast data streams from the same source is called a multicast group. Queries and hosts use IGMP messages to join and leave multicast groups.

IGMP supports two specific message structures:

- Query messages are used to discover which network devices are members of a given multicast group.
- Report messages are sent by hosts in response to query messages to inform the querier of a host membership.

Within the IP multicast model, there is no notion of membership between a source and the receivers. A source does not have to be a member of a group to send traffic to that group. Conversely, receivers do inform routers what groups the receivers want to have membership in so that the router can forward the appropriate traffic flows.

There are two versions of IGMP; each version has its own set of behavior characteristics.

IGMPv1

IGMPv1 is a basic protocol designed for facilitating a device joining a multicast group. It is responsible for communication between the host and the router that allows the host to join a multicast group and allows the router to determine when the host no longer needs to be part of a multicast group.

NOTE   From the router's perspective, it is not a host that joins the multicast group, but an interface. All the router wants to know is if an interface is supposed to receive the multicast traffic. It does not keep track of the exact hosts that are making the multicast request. The multicast traffic is sent to an entire cable segment, not to a single host.

IGMPv1: Packet Format

IGMP uses IP datagrams to transmit information about multicast groups. The datagram consists of a 20-byte IP header and an 8-byte IGMP message. Figure 8-7 shows the IGMPv1 packet format.

Figure 8-7   *IGMPv1 Packet Format*

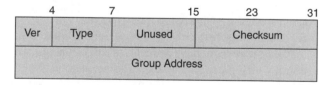

According to the IGMPv1 specification, one multicast router per LAN must periodically transmit host membership query messages to determine which host groups have members on the querier's directly attached networks. IGMP query messages are addressed to the all-host group (224.0.0.1) and have an IP Time To Live (TTL) equal to 1. This TTL ensures that the query messages sourced from a router are transmitted onto the directly attached network but are not forwarded by any other multicast routers.

When the end station receives an IGMP query message, the end station responds with a host membership report for each group in which the end station belongs.

IGMP messages are specified in the IP datagram with a protocol value of 2. Table 8-2 describes the fields of the IGMP message shown in Figure 8-7.

Table 8-2 *IGMPv1 Message Format Fields*

Field Name	Value
Ver	Indicates the IGMP version number.
Type	There are two types of IGMP messages of concern to hosts: 1 = Host Membership Query 2 = Host Membership Report
Unused	Unused field. Zeroed when sent; ignored when received.
Checksum	The checksum is the 16-bit 1's complement of the 1's complement sum of the eight-octet IGMP message. For computing the checksum, the checksum field is zeroed.
Group Address	In a host membership query message, the group address field is zeroed when sent and ignored when received. In a host membership report message, the group address field holds the IP host group address of the group being reported.

IGMPv1: Joining a Group

Hosts joining a group do not have to wait for a query in order to join. When a host wants to join a multicast group, the host sends a host membership report to the all-router group address 224.0.0.2. This unsolicited request reduces join latency for the end system when no other members of that group are present on that network segment.

IGMPv1: General Queries

Multicast routers send host membership query messages to discover which host groups have members on their attached local networks. General queries go to the all-hosts (224.0.0.1) multicast address and carry a TTL of 1. One member from each group on the segment responds with a report. General queries are sent out periodically based on the setting of the **ip igmp** *query-interval* command. (The default setting is 60 seconds.)

There is no formal IGMP query router election process within IGMPv1 itself. Instead, the election process is left up to the multicast routing protocol, and different protocols use different mechanisms. This often results in multiple queriers on a single network segment supporting multiple multicast-enabled routers.

IGMPv1: Maintaining a Group

To ensure the viability of group membership on a given network segment, the router multicasts periodic IGMPv1 membership queries to the all-hosts (224.0.0.1) group address. Only one member per group responds with a report to a query. This action saves bandwidth on the network segment and processing by the hosts. This process is called *response suppression*. The report suppression mechanism is accomplished as follows.

When a host receives the query, it starts a countdown timer for each multicast group for which the host is a member. The countdown timers are each initialized to a random count within a given time range. In IGMPv1, this is a fixed range of 10 seconds. Therefore, the countdown timers are randomly set to some value between 0 and 10 seconds.

When a countdown timer reaches zero, the host sends a membership report for the group associated with the countdown timer to notify the router that the group is still active. However, if a host receives a membership report before the associated countdown timer reaches zero, the host cancels the countdown timer associated with the multicast group, thereby suppressing the host's own report.

IGMPv1: Leaving a Group

No special leave mechanism was defined in version 1 of IGMP. Instead, IGMPv1 hosts leave a group passively or quietly at any time without any notification to the router.

Multicast routers periodically transmit IGMP queries to refresh their knowledge of which group members are present on each network interface. This process updates the router's local group database. Eventually, the router should be able to detect that no members of a group are any longer present on an interface and, if possible, remove itself from the multicast delivery tree for this group. If the router does not receive a report from any members of a group after a number of queries, the router assumes that no group members are present on a particular interface.

NOTE   When a router is just starting up, or if multicast routing has just been enabled, a router can, in order to quickly learn which groups have local members, send several IGMP queries in rapid succession.

IGMPv2

As a result of some of the limitations discovered in IGMPv1, work began on IGMPv2 in an attempt to remove these limitations. Most of the changes between IGMPv1 and IGMPv2 are primarily to address the issues of leave and join latencies, as well as to address ambiguities in the original protocol specification.

IGMPv2: Packet Format

Version 2 of IGMP made some enhancements to the previous version, including the definition of a group-specific query. This type of message allows the router to transmit a specific query to one particular group. IGMPv2 also defines a leave group message for the hosts, which results in lower leave latency. Figure 8-8 shows the IGMPv2 packet format.

There are four types of IGMP messages of concern to the host-router interaction:

- Membership query
- Version 2 membership report
- Leave report
- Version 1 membership report

The version 1 membership report is used for backward compatibility with IGMPv1. New message types can be used by newer versions of IGMP or by multicast routing protocols. Any other message type or unrecognized message types are ignored.

Figure 8-8   *IGMPv2 Frame Format*

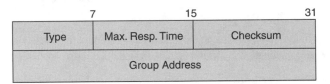

Table 8-3 describes the IGMPv2 message fields shown in Figure 8-8.

Table 8-3   *IGMPv2 Message Format Fields*

Field Name	Value
Type	0 x 11 = Membership query.
	0 x 12 = Version 1 membership report.
	0 x 16 = Version 2 membership report.
	0 x 17 = Leave report.
	0 x 12 = Version 1 membership report.
Max. Resp. Time (Maximum Response Time)	10 seconds = Default value. Meaningful only in a membership query. Specifies the maximum allowed time before sending a responding report in units of 1/10 second. 0 = All other messages.
Checksum	Calculated the same as for the ICMP checksum.
Group Address	0 in a general query. Group address queried in a group-specific query. Multicast group address in a report.

IGMPv2: Joining a Group

The process of joining a multicast group is the same in IGMPv2 as it is in IGMPv1. Like IGMPv1, IGMPv2 hosts joining a group do not have to wait for a query to join. When a host wants to join a multicast group, it sends a host membership report to the all-router group address 224.0.0.1.

A host sends an IGMP join message when it wants to join a multimedia group. If the host and server reside in different subnets, the join message must go to a router. When the router intercepts the message, it looks at its IGMP table. If the network number is not in the table, the router adds the information contained in the IGMP message.

Using queries and reports, a multicast router builds a table detailing which of the router interfaces has one or more hosts in a multicast group. When the router receives a multicast datagram, it forwards the datagram to only those interfaces that have hosts with processes belonging to that group.

After a host has joined a multicast group, it appears in the router's group database.

In Figure 8-9, group 224.1.1.1 has been active on Ethernet 0 for 6 days and 17 hours. This entry expires and will be deleted from the database in 2 minutes and 31 seconds if an IGMP host membership report for this group is not heard in that time. The last host to report membership was 172.16.41.2 (H2).

Figure 8-9   *IGMPv2 Join Process*

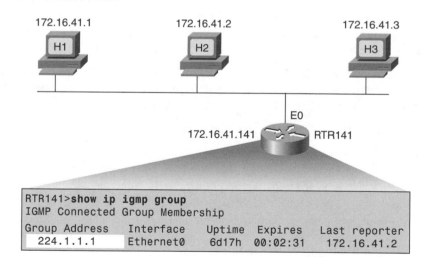

NOTE	Joining and leaving groups does not reflect the host's joining and leaving a group. It more accurately reflects a subnet joining and leaving a group. The host device indicates that it needs to receive a multicast group address. The router is notified that someone on the subnet needs the address. The subnet is then added to the router's multicast routing table as long as a single host is requesting the address.

IGMPv2: Querier Election

IGMPv2 defines a procedure for electing the multicast querier for each network segment. In IGMPv2, the multicast router with the lowest IP address on the LAN segment is elected the multicast querier.

Initially, every router on the segment believes itself to be the querier for every one of the router's interfaces that are multicast-enabled. When a router is first multicast-enabled, it begins transmitting query messages. If the router subsequently detects a queried message that is sourced from a numerically lower IP address, it ceases to act as a querier on that interface.

The query-interval response time has been added to IGMPv2 to control the burstiness of reports. This value is indicated in queries to convey to the membership the time interval in which members must respond to a query with a report message.

A group-specific query also was added in IGMPv2 to allow the router to query membership in only a single group instead of all groups. This is an optimized way to quickly find out if any members are left in a group without asking all groups for a report.

The difference between the group-specific query and the general query is that a general query is multicast to the all-hosts (224.0.0.1) address, while a group-specific query for group G is multicast to the group G multicast address.

To locate and verify the elected querier, enter the following command in user or privileged EXEC mode:

```
RTR141>show ip igmp interface type number
```

Example 8-1 shows the output of the **show ip igmp** *interface type number* command. This command indicates whether IGMP is enabled for the interface, the version number that is being used, and the current timers. The designated router is a different function and is listed separately from Example 8-1. The concept of designated routers is discussed in more detail in Chapter 9, "Configuring IP Multicast."

Example 8-1 *Locating the Designated Querier Router*

```
RTR141>show ip igmp interface e0
Ethernet0 is up, line protocol is up
  Internet address is 172.16.41.141, subnet mask is 255.255.255.0
  IGMP is enabled on interface
  Current IGMP version is 2
```

Example 8-1   *Locating the Designated Querier Router (Continued)*

```
CGMP is disabled on interface
IGMP query interval is 60 seconds
IGMP querier timeout is 120 seconds
IGMP max query response time is 10 seconds
Inbound IGMP access group is not set
Multicast routing is enabled on interface
Multicast TTL threshold is 0
Multicast designated router (DR) is 172.16.41.141 (this system)
IGMP querying router is 172.16.41.141 (this system)
Multicast groups joined: 224.0.1.40 224.2.127.254
```

IGMPv2: Maintaining a Group

Similar to IGMPv1, the IGMPv2 router multicasts periodic membership queries to the all-hosts (224.0.0.1) group address. Only one member per group responds with a report to a query. All other group members suppress their membership reports.

When a host receives a general query, it sets delay timers for each group, excluding the all-systems group, of which the host is a member on the interface from which the query was received. Each timer is set to a different random value, using the highest clock granularity available on the host.

When a host receives a group-specific query, it sets a delay timer to a random value for the group being queried if the host is a member of that group. If a timer for the group is already running, the host timer is reset to the random value only if the requested max response time is less than the remaining value of the running timer. When a group timer expires, the host multicasts a version 2 membership report to the group, with an IP TTL of 1.

IGMPv2: Leaving a Group

A leave group message was also added in IGMPv2. Whenever any end station wants to leave a group, the host transmits a leave group message to the all-routers (224.0.0.2) group, with the group field indicating the group being left. This allows end systems to tell the router that the hosts are leaving the group. This action reduces the leave latency for the group on the segment when the member leaving is the last member of the group.

Figure 8-10 shows the state of the router database before a leave group message has been issued. Both Hosts H2 (172.16.41.2) and H3 (172.16.41.3) are members of multicast group 224.1.1.1. Because Host H2 was the last member to send a host report message, Host H2's IP address is recorded in the router database.

Figure 8-10   *IGMPv2 Leave*

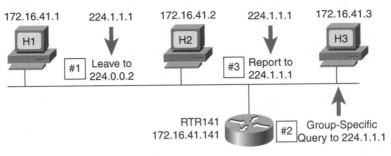

In Figure 8-11, Host H2 has issued a group leave message to the all-router IP address 224.0.0.2. In response to a leave group message, the elected querier begins transmitting group-specific query messages on the interface from which the querier received the leave group message. This action allows the router to discover if any members of that group remain on that directly attached network segment.

Figure 8-11   *H2 Issues a Group Leave Message*

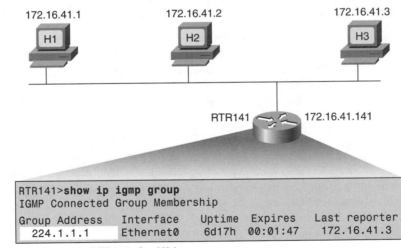

• IGMP state in RTR141 after H2 leaves

If Host H3 is still a member of the group, it responds to the group-specific query, and this subnet remains in the multicast routing table for this group.

When the last host leaves the multicast group on this subnet, the querier transmits a group-specific query to which there will be no response. After the hold-down timer expires, all routers on this subnet will remove this subnet from their multicast routing tables. This process is called *pruning*.

Handling Multicast Traffic in a Switch

In the multilayer campus model, IP multicast traffic traverses a Layer 2 switch, especially at the access layer. Because IP multicast traffic maps to a corresponding Layer 2 multicast address, multicast traffic is delivered to all ports of a Layer 2 switch.

For example, suppose a video client wants to watch a 1.5 Mbps IP multicast-based video feed sent from a corporate video server. The video client sends an IGMP join message to all routers indicating that it would like to join a multicast group. The next-hop router for the client logs the IGMP join message. IP multicast traffic is transmitted downstream to the video client. The switch detects the incoming traffic and examines the destination MAC address to determine where the traffic should be forwarded. Because the destination MAC address is a multicast address and there are no entries in the switching table for where the traffic should go, the 1.5 Mbps video feed is simply sent to all ports.

Switches must have an architecture that allows multicast traffic to be forwarded to a large number of attached group members without unduly loading the switch fabric. This function allows the switch to provide support for the growing number of new multicast applications without affecting other traffic. Layer 2 switches also need some degree of multicast awareness to avoid flooding multicasts to all switch ports.

Multicast control in Layer 2 switches can be accomplished in several ways:

- VLANs can de defined to correspond to the boundaries of the multicast group. This is a simple approach, but it does not support dynamic changes to group membership and adds to the administrative burden of unicast VLANs.

- Layer 2 switches can snoop IGMP queries and reports to learn the port mappings of multicast group members. This allows the switch to dynamically track group membership. However, snooping every multicast data and control packet consumes much switch processing capacity and therefore can degrade forwarding performance and increase latency.

The traditional role of the router as a control point in the network can be maintained by defining a multicast router-to-switch protocol. The Cisco Group Management Protocol (CGMP) allows the router to configure the Content Addressable Memory (CAM) table in the switch to correspond with the current group membership.

CGMP

CGMP is a Cisco-developed protocol that allows Catalyst switches to learn about the existence of multicast clients from Cisco routers and Layer 3 switches.

CGMP is based on a client/server model. The router is considered a CGMP server, with the switch taking on the client role. The basis of CGMP is that the IP multicast router sees all IGMP packets and therefore can inform the switch when specific hosts join or leave multicast groups. The switch then uses this information to construct a forwarding table.

When the router sees an IGMP control packet, it creates a CGMP packet. This CGMP packet contains the request type (either a join or a leave), the multicast group address, and the client's actual MAC address. The packet is sent to a well-known address to which all switches listen. Each switch then interprets the packet and creates the proper entries in a forwarding table.

In Figure 8-12, the client starts by sending an IGMP join message to the video server. However, now when the next-hop router receives the IGMP join message, the router records the source MAC address of the IGMP message and issues a CGMP join message downstream to the Catalyst switch. The Catalyst switch uses the CGMP message to dynamically build an entry in the switching table that maps the multicast traffic to the client's switch port. In this example, the server delivers the 1.5 Mbps video feed only to those switch ports that are in the switching table. The ports on the switch that do not support any hosts in the multicast group do not propagate the traffic.

Figure 8-12   *The Receipt of an IGMP Control Packet Causes the Router to Create a CGMP Packet*

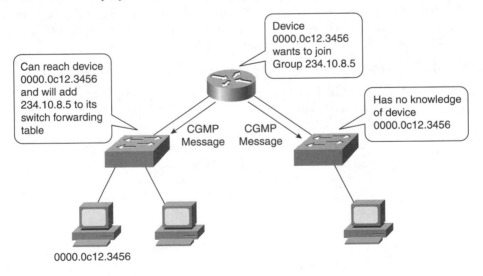

Routing Multicast Traffic

The campus network is composed of a collection of subnetworks connected by routers. When the source of a video data stream is located on one subnet and the host devices are located on different subnets, there needs to be a way of determining how to get from the source to the destinations. This is the function of the IP protocol.

Each host on the Internet has an address that identifies the physical location of the host. Part of the address identifies the subnet on which the host resides, and part identifies the individual host on that subnet. Routers periodically send routing update messages to adjacent routers, conveying the state of the network as perceived by that particular router. This data is recorded in routing tables that are then used to determine optimal transmission paths for forwarding messages across the network.

Unicast transmission involves transmission from a single source to a single destination. The transmission is directed toward a single physical location that is specified by the host address. This routing procedure is relatively straightforward because of the binding of a single address to a single host.

Routing multicast traffic is a more complex problem. A multicast address identifies a particular transmission session rather than a specific physical destination. An individual host can join an ongoing multicast session by using IGMP to communicate this desire to the subnet router.

Because the number of receivers for a multicast session can potentially be quite large, the source should not need to know all the relevant addresses. Instead, the network routers must somehow be able to translate multicast addresses into host addresses. The basic principle involved in multicast routing is that routers interact with each other to exchange information about neighboring routers.

Distribution Trees

For efficient transmission, designated routers construct a tree that connects all members of an IP multicast group. A distribution tree specifies a unique forwarding path between the source's subnet and each subnet containing members of the multicast group.

A distribution tree has just enough connectivity so that there is only one loop-free path between every pair of routers. Because each router knows which of its lines belong to the tree, the router can copy an incoming multicast datagram onto all the outgoing branches. This action generates the minimum needed number of datagram copies. Because messages are replicated only when the tree branches, the number of copies of the messages transmitted through the network is minimized.

Because multicast groups are dynamic, with members joining or leaving a group at any time, the distribution tree must be dynamically updated. Branches that contain new members must be added. Branches in which no listeners exist must be discarded, or pruned.

Two basic tree-construction techniques exist: source-specific trees and shared, or center-specific, trees.

Source Distribution Tree

Source-specific trees require finding the shortest path from the sender to each receiver, resulting in multiple minimal delay trees for a group.

The source-specific method builds a Spanning Tree for each potential source, or subnetwork. These Spanning Trees result in source-based delivery trees emanating from the subnetworks directly connected to the source stations. Since there are many potential sources for a group, a different delivery tree is constructed, rooted at each active source.

Source-based trees are constructed using a technique called Reverse Path Forwarding (RPF). If a packet arrives on a link that the local router believes to be on the shortest path back toward the source of the packet, the router forwards the packet on all interfaces except the incoming interface. If the packet does not arrive on the interface that is on the shortest path back toward the source, the packet is discarded.

The interface over which the router expects to receive multicast packets from a particular source is referred to as the parent link. The outbound links over which the router forwards the multicast packet are called the child links for this source.

The RPF algorithm also reduces unnecessary packet duplication. If the local router making the forwarding decision determines that a neighboring router on a child link is downstream, the packet is not forwarded to the upstream neighboring router. A downstream neighbor is a neighboring router that considers the local router to be on the shortest path back toward a given source. Figure 8-13 shows the loop-free tree that is built to the source device.

Figure 8-13   *Source-Based Trees Build a Spanning Tree Based on the Source of the Multicast*

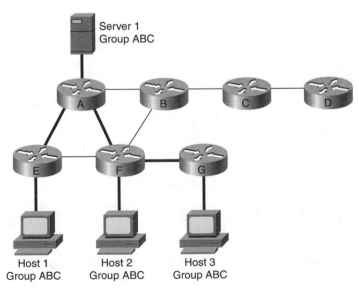

If the link between the local router and the neighboring router is not the shortest path, the packet is not forwarded on that child link.

Shared Distribution Tree

Shared trees use distribution centers and construct a single multicast tree, resulting in a low-overhead method but sacrificing minimal end-to-end delay.

Unlike source (or shortest-path) tree algorithms, which build a source-based tree for each source or each (source, group) pair, shared-tree algorithms construct a single delivery tree that is shared by all members of a group. The shared-tree approach is similar to the Spanning-Tree algorithm, except the shared-tree approach allows the definition of a different shared tree for each group. Devices wanting to receive traffic for a multicast group must explicitly join the shared delivery tree. Multicast traffic for each group is sent and received over the same delivery tree, regardless of the source. Figure 8-14 shows the single tree that is constructed in a shared distribution tree mode.

Figure 8-14   *Shared Distribution Trees Construct a Single Tree Based on a Rendezvous Point*

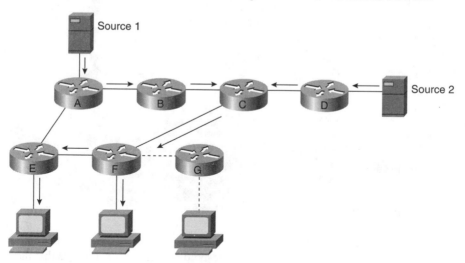

A shared tree can involve a single router (or set of routers) that comprises the core of a multicast delivery tree. Shared-tree algorithms make efficient use of router resources, because this technique requires a router to maintain state information only in each group, not each (source, group) pair.

Multicast routing protocols build distribution trees by examining a unicast reachability protocol routing table.

Managing the Scope of Delivery

In a campus network, limiting high-bandwidth traffic to specific LANs or regions within the network is essential to containing or eliminating unnecessary consumption of resources. One method of containing multicast traffic is to put constraints around the forwarding of that traffic by using the TTL field in the IP packet.

As in unicast routing, the multicast TTL field controls the packet's live time. The function of TTL is to prevent packets from being looped forever due to routing errors. However, the TTL field in multicasting also carries the concept of a threshold. Figure 8-15 shows how a scope of delivery defines how far multicast traffic can traverse the network.

Figure 8-15   *Scope of Delivery*

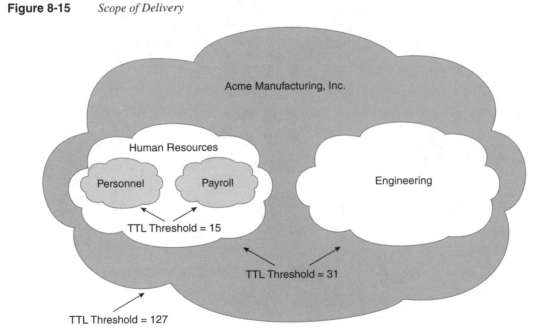

Multicast-enabled routers have a TTL threshold assigned to each interface. Packets that have a TTL greater than the interface threshold are forwarded. Packets that have a TTL equal to or less than the interface threshold are discarded. The packet TTL is compared to the interface threshold first. The router then decrements the packet TTL upon sending the packet out the interface.

Table 8-4 lists TTL thresholds and their associated scope.

Table 8-4   *TTL Thresholds*

Value	Action
0	Restricted to the same host. Not output by any interface.
1	Restricted to the same subnet. Not forwarded by a router.
15	Restricted to the same site, organization, or department.
63	Restricted to the same region.
127	Worldwide.
191	Worldwide; limited bandwidth.
255	Unrestricted in scope; global.

For example, a multicast packet with a TTL of less than 16 is restricted to the same department, or site, and should not be forwarded across an interface to other sites in the same region. Defining the scope of a site or region is the responsibility of the network administrator.

A multicast router forwards a multicast packet across an interface only if the TTL field in the IP header is greater than the TTL threshold assigned to the interface. If the TTL field in the IP header of the packet is equal to or less than the TTL threshold assigned to the interface, the packet is discarded. If the interface has no assigned TTL threshold, the packet is forwarded.

In Figure 8-16, the interfaces on the router have been configured with the following TTL thresholds:

- E1: TTL Threshold = 16
- E2: TTL Threshold = 0 (none)
- E3: TTL Threshold = 64

An incoming multicast packet for Group XYZ is received on interface E0 with a TTL of 24, as shown in Figure 8-16. The outgoing interface list for Group XYZ contains interfaces E1, E0, and E2. The TTL threshold check is performed on each outgoing interface as follows:

- E1: TTL (24) > TTL Threshold (16). FORWARD
- E2: TTL (24) > TTL Threshold (0). FORWARD
- E3: TTL (24) < TTL Threshold (64). DROP

The TTL is then decremented to 23 by the normal router IP packet processing.

Figure 8-16   *The Time To Live Threshold Determines the Scope of Delivery for Multicast Traffic*

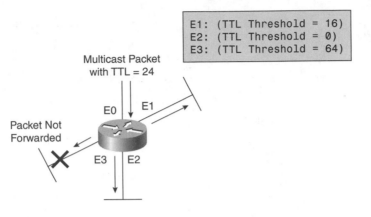

NOTE	By default, the IP protocol sets the TTL value to 255. Each Layer 3 device decrements the TTL during the frame's rewrite process. Different routing protocols look for different things inside the TTL. For example, if RIP has a maximum hop count of 15, it looks for a TTL value that is 255–16, or 239, in order to indicate that the TTL for that packet has expired. Some packets, such as broadcasts, set the TTL to 1 in order to prevent the packet from crossing a router. Other applications, such as traceroute, modify the TTL in order to produce an ICMP message if TTL expired. This message is used to indicate the device that actually received the packet by watching for ICMP TTL expired packets.

Multicast Routing Protocols

Just as there are different routing protocols for unicast routing, there are different routing protocols for multicast routing. This section describes how the different multicast routing protocols construct multicast delivery trees and enable multicast packet forwarding.

A multicast routing protocol is responsible for constructing multicast delivery trees and enabling multicast packet forwarding. Different IP multicast routing protocols use different techniques to construct multicast Spanning Trees and forward packets.

IP multicast routing protocols generally follow one of two basic approaches, depending on the distribution of multicast group members on the network: dense mode and sparse mode routing protocols.

Dense Mode Routing Protocols

The first approach is based on the assumption that the multicast group members are densely distributed throughout the network and bandwidth is plentiful, meaning that almost all hosts on the network belong to the group. These dense mode multicast routing protocols rely on periodic flooding of the network with multicast traffic to set up and maintain the distribution tree.

Dense mode routing protocols include the following:

- Distance Vector Multicast Routing Protocol (DVMRP)
- Multicast Open Shortest Path First (MOSPF)
- Protocol-Independent Multicast Dense Mode (PIM DM)

Dense mode operations assume that almost all routers in the network need to distribute multicast traffic for each multicast group. Dense mode protocols are most appropriate in environments with densely clustered receivers and the bandwidth to tolerate flooding. An example of when a dense mode protocol can be used is when a CEO of a company wants to broadcast a message to all employees within the headquarters campus network.

Distance Vector Multicast Routing Protocol

Distance Vector Multicast Routing Protocol (DVMRP) is described in RFC 1075. DVMRP is widely used on the Internet multicast backbone (MBONE).

DVMRP uses reverse path flooding. When a router receives a packet, it floods the packet out of all paths except the one that leads back to the packet source. This technique allows a data stream to reach all LANs. If a router is attached to a set of LANs that do not want to receive a particular multicast group, the router can send a prune message back up the distribution tree to stop subsequent packets from traveling where there are no members.

DVMRP periodically floods packets in order to reach any new hosts that want to receive a particular group. There is a direct relationship between the time it takes for a new receiver to get the data stream and the frequency of flooding.

DVMRP implements its own unicast routing protocol in order to determine which interface leads back to the source of the data stream. This unicast routing protocol is similar to RIP and is based purely on hop counts. As a result, the path that the multicast traffic follows might not be the same as the path that the unicast traffic follows.

NOTE	Cisco routers run PIM. Cisco routers know enough about DVMRP to successfully forward multicast packets to and receive packets from a DVMRP neighbor. Cisco routers can also propagate DVMRP routes into and through a PIM cloud. However, only the PIM protocol uses this information. Cisco routers do not implement DVMRP to forward multicast packets.

Multicast Open Shortest Path First

Multicast Open Shortest Path First (MOSPF) is described in RFC 1584. MOSPF is intended for use within a single routing domain, such as a network controlled by a single organization. MOSPF is dependent on the use of OSPF as the accompanying unicast routing protocol. In an OSPF/MOSPF network, each router maintains an up-to-date image of the topology of the entire network. MOSPF works by including multicast information in OSPF link-state advertisements. An MOSPF router learns which multicast groups are active on which LANs.

This link-state information is used to construct multicast distribution trees. MOSPF builds a distribution tree for each (source, group) pair and computes a tree for active sources sending to the group. The tree state is cached, and trees must be recomputed when a link-state change occurs or when the cache times out.

MOSPF is best suited for environments that have relatively few (source, group) pairs active at any given time. This protocol doesn't work as well in environments that have many active sources or in environments that have unstable links.

NOTE	Cisco routers do not support MOSPF.

Protocol-Independent Multicast Dense Mode

Protocol-Independent Multicast Dense Mode (PIM DM) is similar to DVMRP. This protocol works best when numerous members belong to each multimedia group, as shown in Figure 8-17. PIM floods the multimedia packet out to all routers in the network and then prunes routers that do not support members of that particular multicast group.

Figure 8-17   *Protocol-Independent Multicast Dense Mode*

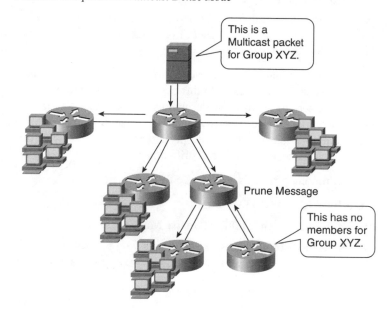

PIM dense mode is most useful when the following are true:

- Senders and receivers are in close proximity to one another.
- There are few senders and many receivers.
- The volume of multicast traffic is high.
- The stream of multicast traffic is constant.

Two Internet standard track drafts describe PIM, a multicast protocol that can be used in
conjunction with all unicast IP routing protocols. These documents are "Protocol-
Independent Multicast (PIM): Motivation and Architecture" and "Protocol-Independent
Multicast (PIM): Protocol Specification."

Sparse Mode Routing Protocols

The second approach to multicast routing is based on the assumption that the multicast group members are sparsely distributed throughout the network and bandwidth is not necessarily widely available.

It is important to note that sparse mode does not imply that the group has a few members—just that they are widely dispersed. In this case, flooding would waste network bandwidth and could cause serious performance problems. Therefore, sparse mode multicast routing protocols must rely on more selective techniques to set up and maintain multicast trees. Sparse mode protocols begin with an empty distribution tree and add branches only as the result of explicit requests to join the distribution.

Sparse mode routing protocols include the following:

- Core-Based Trees (CBT)
- Protocol-Independent Multicast Sparse Mode (PIM SM)

Because sparse mode protocols assume that relatively few routers in the network will be involved in each multicast, these protocols are more appropriate in WAN environments.

Core-Based Trees

Core-Based Trees (CBT) are described in RFC 2201. The CBT protocol constructs a single tree that is shared by all members of the group. Multicast traffic for the entire group is sent and received over the same tree, regardless of the source. This use of a shared tree can provide significant savings in terms of the amount of multicast state information that is stored in individual routers.

A CBT shared tree has a core router that is used to construct the tree. Routers join the tree by sending a join message to the core. When the core receives a join request, it returns an acknowledgment over the reverse path, thus forming a branch of the tree. Join messages need not travel all the way to the core before being acknowledged. If a join message encounters a router on the tree before the message reaches the core, that router terminates the join message and acknowledges it. The router that sent the join is then connected to the shared tree.

Protocol-Independent Multicast Sparse Mode

Protocol-Independent Multicast Sparse Mode (PIM SM) is optimized for environments that have many multipoint data streams. Sparse multicast is most useful when the following are true:

- There are few receivers in a group.
- The type of traffic is intermittent.

In sparse mode, each data stream goes to a relatively small number of segments in the campus network, as shown in Figure 8-18. Instead of flooding the network to determine the status of multicast members, PIM SM defines a rendezvous point. When a sender wants to send data, it first sends to the rendezvous point. When a receiver wants to receive data, it registers with the rendezvous point. Once the data stream begins to flow from sender to rendezvous point to receiver, the routers in the path optimize the path automatically to remove any unnecessary hops. PIM SM assumes that no hosts want the multicast traffic unless they specifically ask for it.

Figure 8-18   *Protocol-Independent Multicast Sparse Mode*

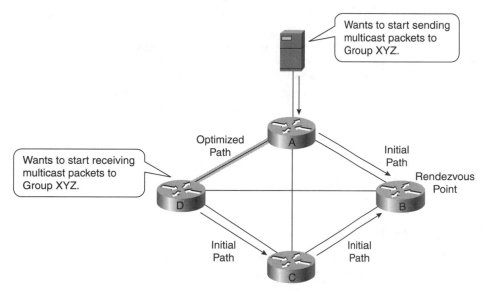

PIM can simultaneously support dense mode for some multicast groups and sparse mode for others.

Summary

Because of its unique capability to send out a single data stream to multiple clients, the multicast method has become the transmission method of choice for most multimedia applications.

IP multicasting is the transmission of an IP data frame to a host group, which is identified by a single IP address. Because the host group is identified by a single IP address rule, the IP multicast contains a specific combination of the destination MAC address and a destination IP address.

Multicasting uses the following methods and protocols:

- IGMP provides a way for clients to join and leave multicast groups.

- CGMP allows the router to configure the multicast forwarding table in the switch to correspond with the current group membership.

- For efficient transmission, designated routers construct a tree that connects all members of an IP multicast group. A distribution tree specifies a unique forwarding path between the source's subnet and each subnet containing members of the multicast group.

- Multicast routing protocols fall into two categories: dense mode (DM) and sparse mode (SM).

- Dense mode protocols assume that almost all routers in the network will need to distribute multicast traffic for each multicast group. Sparse mode protocols assume that relatively few routers in the network will be involved in each multicast. The hosts belonging to the group are widely dispersed, as might be the case for most multicasts in the Internet.

- Dense mode protocols are most appropriate in LAN environments that have densely clustered receivers and the bandwidth to tolerate flooding.

- Sparse mode protocols are most appropriate in LAN environments in which relatively few routers in the network will be involved in each multicast.

Review Questions

The following questions test your retention of the material presented in this chapter. The answers to the Review Questions can be found in Appendix A, "Answers to Review Questions."

1 Discuss the three types of transmission methods and the effect each one has on network bandwidth.

2 Explain how routers and switches handle the impact of multicast addressing techniques.

3 Discuss different multicast routing protocols, and identify which ones are most effective in a campus network.

Written Exercises: Multicasting Overview

Complete the following written exercises to practice what you learned in this chapter. The answers to each task can be found at the end of this chapter.

Task 1: Transmission Characteristics

Read each transmission characteristic statement. From the following list, choose the transmission method that most accurately supports each statement, and place the letter representing that transmission method next to the appropriate statement.

A. Unicast
B. Broadcast
C. Multicast

Transmission Characteristic Statement	Answer
Packets are replicated on an as-needed basis.	
Sends a separate video stream for a requesting client.	
Sends one copy of each packet to every client address.	
Sends one copy of each packet to all hosts on the network.	
Sends one copy of each packet to a specific group of clients.	
Used when a defined set of users needs access to the application.	
Requires clients to process large packets whether requested or not.	
Used when only a few clients need to access the application.	

Task 2: Reconcile Multicast IP Addresses to Ethernet Addresses

Match the correct MAC address to its corresponding IP multicast address. Use the binary representation and the decimal-to-hexadecimal conversion chart in Table 8-5 to help you resolve the addresses. The first address has been filled in for you.

IP Multicast Address	Binary Representation	MAC Address
224.10.8.5	1110 0000 0000 1010 0000 1000 0000 0101	01-00-5E-0A-08-05
224.163.163.45	1110 0000 1010 0011 1010 0011 0010 1101	
224.138.137.45	1110 0000 1000 1010 1000 1001 0010 1101	
224.2.239.45	1110 0000 0000 0010 1110 1111 0010 1101	
224.192.255.45	1110 0000 1100 0000 1111 1111 0010 1101	
224.35.35.45	1110 0000 0010 0011 0010 0011 0010 1101	

IP Multicast Address	Binary Representation	MAC Address
224.64.255.45	1110 0000 0100 0000 1111 1111 0010 1101	
224.0.9.45	1110 0000 0000 0000 1010 0101 0010 1101	
224.124.9.45	1110 0000 0111 1100 0000 1001 0010 1101	
224.252.9.45	1110 0000 1111 1100 0000 1001 0010 1101	

Here are the MAC addresses:

- 01-00-5E-00-09-2D
- 01-00-5E-02-89-2D
- **01-00-5E-0A-08-05**
- 01-00-5E-02-EF-2D
- 01-00-5E-23-A3-2D
- 01-00-5E-40-FF-2D
- 01-00-5E-7C-09-2D
- 01-00-5E-A3-A3-2D
- 01-00-5E-C0-FF-2D
- 01-00-5E-FC-09-2D

Table 8-5   *Decimal-to-Hexadecimal Conversion Chart*

DEC = HEX	DEC = HEX	DEC = HEX	DEC = HEX	DEC = HEX
0 = 00	52 = 34	104 = 68	156 = 9C	208 = D0
1 = 01	53 = 35	105 = 69	157 = 9D	209 = D1
2 = 02	54 = 36	106 = 6A	158 = 9E	210 = D2
3 = 03	55 = 37	107 = 6B	159 = 9F	211 = D3
4 = 04	56 = 38	108 = 6C	160 = A0	212 = D4
5 = 05	58 = 3A	110 = 6E	162 = A2	214 = D6
7 = 07	59 = 3B	111 = 6F	163 = A3	215 = D7
8 = 08	60 = 3C	112 = 70	164 = A4	216 = D8
9 = 09	61 = 3D	113 = 71	165 = A5	217 = D9
10 = 0A	62 = 3E	114 = 72	166 = A6	218 = DA
12 = 0C	64 = 40	116 = 74	168 = A8	220 = DC

Table 8-5   *Decimal-to-Hexadecimal Conversion Chart (Continued)*

DEC = HEX	DEC = HEX	DEC = HEX	DEC = HEX	DEC = HEX
13 = 0D	65 = 41	117 = 75	169 = A9	221 = DD
14 = 0E	66 = A8	118 = 76	170 = AA	222 = DE
15 = 0F	67 = 43	119 = 77	171 = AB	223 = DF
16 = 10	68 = 44	120 = 78	172 = AC	224 = E0
17 = 11	69 = 45	121 = 79	173 = AD	225 = E1
18 = 12	70 = 46	122 = 7A	174 = AE	226 = E2
19 = 13	71 = 47	123 = 7B	175 = AF	227 = E3
20 = 14	72 = 48	124 = 7C	176 = B0	228 = E4
21 = 15	73 = 49	125 = 7D	177 = B1	229 = E5
22 = 16	74 = 4A	126 = 7E	178 = B2	230 = E6
23 = 17	75 = 4B	127 = 7F	179 = B3	231 = E7
24 = 18	76 = 4C	128 = 80	180 = B4	232 = E8
25 = 19	77 = 4D	129 = 81	181 = B5	233 = E9
26 = 1A	78 = 4E	130 = 82	182 = B6	234 = EA
27 = 1B	79 = 4F	131 = 83	183 = B7	235 = EB
28 = 1C	80 = 50	132 = 84	184 = B8	236 = EC
29 = 1D	81 = 51	133 = 85	185 = B9	237 = ED
30 = 1E	82 = 52	134 = 86	186 = BA	238 = EE
31 = 1F	83 = 53	135 = 87	187 = BB	239 = EF
32 = 20	84 = 54	136 = 88	188 = BC	240 = F0
33 = 21	85 = 55	137 = 89	189 = BD	241 = F1
34 = 22	86 = 56	138 = 8A	190 = BE	242 = F2
35 = 23	87 = 57	139 = 8B	191 = BF	243 = F3
36 = 24	88 = 58	140 = 8C	192 = C0	244 = F4
37 = 25	89 = 59	141 = 8D	193 = C1	245 = F5
38 = 26	90 = 5A	142 = 8E	194 = C2	246 = F6
39 = 27	91 = 5B	143 = 8F	195 = C3	247 = F7
40 = 28	92 = 5C	144 = 90	196 = C4	248 = F8
41 = 29	93 = 5D	145 = 91	197 = C5	249 = F9
42 = 2A	94 = 5E	146 = 92	198 = C6	250 = FA

continues

Table 8-5 *Decimal-to-Hexadecimal Conversion Chart (Continued)*

DEC = HEX	DEC = HEX	DEC = HEX	DEC = HEX	DEC = HEX
43 = 2B	95 = 5F	147 = 93	199 = C7	251 = FB
44 = 2C	96 = 60	148 = 94	200 = C8	252 = FC
45 = 2D	97 = 61	149 = 95	201 = C9	253 = FD
46 = 2E	98 = 62	150 = 96	202 = CA	254 = FE
47 = 2F	99 = 63	151 = 97	203 = CB	255 = FF
48 = 30	100 = 64	152 = 98		
49 = 31	101 = 65	153 = 99		
50 = 32	102 = 66	154 = 9A		
51 = 33	103 = 67	155 = 9B		

Task 3: The Functional Differences Between IGMPv1 and IGMPv2

Read each statement in the table. From the following list, choose the protocol version that most accurately supports each statement, and place the letter representing that protocol version next to the appropriate statement.

A. IGMPv1
B. IGMPv2
C. Both IGMPv1 and IGMPv2

Statement	Answer
This unused field in the IGMP packet is zeroed when sent and ignored when received.	
Routers use group-specific queries to query membership in a single group instead of all groups.	
If a host receives a membership report before the associated timer reaches 0, the host cancels the countdown timer associated with that group.	
No leave mechanism is defined. Instead, hosts leave a group passively or quietly at any time without any notification to the router.	
Defines a procedure for election of the multicast querier for each network segment. The router with the lowest IP address is elected the multicast querier for that LAN segment.	
One multicast router per LAN must periodically transmit host membership query messages to determine which host groups have members on the querier's directly attached networks.	

Task 4: The Setup Procedure in Which Routers and Switches Facilitate Multicast Traffic

Read each multicast operation statement listed in the following table. Using the numbers 1 through 6, number each statement in the order of its occurrence, with 1 being the first step.

Multicast Operation	Step
The switch builds an entry in the switching table that maps the multicast traffic to the client's switch port.	
The router logs the join message and uses PIM or another multicast routing protocol to add this segment to the multicast distribution tree.	
IP multicast traffic transmitted from the server is distributed via the designated router to the client's subnet. The destination MAC address corresponds to the group's Class D address.	
The router creates a CGMP packet with a join request type, the requested multicast group address, and the actual MAC address of the client and sends it to a well-known address to which all switches listen.	
The client sends an IGMP join message to the designated multicast router. The destination MAC address maps to the Class D address of the group being joined rather than the router's MAC address. The body of the IGMP datagram also includes the Class D group address.	
The switch receives the multicast packet and examines the forwarding table. If no entry exists for the MAC address, the packet is flooded to all ports within the broadcast domain. If an entry does exist in the switch table, the packet is forwarded only to the designated ports.	

Task 1 Answers: Transmission Characteristics

Transmission Characteristic Statement	Answer
Packets are replicated on an as-needed basis.	C
Sends a separate video stream for a requesting client.	A
Sends one copy of each packet to every client address.	A
Sends one copy of each packet to all hosts on the network.	B
Sends one copy of each packet to a specific group of clients.	C
Used when a defined set of users needs access to the application.	C
Requires clients to process large packets whether requested or not.	B
Used when only a few clients need to access the application.	A

Task 2 Answers: Reconcile Multicast IP Addresses to Ethernet Addresses

IP Multicast Address	Binary Representation	MAC Address
224.10.8.5	1110 0000 0000 1010 0000 1000 0000 0101	01-00-5E-0A-08-05
224.163.163.45	1110 0000 1010 0011 1010 0011 0010 1101	01-00-5E-23-A3-2D
224.138.137.45	1110 0000 1000 0010 1000 1001 0010 1101	01-00-5E-02-89-2D
224.2.239.45	1110 0000 0000 0010 1110 1111 0010 1101	01-00-5E-02-EF-2D
224.192.255.45	1110 0000 1100 0000 1111 1111 0010 1101	01-00-5E-40-FF-2D
224.35.35.45	1110 0000 0010 0011 0010 0011 0010 1101	01-00-5E-23-23-2D
224.64.255.45	1110 0000 0100 0000 1111 1111 0010 1101	01-00-5E-40-FF-2D
224.0.9.45	1110 0000 0000 0000 1010 0101 0010 1101	01-00-5E-00-09-2D
224.124.9.45	1110 0000 0111 1100 0000 1001 0010 1101	01-00-5E-7C-09-2D
224.252.9.45	1110 0000 1111 1100 0000 1001 0010 1101	01-00-5E-7C-09-2D

Task 3 Answers: The Functional Differences Between IGMPv1 and IGMPv2

Statement	Answer
This unused field in the IGMP packet is zeroed when sent and ignored when received.	A
Routers use group-specific queries to query membership in a single group instead of all groups.	B
If a host receives a membership report before the associated timer reaches 0, the host cancels the countdown timer associated with that group.	C
No leave mechanism is defined. Instead, hosts leave a group passively or quietly at any time without any notification to the router.	A
Defines a procedure for election of the multicast querier for each network segment. The router with the lowest IP address is elected the multicast querier for that LAN segment.	B
One multicast router per LAN must periodically transmit host membership query messages to determine which host groups have members on the querier's directly attached networks.	B

Task 4 Answers: The Setup Procedure in Which Routers and Switches Facilitate Multicast Traffic

Multicast Operation	Step
The switch builds an entry in the switching table that maps the multicast traffic to the client's switch port.	4
The router logs the join message and uses PIM or another multicast routing protocol to add this segment to the multicast distribution tree.	2
IP multicast traffic transmitted from the server is distributed via the designated router to the client's subnet. The destination MAC address corresponds to the group's Class D address.	5
The router creates a CGMP packet with a join request type, the requested multicast group address, and the actual MAC address of the client and sends it to a well-known address to which all switches listen.	3
The client sends an IGMP join message to the designated multicast router. The destination MAC address maps to the Class D address of the group being joined rather than the router's MAC address. The body of the IGMP datagram also includes the Class D group address.	1
The switch receives the multicast packet and examines the forwarding table. If no entry exists for the MAC address, the packet is flooded to all ports within the broadcast domain. If an entry does exist in the switch table, the packet is forwarded only to the designated ports.	6

CHAPTER 9

Configuring IP Multicast

Chapter 8, "Multicast Overview," provided an overview of how multicasting and multicast routing work. This chapter describes how to configure IP multicast routing for Cisco routers, including PIM in both sparse and dense mode and in CGMP. This chapter covers the following topics:

- Planning for multicasting
- Configuring IP multicast routing
- Enhancing the route processor
- Enabling CGMP

Upon completion of this chapter, you will be able to configure the primary distribution router to forward multicast traffic using the Protocol-Independent Multicast Dense Mode (PIM DM) protocol, configure the primary distribution router to forward multicast traffic using the PIM Sparse Mode (PIM SM) protocol, and enable the Cisco Group Management Protocol (CGMP) on the distribution layer devices.

NOTE   For a complete description of the IP multicast routing commands discussed in this chapter, refer to the "IP Multicast Routing Commands" chapter of the *Network Protocols Command Reference,* Part I. For a complete description of the switch-related commands discussed in this chapter, refer to the "Configuring Multicast Services" chapter of the *Catalyst 5000 Series Software Configuration Guide* (4.3). Both of these guides are published by Cisco and can be found on the Universal Documentation CD or on CCO at www.cisco.com.

Planning for Multicasting

Support for IP multicasting requires that the server, client, and network infrastructure of Layer 2 and Layer 3 switches and routers have multicasting enabled. Before you can configure the different entities within your campus network to support IP multicasting, these entities must be able to identify and support multicast traffic. Figure 9-1 shows the entities that must be configured in order to support multicast routing.

Figure 9-1   *Planning for Multicasting*

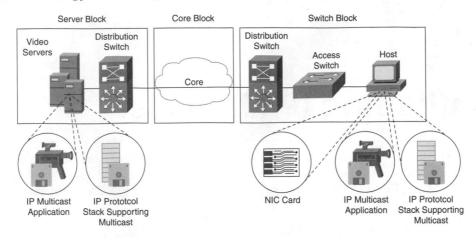

The following requirements must be satisfied before you can enable IP multicasting:

- Server and client hosts must have an IP protocol stack that supports multicasting, as specified in Internet RFC 1112. Full support of this RFC allows hosts to both send and receive multicast data. TCP/IP stacks supporting Windows Sockets V1.1 and V2.0 are multicast-enabled.

- Servers and clients must have applications—such as audio broadcast, video broadcast, or videoconferencing—that support IP multicasting. These applications might have special requirements for system resources, such as processor speed, memory size, and, in some cases, recommended network interface cards (NICs) or graphics accelerator cards.

- NICs on all receiving hosts must be configured to monitor multicast packets in addition to the usual unicast and broadcast packets. Depending on the network infrastructure, receiving hosts might also benefit from having intelligent NICs that can filter out multicasts to unwanted groups, preventing unnecessary interruption to the host CPU.

- The network must have a high-performance backbone with a Layer 2 or Layer 3 switched connection from the backbone to both the sender and receiver hosts, which provides a highly scalable LAN infrastructure for multicasting. The switched infrastructure is desirable because it can provide enough bandwidth to allow unicast and multimedia applications to coexist within the subnet. With dedicated bandwidth to each desktop, switching vastly reduces Ethernet collisions that can disrupt real-time multimedia traffic. A shared media network might prove adequate for low-bandwidth audio applications or limited pilot projects.

- The network must have switches that are appropriate for multicasting. The most appropriate switches have a switch architecture that allows multicast traffic to be forwarded to a large number of attached group members without unduly loading the switch fabric. This allows the switch to provide support for the growing number of new multicast applications without affecting other traffic. Layer 2 switches also need some degree of multicast awareness to avoid flooding multicasts to all switch ports.

Widespread deployment of multicasting in campus networks involves traversing multiple subnet boundaries and router hops. Intermediate routers and/or Layer 3 switches between senders and receivers must be IP multicast-enabled. Although most recent releases of router software include support for IP multicasting, an industry standard multicast routing protocol supported by all vendors is not yet available, making interoperability an issue in multivendor router backbones. The choice of multicast routing protocol among the Distance Vector Multicast Routing Protocol (DVMRP), Multicast Open Shortest Path First (MOSPF), Protocol-Independent Multicast (PIM), and Core-Based Trees (CBT) should be based on the characteristics of the multicast application being deployed, as well as the density and geographical location of the receiving hosts.

End-to-End IP Multicasting

The Cisco IOS software supports the following protocols to implement IP multicast routing:

- PIM is used between routers so that they can track which multicast packets to forward to each other and to their directly connected LANs.

- Internet Group Management Protocol (IGMP) is used between hosts on a LAN and the router(s) on that LAN to track the multicast groups of which the hosts are members.

- CGMP is a protocol used on routers connected to Cisco Catalyst switches. CGMP allows the router to notify the switch with the host addresses that are participating in a multicast group.

- DVMRP is the protocol used on the MBONE (multicast backbone). The MBONE is the Internet's multicast backbone. The Cisco IOS software supports PIM-to-DVMRP interaction.

Figure 9-2 shows where each multicast protocol operates in the network infrastructure in order to provide end-to-end multicast services.

Figure 9-2 *End-to-End Multicasting*

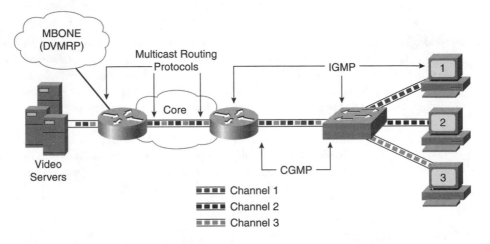

Configuring IP Multicast Routing

IP multicast routing tasks are divided into basic and advanced tasks. This book and the BCMSN course cover the basic tasks you must perform to set up a multicast session. For more information regarding the advanced tasks, refer to the "IP Routing Protocols" chapter of the *Network Protocols Configuration Guide,* Part I. This documentation is published by Cisco Systems and can be found on the Universal Documentation CD or on CCO at www.cisco.com.

The first two basic tasks in the following list are required to configure IP multicast routing; the remaining tasks are optional:

Step 1 Enable IP multicast routing.

Step 2 Enable PIM on an interface.

Step 3 Configure a rendezvous point.

Step 4 Configure the TTL threshold.

Step 5 Join a multicast group.

Step 6 Change the IGMP version.

Step 7 Enable CGMP.

The remainder of this chapter discusses these steps in more detail.

Enabling Multicasting

The first step in configuring Layer 3 devices for multicasting is to enable multicast routing. To enable IP multicast routing on the router, enter the following command in global configuration mode:

```
Router(config)#ip multicast-routing
```

To disable IP multicast routing, enter the **no ip multicast-routing** command.

NOTE   By default, multicast routing is disabled on an interface. Enabling IP multicasting on the router does not automatically enable multicasting for each of the interfaces.

Configuring Multicast Interfaces

An interface can be configured to be in dense mode, sparse mode, or sparse-dense mode. The mode determines how the router populates its multicast routing table and how the router forwards multicast packets received from directly connected LANs. You must enable PIM in one of these modes for an interface to perform IP multicast routing.

Routers forward multicast data on a per-interface basis. Therefore, the multicast routing protocol must be specifically assigned to an interface. To enable PIM on an interface, enter the following command in interface configuration mode:

```
Router (config-if)# ip pim {dense-mode | sparse-mode | sparse-dense-mode}
```

Table 9-1 explains the elements of this command.

Table 9-1   *ip pim Command Elements*

Element	Description
dense-mode	Enables the dense mode of operation. Dense mode is used when all routers in the network need to distribute multicast traffic for each multicast group.
sparse-mode	Enables the sparse mode of operation. Sparse mode is used when relatively few routers in the network will be involved in each multicast.
sparse-dense-mode	The interface is treated in the mode in which the group operates.

In sparse-dense mode, the interface is treated as dense mode if no rendezvous point is detected; the interface is treated as sparse mode if a rendezvous point is detected.

To disable PIM on the interface, enter the **no ip pim** command.

NOTE	Enabling PIM on an interface also enables IGMP operation on that interface.

Dense Mode

In dense mode, a router assumes that all other routers want to forward multicast packets for a group. If a router receives a multicast packet and has no directly connected members or PIM neighbors present, a prune message is sent back to the source. Subsequent multicast packets are not flooded to this router on this pruned branch.

In populating the multicast routing table, dense mode interfaces are always added to the routing table.

All multicast-enabled routers maintain an outgoing interface list (oilist). An interface is placed in the oilist for a multicast group if one of the following conditions occurs:

- A PIM neighbor was heard on an interface
- A host serviced by the interface has joined a group
- The interface was manually configured to join a group

If a PIM neighbor is present, dense mode assumes that all hosts want to receive the group, so the stream is flooded to that link, as shown in Figure 9-3.

Figure 9-3   *Dense Mode*

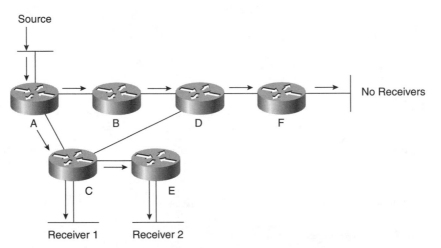

Initially, the multicast-enabled router floods the multicast (source group) packets to all interfaces in the oilist. The source field indicates where the packet originated; the group field contains the multicast address. Because dense mode is a source-based Spanning Tree, the source field contains the address of the source system. However, a (*,G) entry is created automatically as soon as the first packet from any source arrives for group G, or when a locally connected host has joined the group via IGMP. Figure 9-4 shows the corresponding outgoing interface list that occurs during the initial flood of a router configured for dense mode.

Figure 9-4   *Outgoing Interface List*

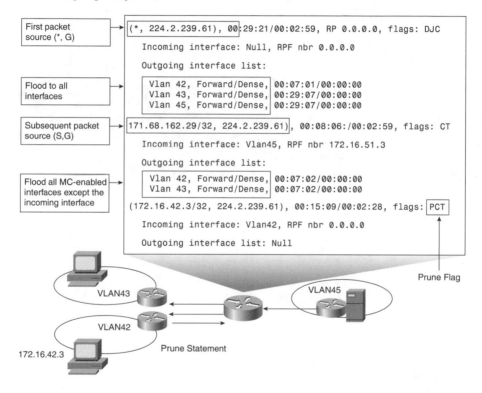

If a downstream router is a leaf node without any receivers, the downstream router sends a prune message back upstream. The upstream router receives the prune message and immediately prunes that interface in the oilist.

Sparse Mode

In sparse mode, a router assumes that other routers do not want to forward multicast packets for a group unless there is an explicit request for the traffic. Rendezvous points are used by senders to a multicast group to announce their existence and by receivers of multicast packets to learn about new senders.

The rendezvous point (RP) keeps track of multicast groups. Hosts that send multicast packets are registered with the RP. The RP sends join messages toward the source. Packets are then forwarded on a shared distribution tree. When no RP is known, the packet is flooded in a dense-mode fashion.

Sparse mode interfaces are added to the table only when periodic join messages are received from downstream routers, or when there is a directly connected member on the interface.

In Figure 9-5, the source begins sending traffic to group G.

Figure 9-5   *Sparse Mode Oilist*

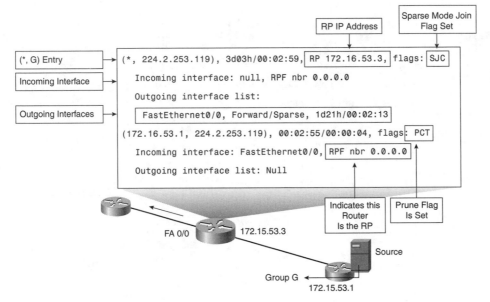

The router interface 172.16.53.1 creates a (*,G) and (S,G) state, encapsulates the multicast packets in PIM register message(s), and unicasts the packet to the RP.

The RP interface 172.16.53.3 de-encapsulates the packets and detects that the packet is for group G, for which the RP already has a (*,G) state. The RP then forwards the packets down the shared tree.

Verifying PIM Configuration

To display information about interfaces configured for PIM, enter the following command in EXEC mode:

```
Router#show ip pim interface [type number] [count]
```

type (optional) indicates the type of interface.

number (optional) indicates the number of the interface.

count (optional) displays the number of packets received and sent out the interface.

The results of this command display the following items:

- IP address of the next-hop router.
- Interface type. On an RSM, this value is the VLAN designation.
- PIM mode configured on each interface.
- Number of PIM neighbors that have been discovered through this interface.
- Frequency, in seconds, of PIM router-query messages.
- IP address of the designated router on the LAN.

Example 9-1 shows sample output from the **show ip pim interface** command.

Example 9-1   *Verifying the PIM Interface Configuration*

```
RSM144#show ip pim interface

Address          Interface     Mode          Nbr    Query   DR
                                             Count  Intvl
172.16.1.144     Vlan1         Sparse-Dense 1       30      172.16.1.145
172.16.41.144    Vlan41        Sparse-Dense 1       30      172.16.11.145
172.16.42.144    Vlan42        Sparse-Dense 0       30      172.16.12.145
172.16.43.144    Vlan43        Sparse-Dense 1       30      172.16.13.145
172.16.44.144    Vlan44        Sparse-Dense 1       30      172.16.14.145
172.16.51.144    Vlan51        Sparse-Dense 4       30      172.16.51.145
172.16.52.144    Vlan52        Sparse-Dense 4       30      172.16.52.145
```

Selecting a Designated Router

Cisco routers use the PIM routing protocol to forward multicast traffic. Two PIM routers are neighbors if there is a direct connection between them.

Each multicast-enabled router is configured to know which interfaces will be using PIM. These interfaces connect to neighboring PIM routers in the network or to host systems on a LAN. If there are multiple PIM routers on a LAN, they are considered to be neighbors. Designated routers are elected based on their IP address on each multiaccess segment, as shown in Figure 9-6.

Figure 9-6   *Designated Routers Are Elected on Multiaccess Segments for Both PIM SM and PIM DM Based on IP Address*

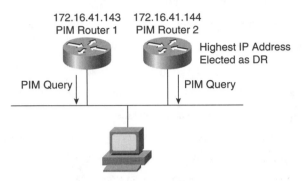

The procedure for electing the designated router (DR) is the same for both PIM SM and PIM DM. Each PIM router connected to a multiaccess LAN issues periodic PIM router queries to the LAN. The PIM router with the highest IP address becomes the DR for the LAN. If the DR becomes inoperable, a new DR is elected from the alternate PIM routers on the LAN.

NOTE   DR election is necessary only on multiaccess networks. It is not required for point-to-point links because the connected router is effectively the DR for directly connected host systems.

On a multiaccess LAN, one router is selected to poll the LAN for host group membership. However, all PIM routers on a single subnet receive replies from the host. The router selected to poll the LAN is called the designated router. The DR is responsible for sending IGMP host-query messages to all hosts on the LAN. There can be many DRs in a campus network—one for each leaf subnet of the distribution tree.

Displaying a PIM Neighbor

The Cisco IOS software can be used to discover the PIM neighbors in the network. To display a table of the neighboring routers from a specific router, enter the following command in privileged EXEC mode:

```
Router#show ip pim neighbor [type] [number]
```

type (optional) indicates the type of interface.

number (optional) indicates the number of the interface.

NOTE	On the RSM, the interface is defined as the keyword **vlan** followed by the VLAN number.

Example 9-2 shows a sample table of neighboring PIM routers for a distribution router.

Example 9-2   *Use the show ip pim neighbor Command to Discover Multicast Neighbors*

```
RSM145>show ip pim neighbor
PIM Neighbor Table
Neighbor Address   Interface        Uptime    Expires    Mode

172.16.51.143      FastEthernet1/0    2d02h    00:01:08   v1   Sparse-Dense
172.16.51.144      FastEthernet1/0    3d01h    00:01:24   v1   Sparse-Dense (DR)
172.16.51.143      FastEthernet1/0    3d01h    00:01:02   v1   Sparse-Dense
172.16.51.144      FastEthernet1/0    3d01h    00:01:19   v1   Sparse-Dense
172.16.52.143      FastEthernet2/0    2d02h    00:01:08   v1   Sparse-Dense
172.16.52.144      FastEthernet2/0    3d01h    00:01:24   v1   Sparse-Dense (DR)
172.16.52.143      FastEthernet2/0    3d01h    00:01:02   v1   Sparse-Dense
172.16.52.144      FastEthernet2/0    3d01h    00:01:19   v1   Sparse-Dense
```

Table 9-2 explains the information shown in Example 9-2.

Table 9-2   *show ip pim neighbor Command Explanation*

Element	Description
Neighbor Address	IP address of the PIM neighbor.
Interface	Interface where the PIM query of this neighbor was received.
Uptime	Period of time that this PIM neighbor has been active.
Expires	Period of time after which this PIM neighbor will no longer be considered active. (Reset by the receipt of another PIM query.)
Mode	PIM mode (sparse, dense, or sparse-dense) that the PIM neighbor is using.
(DR)	This PIM neighbor is the designated router for the network.

Configuring a Rendezvous Point

If you configure PIM to operate in sparse mode, you must also choose one or more routers to act as rendezvous points (RPs).

The IP address of the rendezvous points must be configured on leaf routers. Leaf routers are routers that are directly connected to either a multicast group member or a sender of multicast messages.

The RP address is used in either of the following scenarios:

- First-hop routers use the RP address to send PIM register messages on behalf of a host sending a packet to the group.

- Last-hop routers use the RP address to send PIM join or prune messages to the RP to inform it of group membership.

The RP does not need to know it is an RP. A PIM router can be an RP for more than one group. A group can have more than one RP. The conditions specified by the access list determine for which groups the router is an RP.

To designate the RP address on a leaf router, enter the following command in global configuration mode:

```
Router(config)#ip pim rp-address ip-address [group-access-list-number] [override]
```

Table 9-3 explains the elements in the **ip pim rp-address** command.

Table 9-3   *ip pim rp-address Command Elements*

Element	Description
ip-address	Designates the IP address of a router to be a PIM RP. This is a unicast IP address in four-part dotted notation.
group-access-list-number	(Optional) Number of an access list that defines for which multicast groups the RP should be used. This is a standard IP access list. The number can be from 1 to 100.
override	(Optional) Indicates that if there is a conflict between the RP configured with this command and one learned by auto-RP, the RP configured with this command prevails.

To remove an RP address, enter the command **no ip pim rp-address** *ip-address* [*group-access-list-number*].

Auto-RP

Manually configuring multiple rendezvous points in a large campus network can result in inconsistent RP configurations and cause connectivity problems. Auto-RP is a Cisco proprietary standalone protocol that automates the distribution of group-to-RP mappings in a network running sparse mode PIM. Auto-RP facilitates the use of multiple RPs within a network to serve different group ranges. Auto-RP also allows load splitting among different RPs and arrangement of RPs according to the locations of group participants. Auto-RP automates the distribution of group-to-RP mappings, as shown in Figure 9-7, so that the network administrator does not have to manage all the rendezvous points for different multicast groups.

Figure 9-7   *Auto-RP*

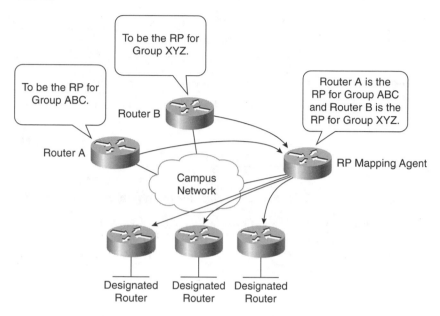

With the auto-RP mechanism, an RP **announce** command must be entered on the router to act as an RP for a certain range of multicast group addresses. Multiple RPs can be used to serve different group ranges, or as backups of each other. An RP mapping agent is assigned to a router to receive the RP announcement messages. The RP mapping agent then sends the consistent group-to-RP mappings to all designated routers. This method allows all designated routers to automatically discover which RP to use for attached receivers and senders.

With the auto-RP mechanism, an RP **announce** command must be entered on the router. This command announces the router as a candidate RP to act as a rendezvous point for a certain range of multicast group addresses. Multiple RPs can be used to serve different group ranges.

Auto-RP is disabled by default. To enable auto-RP on a router, enter the following command in global configuration mode:

```
Router(config)#ip pim send-rp-announce type number scope
    ttl group-list access-list-number
```

Table 9-4 explains the elements in the **ip pim send-rp-announce** command.

Table 9-4 *ip pim send-rp-announce Command Elements*

Element	Description
type	Type of interface for the RP address.
number	Number of the interface for the RP address.
ttl	Time To Live (TTL) value that limits the scope of the announcements.
access-list-number	Access list that describes the group ranges for which this router is the RP.

To disable a router as a candidate RP, enter the **no ip pim send-rp-announce** command.

In Figure 9-8, candidate RPs send an auto-RP RP announcement message to the well-known group CISCO-RP-ANNOUNCE (224.0.1.39). A router configured as an RP mapping agent listens on this well-known group address to determine which RPs act for the various ranges of multicast group addresses.

Figure 9-8 *Auto-RP Discovery*

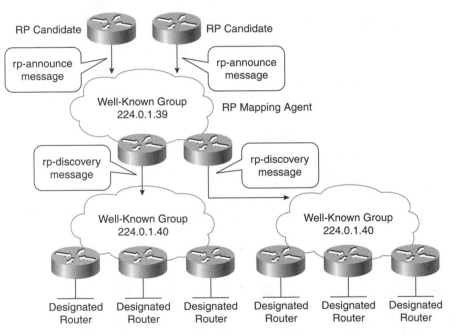

The RP mapping agent then sends the RP-to-group mappings in an auto-RP RP discovery message to the well-known group CISCO-RP-DISCOVERY (224.0.1.40). PIM DRs listen to the well-known group CISCO-RP-DISCOVERY (224.0.1.40) to determine which RPs to use.

By default, a router is not configured as a PIM RP mapping agent. To configure a router to send auto-RP RP discovery messages, enter the following command in global configuration mode:

```
Router#(config)ip pim send-rp-discovery scope ttl
```

ttl is the Time To Live value that limits the scope of the discovery message.

Example 9-3 shows that router 172.16.2.146 is an RP mapping agent. The scope of the discovery messages is 16 router hops.

Example 9-3   *Configuration of Mapping Agent*

```
hostname Router
!
!
ip multicast-routing
!
(text deleted)

ip pim send-rp-discovery scope 16
```

To disable a router as an RP mapping agent, enter the **no ip pim send-rp-discovery** command.

Defining the Scope of Delivery

The function of the Time To Live parameter on a multicast-enabled interface controls whether packets are forwarded out of that interface.

Only multicast packets with a TTL greater than the interface TTL threshold are forwarded on the interface. Packets with a TTL equal to or less than the interface threshold are discarded. The packet TTL is compared to the interface threshold first. The router then decrements the packet TTL upon sending the packet out the interface.

The default value for the TTL threshold on an interface is 0. A value of 0 means that all multicast packets are forwarded on the interface. To change the default TTL threshold value, enter the following command in interface configuration mode:

```
Router(config-if)#ip multicast ttl-threshold ttl
```

ttl signifies the Time To Live value in router hops. This value can range from 0 to 255 hops.

To restore the default value of 0, enter the **no ip multicast ttl-threshold** command in interface configuration mode.

NOTE	Because the Time To Live field is used to limit the range, or scope, of a multicast transmission, configure the TTL threshold only on border routers. Routers on which a TTL threshold value is configured automatically become border routers.

Verifying Multicast Configuration

Each PIM router maintains a multicast routing table. The routing table contains entries known as (S,G) entries, where S indicates the source of the datagram and G indicates the destination multicast group.

When a source sends a join message for a specific multicast group, the DR registers both the source address and the multicast group address (S,G) in the routing table. When a host wants to join a multicast group, it sends a join message to the DR. The DR for the host registers the multicast group address (*,G) in the routing table.

To display the contents of the IP multicast routing table for a specific router, enter the following command in EXEC mode:

```
Router#show ip mroute [group-name | group-address] [source]
        [summary] [count] [active kbps]
```

Table 9-5 explains the elements in the **show ip mroute** command.

Table 9-5   *show ip mroute Command Elements*

Element	Description
group-name and *group-address*	(Optional) IP address, name, or interface of the multicast group, as defined in the DNS host table.
source	(Optional) IP address or name of a multicast source.
summary	(Optional) Displays a one-line, abbreviated summary of each entry in the IP multicast routing table.
count	(Optional) Displays statistics about the group and source, including number of packets, packets per second, average packet size, and bits per second.
active *kbps*	(Optional) Displays the rate that active sources are sending to multicast groups. Active sources are those sending at a rate of *kbps* or higher. The *kbps* argument defaults to 4 Kbps.

To log all IP multicast packets received and transmitted by a router, enter the following command in EXEC mode:

```
Router# debug ip mpacket [detail] [acl] [group]
```

Table 9-6 explains the elements in the **debug ip mpacket** command.

Table 9-6   *debug ip mpacket Command Elements*

Elements	Description
detail	(Optional) Monitors IP header information as well as MAC address information.
acl	(Optional) Monitors only those multicast packets from sources described by the access list.
group	(Optional) Monitors multicast packets generated by a single group.

WARNING   The **debug ip mpacket** command generates a substantial number of messages and can affect router performance.

The Cisco IOS software provides several **debug** commands that allow you to track and log multicast activity in a router. These commands are documented in the *Cisco IOS Release 11.3 Debug Command Reference Guide*. This guide can be found on the Universal Documentation CD or on CCO.

Enhancing the Route Processor

Several additional commands can be entered in order to enhance the router's configuration. These include the capability of the router to join a multicast group for testing purposes and the manipulation of each interface's IGMP version.

Joining a Multicast Group

Cisco routers can be configured to be members of a multicast group. Being a member of a multicast group is useful in determining multicast reachability in a network. If a router is configured to be a member of a specific multicast group, that router can respond to commands addressed to that group, such as ping and Internet Control Message Protocol (ICMP) echo requests. A group member router can also participate in multicast Cisco IOS traceroute actions.

To have the router join a multicast group, enter the following command in interface configuration mode:

```
Router(config-if)#ip igmp join-group group-address
```

group-address is the address of the multicast group.

Issuing a **ping** command specifying that multicast group address causes all routers in that group to respond.

To cancel a router's membership in a multicast group, enter the **no ip igmp join-group** *group-address* command.

NOTE   The term *interface* describes the primary interface on an attached network. If a router has multiple physical interfaces on a single network, this protocol needs to run on only one of the interfaces. Hosts, on the other hand, need to perform their actions on all interfaces that have memberships associated with them.

Manipulating the IGMP Version

How multicast-enabled routers handle group membership in the network differs between IGMP versions 1 and 2. IGMP version 1 is described in RFC 1112. IGMP version 2 is described in RFC 2236. Figure 9-9 shows that the IGMP version might have to be configured if not all hosts support IGMP version 2.

Figure 9-9   *IGMPv2 and IGMPv1 Devices in the Same Subnet*

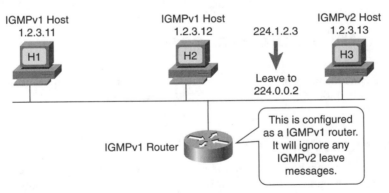

Cisco routers do not automatically detect the IGMP version of systems on the subnet and dynamically switch between versions. If some hosts on the subnet support only IGMPv1, the designated router must be configured for IGMPv1. However, as soon as the router is statically configured for IGMPv1, it will ignore any IGMPv2 leave group messages it receives from any IGMPv2 hosts on the same subnet.

IGMP version 2 mode is the default for all systems using Cisco IOS release 11.3(2)T or later. To determine the current version setting for an interface, enter the following command in privileged EXEC mode:

```
Router#show ip igmp interface type-number
```

type-number represents the name of the interface on which the IGMP protocol is configured.

Example 9-4 shows sample output from the **show ip igmp interface** command.

Example 9-4   *Determining the IGMP Version*

```
Router#show ip igmp interface
Vlan101 is up, line protocol is up
  Internet address is 172.16.1.113, subnet mask is 255.255.255.0
  IGMP is enabled on interface
  Current IGMP version is 2
  CGMP is enabled on interface
  IGMP query interval is 60 seconds
  IGMP querier timeout is 120 seconds
  IGMP max query response time is 10 seconds
  Inbound IGMP access group is not set
  Multicast routing is enabled on interface
  Multicast TTL threshold is 16
  Multicast designated router (DR) is 172.16.1.114
  IGMP querying router is 172.16.1.113 (this system)
  Multicast groups joined: 224.0.1.40 224.0.1.39 224.1.2.3
```

If you must reenable IGMP version 2 or specify IGMP version 1, enter the following command in interface configuration mode:

```
Router(config-if)#ip igmp version {2 | 1}
```

To restore the default value of version 2, enter the **no ip igmp version** command.

Enabling CGMP

Cisco Group Management Protocol allows Catalyst switches to leverage IGMP information on Cisco routers to make Layer 2 forwarding decisions. With CGMP, IP multicast traffic is delivered only to Catalyst switch ports that are interested in the traffic. All other ports that have not explicitly requested the traffic will not receive it. CGMP filtering requires a network connection from the switch to a router running CGMP.

This section covers how to enable CGMP on a router and as a switch.

Enabling CGMP on the Router

CGMP can run on an interface only if PIM is configured on the same interface. CGMP is disabled by default. To enable CGMP on the router, enter the following command in interface configuration mode:

```
Router(config-if)#ip cgmp
```

This command enables the CGMP for IP multicasting on a router and triggers a CGMP join message. The configuration output for CGMP is shown in Example 9-5.

Example 9-5 *CGMP Configuration*

```
Router#show run
Building configuration...
Current configuration:
!
(text deleted)
interface VLAN41
 ip cgmp
 ip address 172.16.41.143 255.255.255.0
 ip pim sparse-dense-mode
 ip multicast ttl-threshold 16
 ip cgmp
```

When a **no ip cgmp** command is issued, a triggered CGMP leave message for group 0000.0000.0000 is sent with the router's MAC address on the interface.

Enabling CGMP on the Switch

Configuring CGMP on the switch allows IP multicast packets to be switched only to those ports that have IP multicast clients. Directing multicast traffic only to user segments that have interested clients reduces the consumption of network bandwidth by not propagating IP multicast traffic throughout the broadcast domain.

In order for CGMP to operate correctly on a switch, the switch must have a network connection to a router running CGMP. A CGMP-capable IP multicast router detects all IGMP packets and informs the switch when specific hosts join or leave IP multicast groups. When the CGMP-capable router receives an IGMP control packet, the router creates a CGMP packet that contains the request type, the multicast group address, and the host's actual MAC address. The router then sends the CGMP packet to a well-known address to which all Catalyst series switches listen. In Figure 9-10, the router sends a CGMP packet to all switches. The CGMP packet contains the MAC address of the host sending the IGMP join request, as well as the multicast address it is joining. Each switch checks its CAM table to determine if it has knowledge of the MAC address that sent the IGMP request. If it does have knowledge of the MAC address, it adds the multicast MAC address to its CAM table destined for the same port.

CGMP on the switch automatically identifies the ports to which the CGMP-capable router is attached. However, static multicast router ports can be statically configured.

To enable CGMP on a switch, enter the following command in EXEC mode:

```
Switch(enable) set cgmp enable
```

NOTE	IGMP snooping must be disabled before you can enable CGMP.

Figure 9-10   *CGMP Join Process*

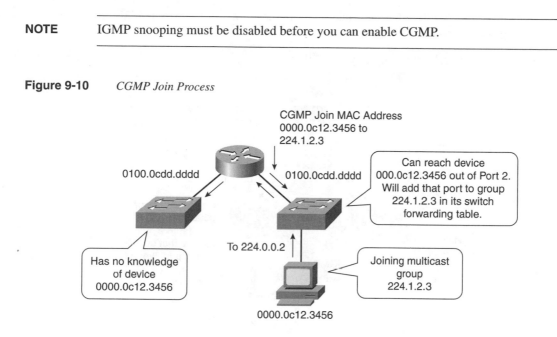

The running configuration in Example 9-6 indicates that the specific switch has been configured for CGMP.

Example 9-6   *Checking for CGMP Configuration*

```
Switch (enable) show config
(text deleted)
!
#cgmp
set cgmp enable
set cgmp leave disable
```

To disable CGMP on a switch, enter the **set cgmp disable** command.

Enabling CGMP Leave

The CGMP/IGMP-capable router sends periodic multicast group queries. If a host wants to remain in a multicast group, it responds to the query from the router. If a host does not want to remain in the multicast group, it does not respond to the router query.

If, after a number of queries, the router receives no reports from any host in a multicast group, the router sends a CGMP/IGMP command to the switch, telling it to remove the multicast group from its forwarding tables, as shown in Figure 9-11. The router does not send a CGMP/IGMP command to remove the multicast group until all the hosts in the group ask to leave the group.

Figure 9-11 *CGMP Leave Process*

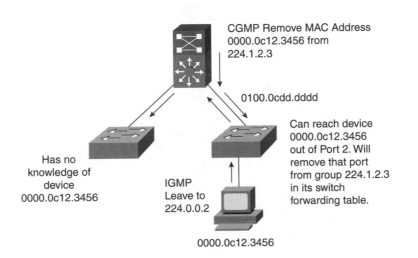

CGMP fast-leave processing allows the switch to detect IGMPv2 leave messages. When the switch receives a leave message, it starts a query-response timer. If this timer expires before a CGMP join message is received, the port is pruned from the multicast tree for the multicast group specified in the original leave message. Fast-leave processing ensures optimal bandwidth management for all hosts on a switched network, even when multiple multicast groups are in use simultaneously.

To enable the CGMP leave function on the switch, enter the following command in privileged EXEC mode:

```
Switch (enable) set cgmp leave enable
```

The **show cgmp leave** command provides verification that CGMP fast-leave has been configured. This command can be entered in either user or privileged EXEC mode.

To disable the CGMP fast-leave function, enter the **set cgmp leave disable** command.

Verifying CGMP Configuration

Several commands are available to help you verify the CGMP configuration on the switch. These commands allow you to view the relationships between VLANs, CGMP-enabled routers, and switch ports. Refer to the "Configuring Multicast Services" section in the *Catalyst 5000 Series Software Configuration Guide (4.3)* for a complete list of these commands.

The **show cgmp statistics** *vlan* and **show multicast group cgmp** *vlan* commands are useful in helping you verify the CGMP configuration on the switch.

The **show cgmp statistics** *vlan* command displays the ongoing CGMP activity for a designated VLAN. Example 9-7 shows sample output from using this command. CGMP statistics display only the information that has been learned automatically through CGMP.

Example 9-7 *Verifying CGMP on the Switch*

```
Switch (enable) show cgmp statistics 41
CGMP enabled
CGMP statistics for vlan 41:
valid rx pkts received            211915
invalid rx pkts received          0
valid cgmp joins received         211729
valid cgmp leaves received        186
valid igmp leaves received        0
valid igmp queries received       3122
igmp gs queries transmitted       0
igmp leaves transmitted           0
failures to add DSW144 to RTR144  0
topology notifications received   80
number of CGMP packets dropped    2032227
```

The **show multicast group cgmp** *vlan command* displays only the multicast router information that has been learned automatically through CGMP. The results of this command show the multicast group MAC addresses associated with a specific VLAN and the ports associated with those groups.

Summary

The configuration of multicast routing grows in importance as the number of multicast applications in the enterprise network increases. One of the most important steps in implementing multicast routing is planning for these multicast applications and determining if their behavior is sparse or dense. As soon as an application's sparseness or denseness has been determined, PIM is configured on each interface to reflect its sparse or dense state.

The following summarizes the protocols and configurations discussed in this chapter:

- PIM is used between routers so that they can track which multicast packets to forward to each other and to their directly connected LANs.

- IGMP is used between hosts on a LAN and the router(s) on that LAN to track of which multicast groups the hosts are members.

- CGMP is a protocol used on routers connected to Cisco Catalyst switches to perform tasks similar to those performed by IGMP.

- On a multiaccess LAN, one router is selected to poll the LAN for host group membership. However, all PIM routers on a single subnet receive replies from the host. The router selected to poll the LAN is called the designated router (DR). The DR is responsible for sending IGMP host query messages to all hosts on the LAN.

- An interface can be configured to be in dense mode, sparse mode, or sparse-dense mode. The mode determines how the router populates its multicast routing table and how it forwards multicast packets received from directly connected LANs. You must enable PIM in one of these modes in order for an interface to perform IP multicast routing.

- In sparse-dense mode, the interface is treated as dense mode if no rendezvous point is detected. It is treated as sparse mode if a rendezvous point is detected.

- With the auto-RP mechanism, an RP **announce** command must be entered on the router to act as an RP for a certain range of multicast group addresses. Multiple RPs can be used to serve different group ranges or serve as backups of each other. An RP mapping agent is assigned to a router to receive the RP-announcement messages. The RP mapping agent then sends the consistent group-to-RP mappings to all designated routers. This method allows all designated routers to automatically discover which RP to use for attached receivers and senders.

- Configuring CGMP on the switch allows IP multicast packets to be switched to only ports that have IP multicast clients. Directing multicast traffic only to user segments that have interested clients reduces the consumption of network bandwidth by not propagating IP multicast traffic throughout the broadcast domain. CGMP can run on an interface only if PIM is configured on the same interface.

Review Questions

The following questions test your retention of the material presented in this chapter. The answers to the Review Questions can be found in Appendix A, "Answers to Review Questions."

1   Discuss the basic tasks required to set up a multicast session within the network.

2   Describe the three PIM modes.

3   Explain how auto-RP automates the distribution of group-to-RP mappings in a network.

4   Discuss how CGMP leverages IGMP information to facilitate Layer 2 forwarding decisions.

Case Study: Configuring IP Multicast

Work through this case study to practice what you learned in this chapter.

In this case study, you will examine the configuration of multicast routing for Cisco IP/TV. The Cisco IP/TV product family streams high-quality video programs to PC users over the enterprise network. It is an example of the common usage of multicast applications. You will complete the following tasks:

- Configure the RSMs to forward multicast traffic using the PIM DM protocol on your assigned interfaces.

- Configure the RSMs to forward multicast traffic using the PIM SM protocol on your assigned interfaces.

- Verify the configuration.

- Enable CGMP on RSM interfaces and the distribution switch.

- Verify the operation of CGMP on both access and distribution switches.

Scenario

Figure 9-12 displays the configuration you will complete in this case study.

Figure 9-12   *Case Study Visual Objective*

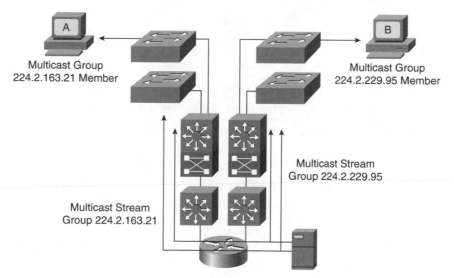

Command List

The commands listed in Tables 9-7 through 9-9 are used in this case study.

Table 9-7 *Access Switch Commands*

Command	Description
show cgmp	Displays current CGMP settings.
cgmp hold-time *seconds*	Global configuration command to set the holdtime.
Ctrl-Shift-6-x	Escape sequence to return to the terminal server or switch block menu.

Table 9-8 *Distribution Switch Commands*

Command	Description
set cgmp enable	Enables CGMP processing on the distribution switch.
show cgmp statistics *vlan*	Displays the CGMP statistical information on a per-VLAN basis.
show config	Displays the switch's configuration.
Ctrl-Shift-6-x	Escape sequence to return to the terminal server or switch block menu.

Table 9-9 *Distribution RSM Commands*

Command	Description
ip cgmp	Router interface command that enables support of CGMP.
ip multicast-routing	Enables IP multicast routing.
ip pim sparse-dense-mode	Enables the PIM protocol on an interface.
ip pim rp-address	Specifies an RP address to enable PIM sparse mode.
show ip igrp interface vlan num	Displays the current interface status.
show ip mroute	Displays the contents of the multicast routing table.
show ip mroute *host ip group ip*	Displays the contents of the multicast routing table for a specified IP host address and specified IP address.
show run	Displays the current configuration.
Ctrl-Shift-6-x	Escape sequence to return to the terminal server or switch block menu.

Task 1: Configure the Primary Distribution Router to Forward Multicast Traffic Using the PIM DM Protocol

This task will enable multicast routing on the distribution router. You will configure your specific VLAN interface with the PIM dense mode protocol and view the mroute information.

There are two RSMs in each switch block. This case study covers the configuration of only one RSM, because the steps to configure them are identical:

Step 1   In global configuration mode, enter the **ip multicast-routing** command.

Step 2   In privileged mode, enter the **show run** command to confirm that multicast routing is enabled. Your configuration should resemble the output shown in Example 9-8.

Example 9-8   *show run Command Output*

```
Building configuration...

Current configuration:
!
version 11.3
service timestamps debug uptime
service timestamps log uptime
no service password-encryption
!
hostname RSM143
!
enable password san-fran
!
ip multicast-routing
```

Step 3   In privileged mode, enter the **show ip mroute** command to display the multicast routing information. Your configuration should resemble the output shown in Example 9-9.

Example 9-9   *show ip mroute Command Output*

```
RSM143#show ip mroute
IP Multicast Routing Table
Flags: D - Dense, S - Sparse, C - Connected, L - Local, P - Pruned
       R - RP-bit set, F - Register flag, T - SPT-bit set, J - Join SPT
Timers: Uptime/Expires
Interface state: Interface, Next-Hop or VCD, State/Mode

RSM143#
```

Step 4   In interface configuration mode, enter the **ip pim sparse-dense-mode** command to enable the PIM protocol on the VLAN51 interface.

Step 5 In privileged mode, enter the **show ip mroute** command to display the multicast routing information. Your configuration should resemble the output shown in Example 9-10.

Example 9-10 *show ip mroute Command Output*

```
RSM123#show ip mroute
IP Multicast Routing Table
Flags: D - Dense, S - Sparse, C - Connected, L - Local, P - Pruned
       R - RP-bit set, F - Register flag, T - SPT-bit set, J - Join SPT
Timers: Uptime/Expires
Interface state: Interface, Next-Hop or VCD, State/Mode

(*, 224.2.210.17), 00:01:00/00:02:59, RP 0.0.0.0, flags: DJ
  Incoming interface: Null, RPF nbr 0.0.0.0
  Outgoing interface list:
    Vlan51, Forward/Sparse-Dense, 00:00:50/00:00:00

(172.16.53.1/32, 224.2.210.17), 00:00:43/00:02:16, flags: PT
  Incoming interface: Vlan51, RPF nbr 172.16.51.3
  Outgoing interface list: Null
 (*, 224.2.182.213), 00:01:00/00:02:59, RP 0.0.0.0, flags: DJ
  Incoming interface: Null, RPF nbr 0.0.0.0
  Outgoing interface list:
    Vlan51, Forward/Sparse-Dense, 00:00:51/00:00:00

(172.16.53.1/32, 224.2.182.213), 00:00:50/00:02:09, flags: PT
  Incoming interface: Vlan51, RPF nbr 172.16.51.3
  Outgoing interface list: Null

(text deleted)

(*, 224.0.1.40), 00:01:10/00:00:00, RP 0.0.0.0, flags: DJCL
  Incoming interface: Null, RPF nbr 0.0.0.0
  Outgoing interface list:
    Vlan51, Forward/Sparse-Dense, 00:01:10/00:00:00
```

Step 6 In interface configuration mode, enter the **ip pim sparse-dense-mode** command to enable the PIM protocol on your VLAN52 interface.

Step 7 In privileged mode, enter the **show ip mroute** command to display the multicast routing information. Notice that VLAN52 has been added to the (*,G) entries. Your display should resemble the output shown in Example 9-11. This depends on other RSMs in your block.

Example 9-11 *show ip mroute Command Output*

```
RSM123#show ip mroute
IP Multicast Routing Table
Flags: D - Dense, S - Sparse, C - Connected, L - Local, P - Pruned
       R - RP-bit set, F - Register flag, T - SPT-bit set, J - Join SPT
Timers: Uptime/Expires
```

Example 9-11   *show ip mroute Command Output (Continued)*

```
Interface state: Interface, Next-Hop or VCD, State/Mode

(*, 224.2.210.17), 00:13:12/00:02:59, RP 0.0.0.0, flags: DJ
  Incoming interface: Null, RPF nbr 0.0.0.0
  Outgoing interface list:
    Vlan52, Forward/Sparse-Dense, 00:00:24/00:00:00
    Vlan51, Forward/Sparse-Dense, 00:13:02/00:00:00

(172.16.53.1/32, 224.2.210.17), 00:00:39/00:02:42, flags: PT
  Incoming interface: Vlan51, RPF nbr 172.16.51.3
  Outgoing interface list:
    Vlan52, Prune/Sparse-Dense, 00:00:25/00:02:42

(*, 224.2.182.213), 00:13:12/00:02:59, RP 0.0.0.0, flags: DJ
  Incoming interface: Null, RPF nbr 0.0.0.0
  Outgoing interface list:
    Vlan52, Forward/Sparse-Dense, 00:00:25/00:00:00
    Vlan51, Forward/Sparse-Dense, 00:13:03/00:00:00

(text deleted)
```

Step 8   In interface configuration mode, enter the **ip pim sparse-dense-mode** command to enable the PIM protocol on the rest of the VLAN interfaces.

Step 9   In privileged mode, enter the **show run** command to display the current configuration and verify that all interfaces are either running PIM or are shut down.

Run IP/TV Viewer from Your PC

This set of steps begins a multicast application. For the purposes of this case study, the application is Cisco IP/TV. However, you could use any multicast application. Cisco IP/TV is presented here for the sole purpose of starting a multicast for the case study.

NOTE   There are applications available on the Internet that allow you to test multicast routing in your network if you do not have access to Cisco IP/TV. A good search would be for applications that stream MP3 files via multicasting.

Follow these steps:

Step 1   From your PC, select Start, Programs, IP/TV Viewer.

Step 2   In the IP/TV window, select Settings, Content Manager. Select the Content Manager tab, and click the Add Content Manager button.

Step 3   Add the Content Manager IP address in the space provided, using IP address 172.16.53.1. Leave the poll parameter at 10 minutes.

Step 4   In the IP/TV window, select the first program listed in the Content list.

Step 5   Right-click the Program Information prompt. Write down the description of the multicast address.

Step 6   Repeat Step 5 for the other three programs. You will need this information when using the **ip mroute** command for a specific group.

Step 7   Right-click the program name and select the Watch Program prompt.

Step 8   From your PC, open a second Telnet window and connect to the first RSM.

Step 9   You have enabled PIM on both RSM VLAN interfaces. The protocol will forward only toward other active members of the group over the shortest-path tree. Displaying the **show ip mroute** command will allow you to see which interfaces are forwarding and which are pruned.

Step 10 In privileged mode, enter the **show ip mroute** *host mc-group* command to display only the information for your host PC IP address to the selected IPmc address. Use the group address of the video channel for the program you've decided to watch. Your display should resemble the output shown in Example 9-12.

Example 9-12   *show ip mroute Command Output*

```
RSM144#show ip mroute 172.16.41.3 224.2.159.93
IP Multicast Routing Table
Flags: D - Dense, S - Sparse, C - Connected, L - Local, P - Pruned
       R - RP-bit set, F - Register flag, T - SPT-bit set, J - Join SPT
Timers: Uptime/Expires
Interface state: Interface, Next-Hop or VCD, State/Mode

(172.16.41.3/32, 224.2.159.93), 00:13:01/00:02:58, flags: CT
  Incoming interface: Vlan41, RPF nbr 0.0.0.0
  Outgoing interface list:
    Vlan1, Prune/Sparse-Dense, 01:38:16/00:00:11
    Vlan42, Prune/Sparse-Dense, 01:38:16/00:00:11
    Vlan43, Prune/Sparse-Dense, 01:38:16/00:00:11
    Vlan44, Prune/Sparse-Dense, 01:38:17/00:00:11
    Vlan51, Prune/Sparse-Dense, 01:38:17/00:02:57
    Vlan52, Forward/Sparse-Dense, 01:38:17/00:00:00
```

Step 11 Telnet to the second RSM and repeat the **show ip mroute** command.
Notice that the flags have P for pruned. Your output depends on how
many groups have active video streams at the time the command is
issued, but it should resemble the output shown in Example 9-13.

Example 9-13   *show ip mroute Command Output*

```
RSM143#show ip mroute 172.16.41.3 224.2.159.93
IP Multicast Routing Table
Flags: D - Dense, S - Sparse, C - Connected, L - Local, P - Pruned
       R - RP-bit set, F - Register flag, T - SPT-bit set, J - Join SPT
Timers: Uptime/Expires
Interface state: Interface, Next-Hop or VCD, State/Mode

(172.16.41.3/32, 224.2.159.93), 00:04:39/00:02:53, flags: PCT
  Incoming interface: Vlan41, RPF nbr 0.0.0.0
  Outgoing interface list:
    Vlan1, Prune/Sparse-Dense, 01:34:23/00:00:23
    Vlan42, Prune/Sparse-Dense, 01:34:23/00:00:23
    Vlan43, Prune/Sparse-Dense, 01:34:23/00:02:56
    Vlan44, Prune/Sparse-Dense, 01:34:24/00:00:23
    Vlan51, Prune/Sparse-Dense, 01:34:24/00:02:55
    Vlan52, Prune/Sparse-Dense, 01:34:24/00:02:55
```

Step 12 In privileged mode, enter the **copy run start** command to save your
configuration on the second RSM.

Step 13 Return to the higher RSM. In privileged mode, enter the **copy run start**
command to save your configuration on the higher-numbered RSM.

Step 14 Return to your PC. In the IP/TV application, watch the second of your
assigned programs.

You have completed this task if you have done the following:

• Configured PIM dense mode on your assigned RSM interfaces

• Successfully run the IP/TV viewer and received the video streams

• Seen from inspection of the **ip mroute** command output how PIM routers display the
state information about multicast groups in the network

• Created two video streams on your desktop

Task 2: Configure Multicast Traffic Using PIM SM

In this task, you will change the multicast routing from dense mode to sparse mode and configure a rendezvous point to support sparse mode. Follow these steps:

Step 1 From your PC Telnet window, connect to your RSM.

Step 2 In global configuration mode, enter the **ip pim rp-address** *ip address* command to designate the rendezvous point for the RSM. Use IP address 172.16.53.3. The system will return the following message as soon as the **ip pim rp-address** command has successfully executed:

```
00:37:52: %AUTORP-5-MAPPING: RP for 224.0.1.39/32 is now 172.16.53.3
00:37:52: %AUTORP-5-MAPPING: RP for 224.0.1.40/32 is now 172.16.53.3
```

Step 3 In privileged mode, enter the **show run** command to verify your configuration. Your configuration should resemble the output shown in Example 9-14.

Example 9-14 *show run Command Output*

```
Building configuration...

Current configuration:
!
(text deleted)
ip multicast-routing
ip dvmrp route-limit 20000
mls rp ip
!!
no ip classless
ip pim rp-address 172.16.53.3
```

Step 4 In privileged mode, enter the **show ip mroute** command, locate the flags in the command output, and verify that the RSM is routing packets in PIM sparse mode. Your display should resemble the output shown in Example 9-15. Output can vary, depending on the number of multicast streams detected.

Example 9-15 *show ip mroute Command Output*

```
(*, 224.2.239.61), 00:37:29/00:02:59, RP 172.16.53.3, flags: SJC
  Incoming interface: Vlan51, RPF nbr 172.16.51.3
  Outgoing interface list:
    Vlan12, Forward/Sparse-Dense, 00:15:09/00:01:57

(171.68.162.29/32, 224.2.239.61), 00:16:15/00:02:59, flags: CT
  Incoming interface: Vlan51, RPF nbr 172.16.51.3
  Outgoing interface list:
    Vlan12, Forward/Sparse-Dense, 00:15:09/00:01:57
```

Step 5 In privileged EXEC mode, enter the **copy run start** command to save the configuration.

Task 3: Enable CGMP

Complete the following steps.

Enable CGMP on RSM Interfaces

Step 1   Telnet to the RSM.

Step 2   In interface configuration mode for your assigned VLAN, enter the **ip cgmp** command to enable processing of CGMP on the interface.

Step 3   In privileged EXEC mode, enter the **show ip igmp interface 41** command to display current settings. You are looking for the CGMP status. Your display should resemble the output shown in Example 9-16.

Example 9-16   *show ip igmp interface Command Output*

```
RSM143#show ip igmp interface vlan 41
Vlan41 is up, line protocol is up
  Internet address is 172.16.41.123/24
  IGMP is enabled on interface
  Current IGMP version is 2
  CGMP is enabled on interface
  IGMP query interval is 60 seconds
  IGMP querier timeout is 120 seconds
  IGMP max query response time is 10 seconds
  Inbound IGMP access group is not set
  IGMP activity: 10 joins, 1 leaves
  Multicast routing is enabled on interface
  Multicast TTL threshold is 0
  Multicast designated router (DR) is 172.16.41.124
  IGMP querying router is 172.16.41.123 (this system)
  Multicast groups joined: 224.0.1.40
```

Step 4   Telnet to the second RSM.

Step 5   In interface configuration mode for your assigned VLAN, enter the **ip cgmp** command to enable processing of CGMP on the interface.

Step 6   In privileged EXEC mode, enter the **show ip igmp interface vlan 41** command to display current settings. Your display should resemble the output shown in Example 9-17.

Example 9-17   *show ip igmp interface Command Output*

```
RSM144#show ip igmp interface vlan 41
Vlan41 is up, line protocol is up
  Internet address is 172.16.41.124/24
  IGMP is enabled on interface
  Current IGMP version is 2
  CGMP is enabled on interface
  IGMP query interval is 60 seconds
```

continues

Example 9-17   *show ip igmp interface Command Output (Continued)*

```
IGMP querier timeout is 120 seconds
IGMP max query response time is 10 seconds
Inbound IGMP access group is not set
IGMP activity: 10 joins, 1 leaves
Multicast routing is enabled on interface
Multicast TTL threshold is 0
Multicast designated router (DR) is 172.16.41.124 (this system)
IGMP querying router is 172.16.41.123
No multicast groups joined
```

Step 7   Return to your PC.

Enable CGMP on Distribution Switches

Follow these steps:

Step 1   Telnet to the distribution switch DSW141.

Step 2   In privileged mode, enter the **set cgmp enable** command to enable
CGMP on the distribution switch.

Step 3   In privileged mode, enter the **show config** command. Your display should
resemble the output shown in Example 9-18.

Example 9-18   *show config Command Output*

```
(text deleted)
#vlan 1005
set spantree fwddelay 15    1005
set spantree hello    2     1005
set spantree maxage   20    1005
set spantree priority 32768 1005
set spantree multicast-address 1005 ieee
!
#cgmp
set cgmp enable
set cgmp leave disable

(text deleted)
```

Step 4   Telnet to the distribution switch, DSW142.

Step 5   In privileged mode, enter the **set cgmp enable** command to enable
CGMP on the distribution switch.

Step 6 In privileged mode, enter the **show config** command. The display should resemble the output shown in Example 9-19.

Example 9-19   *show config Command Output*

```
(text deleted)

#vlan 1005
set spantree fwddelay 15      1005
set spantree hello     2      1005
set spantree maxage    20     1005
set spantree priority 32768 1005
set spantree multicast-address 1005 ieee
!
#cgmp
set cgmp enable
set cgmp leave disable

(text deleted)
```

Step 7 After a few minutes, you should see the output shown in Example 9-20 when you enter the **show cgmp statistics 41** command.

Example 9-20   *show cgmp statistics Command Output*

```
DSW142> (enable) show cgmp statistics 41
CGMP enabled

CGMP statistics for vlan 41:
valid rx pkts received          3
invalid rx pkts received        0
valid cgmp joins received       3
valid cgmp leaves received      0
valid igmp leaves received      0
valid igmp queries received     0
igmp gs queries transmitted     0
igmp leaves transmitted         0
failures to add GDA to EARL     0
topology notifications received 0
number of CGMP packets dropped  0
DSW142> (enable)
```

Step 8 Return to your PC.

Enable CGMP on Your Access Switch

Follow these steps:

Step 1 Telnet to the access switch.

Step 2 In privileged EXEC mode, enter the **show cgmp** command. Your display should resemble the output shown in Example 9-21. CGMP is enabled by default.

Example 9-21 *show cgmp Command Output*

```
ASW21#show cgmp
CGMP Status :    Enabled

CGMP Holdtime (secs) : 600
VLAN    Address               Destination
-----------------------------------------
!
(text deleted)
```

Step 3 In global configuration mode, enter the **cgmp hold-time 300** command to lower the holdtime from 600 seconds to 300 seconds.

Step 4 In privileged EXEC mode, enter the **show cgmp** command. Your display should resemble the output shown in Example 9-22.

Example 9-22 *show cgmp Command Output*

```
ASW41#show cgmp
CGMP Status :    Enabled

CGMP Holdtime (secs) : 300
VLAN    Address               Destination
-----------------------------------------
42      0100.5E02.D211        Fa0/27
43      0100.5E02.9F5D        Fa0/26
41      0100.5E02.ED93        Et0/3, Fa0/26
41      0100.5E02.D211        Et0/3, Fa0/26
41      0100.5E02.9F5D        Et0/3, Fa0/26
42      0100.5E02.E3B1        Fa0/27
44      0100.5E02.D211        Fa0/27
44      0100.5E02.B9A7        Fa0/27
41      0100.5E02.E3B1        Et0/3, Fa0/26
43      0100.5E02.860D        Fa0/26
42      0100.5E02.FD77        Fa0/27
42      0100.5E02.B9A7        Fa0/27
41      0100.5E02.860D        Et0/3, Fa0/26
43      0100.5E02.B6D5        Fa0/26
41      0100.5E02.FD77        Et0/3, Fa0/26
44      0100.5E02.E3B1        Fa0/27
41      0100.5E02.B9A7        Et0/3, Fa0/26
41      0100.5E02.B6D5        Et0/3, Fa0/26
```

Example 9-22   *show **cgmp** Command Output (Continued)*

```
41      0100.5E00.0128      Fa0/26
44      0100.5E02.FD77      Fa0/27
43      0100.5E02.ED93      Fa0/26
```

Step 5   Return to your PC.

Step 6   Close and reopen some of the video streams. Watch them for two minutes, and then close the IP/TV application completely.

Step 7   Telnet to your access switch.

Step 8   In privileged mode, enter the **show cgmp** command. Observe that the host interface e0/3 is not on the list anymore. It will take about five minutes for the VLAN entries to expire. Notice that 0100.5E00.0128 does not go away (it's the 224.0.1.40 group).

CHAPTER 10

Controlling Access to the Campus Network

When the campus network has been implemented, you need to implement a security policy to protect the network. The need to control access to the network increases as the applications used on the network increase in both quantity and size. An access policy is used for many reasons other than security. It allows the network administrator to control the amount and type of traffic that uses each link, allowing for the deterministic growth of the link. It prevents fraudulent routes from making it out of the switch block to the core. A good access policy allows the network to act and grow in a predictable manner.

This chapter focuses on some of the methods used to implement access control policies in the campus network. First is a definition of the components of an access policy. Then, there is a discussion of some of the methods of policy implementation for each component.

Securing the campus network involves managing physical devices through passwords and access lists, as well as securing the physical access to the network through port security. Traffic management control is accomplished through the applied use of access lists to interfaces and routing tables.

This chapter covers the following topics:

- Definition of an access policy
- Managing network devices
- Access layer policy
- Distribution layer policy
- Core layer policy

Definition of an Access Policy

Access control cannot be implemented until a standard access policy has been created.

An access policy is a corporation's documented standard of network access for its users. Just as corporations vary widely, so will their standards for access to the network.

An access policy might define some or all of the following:

- Management of network devices, including physical security and access control
- User access to the network through the use of mechanisms such as port security and VLAN management
- Access to distributed and enterprise services
- The traffic that is allowed out of the switch block and onto the core block and providing for traffic management
- Route filtering to determine the routes that should be seen by the core block and other switch blocks

The access policy is designed to secure the campus network and to prevent unwanted or unneeded traffic from getting to the most expensive (and sometimes slowest) areas of the network. An access policy allows a network administrator to provide a level of service to users based on a set of defined traffic standards. In addition, an access policy provides a level of security to campus network devices.

Applying Policies in a Hierarchical Model

Each layer can have a different access policy, because each layer is responsible for a different task. Some of the policies in the access policy, such as controlling physical access, apply to all devices in the campus network. Other policies, however, should be defined at specific layers. As shown in Figure 10-1, each block of the campus network should have an access policy defined.

Access Layer

The access layer is the entry point to the network for the users. The access policy at this layer should allow legitimate users into the network while keeping other users out. Controlling access here should be done through the use of port security and passwords to protect network devices.

Distribution Layer

The distribution layer is the primary handler of Layer 3 routing decisions for the network. It should also be the home of most of your access policy. The access policy at this layer can be as simple as saying that Engineering's traffic is not allowed to be carried on XYZ network or as complicated as defining the exact path that information should take. The access policy at the distribution layer should be responsible for ensuring that only necessary traffic makes it to the core or to another switch block. The distribution layer is also responsible for advertising the correct routing and services information to the core.

It should limit the information sent to the core as much as possible. The distribution layer also deploys some of the same device management techniques as the access layer.

Figure 10-1   *An Access Policy Should be Created for Each Layer in the Hierarchical Model*

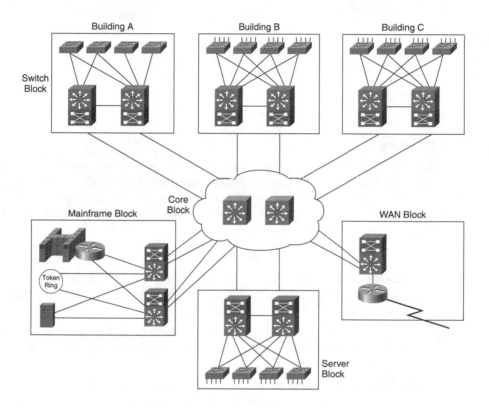

Core Layer

The core layer should have little to no policy control. The core's job is to pass information as quickly as possible. Any policy implemented at the core will only serve to slow down the data that is traversing the core. The core relies on the distribution layer to prevent unwanted traffic from making it to the core block.

Managing Network Devices

The policy to control access to network devices should be one of the first components of the access policy. All devices at every layer of the campus network should have a plan to provide for the following:

- Physical security
- Passwords
- Privilege levels to allow limited access to a network device
- Limiting virtual terminal or Telnet access

Physical Security

Given physical access to any device, be it a switch, router, server, or workstation, a person knowledgeable about that device can gain complete control over it. Almost all devices have a mechanism, or back door, for getting in without a password. A security policy is of little use without physical security for network devices. A physical security policy should be defined for every device in your network.

Physically secure your network by doing the following:

- **Establish configurations for the access policies**—This should be done for devices at each layer of the hierarchical model. Have a security plan for each site that details how the device and the links will be secured.

- **Provide the proper physical environment**—The physical environment should have provisions for locking the room, proper ventilation and temperature controls, and backup power.

- **Control direct access to the device**—Lock racks when possible, and apply passwords to console and auxiliary ports. Disable ports such as the auxiliary port if they are not being used.

- **Secure access to network links**—Provide the same type of security for the wiring closets that you would provide for the physical equipment.

Assigning Passwords

There are several different ways to access every Cisco device. Every method of accessing the device should have a password applied in order to prevent unauthorized access.

Out-of-band management options include the following:

- Console 0
- Auxiliary 0

In-band management options include the following:

- TFTP servers
- Network management software such as CiscoWorks 2000
- Virtual terminal ports that are used for terminal access and are referred to as vty ports. There are five vty ports by default on each Cisco device. You can create more virtual terminal ports if you need to have more than five users assessing a device simultaneously.

Most Cisco routers can support more than five vty ports. There are, however, some exceptions in which the router can support a total of only five vty ports.

Each method of access into the network device should have a login and password applied, as shown in Figure 10-2.

Figure 10-2 *A Password and Login Method Should Be Set at Every Entry Point into a Network Device*

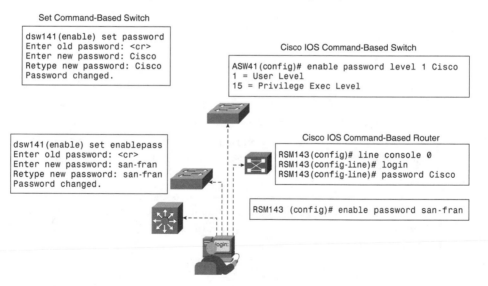

The login option indicates where to find the login information. If **login** is specified without any keyword, as in the case of the console port, **login** will be used the login. The user will be prompted for the password of the line itself (in the case of Figure 10-2, **Cisco**). The other options indicate that the specific user must log in. The keyword after **login** indicates where to find the user information. The **login local** statement indicates that the information will be found locally in the **username student password cisco** statement. Another option is

login authentication. This option indicates that the login information is contained on a centralized authentication server and requires that additional AAA commands be issued. Centralizing usernames, passwords, and profile information makes it easier to maintain a large number of users or devices.

It is recommended that users log into the system with a username and password rather than having everyone use the line's password. Having users log into the device makes it easier to track down who is accessing the device and what changes they have made.

NOTE   Although usernames and passwords can be configured on the network device, it is recommended that security be handled in a centralized location. This is done through the use of a process called AAA (authentication, authorization, and accounting). AAA allows all facets of user security, including access to resources, to be defined in a centralized, controlled place. TACACS+ is a protocol providing detailed accounting information and flexible administrative control over the authentication and authorization process. TACACS+ is facilitated through AAA and is enabled with AAA commands. CiscoSecure provides AAA, Radius, and TACACS+ services for network devices as well as for remote access. Use caution when implementing AAA authentication services. If authentication is configured incorrectly, you can be locked out of the network device.

By default, passwords are stored in cleartext format in the router's configuration. The only exception to this is the enable secret password, which is automatically encrypted. To encrypt all passwords, issue the following command:

```
Router(config)#service password-encryption
```

Password encryption can be compromised, so it should be used in combination with other methods of security.

NOTE   More information on TACACS+ and other authentication services can be found in the Managing Cisco Network Security course. Contact your Cisco authorized training partner for more information.

Controlling Session Timeouts

Assigning passwords prevents users from initiating a session with the network device. If, however, the console is left unattended in privileged mode, any user can modify the network device's configuration. A timeout for an unattended session provides additional security.

The default timeout is 10 minutes. To change the default timeout, enter the following command:

```
Router(config-line)#exec-timeout minutes seconds
```

NOTE   You can also prevent access to your terminal session while keeping the session open by issuing the lock command. You will be prompted for a password. Reenter the password when you return to your session.

Privilege Levels

The two default levels of access are user and privileged. User level allows the user to perform certain commands but does not give him or her the ability to modify the configuration or perform a debug. At the other end of the spectrum, privileged level allows the user to issue all commands, including configuration and debug commands.

The Cisco IOS command set can provide users with additional levels of privilege with the use of the **privilege level** command. This allows network administrators to provide a more granular set of rights to Cisco network devices.

NOTE   Privilege levels are particularly useful in large networks where there are many people who might need access to a network device. A user can be given the ability to perform trouble-shooting commands such as **show line** and **show interface** without being given the rights to modify the entire device.

Sixteen different levels of privilege can be set, ranging from 0 to 15. Level 1 is the default user EXEC privilege. The highest level, 15, allows the user to have all rights to the device. Level 0 can be used to specify a more limited subset of commands for specific users or lines. For example, you can allow user "guest" to use only the **show users** and **exit** commands.

NOTE   Five commands are associated with privilege level 0: **disable**, **enable**, **exit**, **help**, and **logout**. If you configure a centralized authorization server, such as AAA authorization, for a privilege level greater than 0, these five commands will not be included.

At other privilege levels, you must specify the commands that are to be assigned to that privilege level.

Use the **privilege** command to define the commands that are assigned to a specific privilege level:

```
Router(config)privilege mode level level command
```

mode can have the values listed in Table 10-1.

Table 10-1 *Mode Values for the **privilege** Command*

Mode	Description
configuration	Global configuration
controller	Controller configuration
exec	EXEC
hub	Hub configuration
interface	Interface configuration
ipx-router	IPX router configuration
line	Line configuration
map-class	Map class configuration
map-list	Map list configuration
route-map	Route map configuration
router	Router configuration

Use the **enable secret level** *level password* command to set the password for the privilege level.

Example 10-1 shows a user named student logging in with a privilege level of 3. Privilege level 3 has been assigned a password of san-jose. The user will inherit all of the commands that have been configured under **privilege** *mode* **level 3** *command*.

Example 10-1   *A User Named student Logs in with a Privilege Level of 3*

```
Router(config)# privilege exec level 3 show ip route
Router(config)# privilege exec level 3 ping
Router(config)# privilege exec level 3 trace
Router(config)#enable secret level 3 san-jose
Router(config)#enable secret san-fran
Router(config)#username student password cisco

Trying x.x.x.x ... Open

Username: student
Password: cisco          ◄────────────
Router>enable 3
Password: san-jose       ◄────────────
Router#show privilege
Current privilege level is 3
```

Banner Messages

As a user enters the network device, a banner or message should greet that person. This is referred to as the message of the day. The greeting should indicate how serious security breaches are to your corporation. Do not use the word "welcome" in the message or in any way indicate that you are welcoming someone to the system. Intruders have been found not guilty in court based on the fact that the network administrator welcomed them with the message of the day banner. Instead, use a statement such as ******Unauthorized access will be vigorously prosecuted******.

To configure the message of the day, enter the following command:

```
Router(config)#banner motd ^c message ^c
```

The **^c** is the delimiter in the command. It is used to indicate the beginning and end of the message. Any character is valid in the message, except the delimiter. The delimiter can be any character, as long as it is not used anywhere else in the message.

NOTE   Entering the banner command is sometimes less than intuitive. The delimiter is any character that will not be repeated in the banner. Good characters to use include symbols such as #, $, and %. After you issue the **banner motd ^c** command, press the Enter key. You should be able to tell that you are in banner configuration mode by the lack of a router prompt. Type in the banner the way you would like it to appear as someone enters the system. The banner will be displayed exactly the way you type it in. When you are done creating the banner, type in your delimiter key. You will now be back at the router prompt. Banners can also be applied to other functions, such as the login process and EXEC.

Controlling Virtual Terminal Access

By default, each Cisco device has five virtual terminal lines. On most routers, you can create more than five vty lines.

The virtual terminal line that you received is based on the number of vtys that are currently in use. Because you will never know exactly which vty line you are using, you should set identical restrictions on all lines. An access control list applied to virtual terminal lines will control who can Telnet to a specific device, as shown in Figure 10-3.

Figure 10-3 *Access List Applied to vty Lines*

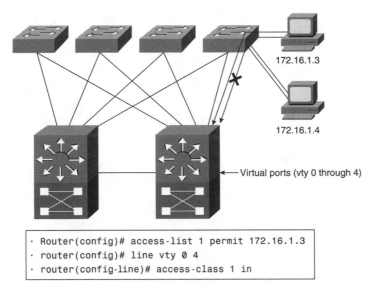

```
· Router(config)# access-list 1 permit 172.16.1.3
· router(config)# line vty 0 4
· router(config-line)# access-class 1 in
```

The **line vty** *vty-number vty-range* command takes you into the selected configuration mode of the virtual terminal lines. The most common version of this command is **line vty 0 4**. It indicates that you are modifying the first five virtual terminal lines.

The **access-class in|out** command applies the access list to the virtual terminal lines. The access list is a standard access list that indicates which source addresses are either permitted or denied. The **in|out** condition at the end of the **access-class** statement indicates whether the source address should be allowed to establish a Telnet session with this device or allowed to Telnet out of this device.

NOTE   Access lists that are applied to interfaces (with the **access-group** command) do not affect traffic that is originated from that device. For that reason, it is important to apply the virtual terminal control both inbound and outbound on the virtual terminal lines. Inbound indicates who can Telnet to this device. Outbound indicates where someone can Telnet to after he is inside the network device. Use caution when implementing virtual terminal access lists. You might inadvertently prevent yourself from getting to the device.

Controlling HTTP Access

Cisco IOS software now allows you to use a Web browser to issue Cisco IOS commands to your network device. The HTTP server software required to do this is found in IOS releases

11.0(6) and later. This might make configuring network devices easier, but it opens some security holes at the same time.

By default, HTTP access is off. To enable HTTP access, enter the following command:

```
Switch(config)#ip http server
```

An access list can then be used to filter the access to the HTTP management of the network device. In Figure 10-4, the access list explicitly permits the station 172.16.1.3 and implicitly denies all others. Applying the access list with the **ip http access-class 1** statement means that all stations other than 172.16.1.3 will be denied access to the HTTP software.

Figure 10-4   *Controlling HTTP Access*

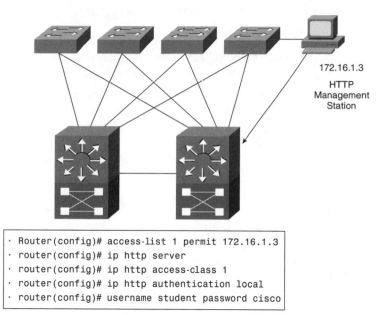

```
· Router(config)# access-list 1 permit 172.16.1.3
· router(config)# ip http server
· router(config)# ip http access-class 1
· router(config)# ip http authentication local
· router(config)# username student password cisco
```

Password security for Web access is similar to console and virtual terminal access. Use the following command to specify where the authentication information is contained:

```
Switch(config)#ip http authentication [aaa | enable | local | tacacs]
```

Table 10-2 explains the options in this command.

Table 10-2   *ip http authentication Command Options*

Option	Description
aaa	Indicates that AAA should be used for authentication.
enable	Indicates that the enable password should be used. This is the default method.

continues

Table 10-2 *ip http authentication Command Options (Continued)*

Option	Description
local	Indicates that the local user database is used for authentication information.
tacacs	Indicates that a TACACS server should be used for authentication.

Access Layer Policy

The access layer is the entry point for users to get onto the network. Cable connections are generally pulled from an access layer switch to offices and cubicles in a company. For this reason, the network devices of the access layer are the most physically vulnerable. Anyone can plug a station into an access layer switch.

Several precautions should be taken at the access layer:

- **Port security**—Limit the MAC addresses that are allowed to use the switch to prevent unauthorized users from gaining access to the network.

- **VLAN management**—VLAN 1 is the default VLAN of all ports. VLAN 1 is traditionally the management VLAN. This means that users who enter the network on ports that are not configured will be in the management VLAN of the switch block. It is recommended that the management VLAN be moved to another VLAN in order to prevent users from entering the network on VLAN 1 on a port that is unconfigured.

NOTE By default, all ports on a switch are enabled and in VLAN 1. Anyone who walks up to an unused port will be enabled and in VLAN 1 by default. This would result in a security problem if the switches were left in the default management VLAN. There are two different philosophies on the handling of this issue. Some companies move the management VLAN from VLAN 1 to some other VLAN. This allows users to come into the default VLAN but keeps them from harming any of the network devices. Other companies leave the switches in VLAN 1 but disable the ports that are not in use. Both methods have their advantages and disadvantages. When all devices are placed in a VLAN other than VLAN 1, you run the risk that the VLAN will be deleted, disabling the ports. When you leave the management VLAN as VLAN 1 and disable all the ports, you have the added administration task of enabling the ports any time the network changes. The solution is the classic answer to any network problem: It depends.

Port Security

Port security is a feature of the Cisco Catalyst switches that allows the switch to block input from a port when the MAC address of a station attempting to access the port is different from the configured MAC address for that port. This is referred to as a *MAC address lockdown*.

When a port receives a frame, it compares the frame's source address to the secure source address that was originally learned by the port. If the addresses do not match, the port is disabled, and the port's LED turns orange.

NOTE   Port security cannot be applied to trunk ports where addresses might change frequently. Not all hardware supports port security. Check your documentation or the CCO Web site to see if your hardware supports this feature.

By default, the switch allows all MAC addresses to access the network. It relies on other types of security, such as file server operating systems and applications, to provide network security. Port security allows a network administrator to configure a set of allowed devices or MAC addresses to provide additional security. If port security is enabled, only the MAC addresses that are explicitly allowed can use the port. A MAC address can be allowed by the following:

- **Static assignment of the MAC address**—The network administrator can code the MAC address when port security is assigned. This is the more secure of the two methods, but it is difficult to manage.

- **Dynamic learning of the MAC address**—If the MAC address is not specified, the port turns on learning for security. The first MAC address seen on the port becomes the secure MAC address.

To enable port security using the set CLI, use the following command:

```
Switch>(enable)set port security mod_num/port_num enable mac address
```

To verify port security using the set CLI, use the following command:

```
Switch>(enable)show port mod_num/port_num
```

To enable port security on IOS-based switches, use the following command:

```
Switch(config-if)#port secure [max-mac-count maximum_mac_count]
```

To verify port security on IOS-based switches, use the following command:

```
Switch#show mac-address-table security [type module/port]
```

The **port secure [max-mac-count** *maximum_mac_count*] command allows the network administrator to define the maximum number of MAC addresses that can be supported by this port. The maximum number can range from 1 to 132. The default value is 132.

Distribution Layer Policy

This section discusses the methods for controlling access at the distribution layer.

Most of the access control policy is implemented at the distribution layer. This layer is also responsible for ensuring that data stays in the switch block unless it is specifically permitted outside the switch block. It is also responsible for sending the correct routing and service information to the core.

A good policy at the distribution layer ensures that the core block or the WAN blocks are not burdened with traffic that has not been explicitly permitted. It also protects the core and the other switch blocks from receiving incorrect information, such as incorrect routes, that might harm the rest of the network.

Access control at the distribution layer falls into several different categories. They can do the following:

- Define which user traffic makes it between VLANs and thus ultimately to the core. This can be done in the form of an access list applied to an interface to permit only certain data to pass through.

- Define which routes are seen by the core block and ultimately by the switch block. This can be done through the use of distribution lists to prevent routes from being advertised to the core.

- Define which services the switch block will advertise to the rest of the network. Service control could also be used to define how the network finds the server-aggregation block in order to get services such as Dynamic Host Configuration Protocol (DHCP) and Domain Name System (DNS).

Controlling Information with Filters

Many of the access control methods used at the distribution layer rely on the creation of an access control list. There are two types of IP access lists:

- Standard
- Extended

Each type of access list is a series of permits and denies based on a set of test criteria. The standard access list allows for a test criteria of only the source address. The extended access list allows a greater degree of control by checking the source and destination addresses as well as the protocol type and the port number or the packet's application type. A standard access list is easier for the router to process, but an extended access list provides a greater degree of control.

NOTE	An access list is a way of defining traffic based on protocols, addressing, and port numbers. It does nothing to the router until it is applied. Access lists can have many different applications, including traffic filtering, defining interesting traffic, defining priority traffic, and so on. The creation of the access list is always the same process. It is the application of the access list that determines how it will be used.

An access list does nothing until it is applied. Access lists are created for a variety of applications. They can be used to control access in the campus network by being applied in different capacities. These include, but are not limited to, the following:

- Applying the access list to the interface for traffic management purposes through the use of the *protocol_***access-group** command, where *protocol* is the Layer 3 protocol that is being managed.

- Applying the access list to a line for security purposes through the use of the **access-class** command. This determines the users of a specific line. This book focuses on the virtual terminal lines.

- Managing routing update information through the use of the **distribute-list** command. This determines which routes are learned by the router and which routes are advertised out of the router.

- Managing services update information through the use of commands such as **ipx output-sap-filter** in order to determine which services are advertised.

Standard Access Lists

IP standard access lists have the following characteristics:

- The test condition is based on the source address only.

- Numbered standard access lists are 1 to 99.

- The access list is processed top-down, line by line. As soon as a match is found, the access list stops processing.

- There is an implicit deny of everything at the end of every access list. If no match is found in the access list, it will ultimately match the implicit deny at the end of the list.

- The creation of the access list does nothing until the access list is applied.

Figure 10-5 shows that standard access lists check on the source address, either inbound or outbound. This access list allows only the source address of 172.16.1.3. It denies everything else.

Figure 10-5   *IP Standard Access List Overview*

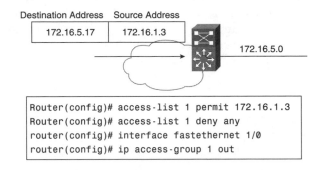

```
Router(config)# access-list 1 permit 172.16.1.3
Router(config)# access-list 1 deny any
router(config)# interface fastethernet 1/0
router(config)# ip access-group 1 out
```

Access lists can be applied either inbound or outbound. An inbound access list checks the packet as it enters the interface, before it has been routed. An outbound access list checks the packet as it goes out the interface, after it has been routed.

Extended Access Lists

An extended access list follows many of the same principles as a standard access list. An extended list, however, provides for a higher degree of control by enabling filtering based on the source address as well as the destination address, the protocol type, and the application or port number.

Extended access lists have the following characteristics:

- Top-down processing of the access list. As soon as a match is made in the access list, it stops processing and either permits or denies the packet based on the statement in the access list.

- Numbered access lists use a range of 100 to 199.

- Test conditions include protocol type, source address, destination address, application port, and session layer information.

- There is an implicit deny of everything at the end of the access list.

- The creation of the access list does nothing until the access list is applied using the appropriate command.

Use the **access-list** command to create an entry in an extended traffic filter list:

```
Router(config)# access-list access-list-number { permit | deny
    { protocol | protocol-keyword }}{ source source-wildcard | any }
    { destination destination-wildcard | any }
    [ protocol-specific options ] [ log ]
```

Table 10-3 explains the options in this command.

Table 10-3   *access-list Command Options*

Option	Description
access-list-number	Identifies the list to which the entry belongs. For an IP extended access list, use a number from 100 to 199.
**permit	deny**	Indicates what the result will be if the test condition is matched. A permit allows the packet either into or out of the interface. A deny drops the packet and sends an ICMP message back to the source.
protocol	Indicates the protocol type to match. Options include **ip**, **tcp**, **udp**, **icmp**, **igrp**, **eigrp**, **ospf**, **nos**, and any number in the range of 0 to 255. To match any protocol, use the keyword **ip**.
source and *destination*	IP addresses of both the source and the destination.
source-wildcard and *destination-wildcard*	Wildcard mask that indicates the number of address bits to match. 0 indicates to match the bit exactly; 1 indicates that the bit can be anything.
log	Results in informational logging messages about the packet that matches the entry. Use this command with caution, because it consumes CPU cycles.

Filtering Data Traffic

An access list can be applied to an interface in order to keep data traffic from either entering or leaving the interface. You apply an access list to the interface using the command **ip access-group** *access-list-number* [**in | out**].

NOTE   It is recommended that, whenever possible, the access control list be applied on the outbound interface rather than the inbound interface. In general, an outbound access list processes more efficiently than an inbound access list.

For example, the access list shown in Figure 10-6 does the following:

- Allows all TCP traffic coming from any host going to the subnetwork of 172.16.2.0 255.255.255.0
- Allows any device to reach the host of 172.16.1.2 if the application is SMTP (mail)
- Permits UDP packets with the application type of Domain (DNS)
- Allows ICMP echo and echo reply (ping)
- Denies all other traffic

Figure 10-6 *Extended Access Lists Allow for a More Granular Check of the Packet*

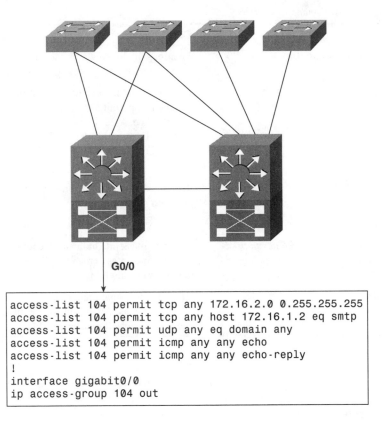

```
access-list 104 permit tcp any 172.16.2.0 0.255.255.255
access-list 104 permit tcp any host 172.16.1.2 eq smtp
access-list 104 permit udp any eq domain any
access-list 104 permit icmp any any echo
access-list 104 permit icmp any any echo-reply
!
interface gigabit0/0
ip access-group 104 out
```

Filtering Routing Update Traffic

Controlling the core block's routing table has several advantages:

- Reduces the size of the routing table at the core block, allowing it to process packets faster

- Prevents users from getting to networks that have not been advertised unless they have a static or default route to get there

- Prevents incorrect information from propagating through the core block

There are several ways to control the routing information that is sent to the core block:

- **Route summarization**—Depending on the routing protocol used, a summarized entry of all the switch block's available routes can be sent from the distribution layer to the core.

- **Distribution lists**—A distribution list can be used to indicate which routes the distribution layer can advertise to the core or, conversely, what the core can accept from the switch block.

NOTE   Route summarization is not covered in the BCMSN course or this book due to the large number of differences between routing protocols. For more information on route summarization, see the Advanced Cisco Router Configuration coursebook from Cisco Press.

You can filter routing update traffic for any protocol by defining an access list and applying it to a specific routing protocol with the **distribute-list** command.

To configure a filter, follow these steps:

Step 1   Identify the network addresses that you want to filter, and create a standard access list.

Step 2   Determine whether the routing protocol should be filtered incoming or outgoing on the interface.

Step 3   Assign the access filter to routing updates.

Step 4   To apply a distribution list, use the following command in router configuration mode:

```
Router(config-router)#distribute-list access_list_number in |out
    [interface | routing_process autonomous_system_number]
```

Table 10-4 explains the options in this command.

Table 10-4   *distribute-list Command Options*

Option	Description
access_list_number	Number of the previously created standard access list.
**in	out**	Defines the filtering on either incoming routing updates (**in**) or outgoing routing updates (**out**).
interface	Name of the interface. Indicates that the networks in the access list will be filtered if they came from or are going to a specific interface.
routing_process autonomous_system_ number	Name of the routing process, including the keywords **static** and **connected**. This option applies to outbound distribution filters only. If the routing process uses autonomous system numbers, this must be specified in the command. IGRP is an example of a routing process that uses an autonomous system number. If the autonomous system number is 100, this variable is IGRP 100.

NOTE	Distribute lists can be applied to any routing process, but their function varies with different routing protocols. In general, for distance vector routing protocols, the distribute list determines what gets added to the routing table or what gets advertised out of the routing table. The **distribute-list** command works differently with a link-state routing protocol. A link-state routing protocol builds a database of the topology and uses that to build its routing table. All routers in an area must have the same topological database and therefore have the same routes in their routing tables. A **distribute-list** statement in a link-state routing protocol doesn't indicate which routes to either send out or accept because the link-state protocol doesn't send routing updates. It sends topological updates. In a link-state environment, the **distribute-list** command actually indicates which routes can be redistributed via another routing process into the link-state routing protocol. For example, if EIGRP were redistributed into OSPF, the **distribute-list** command under OSPF would indicate which EIGRP routes could be placed into OSPF as external routes.

Figure 10-7 indicates that the routing process of EIGRP sends the network of 172.16.2.0 0.0.0.255 in its routing updates out G0/0 (Gigabit Ethernet) but filters all other networks. If the core is connected to G0/0, it will receive only 172.16.2.0, and only 172.16.2.0 will be allowed to traverse the core. Route filtering allows you to control which networks are accessible and prevents fraudulent routes from being entered into the core layer.

Figure 10-7   *IP Route Filtering Example*

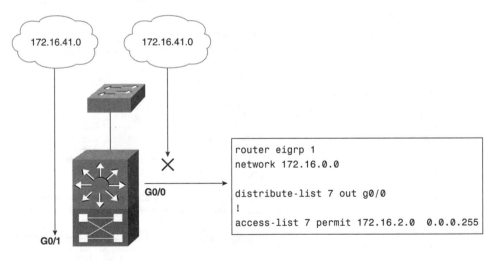

In Figure 10-7, the options for the networks of 172.16.x.0 (except 172.16.2.0) include the following:

- All other networks will be able to send and receive data in the switch block but will not be allowed to get to any other switch block or get to the core block. In order for this to work, a static or default route will have to be configured.

- No other networks will be seen by the core block and other switch blocks. A default or static route will allow them to send data to and receive data from other switch blocks, including the core.

Core Layer Policy

The core layer is responsible for moving data as quickly as possible. All the devices that are designed to be core layer solutions are optimized to move data as quickly as possible. For this reason, the core layer should have little to no policy.

The only policies that should be applied at the core layer are those that relate to quality of service (QoS) commands for congestion management and congestion avoidance.

NOTE   The implementation of QoS at the core layer varies greatly, depending on the Cisco device deployed at the core and which version of IOS is running. Check the CCO Web site for device-specific information.

Summary

This chapter covered the access policies that can be applied to each layer in the campus switch model. Defining and documenting a corporate access policy is an important step in maintaining a secure and predictable campus network. This chapter covered the following:

- Controlling physical devices at all layers with the use of passwords, logins, and privilege levels to allow for a more granular set of rights for network administrators

- Preventing unauthorized access to your network through the use of port security

- Controlling access at the distribution layer using access lists in a variety of ways, including route distribution, traffic management at the interface, and virtual terminal management

Review Questions

The following questions test your retention of the material presented in this chapter. The answers to the Review Questions can be found in Appendix A, "Answers to Review Questions."

1 List and define the different methods of login.

2 List the steps necessary to assign security to a virtual terminal port.

3 What types of polices exist at the distribution layer? At the core?

4 What are the different uses of access lists at the distribution layer?

Answers to Review Questions

This appendix contains the answers to each chapter's review questions. Because most of the questions are in short answer format, your answers will vary. The author has given the best possible answer and explanation for each question.

Chapter 1 Answers to Review Questions

1 Discuss the various trends that have forced the redesign of campus networks.

The use of LAN switches increases bandwidth per user, causing explosive growth and increasing traffic on the network.

The increased use of multifaceted applications, such as desktop publishing, videoconferencing, and WebTV broadcast programs, consumes large amounts of bandwidth. This congests the network.

Emerging traffic patterns show that 80 percent of the traffic in today's network is remote. Information now comes from anywhere in the network. This creates massive amounts of traffic that must travel across subnet boundaries.

Enterprise servers are being deployed to centralized server farms because of the reduced cost of ownership, security, and ease of management.

Customer requirements for the campus network create pressure for a new design. These requirements are as follows:

— **Fast convergence**

— **Deterministic paths**

— **Deterministic failover**

— **Scalable size and throughput**

— **Centralized applications—This requirement dictates that centralized applications are available to support most or all users on the network**

— **The new 20/80 rule**

— **Multiprotocol support**

— **Multicasting**

2 Describe the different switching technologies and how they enable multilayer switching.

Layer 2 switching is hardware-based bridging. Layer 2 switches give network managers the ability to increase bandwidth.

Layer 2 switching, also called bridging, forwards packets based on the unique MAC address of each end station. Data packets consist of infrastructure content, such as MAC addresses, other information, and end-user content.

The high performance of Layer 2 switching can produce network designs that increase the number of hosts per subnet. Increasing the hosts leads to a flatter design with fewer subnets or logical networks in the campus.

Layer 2 switching still has all the same characteristics and limitations as bridging. Broadcast domains built with Layer 2 switches still experience the same scaling and performance issues as the large bridged networks of the past.

Layer 3 switching is hardware-based routing. The primary difference between the packet-switching operation of a router and a Layer 3 switch is the physical implementation.

A simple definition of Layer 4 switching is the ability to make forwarding decisions based not just on the MAC address (Layer 2 bridging) or source/ destination IP addresses (Layer 3 routing) but on the TCP/UDP (Layer 4) application port number.

Layer 4 gives the network the ability to differentiate between applications when performing routing decisions. To be effective in enterprise networks, Layer 4 switching must provide performance comparable to Layer 3 wirespeed routers. In other words, Layer 4 switching must be performed at full media speeds across all ports.

By implementing Layer 4 switching in hardware, these switches can apply security filters at wire speeds.

Layer 4 switching enables the prioritization of traffic based on specific applications. This provides a more granular approach to policy-based quality of service (QoS) mechanisms.

Layer 4 switching provides a way of differentiating between types of applications. This information can be taken into consideration when performing forwarding decisions.

Multilayer switching combines Layer 2 switching, Layer 3 routing, and, sometimes, Layer 4 application functionality in the same device.

Multilayer switching interrogates the first packet in a flow using normal Layer 3 switching functions in sequence. If a network flow is identified, the characteristics determined for the initial packet are forwarded to a cache. All subsequent packets are switched to that same destination at Layer 2.

3 Explain the multilayer model and how it affects traffic flows in the network.

The multilayer model consists of the access layer, the distribution layer, and the core layer. This model allows designers to define building blocks that interconnect users and services.

The access layer of the network is the point at which end users are allowed into the network. The distribution layer of the network marks the point between the access and core layers of the network. The distribution layer also helps define and differentiate the core. The sole purpose of the core layer is to switch packets as fast as possible.

The switch block contains a balanced implementation of scalable Layer 2 switching and Layer 3 services. If the switch block experiences a broadcast storm, the router prevents the storm from propagating into the core and into the rest of the network. Each block is protected from the other blocks when failures occur.

The core block is responsible for transferring cross-campus traffic without any processor-intensive operations, such as routing.

The location of servers and their functions impacts traffic patterns. Enterprise servers are placed close to the backbone. Maintaining a consistent administrative distance between all end users and enterprise servers results in more consistent performance for all users. Distributed servers reside at the access or distribution layer of the network.

Because a distributed server is connected to the same switch as the supported end users, the traffic is never routed to another location. This configuration lowers the amount of traffic on the backbone, increasing network performance and response times.

Chapter 2 Answers to Review Questions

1 Describe the three major link technologies and where they are used in the campus network.

The three major link technologies currently used in the campus network are Ethernet, Fast Ethernet, and Gigabit Ethernet. Ethernet is typically found at the access layer. Fast Ethernet can be found at the access layer and in the uplinks from the access layer to the distribution layer. Gigabit Ethernet can be found in the uplinks from the access layer to the distribution layer and at the core layer.

2 List the steps necessary to configure an Ethernet connection on an access-layer switch.

Follow these steps to configure an Ethernet port on an access switch:

1. Set the port speed:

— The speed of the ports is 10/100 on an IOS-based switch and cannot be altered. Connect the cable to the 10Base port.

— On a set command-based system, enter the following command:

```
Switch(enable) set port speed mod-num/port-num 10
```

2. Set the duplex mode:

— On an IOS command-based system, enter the following command:

```
Switch(config-if)# duplex {auto | full | full-flow-control | half}
```

— On a set command-based system, enter the following command:

```
Switch(enable) set port duplex mod-num/port-num {full | half}
```

You can also define an interface/port description, but this command is not required.

Chapter 3 Answers to Review Questions

1 Explain how VTP enables propagation of VLAN data across the network.

VTP uses trunk links to advertise a VTP database. Each switch listens to VTP updates that are in the same domain and that have the correct password. Using the configuration revision number, the switches determine whether they need to update their database with the most current VLAN information.

2 Discuss how frame identification enables VLAN membership association.

Frame identification is the process of marking the frame with the VLAN number in order to indicate its VLAN membership. The two frame identification techniques currently supported are ISL and 802.1Q. ISL uses an encapsulation around the existing frame to identify the VLAN. 802.1Q inserts the VLAN information into the standard Ethernet frame and recalculates the CRC.

3 Define the three VTP modes of operation and describe how they work.

The three modes of VTP operation are server, client, and transparent:

— **Server mode allows the network administrator to add, delete, and rename VLANs. Each modification to the VLANs increments the configuration revision number by 1. In addition, a server switch retains VLAN information in NVRAM. This means that it will boot with the VLAN information that it had before it was turned off.**

— **Client mode does not allow the network administrator to add, delete, and rename VLANs. It furthermore does not save VLAN information to NVRAM, and it requires another device (such as a server) to advertise the VLANs to it when it boots. A client does, however, advertise VTP information to other switches.**

— **Transparent mode means that the switch does not participate with other switches in the VTP domain. VLANs can be created, deleted, and renamed, and they are stored to NVRAM. Transparent switches do not advertise their VLANs, nor do they accept VTP update information from other switches.**

4 Describe the use of VTP pruning. Explore the same solution without VTP pruning.

VTP pruning is used to stop broadcasts, multicasts, and flooded unicasts from being sent to switches that do not have ports in that VLAN. Clearing the VLAN from the trunk link would accomplish the same goal, with the added benefit that the link no longer participates in the Spanning-Tree Protocol for that VLAN, increasing the convergence time of STP.

Chapter 4 Answers to Review Questions

1 List the five Spanning Tree port states.

The five Spanning Tree states are blocked, listen, learn, forward, and disabled.

2 Identify at least one network problem caused by STP.

The following are three network problems caused by Spanning Tree:

— **Convergence time after a network failure.**

— **The time that it takes a port to move into forwarding mode causes many workstations to time out while attempting to attach to a service.**

— **Paths can be suboptimal if the network is not designed correctly.**

3 Explain the solutions developed to improve STP operation.

The following solutions improve Spanning Tree:

— **PortFast—Lets a port bypass Spanning Tree operations.**

— **UplinkFast—Creates an UplinkFast group of ports that can be used to perform a rapid failover in the case of a direct link failure.**

— **BackboneFast—Expires the max age timer when it stops hearing the superior BPDU but continues hearing the inferior BPDU.**

— **EtherChannel—Bundles parallel ports, which allows Spanning Tree to treat them as one port.**

— **Root bridge—Correct placement of the root bridge and modification of the diameter will improve path selection and convergence time.**

— **Port priority and port cost—Used to influence the path selections made by Spanning Tree.**

4 Discuss the purpose of an inferior BPDU.

The loss of a superior BPDU and the receipt of an inferior BPDU triggers the BackboneFast process.

BackboneFast is initiated when a root port or blocked port on a switch receives inferior BPDUs from its designated bridge. An inferior BPDU identifies one switch as both the root bridge and the designated bridge.

When a switch receives an inferior BPDU, it indicates that a link to which the switch is not directly connected (an indirect link) has failed (that is, the designated bridge has lost its connection to the root bridge). Under normal Spanning Tree rules, the switch ignores inferior BPDUs for the configured maximum aging time.

5 Identify the purpose of PortFast, and describe its operation.

PortFast is used for workstation and server ports to allow them to more quickly connect to the network. Without PortFast, workstations might have problems with DHCP and server connections when they are first booted.

PortFast immediately places the port in a forwarding state. It then performs listening and learning to determine if there is a loop. If there is, the port is taken out of a forwarding state and placed in a blocked state.

6 Explain the difference between BackboneFast and UplinkFast.

UplinkFast is configured only on access layer switches. It is used for direct link failure. It transitions a blocked port into a forwarding state if it detects a link loss on the forwarding port.

BackboneFast is configured on all switches in the switch block. It is used for indirect link failure. It is triggered by the receipt of an inferior BPDU on a root port.

Chapter 5 Answers to Review Questions

1 List at least two problems that can impede communications between VLANs, and identify a solution for each problem.

VLANs are associated with individual networks or subnetworks; therefore, network devices in different VLANs cannot communicate with one another.

Because VLANs isolate traffic to a defined broadcast domain or subnet, network devices in different VLANs cannot communicate with one another without some intervening device to forward packets between subnets.

In switched networks, route processors are used to provide communications between VLANs. Route processors provide VLAN access to shared resources and connect to other parts of the network that are either logically segmented with the more traditional subnet approach or that require access to remote sites across wide-area links.

Connecting the separate subnets through a route processor introduces the issue of how end-user devices can communicate with other devices through multiple LAN segments.

So that each end device does not have to manage its own routing tables, most devices are configured with the IP address of a designated route processor. This designated route processor is the default router to which all non-local network packets are sent.

2 Identify at least two Cisco platform solutions for an internal route processor topology at the distribution layer.

Any of the following solutions are viable:

— **A Catalyst 5000 with an RSM**

— **A Catalyst 5000 with an RSFC**

— **A Catalyst 6000 with an MSM**

— **A Catalyst 6500 with an MSFC**

3 Compare and contrast the steps used to configure an interface on an RSM and an ISL link on an external router.

For an internal route processor:

— **Enter the VLAN number as part of the interface command.**

— **Assign a unique IP address to that interface.**

— **Administratively enable the interface.**

For an external route processor:

— **Identify the interface type and subinterface number.**

— **Define the VLAN encapsulation type and VLAN number.**

— **Assign an IP address to the interface.**

— **Administratively enable the interface.**

Chapter 6 Answers to Review Questions

1 Explain how the routing and switching functions of a Cisco MLS switch work together to enable multilayer switching.

Multilayer switching is a technique used to increase IP routing performance by handling the packet switching and rewrite function in ASICs.

In MLS, the frame forwarding and rewrite process functions previously handled by a router have been moved to switch hardware.

The Cisco implementation of MLS is comprised of three components:

— **Multilayer Switching Switch Engine (MLS-SE)—The MLS-SE is the switching entity that handles the function of moving and rewriting the packets. The MLS-SE is a NetFlow Feature Card residing on a Supervisor Engine III card in a Catalyst switch.**

— **Multilayer Switching Route Processor (MLS-RP)—This component is a Route Switch Module or an externally connected Cisco 7500, 7200, 4500, 4700, or 8500 series router with software that supports multilayer switching. The MLS-RP sends MLS configuration information and updates, such as the router MAC address and VLAN number, flow mask, and routing and access list changes.**

— **Multilayer Switching Protocol—This protocol operates between the MLS-SE and MLS-RP to enable multilayer switching. The Multilayer Switching Protocol is the method by which the RSM or router advertises routing changes and the VLANs or MAC addresses of the interfaces that are participating in MLS.**

An MLS cache entry is created for the initial packet of each flow. This packet is called the candidate packet. The switch forwards the frame to the MLS-RP.

If the MLS-RP finds an entry for the destination address in the routing table, the MLSP-RP rewrites the packet and returns the frame to the switch.

The MLS-SE compares the XTAGs for both the candidate entry in the MLS cache and the returned frame. If the two XTAGs match, the frame came from the same router for the same flow. This second frame becomes the enable entry in MLS cache, and the partial entry for that flow is completed.

2 Describe the three flow mask modes and the impact that ACLs have on those modes.

The three flow mask types supported by the MLS-SE are as follows:

— **Destination-IP mode—This mode represents the least-specific flow mask. The MLS-SE maintains one MLS entry for each destination IP address. All flows to a given destination IP address use this MLS entry. This mode is used if no access lists are configured on any of the MLS router interfaces.**

— **Source-Destination-IP mode**—The MLS-SE maintains one MLS entry for each source/destination IP address pair. All flows between a given source and destination use this MLS entry, regardless of the IP protocol ports. This mode is used if there is a standard access list on any of the MLS interfaces.

— **IP-Flow mode**—This mode represents the most specific flow mask. The MLS-SE creates and maintains a separate MLS cache entry for every IP flow. An IP-Flow entry includes the source IP address, destination IP address, protocol, and protocol ports. This mode is used if there is extended access switching.

3 Discuss how various router/switch configurations can affect multilayer switching.

There is a dependency between the router and the switch at the distribution layer. How these devices are placed in relation to each other is critical to multilayer switching.

As long as the MLS-SE can detect both candidate and enable packets, multilayer switching takes place. However, if the configuration is designed so that the enabling packet is never returned to the MLS-SE, the candidate packet ages out of the MLS cache, and all packets in that flow are routed.

Changes to the routing table might affect the behavior of MLS. Whenever a route change takes place, the MLS cache is flushed for any flow entries affected by the route change.

As long as the MLS-SE detects both the candidate and enable packets for the new route, a flow entry is entered into the MLS cache.

Chapter 7 Answers to Review Questions

1 Discuss the basic tasks required to configure HSRP in the network.

The basic tasks of configuring HSRP include the following:

— **Choose the IP address of the virtual router. This IP address must be on the same subnet as the standby and active router but must be a unique address.**

— **Assign the virtual IP address to the standby and active routers using the standby** *group-number* **ip** *virtual-ip-address* **command.**

— **Assign a priority to indicate which router should be active using the standby** *group-number* **priority** *priority-value* **command.**

2 Explain the purpose of active and standby routers and how these two entities interact.

The active router is responsible for responding to packets that are sent to the virtual router's IP address and MAC address. It is also responsible for sending out hello packets to the all-router multicast address in order to indicate to the standby router that it is still available. The standby router is responsible for sending out hello packets to the all-router multicast address in order to indicate that it is available. It is also responsible for becoming the active router if it has not heard from the active router during the hold-down time.

3 Describe the six HSRP router states and the actions an HSRP router takes in each state.

The six HSRP states are initial, learn, listen, speak, standby, and active:

— **Initial state—All routers begin in the initial state. This is the starting state, and it indicates that HSRP is not running. This state is entered via a configuration change or when an interface first comes up.**

— **Learn state—In the learn state, the router is still waiting to hear from the active router. The router has not yet seen a hello message from the active router, nor has it learned the IP address of the virtual router.**

— **Listen state—In the listen state, the router knows the virtual IP address but is neither the active router nor the standby router. The router listens for hello messages from those routers. Routers other than the active and standby router remain in listen state.**

— **Speak state—In the speak state, the router sends periodic hello messages and actively participates in the election of the active and/or standby router. A router cannot enter the speak state unless the router has the IP address of the virtual router.**

— **Standby state—In the standby state, the router is a candidate to become the next active router and sends periodic hello messages. There must be one, and only one, standby router in the HSRP group.**

— **Active state—In the active state, the router forwards packets that are sent to the group's virtual MAC address. The active router sends periodic hello messages. The must be one, and only one, active router in the HSRP group.**

Chapter 8 Answers to Review Questions

1 Discuss the three types of transmission methods and the effect each one has on network bandwidth.

With a unicast design, an application sends one copy of each packet to every client unicast address. Replicated unicast transmissions consume bandwidth within the network.

In a broadcast design, an application sends only one copy of each packet using a broadcast address. End stations not using a multimedia application must process the broadcast traffic.

Multicasting sends one copy of each packet to a special address. Multicasting saves bandwidth and controls network traffic by forcing the network to replicate packets only when necessary. By eliminating traffic redundancy, multicasting reduces network and host processing.

2 Explain how routers and switches handle the impact of multicast addressing techniques.

IP multicasting uses Class D addresses.

This multicast group ID is a single address typically written as decimal numbers in the range 224.0.0.0 through 239.255.255.255. The high-order bits in the first octet identify this 224-base address.

The last 28 bits of a Class D address identify the multicast group ID.

The lower 23 bits of the Class D address are mapped into a block of Ethernet addresses.

Because IP multicast groups are 28 bits long, the mapping cannot be one-to-one. Only the 23 least-significant bits of the IP multicast group are placed in the frame. The remaining 5 high-order bits are ignored, resulting in 32 different multicast groups being mapped to the same Ethernet address.

There is a small chance of collisions should multiple groups happen to pick Class D addresses that map to the same MAC-layer multicast address.

Usually, higher-layer protocols let hosts interpret which packets are for the application. The chance of two different groups picking the same Class D address and the same set of UDP ports is extremely unlikely.

3 Discuss different multicast routing protocols, and identify which ones are most effective in a campus network.

Routing protocols fall into two categories: dense and sparse.

Dense mode multicast routing protocols are designed to work well in environments that have plentiful bandwidth and where receivers are densely distributed, such as campus networks.

Sparse mode routing protocols are more suited to scaling over large WANs, where bandwidth is scarce and expensive.

DVMRP is widely used on the Internet multicast backbone.

MOSPF is best suited for environments that have relatively few (source, group) pairs active at any given time. This protocol works less well in environments that have many active sources, or environments that have unstable links. Although this is a good protocol for campus LANs, Cisco does not support MOSPF.

PIM DM works best when numerous members belong to each multimedia group, and resources, such as bandwidth, are plentiful. This is a good routing protocol for a campus LAN.

PIM SM is optimized for environments that have many multipoint data streams. Sparse multicasting is most useful when the following are true:

— There are few receivers in a group.

— Senders and receivers are separated by WAN links.

— The type of traffic is intermittent.

The CBT protocol is designed to operate efficiently over a wide-area network where bandwidth is scarce and group members can be sparsely distributed.

Chapter 9 Answers to Review Questions

1 Discuss the basic tasks required to set up a multicast session within the network.

Only two basic tasks must be accomplished in order to get multicasting to work. IP multicasting must be enabled globally, and then PIM must be enabled at the interfaces. Sparse mode requires the additional configuration of a rendezvous point.

2 Describe the three PIM modes.

The three PIM modes are dense mode, sparse mode, and sparse-dense mode.

Dense mode assumes that all interfaces should receive the multicast information unless it is specifically instructed to prune a segment. Dense mode uses a source-distribution tree.

Sparse mode requires the configuration of a rendezvous point and assumes that the segment does not need to receive the multicast unless it requests it. In addition, sparse mode uses a shared distribution tree.

Sparse-dense mode allows for both configurations. If there is a rendezvous point for a multicast group, it uses sparse mode. If there is no rendezvous point, dense mode is used.

3 Explain how auto-RP automates the distribution of group-to-RP mappings in a network.

Candidate RPs send an auto-RP RP announcement message to the well-known group. A router configured as an RP-mapping agent listens on this well-known group address to determine which RPs act for the various ranges of multicast group addresses.

The RP mapping agent then sends the RP-to-group mappings in an auto-RP RP discovery message to the well-known group. PIM DRs listen to the well-known group to determine which RPs to use.

4 Discuss how CGMP leverages IGMP information to facilitate Layer 2 forwarding decisions.

A CGMP-capable IP multicast router detects all IGMP packets and informs the switch when specific hosts join or leave IP multicast groups. When the CGMP-capable router receives an IGMP control packet, the router creates a CGMP packet that contains the request type, the multicast group address, and the host's actual MAC address. The router then sends the CGMP packet to a well-known address to which all Catalyst series switches listen. The CGMP-capable switch then identifies the ports that are to receive the multicast MAC address.

Chapter 10 Answers to Review Questions

1 List and define the different methods of login.

There are two default modes of login: user (privilege level 1) and privilege (privilege level 15). A network administrator can set up additional privilege levels to allow for a more granular set of rights. The privilege levels can be from 0 to 15.

The network device can generally be logged into from the auxiliary port (AUX), the console port (CON), or one of five vtys.

2 List the steps necessary to assign security to a virtual terminal port.

The following are several ways in which you can secure access to a terminal device:

— **Assign a password and a login to the virtual terminal ports.**

— **Create an access list that permits the devices that are allowed to Telnet to this network and denies devices that are not allowed in.**

— **Apply the access class to the virtual terminal port.**

3 What types of polices exist at the distribution layer? At the core?

The distribution layer's policy should determine what traffic and which routes make it into and out of the switch block.

The core layer should have no policy, because its function is to move data from block to block as quickly as possible.

4 What are the different uses of access lists at the distribution layer?

The following are the different uses of access lists at the distribution layer:

— **Traffic filtering at the interfaces**

— **Route filtering of the routing protocol**

— **Service filtering of advertised services**

Switching Architectures and Functional Descriptions

Because this book has not offered a detailed discussion of the hardware components that make up the campus network, this appendix is intended as a supplement that describes the switching architecture of the Catalyst 4000, 5000, 6000, and 8500 family of switches.

This appendix also helps you understand the Catalyst multilayer switching components and their methods of operation.

NOTE   Some of the information presented in this appendix does not appear in the Building Cisco Multilayer Switched Network course presented by Cisco Authorized Training Partners.

Switching Terms and Definitions

Before discussing the different components of multilayer switches, it will be helpful to define some of the terms that are commonly used in the industry to describe switches.

Backplane

The backplane is a series of electrical traces located in a chassis and used as the physical connection points. The easiest way to see the backplane in a Cisco Catalyst switch is to remove some of the line modules and look at the back of the chassis. What you are seeing is actually the backplane.

Local Switching

Each Catalyst series switch has a switching fabric that is used by all ports and line cards in order to transmit frames from the ingress port to the egress port. This means that each port must arbitrate for access to the switching fabric in order to send a frame, even if the frame exits on the same line card where it entered the switch.

Some line cards support a local switch fabric. A local switch fabric can be used to transfer a frame from one port to the next when they are on the same line card without arbitration for the central switch fabric.

Oversubscription

Oversubscription is a condition in which the sum of bandwidth of all the ports is greater than the capacity of the switch fabric. Switches are rarely oversubscribed in production due to the fact that most links use only a percentage of their total bandwidth. Switches handle oversubscription by using input buffers to buffer frames as they wait for access to the switching fabric.

Nonblocking

A nonblocking switching implementation occurs when the switch fabric has a greater capacity than the sum of the bandwidth of all the ports.

Queuing

Queuing is a buffer mechanism inside the switch used to control congestion. Congestion can occur in one of several places. It can occur as the frame enters the switch if the switch is busy processing something else. Congestion can occur as the frame attempts to exit the switch if the cable medium is congested. Buffers allow the switch to hold the frame until the congestion is over rather than dropping the frame.

Switching Decisions

One of the most important steps in the switching process is determining where the information is actually supposed to go. There are two different times when this decision can occur. The first is a central switching decision. A central switching decision occurs at the central processor. An example of this is the Catalyst 5000 series switch. All decisions about what ports should receive a frame are done at one location on the Supervisor Engine.

Switching decisions can also occur locally. A local switching decision is an implementation in which the switching decisions are made at the local line card or at the port. A local switching decision is faster than one that is centralized. An example of a local switching decision is the Catalyst 8540 series switch. Decisions about which ports should receive the frame are made at the line card level without the need to consult a centralized processor.

Switching Fabric

The switching fabric is the highway the data takes as it passes from one port to the next inside the switch. This is frequently referred to as the data plane, D-plane, or D-bus. Many times you hear about backplane capacity when in fact the person is talking about the switching fabric. The size of the switching fabric varies, depending on which switch you are using. It is defined by its width in bits and the speed at which it can transmit those bits, defined in megahertz (MHz). For example, the Catalyst 6000 series switch has a switch fabric that is 256 bits wide operating at 62.5 MHz/sec. This translates into a switch fabric capacity of 256 bits × 62.5 MHz/sec = 16 Gbps. This calculation is considered to be half duplex and is based on a frame moving in one direction. If the switching fabric can support the transmission and receipt of a frame simultaneously, it is calculated at full duplex. This means that the 16 Gbps switching fabric of the 6000 series switch is actually calculated as a 32 Gbps data highway.

Switching Components

Several different components make up every switch. First, there must be some type of congestion management in order to provide a smooth frame flow through the switch. A switching decision about where the frame should go must also be made. Finally, a data highway must be used to move the frame from the ingress port to the egress port.

Congestion Management

Congestion management is used to handle periods of time when the switch fabric or the port is receiving more data than it can handle. Congestion management is needed when multiple ports are trying to access the same port simultaneously. It is also needed when the switch fabric is congested. Finally, one of the most important reasons for congestion management is to handle ports that have different capacities, as well as switching fabrics that have different capacities than the ports. A 100 Mbps port can quickly overwhelm a 10 Mbps port if there is no congestion management. A switching fabric that is moving frames at 32 Gbps will overwhelm a 1 Gbps port if there is no congestion management.

Congestion management is implemented in a variety of ways using buffers or queues. A queue is memory that is allocated in order to hold a frame until the switch or port can process it. Queues can be either dynamic or fixed.

Many Cisco products use a fixed queue size. A fixed amount of memory space is allocated for each frame that is to enter the switch or router. Because the queue size is fixed, it must be large enough to accommodate the largest frame that can enter the switch. It is typically set to the maximum transmission unit (MTU). Each frame, regardless of its size, would take the same amount of memory to be buffered. A fixed queue size requires less-expensive controllers but is an inefficient use of memory. In Figure D-1, each frame must take 2000 bytes of memory space, regardless of its size.

Figure B-1 *Fixed Buffer Queuing*

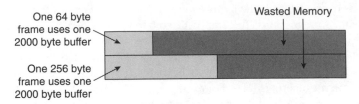

Dynamic queue buffers are fixed in small increments, such as 64 bytes. Each frame entering the switch takes only as many buffers as are needed to queue that frame. For example, a 64-byte frame would take a single buffer, and a 1500-byte frame would take 24 buffers. Dynamic queue buffers allow for a more efficient use of memory, but they require more expensive controllers to manage the location of the complete frame inside the queues. In Figure B-2, the dynamic buffers are 64 bytes in size, allowing frames to use only the memory they need.

Figure B-2 *Dynamic Buffer Queuing*

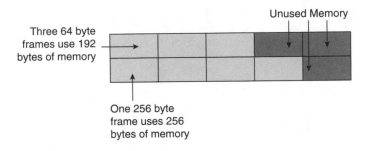

The next section examines some of the different techniques for implementing queues. A switch can implement several of these queuing techniques for its overall congestion management solution.

Queuing Techniques

Fixed and dynamic queues can be implemented in a switch in a variety of ways. This includes input queues, output queues (which are generally located at each of the ports or group of ports), and shared buffers (which are shared by all the ports in the switch).

Input queues are used to handle blocking switch fabrics. Input queues are generally located on each of the switch's ports and are used to buffer the frame as it enters the switch. After the frame has been buffered, an Application-Specific Integrated Circuit (ASIC) on the switch arbitrates for access to the switching fabric.

The use of an input queue allows the sum of all the ports to exceed the capacity of the switching fabric. Buffering the frame as it enters the switch, however, adds latency to the overall process of switching the frame. Throughput is reduced to 60 percent maximum. Figure B-3 shows an input queue buffer.

Figure B-3   *Input Queue Buffer*

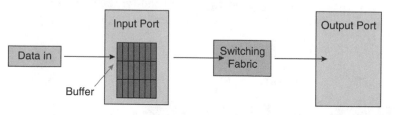

Input queuing also leads to a process called Head of Line Blocking. As frames enter an input queue, they are handled on a first-come, first-served basis. A frame cannot be transmitted until all the frames that entered before it have been transmitted. Moreover, a frame cannot be transmitted until the egress port is available. If the egress port is congested, the frame waits in the input queue, blocking all the frames that come in behind it while it waits for the egress port to become available.

NOTE   What happens in Head of Line Blocking is similar to what happens when you come to a stop light with the intention of turning right. If the stop light is red, and no one is in front of you, you are allowed to make a right turn without waiting for the light to turn green. However, if someone in front of you is going straight, you are blocked from turning right until the car in front of you goes.

In Figure B-4, frames that are destined for Port B have to wait for the congestion at Port A to clear up before they are transmitted to Port B. Frames that are destined for Port A block frames destined for Port B.

Figure B-4   *Head of Line Blocking*

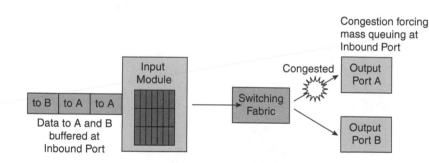

One way to help prevent Head of Line Blocking problems is through the use of output queues. Output queues allow the switch egress port to buffer a frame until the receiving device is ready to accept the frame, thus minimizing the chances of congestion at the port and minimizing the possibility of Head of Line Blocking at the ingress port.

If the destination device is very busy, the egress port output queue might overflow, resulting in Head of Line Blocking at the ingress port and eventually resulting in dropped frames. Figure B-5 illustrates output queue operation.

Figure B-5   *Output Queuing*

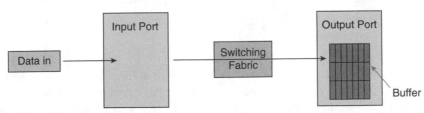

The final method of queuing is a shared output queue. This method is the most efficient of the queuing techniques. All ports on a system share the queues or buffers. As a frame enters the switch, it is placed in the shared buffer space. It can then be switched to the output port without having to move from one buffer to the next. Shared queues also prevent Head of Line Blocking. Frames can be switched to their egress ports as soon as the port is available.

Switching Implementations

Queuing handles the frame as it enters or leaves the switch and is implemented to handle congestion at the switch fabric or at the egress port. The next major component of switching is how and where the decision about the egress port is made. This section discusses where the switching decision occurs and then examines how the switching decision occurs.

The first component of a switching implementation is where the switching decision occurs. This decision can be made in two places:

- Centrally, at the processor
- Distributed to the line cards or ports

Cisco currently has two switching techniques that dominate the campus network:

- Multilayer switching
- Cisco Express Forwarding

NOTE   Multilayer switching is also referred to as flow-based switching. MLS is discussed in Chapter 6, "Improving IP Routing Performance with Multilayer Switching."

Central Switching Decision

A central switching decision occurs at the switch's central processor. This could be at the Supervisor Engine for the Catalyst 5000 and 6000 series switches or at the route processor for the Catalyst 8500 series switches. In a central switching decision process, all frames utilize a centralized table to request forwarding information about the destination. This provides centralized control but requires that all frames come to one place in order to perform table lookups to make forwarding decisions.

Distributed Switching Decision

A distributed switching decision occurs when the switching decision is made on the line card or port. In order for this to occur, the forwarding information, such as the routing table or the content-addressable memory (CAM) table, must be synchronized with the line card. Distributed switching is faster than centralized switching because the line card can make the decision without querying the centralized processor. However, it requires more expensive components at each of the line cards in order to support the forwarding tables. It also requires a process to handle the synchronization of the tables to the line card.

Both centralized and distributed switching decisions are performed in ASICs in order to increase the speed at which the decision is made.

NOTE   A CAM table is the Layer 2 table used by switches to make forwarding decisions. This table contains a MAC address-to-port assignment as well as VLAN information.

Cisco currently has two different methods for handling switching for Layer 2/Layer 3 devices. Each of these devices can make forwarding decisions centrally or at the line cards, as with distributed switches.

Multilayer Switching

The second component of every switch implementation is how it makes the decision. The first method commonly used in the campus network is multilayer switching. Refer to Chapter 6 for an in-depth discussion of this technique.

Cisco Express Forwarding

The second method used in the Catalyst family of switches is a process called Cisco Express Forwarding (CEF). Cisco Express Forwarding is a different switching concept from multilayer switching.

In multilayer switching, the route processor makes all the Layer 3 routing decisions. The Layer 2 process is notified of the Layer 3 information and caches it just as it would cache the MAC address in the Layer 2 CAM table. This gives the switch greater intelligence to make a decision, but it still relies on the route processor to make the Layer 3 routing decision. Information in multilayer switching is cached based on the traffic that passes through the switch, not the route table.

Cisco Express Forwarding looks at improving the switching time from a very different perspective. Rather than caching information based on the traffic flows through the switch, it works to optimize the entire routing process.

There are two Cisco Express Forwarding components:

- Forwarding Information Base
- Adjacency table

Forwarding Information Base

The first step to improving the routing process is to decrease the time it takes to look up a route inside a routing table. A traditional routing table search occurs in a top-down fashion. This means that the routing table is searched entry by entry in order to find a match for the destination. If the routing table is large, this entry-by-entry search can slow the frame's movement through the Layer 3 switch. Cisco Express Forwarding reindexes the routing table into a new table called a Forwarding Information Base (FIB). The FIB is an entry-for-entry match of the routing table that has been reindexed via a binary search algorithm called a Patricia tree. Patricia stands for Practical Algorithm to Retrieve Information in Alphanumeric. A Patricia tree has some of the same characteristics as a binary radix tree. A radix tree stores and searches for items by bit rather than by full comparison.

Adjacency Table

The next step in processing a packet in a Layer 3 device is to determine the Layer 2 information needed to switch the packet to the next hop. This Layer 2 information is generally contained in the ARP cache table. Cisco Express Forwarding creates an adjacency table to prepend the Layer 2 information. The adjacency table maintains Layer 2 next-hop addresses for all FIB entries. Each leaf in the FIB's Patricia tree points to an entry or multiple entries inside the adjacency table. The multiple entries allow Cisco Express Forwarding to handle load balancing when there are multiple next-hop addresses to a destination.

Figure B-6 shows the movement of a packet through three Cisco Express Forwarding routers. At each step, the router looks up the next-hop Layer 3 destination in the FIB and then retrieves that Layer 2 information from the adjacency table. This process is similar to a normal routing process. Cisco Express Forwarding simply optimizes the lookup process in the routing table and then directly ties it to the Layer 2 information that it needs to rewrite the frame in order to make it to its destination.

Figure B-6   *Cisco Express Forwarding*

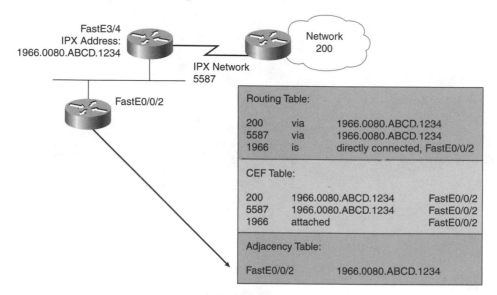

Cisco Express Forwarding Modes

Cisco Express Forwarding can be deployed in one of two modes:

- Centralized CEF
- Distributed CEF

Centralized CEF

When Cisco Express Forwarding is enabled, the FIB and adjacency table exist on the route processor. If the router's line cards do not support CEF, each packet must go to the central route processor in order to be processed through the FIB and the adjacency table. Figure B-7 illustrates centralized CEF.

Distributed CEF

When distributed CEF (dCEF) is enabled, the router's line cards maintain an identical copy of the FIB and the adjacency table. Changes to the FIB or the adjacency table are copied to each of the line cards as the changes occur. This relieves the route processor of any involvement in a packet's forwarding decision. Line cards that support dCEF include the VIP line cards, Gigabit Switch Router (GSR) line cards, and the line cards of the Catalyst 8500 series switch.

Figure B-7   *Centralized CEF*

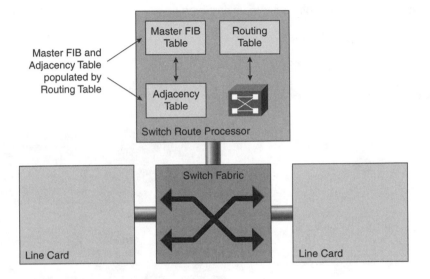

In Figure B-8, the master FIB and adjacency table get copied to each of the line cards.

Figure B-8   *Distributed CEF*

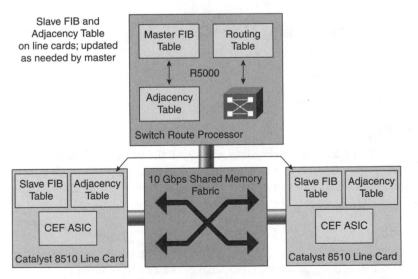

Cisco Express Forwarding is available for IP and IPX traffic.

Catalyst 4000 Series Family

The Catalyst 4000 series switch is an extension of the 5000 series family of switches. It is designed for mid-range wiring closets with fewer than 50 users. The 4000 is a three-slot chassis with two slots available for line cards and one slot for the Supervisor Engine.

The Catalyst 4000 series switch supports EtherChannel, per-VLAN Spanning Tree, and IEEE 802.1Q frame identification. It currently does not support ISL.

The Catalyst 4000 series switch has a 24 Gbps nonblocking shared 8 Mb memory fabric. Each of the two line cards has a 12 Gbps pipe to the shared memory fabric. There is no buffering on the line cards, nor is there a local switching fabric. Frames are sent directly to the shared memory fabric and are buffered there while the forwarding table is consulted to find the destination. After the destination is found, the frame is switched from the shared memory fabric without having to be copied to another buffer. The use of the shared memory fabric decreases the latency experienced with an input queue or buffer.

The Catalyst 4000 series switch makes its switching decision centrally at the switch processor, located on the Supervisor Engine, as shown in Figure B-9.

Figure B-9   *Frame Switching in the Catalyst 4000*

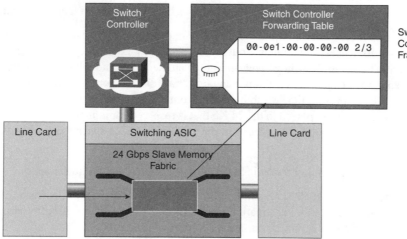

The packet-per-second (pps) throughput of the Catalyst 4000 series switch is approximately 14 million pps for 96 10/100 ports and 17 million pps for 12 Gigabit Ethernet ports.

Catalyst 5000 Series Family

The Catalyst 5000 series switch provides high-density LAN aggregation for the wiring closet or the distribution layer. The Catalyst 5000 supports a variety of line cards, including a Layer 3 Route Switch Module, Token Ring line cards, native ATM, FDDI, 10/100, and Gigabit Ethernet. There are three different models—the 5505, the 5509, and the 5500, which is a 13-slot chassis.

The 5500 has three separate data buses, or switch fabrics. Each data bus is 48 bits wide with a data transfer rate of 25 MHz. A 48-bit-wide database running at 25 MHz is calculated as a 1.2 Gbps bus. The original Catalyst 5000 series switch had one 1.2 Gbps data bus. The release of Gigabit Ethernet meant that the 1.2 Gbps bus of the original Catalyst 5000 could be easily oversubscribed. In order to support a larger port capacity in the 5000 and to also support all the existing line cards, Cisco retained the 1.2 Gbps bus in the Catalyst 5500 but added two additional switch fabrics or data buses. The buses are linked with a Phoenix ASIC in order to allow a line card to use all three data buses. A line card sends its frame to the Phoenix ASIC rather than to an individual switching bus. The Phoenix ASIC is then responsible for sending the frame to the switching fabrics, ensuring that all the 1.2 Gbps data buses are used.

Only the Gigabit Ethernet line cards currently support the use of all three switching fabrics simultaneously. Other line cards use one of the buses but can't use all of them simultaneously.

The 5000 uses a very different queuing mechanism than the Catalyst 4000 series switch. The Catalyst 5000 uses both input and output buffer queues. Each port on a 10/100 line card has a 192 Kb buffer for handling congestion management into and out of the switch. Ports are divided on a 7:1 ratio between input and output. More memory is devoted to output buffers in order to prevent the switching fabric from overwhelming the port. As frames enter the switch, they are placed in the 24 Kb that is reserved for input buffers. As the frame prepares to leave the switch, it is placed in the 168 Kb of queue space that is reserved for output buffers.

In Figure B-10, an incoming frame is buffered in the switch's input queue space.

Each port on the Catalyst 5000 has an ASIC called a SAINT that moves the frame onto the switching fabric and requests destination information. After the frame is buffered in the input queue, the SAINT arbitrates for access to the switching fabric. The frame is transferred to all ports across the switching fabric after it is given access to the switching fabric. As the frame crosses the switching fabric, the SAINT sends a request to the central processor, or supervisor, for destination information. The results of this request are sent on a separate bus used for control information. Ports that are not supposed to receive the frame are told to flush it. This process of sending all frames to all ports first and then checking the results allows the Catalyst 5000 to more quickly move frames across the data bus.

The Catalyst 5000 series switch is capable of a throughput of 2.2 million pps for both 10 and 100 Mbps Ethernet. The RSM that provides Layer 3 functionality in the Catalyst 5000 series switch has a throughput of 175,000 pps. The use of multilayer switching and the NetFlow Feature Card II increases this throughput for IP and IPX to 2 million pps.

Figure B-10   *A Frame Entering a Catalyst 5000*

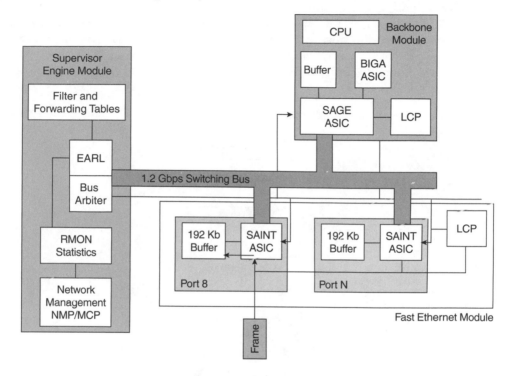

Catalyst 6000 Series Family

The Catalyst 6000 series switch is similar in operation to the Catalyst 5000 series switch. It uses a similar model of input and output queuing to handle congestion control at each of the ports. It also sends frames to each port in the switch in a manner similar to the 5000. There are several major differences between the Catalyst 5000 and Catalyst 6000 that make the Catalyst 6000 the optimum solution for the distribution or core layers in the switch block.

The Catalyst 6000 has a larger switching fabric to handle the aggregation of larger capacity ports such as Gigabit Ethernet. The switching fabric of the 6000 is currently 256 bits and operates at 62.5 MHz. This gives the switch fabric a capacity of 16 Gbps. In addition, the 6000's switching fabric can handle multiple frames simultaneously. Due to this ability, the switching fabric is measured full-duplex and is listed with a total capacity of 32 Gbps. In addition to the data bus, or switching fabric, there are two additional buses—the control bus and the results bus. These buses are used to handle switching functions out-of-band.

Future releases of the Catalyst 6000 series switch will support a switching fabric of up to 256 Gbps and will scale to a throughput of 150 million pps.

The Catalyst 6000 is further optimized to handle quality of service through the use of queues with different priorities. In Figure B-11, the switching fabric passes a frame to an ASIC called a pinnacle. The pinnacle then decides whether the frame should be placed in a low- or high-priority queue. Weighted round robin is then used to schedule between queues. Weighted round robin allows both queues to be handled but gives additional cycles to the high-priority queue. The forwarding rate of the Catalyst 6000 is 15 million pps for Layer 2 frames.

Figure B-11   *QoS Mechanisms in Catalyst 6000*

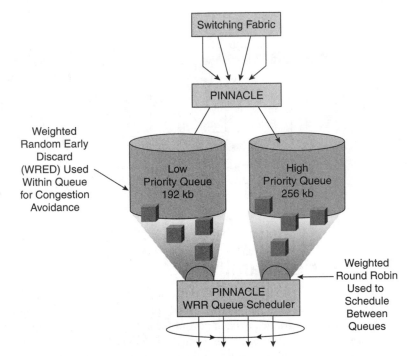

Catalyst 8500 Series Family

The Catalyst 8500 series switch is entirely different from all the other switches in the Catalyst family. It more closely resembles a Layer 3 router, and, in fact, it is called a Layer 3 switch. The Catalyst 5000 and 6000 series switches become Layer 3 switches only with the addition of a routing module.

The Catalyst 8500 series switch uses distributed Cisco Express Forwarding in order to switch packets at Layer 3 and runs the majority of the Cisco IOS routing protocols for both IP and IPX. The Catalyst 8500 also configures using a standard Cisco IOS.

It further deviates from the traditional Catalyst line by using ATM in the switching fabric rather than the traditional Ethernet frames.

The Catalyst 8500 is currently available in two models, with two chassis types in each model. The first model is the 8500 MSR, which is a Multiservice Switch Router. The 8500 MSR is designed as an ATM switch. The second model is the 8500 CSR, or Campus Switch Router. The CSR version is currently for Ethernet, Fast Ethernet, and Gigabit Ethernet port aggregation. It will support ATM line cards in the future. Both models are available in two chassis types:

- **Catalyst 8510**—A five-slot chassis with a single switch-route processor
- **Catalyst 8540**—A 13-slot chassis with two switch processors and one route processor

The Catalyst 8510 has a 3 Mb shared memory architecture with a 10 Gbps switch fabric capacity. Each of the line cards of the 8510 is given 2.5 Gbps of capacity for the switch fabric, allowing for a nonblocking switch fabric. The 2.5 Gbps is divided into two channels of transmit and receive, ensuring that reads and writes to the switch fabric can be handled simultaneously.

The Catalyst 8540 has an architecture that is very similar to the 8510. It has a 12 Mb shared memory architecture with a 40 Gbps switch fabric capacity. Each of the line cards has 5 Gbps of access to the switch fabric. The 5 Gbps line card access is divided into transmit and receive, allowing simultaneous reads and writes to the switch fabric.

Each port also has four queues, allowing the frame scheduler to make QoS decisions. By default, each frame is placed in the lowest-priority queue. The frame scheduler is responsible for scheduling frames into and out of the switch fabric based on queue priority.

Another major component of the Catalyst 8540 series switch is the line cards. Each line card has the intelligence to handle the FIB and the adjacency table generated by Cisco Express Forwarding. The line cards are based on a CEF ASIC (CEFA). The CEF ASIC is responsible for the Ethernet MAC layer functions, address or network lookup in the CAM table, and forwarding of the packet with its correct rewrite information to the fabric interface. The fabric interface is also resident on the line card and is responsible for the packet rewrite, QoS classification, and signaling to the frame scheduler.

The intelligence of the line cards means that after the first 64 bytes of an Ethernet frame is read, the line card can determine the frame's destination information, including the egress port. It also can rewrite the frame with the new source and destination MAC address as well as decrementing TTL. The CEF ASIC also adds an internal tag to the frame, which allows the frame scheduler to determine the egress port and the QoS that is expected for the frame. The frame is then scheduled for access to the switching fabric by the frame scheduler based on its priority information.

For more information on the architecture of the Catalyst 8500 series switch, refer to the white paper on CCO at http://www.cisco.com/warp/public/cc/cisco/mkt/switch/cat/8500/tech/8510_wp.htm.

Numerics

10BaseT, media deployment strategies 51
20/80 rule, switching technologies 13-19
80/20 rule 9-10

A

AC (address copied) 102
access control lists (ACL) 235-237
access
    devices 64-66
    layers
        campus networks 21
        policies 376-377
        security 366
        switching 22-23
    links (VLANs) 96
    lists 378-381
    polices
        campus networks 365, 366
        Hierarchical mode 366
        network devices 368-374
    RSM 197
    See also security
access-class command 379
access-class in/out command 374
access-class statement 374
access-group command 374, 379
accessibility, remote 67
access-list command 380
ACL (access control lists) 235-237
active routers, HSRP 266-271
active states, HSRP 272
adding
    external routers (MLS IDs) 240-241
    switches 109-110
address copied (AC)102
Address Resolution Protocol (ARP) 27, 294
    caches 269
    proxy 261-262
addresses
    Class D 293
    IP 292-295

layers 17
MAC 89, 262
    lockdown 376-377
    searching virtual routers 267-268
SA 101
XTAGs 221
adjacency tables (FIB) 412
advertisements
    MLS-RP 220-221
    VTP 110
agents, RP mapping 341
aging out MLS cache entries 239
algorithms, STA 135
applications
    network traffic 9
    requirements (MLS) 219
Application-Specific Integrated Circuit (ASIC)
  14, 408
applying
    flow masks (MLS-SE) 233-238
    MLS 220-226
    RIP (IP hosts) 263
ARP (Address Resolution Protocol) 27, 294
    caches 269
    proxy 261-262
ASIC (Application-Specific Integrated Circuit)
  14, 408
    Layer 3 switching 18
assigning
    passwords 368-370
    standby priority (HSRP) 273-274
    VLAN
        ID to interfaces 231
        membership 93-94
    XTAGs to multiple MLS-RPs 221
associations, root bridges 137-139
Asynchronous Transfer Mode 99
ATM (Asynchronous Transfer Mode) 99
auto parameter 70
autonegotiation, priority resolution 53
Auto-RP 338-341

M

N

O

T

U

V

W-Z

Cisco Career Certifications

Building Cisco Remote Access Networks
Cisco Systems, Inc., edited by Catherine Paquet
1-57870-091-4 • AVAILABLE NOW

Based on the Cisco Systems instructor-led course available worldwide, *Building Cisco Remote Access Networks* teaches you how to design, set up, configure, maintain, and scale a remote access network using Cisco products. In addition, *Building Cisco Remote Access Networks* provides chapter-ending questions to help you assess your understanding of key concepts and start you down the path for attaining your CCNP or CCDP certification.

Cisco Internetwork Troubleshooting
Cisco Systems, Inc., edited by Laura Chappell and Dan Farkas, CCIE
1-57870-092-2 • AVAILABLE NOW

Based on the Cisco Systems instructor-led course available worldwide, *Cisco Internetwork Troubleshooting* teaches you how to perform fundamental hardware maintenance and troubleshooting on Cisco routers and switches. If you are pursuing CCNP certification and anticipate taking the CCNP Support exam, this book is a logical starting point.

Cisco Internetwork Design
Cisco Systems, Inc., edited by Matthew H. Birkner, CCIE
1-57870-171-6 • AVAILABLE NOW

Based on the Cisco Systems instructor-led course available worldwide, *Cisco Internetwork Design* teaches you how to plan and design a network using various internetworking technologies. Created for those seeking to attain CCDP certification, this book presents the fundamental, technical, and design issues associated with campus LANs; TCP/IP networks; IPX, AppleTalk, and Windows-based networks; WANs, and SNA networks.

Interconnecting Cisco Network Devices
Cisco Systems, Inc., edited by Steve McQuerry
1-57870-111-2 • AVAILABLE NOW

Based on the Cisco course taught worldwide, *Interconnecting Cisco Network Devices* teaches you how to configure Cisco switches and routers in multi-protocol internetworks. ICND is the primary course recommended by Cisco Systems for CCNA #640-507 preparation. If you are pursuing CCNA certification, this book is an excellent starting point for your study.

CISCO SYSTEMS
CISCO PRESS

www.ciscopress.com

CCIE Professional Development

Large-Scale IP Network Solutions

Khalid Raza, CCIE and Mark Turner

1-57870-084-1 • AVAILABLE NOW

Network engineers can find solutions as their IP networks grow in size and complexity. Examine all the major IP protocols in-depth and learn about scalability, migration planning, network management, and security for large-scale networks.

Advanced IP Network Design

Alvaro Retana, CCIE, Don Slice, CCIE, and Russ White, CCIE

1-57870-097-3 • AVAILABLE NOW

Network engineers and managers can use these case studies, which highlight various network design goals, to explore issues including protocol choice, network stability, and growth. This book also includes theoretical discussion on advanced design topics.

Inside Cisco IOS Software Architecture

Vijay Bollapragada, CCIE, Curtis Murphy, CCIE, and Russ White, CCIE

1-57870-181-3 • AVAILABLE NOW

Inside Cisco IOS Software Architecture offers crucial and hard-to-find information on Cisco's Internetwork Operating System (IOS) software. Beyond understanding the Cisco IOS command set, comprehending what happens inside Cisco routers will help you as network designer or engineer to perform your job more effectively. *Inside Cisco IOS Software Architecture* provides essential information that will educate you on the internal aspects of IOS at this level.

Routing TCP/IP, Volume I

Jeff Doyle, CCIE

1-57870-041-8 • AVAILABLE NOW

This book takes the reader from a basic understanding of routers and routing protocols through a detailed examination of each of the IP interior routing protocols. Learn techniques for designing networks that maximize the efficiency of the protocol being used. Exercises and review questions provide core study for the CCIE Routing and Switching exam.

CISCO SYSTEMS

CISCO PRESS

ciscopress.com

Cisco Press Solutions

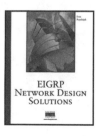

EIGRP Network Design Solutions

Ivan Pepelnjak, CCIE

1-57870-165-1 • AVAILABLE NOW

EIGRP Network Design Solutions uses case studies and real-world configuration examples to help you gain an in-depth understanding of the issues involved in designing, deploying, and managing EIGRP-based networks. This book details proper designs that can be used to build large and scalable EIGRP-based networks and documents possible ways each EIGRP feature can be used in network design, implementation, troubleshooting, and monitoring.

Cisco IOS Releases

Mack Coulibaly

1-57870-179-1 • AVAILABLE NOW

This book is the first comprehensive guide to the more than three dozen types of Cisco IOS releases being used today on enterprise and service provider networks. You will learn to select the best Cisco IOS release for your network and to predict the quality and stability of a particular release. With the knowledge, you'll be able to design, implement, and manage world-class network infrastructures powered by Cisco IOS software.

OpenCable™ Architecture

Michael Adams

1-57870-135-x • AVAILABLE NOW

Whether you're a television, data communications, or telecommunications professional, or simply an interested business person, this book will help you understand the technical and business issues surrounding interactive television services. It will also provide you with an inside look at the combined efforts of the cable, data, and consumer electronics industries' efforts to develop those new services.

Enhanced IP Services for Cisco Networks

Donald C. Lee, CCIE

1-57870-106-6 • AVAILABLE NOW

This is a guide to improving your network's capabilities by understanding the new enabling and advanced Cisco IOS services that build more scalable, intelligent, and secure networks. Learn the technical details necessary to deploy Quality of Service, VPN technologies, IPsec, the IOS firewall, and IOS Intrusion Detection. These services will allow you to extend the network to new frontiers securely, protect your network from attacks, and increase the sophistication of network services.

www.ciscopress.com

Cisco Press Solutions

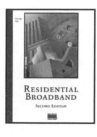

Residential Broadband, Second Edition

George Abe

1-57870-177-5 • AVAILABLE NOW

This book provides a comprehensive, accessible introduction to the topics surrounding high-speed networks to the home. It is written for anyone seeking a broad-based familiarity with the issues of residential broadband. You will learn about the services that are driving the market, the technical issues shaping the evolution, and the network with the home and how it connects to the access network.

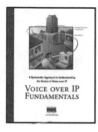

Voice over IP Fundamentals

Jonathan Davidson and Jim Peters

1-57870-168-6 • AVAILABLE NOW

This book will provide you with a thorough introduction to the voice and data technology. You will learn how the telephony infrastructure was built and how it works today. You will also gain an understanding of the major concepts concerning voice and data networking, transmission of voice over data, and IP signaling protocols used to interwork with current telephony systems.

Top-Down Network Design

Priscilla Oppenheimer

1-57870-069-8 • AVAILABLE NOW

Building reliable, secure, and manageable networks is every network professional's goal. This practical guide teaches you a systematic method for network design that can be applied to campus LANs, remote-access networks, WAN links, and large-scale internetworks. Learn how to analyze business and technical requirements, examine traffic flow and Quality of Service requirements, and select protocols and technologies based on performance goals.

www.ciscopress.com

Cisco Press

Committed to being your long-term resource as you grow as a Cisco Networking professional

Help Cisco Press **stay connected** to the issues and challenges you face on a daily basis by registering your product and filling out our brief survey. Complete and mail this form, or better yet ...

CISCO SYSTEMS

CISCO PRESS

Register online and enter to win a **FREE** book!

Jump to **www.ciscopress.com/register** and register your product online. Each complete entry will be eligible for our monthly drawing to win a FREE book of the winner's choice from the Cisco Press library.

May we contact you via e-mail with information about **new releases, special promotions** and customer benefits?

❐ Yes   ❐ No

E-mail address _____

Name _____

Address _____

City _____ State/Province _____

Country _____ Zip/Post code _____

Where did you buy this product?

❐ Bookstore   ❐ Computer store/electronics store
❐ Online retailer   ❐ Direct from Cisco Press
❐ Mail order   ❐ Class/Seminar
❐ Other_____

When did you buy this product? _____ Month _____ Year

What price did you pay for this product?

❐ Full retail price   ❐ Discounted price   ❐ Gift

How did you learn about this product?

❐ Friend   ❐ Store personnel   ❐ In-store ad
❐ Cisco Press Catalog   ❐ Postcard in the mail   ❐ Saw it on the shelf
❐ Other Catalog   ❐ Magazine ad   ❐ Article or review
❐ School   ❐ Professional Organization   ❐ Used other products
❐ Other_____

What will this product be used for?

❐ Business use   ❐ School/Education
❐ Other_____

Cisco Press

How many years have you been employed in a computer-related industry?

❏ 2 years or less ❏ 3-5 years ❏ 5+ years

Which best describes your job function?

❏ Corporate Management ❏ Systems Engineering ❏ IS Management
❏ Network Design ❏ Network Support ❏ Webmaster
❏ Marketing/Sales ❏ Consultant ❏ Student
❏ Professor/Teacher ❏ Other _____

What is your formal education background?

❏ High school ❏ Vocational/Technical degree ❏ Some college
❏ College degree ❏ Masters degree ❏ Professional or Doctoral degree

Have you purchased a Cisco Press product before?

❏ Yes ❏ No

On what topics would you like to see more coverage?

_____

_____

Do you have any additional comments or suggestions?

_____

_____

Thank you for completing this survey and registration. Please fold here, seal, and mail to Cisco Press.

Building Cisco Multilayer Switched Networks (1-57870-093-0)

Cisco Press

Customer Registration—CP050227

P.O. Box #781046

Indianapolis, IN 46278-8046

Place
Stamp
Here

ciscopress.com

Indianapolis, IN 46290

201 West 103rd Street

Cisco Press

CISCO SYSTEMS

NO POSTAGE
NECESSARY
IF MAILED
IN THE
UNITED STATES

BUSINESS REPLY MAIL

FIRST-CLASS MAIL   PERMIT NO. 25788   SAN FRANCISCO CA

POSTAGE WILL BE PAID BY ADDRESSEE

CISCO SYSTEMS / PACKET MAGAZINE
PO BOX 60939
SUNNYVALE CA 94088-9741

PACKET

Packet magazine serves as the premier publication linking customers to Cisco Systems, Inc. Delivering complete coverage of cutting-edge networking trends and innovations, *Packet* is a magazine for technical, hands-on users. It delivers industry-specific information for enterprise, service provider, and small and midsized business market segments. A toolchest for planners and decision makers, *Packet* contains a vast array of practical information, boasting sample configurations, real-life customer examples, and tips on getting the most from your Cisco Systems' investments. Simply put, *Packet* magazine is straight talk straight from the worldwide leader in networking for the Internet, Cisco Systems, Inc.

We hope you'll take advantage of this useful resource. I look forward to hearing from you!

Jennifer Biondi
Packet Circulation Manager
packet@cisco.com
www.cisco.com/go/packet

PACKET